Action Stations Revisited

Action Stations Revisited

The complete history of Britain's
military airfields:
No. 4 South West England

David Berryman

Crécy Publishing Limited

Published in 2009 by Crécy Publishing Limited
All rights reserved

© David Berryman 2009

A CIP record for this book is available from the British Library

ISBN 9 780859 791212

Printed and bound in the UK
by MPG Books Ltd

Crécy Publishing Limited
1a Ringway Trading Estate, Shadowmoss Road, Manchester M22 5LH
www.crecy.co.uk

CONTENTS

ACKNOWLEDGEMENTS

Having written many papers and articles for the Ministry of Defence and Royal Auxiliary Air Force, the inclusion of books to my repertoire resulted in a number of volumes of airfield histories for the Newbury publishers Countryside Books. A commission from Crecy to write this book followed and I feel proud and privileged to follow in the footsteps of Chris Ashworth in accepting it.

As with the other books in the series, this one covers airfields that have at some stage seen military use. Many of these were purpose-built as such, but others were opened as civil airfields and later either requisitioned or used as bases by military aircraft. The main features included at the end of each section are as detailed at 1st December 1944 and are taken from an Air Ministry Publication of that date. This information is therefore only included for those airfields in existence at that time. The longest runway is given first, followed by the others. The hangars are listed generally by size and the accommodation figures give an indication of the overall size of the station and its importance, although off-camp billeting is not included.

The photographs, many of which have not been published before, have been drawn from my own collection or generously made available by other contributors. Prime amongst these are Pete White of the Bellanca Association, Mark Roberts of Aerobilia, Nick Stroud of Aeroplane Magazine and Keith Male of the Museum of Army Flying. I have also been loaned or given material by Mike Phipp (Hurn Airport), Alan Donald (Jersey Airport), Phil Matthews (Cotswold Aero Club, Staverton), Gary Hawkins (Penzance Heliport), John Levesley (Friends of the New Forest Airfields), Robin Gilbert and David Steel (South-West Airfields Trust), Ashley Roy (Bond Air Services), 21 Signals Regiment, Royal Signals Colerne, Leo Marriott, Steve Webster, Chris Thomas, Norman "Spud" Borer, Ian Haskell, Bill Young, Margaret Perry, Colin van Geffen and Roy Nerou.

I should also like to thank the following for their invaluable help and assistance: Terry Heffernan, Terry Booker, Alan Gray, Ross Marven, Sue Carrigan, Dr. Hugh Thomas, Gradon Carter, Peter Amos, Michael Stroud, Jeanette Powell, Richard Lane, Sandy Beatty, Ruth Warren, Adrian King, Roger Day, Norman Parker, Matthew Costard (Channel Islands Occupation Society), Henry Pelham, Pat Hudson and June Harvey (Western Air (Thruxton) Ltd), Air Britain, Airfield Research Group, National Archives Kew, DSTL, RAF College Cranwell, RAF Museum Hendon, Wiltshire County Records Office, Cornwall County Records Office, Salisbury Journal, Salisbury Reference Library, Penzance Reference Library, Plymouth Reference Library, Cambridge University Library (Vickers Archives), 621 and 625 VGS Hullavington, 626 VGS Predannack, 622 VGS Upavon, 2 AEF Boscombe Down. I would especially like to thank Gill Richardson of Crecy Publishing for her advice and understanding, and my wife Karen for all of her support and hard work in helping me get the manuscript together.

GLOSSARY

A	(as in Halifax A9) Airborne forces
A	(as in A-20 Havoc) Attack
A	(as in A4/Deux) US ALG in France
AA	Anti-aircraft
A&AEE	Aeroplane & Armament Experimental Establishment
AAC	Army Air Corps
(AAC) Flt	(Anti-Aircraft Cooperation) Flight
AACU	Anti Aircraft Cooperation Unit
AAP	Air Acceptance Park
AAPC	Anti-Aircraft Practice Camp
AAR	Air-to-Air Refuelling
AASF	Advanced Air Strike Force
ACS	Airfield Construction Squadron
ADGB	Air Defence of Great Britain
AEAF	Allied Expeditionary Air Force
AEF	Air Experience Flight
AES	Air Electronics School
AEW	Airborne Early Warning
AFC	Air Force Cross
AFEE	Airborne Forces Experimental Establishment
AFS	Advanced Flying School
AH	(as in Gazelle AH1) Army Helicopter
AI	Airborne Interception (radar)
AIS	Airborne Interception School
ALG	Advanced Landing Ground
AN/APS	(as in AN/APS20) Designation for US airborne search and detection radar systems, ie no specific meaning for individual letters
ANS	Air Navigation School
Anti-Diver	Patrol to intercept V-1 flying bombs
AOC	Air Officer Commanding
AONS	Air Observer & Navigator School
AOP	Air Observation Post
AOS	Air Observer School
APC	Armament Practice Camp
ARS	Aircraft Repair Shed
ASaC	(as in Sea King ASaC7) Airborne Surveillance and Control
ASR	Air Sea Rescue
ASU	Aircraft Storage Unit
ASW	Anti-Submarine Warfare
ASWDU	Anti-Submarine Warfare Development Unit

ATA	Air Transport Auxiliary
ATC	Air Traffic Control
ATC	Air Training Corps
ATC	Armament Training Camp
ATDU	Aircraft Torpedo Development Unit
ATS	Armament Training Station
ATTDU	Air Transport Tactical Development Unit
B	(as in B-17) Bombardment
B	(as in B3/Ste Croix sur Mer) British ALG in France
Baedeker	German reprisal raid on historic British city
BATDU	Beam Approach Training & Development Unit
BATF	Beam Approach Training Flight
BE	(as in BE2) Bleriot Experimental, ie tractor configuration
BEA	British European Airways
BEAH	British European Airways Helicopters
Bf	Bayerische Flugzeugwerke (of Messerschmitt)
BG	Bombardment Group
B&GS	Bombing & Gunnery School
BIA	British Island Airways
BLEU	Blind Landing Experimental Unit
BN	Britten Norman
BOAC	British Overseas Airways Corporation
BS	Bombardment Squadron
BUA	British United Airways
BUA(CI)	British United Airways (Channel Islands)
BV	Blohm und Voss
BW	Bombardment Wing
C	(as in C-47) Cargo/transport
C	(as in Hastings C.1) transport
CAEC	Casualty Air Evacuation Centre
CAACU	Civilian Anti-Aircraft Cooperation Unit
CANS	Civil Air Navigation School
casevac	Evacuation of casualties by air
CDEE	Chemical Defence Experimental Establishment
CDES	Chemical Defence Experimental Station
CFS	Central Flying School
CG	(as in CG-4A) Cargo Glider
CGS	Central Gunnery School
Circus	Bomber operation with fighter escort to entice enemy response
CLS	Central Landing School
C&M	Care & Maintenance
(C)OTU	(Coastal) Operational Training Unit
D	(as in D-Day) Designated date for an operation; due to its widespread application during the event, it became synonymous with Operation *Overlord*

DERA	Defence Evaluation & Research Agency
DFC	Distinguished Flying Cross
DFM	Distinguished Flying Medal
DH	de Havilland
DHC	de Havilland Canada
DHFS	Defence Helicopter Flying School
DTEO	Defence Trials & Evaluation Organisation
DZ	Drop Zone
EC	Eurocopter
ECFS	Empire Central Flying School
ECM	Electronic Counter-Measures
EFS	Empire Flying School
EFTS	Elementary Flying Training School
ELG	Emergency Landing Ground
ENE	East-north-east
EO-Blister	Extra Over Blister
EOD	Explosive Ordnance Disposal
E&RFTS	Elementary & Reserve Flying Training School
ETO	European Theatre of Operations
ETS	Equipment Training School
ETPS	Empire Test Pilots School
E&WS	Electrical & Wireless School
F	(as in Hunter F.1) Fighter
FA	(as in Sea Harrier FA2) Fighter/Attack
FAA	Fleet Air Arm
FAW	Fleet Air Wing
FAW	Fighter All Weather
FB	(as in Mosquito FBVI) Fighter Bomber
FBTS	Flying Boat Training Squadron
FCP	Ferry Crew Pool
FCST	Fighter Command School of Tactics
FE	(as in FE2) Farman Experimental, ie pusher configuration
FG	(as in Phantom FG1) Fighter Ground-attack
FG	Fighter Group
FGA	(as in Hunter FGA9) Fighter Ground-Attack
FIDO	Fog Investigation & Dispersal Operation
FIS	Flying Instructor School
FIS(A)	Flying Instructor School (Advanced)
Fg Off	Flying Officer
FLS	Fighter Leaders School
Flt Lt	Flight Lieutenant
FOB	Forward Operating Base
FOST	Flag Officer Sea Training
FPP	Ferry Pilots Pool

FPP(ATA)	Ferry Pilots Pool (Air Transport Auxiliary)
(FPT)F	(Ferry Pilot Training) Flight
FRA	Flight Refuelling Aviation
FRADU	Fleet Requirements & Direction Unit
FRS	(as in Harrier FRS1) Fighter Reconnaissance Strike
FRU	Fleet Requirements Unit
FS	Fighter Squadron
FS	Flying School
FSP	Field Staging Post
FTCIS	Flying Training Command Instructors School
FTDU	Ferry Training & Despatch Unit
FTF	Ferry Training Flight
FTS	Flying Training School
FTU	Ferry Training Unit
FU	Ferry Unit
FW	Fighter Wing
FW	Focke Wulf
GCA	Ground-Controlled Approach
GCHQ	Government Communications Headquarters
GCI	Ground-Controlled Interception
Gee	Radio navigation aid employing ground transmitters and airborne receiver
GIS	Glider Instructors School
GP	General Purpose
GPEU	Glider Pilot Exercise Unit
GPR	Glider Pilot Regiment
GPTF	Glider Pilot Training Flight
GR	(as in Warwick GRX) General Reconnaissance
GR	(as in Harrier GR9) Ground-attack Reconnaissance
Gp Capt	Group Captain
GRU	Gunnery Research Unit
GS	General Service
GS	Gliding School
GSU	Ground Support Unit
GTS	Glider Training School
H	(as in H-Hour) Designated time for an operation to commence
H2S	Airborne radar-navigation target location aid
HAAPC	Heavy Anti-Aircraft Practice Camp
HAR	(as in Whirlwind HAR10) Helicopter, Air Rescue
HAS	(as in Sea King HAS5) Helicopter, Anti-Submarine
HAS	Hardened Aircraft Shelter
HC	(as in Belvedere HC1) Helicopter, Transport
HCU	Heavy Conversion Unit
He	Heinkel

HE	High Explosive
HF	(as in Spitfire HFVII) High-altitude Fighter
HGCU	Heavy Glider Conversion Unit
HGMU	Heavy Glider Maintenance Unit
HGSU	Heavy Glider Support Unit
HGU	Heavy Glider Unit
HM	(as in Merlin HM1) Helicopter, Maritime
HMF	Helicopter Maintenance Facility
HMS	Her/His Majesty's Ship
HP	Handley Page
HQ	Headquarters
HQSFP	Headquarters Service Ferry Pools
HR	(as in Sycamore HR12) Helicopter, Rescue
Hs	Henschel
HT	(as in Hiller HT2) Helicopter, Trainer
HT	High-tension (electrical)
HU	(as in Wessex HU5) Helicopter, Utility
IFDU	Intensive Flying Development Unit
IFF	Identification Friend or Foe
IFOR	Implementation Force
IFTU	Intensive Flying Trials Unit
ILS	Instrument Landing System
Instep	Operations over the Western Approaches to intercept German fighters targetting Coastal Command aircraft
ITS	Initial Training School
ITW	Initial Training Wing
JCA	Joint Combat Aircraft
JEHU	Joint Experimental Helicopter Unit
JG	Jagdgeschwader (Luftwaffe fighter squadron)
Ju	Junkers
JWE	Joint Warfare Establishment
Kg	Kilogramme
KG	Kampfsgeschwader (Luftwaffe bomber squadron)
KLM	Koninklijke Luchtvaart Maatschappij (Royal Dutch Airlines)
L	(as in Piper L-4) Liaison
LAA	Light Anti-Aircraft
LAAPC	Light Anti-Aircraft Practice Camp
LAC	Leading Aircraftsman
LAS	Light Aircraft School
lb	Pound (weight)
LCT	Landing Craft Tank
LF	(as in Spitfire LF16) Low-Flying
LG	Landing Ground
Lorenz	Homing and landing system using radio bearings

LRFU	Long Range Ferry Unit
LRMRF	Long Range Meteorological Reconnaissance Flight
MAP	Ministry of Aircraft Production
(M)CU	(Meteor) Conversion Unit
MCU	Marine Craft Unit
Me	Messerschmitt
Met	Meteorological
MHU	Maritime Headquarters Unit
MoA	Ministry of Aviation
MoD	Ministry of Defence
MONAB	Mobile Naval Air Base
MoS	Ministry of Supply
MOTU	Maritime Operational Training Unit
MPSU	Mobile Parachute Servicing Unit
MQM	(as in MQM-74C) Designation for US missiles and drones
MR	Maritime Reconnaissance
MT	Mechanical Transport
MTB	Motor Torpedo Boat
MU	Maintenance Unit
NAAFI	Navy Army and Air Force Institute
NAC	National Air Communications (organisation)
NAFWg	Naval Air Fighter Wing
NE	North-east
NF	(as in Mosquito NFII) Night Fighter
NFG	Night Fighter Group
NFS	Night Fighter Squadron
NW	North-west
Nickel	Leaflet-dropping operation
Noball	Operation against V-1 launch-sites
OADF	Overseas Air Deliveries Flight
OADU	Overseas Aircraft Despatch Unit
(O)AFU	(Observer) Advanced Flying Unit
OAPF	Overseas Aircraft Preparation Flight
OAPU	Overseas Aircraft Preparation Unit
Oboe	Ground-controlled radio aid to blind bombing
OC	Officer Commanding
OCU	Operational Conversion Unit
ODF	Overseas Deliveries Flight
ODU	Overseas Despatch Unit
Operation *Dragoon*	Allied landings in southern France, August 1944
Operation *Jubilee*	Dieppe raid, August 1942
Operation *Market Garden*	Airborne operation to take Arnhem, September 1944
Operation *Overlord*	Invasion of Normandy, June 1944
Operation *Torch*	Invasion of North Africa, November 1942

Operation *Varsity*	Airborne element of the Rhine Crossing, March 1945
OR	Operational Requirement
OR	Other ranks
O&RTU	Operational & Refresher Training Unit
OS	Observation Squadron
OSS	Office of Strategic Services
OTU	Operational Training Unit
P	(as in P-47) Pursuit
(P)AFU	(Pilots) Advanced Flying Unit
PBY	(as in PB4Y-1), Patrol Bomber, Consolidated Aircraft Ltd (as under the USN aircraft designation system of 1922)
PFA	Popular Flying Association
PFS	Primary Flying School
Plt Off	Pilot Officer
PoW	Prisoner of War
PR	(as in Spitfire PR19) Photographic Reconnaissance
PRU	Photographic Reconnaissance Unit
PSP	Pierced Steel Planking
PTS	Parachute Training School
'Q' site	Type of decoy site to mislead German bombers
RAAF	Royal Australian Air Force
RAE	Royal Aircraft Establishment
RAF	Royal Air Force
RAFA	Royal Air Forces Association
Ramrod	Fighter-supported day bomber raid against a specific target
Ranger	Freelance intruder operations at squadron, wing or group strength intended to wear down the enemy fighter force
RATF	Radio Aids Training Flight
RAuxAF	Royal Auxiliary Air Force
RCAF	Royal Canadian Air Force
R&D	Research & Development
RE	(as in RE8) Reconnaissance Experimental
Recce	Reconnaissance
REES	Royal Engineers Experimental Station
REME	Royal Electrical & Mechanical Engineers
RFA	Royal Fleet Auxiliary
RFC	Royal Flying Corps
RFS	Reserve Flying School
Rhubarb	Low-level fighter strike operation, often relying upon low cloud
RLG	Relief Landing Ground
RMS	Royal Mail Ship
RN	Royal Navy
RNAS	Royal Naval Air Service
RNVR	Royal Navy Volunteer Reserve
RNZAF	Royal New Zealand Air Force

Roadstead	Fighter operation to attack enemy shipping
Rodeo	Authorised fighter sweep
Rover	Coastal Command patrol to search and attack enemy shipping
RP	Rocket Projectile
RS	Radio School
RS	Reserve Squadron
SAC	Senior Aircraftsman
SAH	School of Aircraft Handling
SAOEU	Strike Attack Operational Evaluation Unit
SAR	Search and Rescue
SAS	Special Air Service
SBA	Standard Beam Approach
SCI	Smoke Curtain Installation
SCSR	School of Combat Survival & Rescue
SDF	Special Duties Flight
SE	(as in SE5A) Scout Experimental
SE	South-east
SFDO	School of Flight Deck Operations
SFOR	Stabilisation Force
SFP	Service Ferry Pools
(S)FPP	(Service) Ferry Pilots Pool
SFTS	Service Flying Training School
SGR	School of General Reconnaissance
SKTF	Sea King Training Flight
SLAW	School of Land/Air Warfare
SLG	Satellite Landing Ground
SMR	School of Maritime Reconnaissance
SNCO	Senior Non-Commissioned Officer
SOE	Special Operations Executive
SofAC	School of Army Cooperation
SofMR	School of Maritime Reconnaissance
S of ANB&D	School of Aerial Navigation & Bomb Dropping
SofN&BD	School of Navigation & Bomb Dropping
SofTT	School of Technical Training
SSZ	Sea Scout Zero
StG	Stuka Geschwader (Luftwaffe dive-bomber squadron)
SW	South-west
T	(as in Chipmunk T10) Trainer
TAF	Tactical Air Force
TCC	Troop Carrier Command
TCDU	Transport Command Development Unit
TCG	Troop Carrier Group
TCS	Troop Carrier Squadron
TCW	Troop Carrier Wing

TDS	Training Depot Station
TEU	Tactical Exercise Unit
TF	(as in Beaufighter TFX) Torpedo Fighter
TFU	Telecommunications Flying Unit
TPTF	Test Pilot Training Flight
TRE	Telecommunications Research Establishment
TRF	Telecommunications Research Flight
TRG	Tactical Reconnaissance Group
TRS	Tactical Reconnaissance Squadron
TS	Training Squadron
TSR	Tactical Strike Reconnaissance
TSR	Torpedo Strike Reconnaissance
TT	(as in Canberra TT18) Target Towing
(TT) Flight	(Target Towing) Flight
TWU	Tactical Weapons Unit
UAS	University Air Squadron
UAV	Unmanned Aerial Vehicle
U-boat	Untersee Boot (German submarine)
UK	United Kingdom
US	United States
USAAF	United States Army Air Force
USAF	United States Air Force
USN	United States Navy
UXB	Unexploded Bomb
V	(as in V-1 flying bomb) Vergeltungswaffe (revenge weapon)
VE Day	Victory in Europe Day
VHF	Very High Frequency
VJ Day	Victory in Japan Day
VGS	Volunteer Gliding School (later Squadron)
VIP	Very Important Person
VLM	Vlaamse Luchttransportmaatschappij (Flemish Air Transport Company)
VP	Patrol Squadron (USN)
W	West
WAAF	Women's Auxiliary Air Force
Wg Cdr	Wing Commander
WIDU	Wireless Intelligence Development Unit
W/O	Warrant Officer
W/Op	Wireless Operator
W/OpAG	Wireless Operator/Air Gunner
Window	Foil strips dropped to disrupt enemy radar systems
W/T	Wireless Telegraphy
YMCA	Young Men's Christian Association
ZG	Zestorer Geschwader (Luftwaffe pathfinder squadron)

INTRODUCTION

At 09.23 hours on Saturday 18 March 1967 the supertanker *Torrey Canyon* struck the Seven Stones rocks 7 miles ENE of St Martin's Head, Isles of Scilly, 15 miles W of Land's End. The ship was carrying 119,328 tons of crude oil from the Persian Gulf to the BP refinery at Milford Haven. One of the first to spot the stricken tanker was Captain Jim Summerlee, piloting the 0900 BEA Helicopters S-61 flight from Penzance Heliport, passing overhead just after it struck. He radioed St Just that the ship was down by the head and that oil was pouring from her. Two RN SAR Whirlwinds were scrambled from Culdrose, and the Penlee and St Mary's lifeboats were launched.

The tanker was losing vast amounts of its cargo, and to support salvage attempts another S-61N was leased from BEAH, and this also operated from Penzance. It took compressors and other equipment aboard the *Torrey Canyon* on 22 March, but on the 26th the ship started to break up and the remainder of the cargo started to flood out. Soon oil was covering the Cornish coastline from the Lizard right round to Newquay. Salvage attempts were abandoned on 28 March, the ship was evacuated, and at 1600 hours that day eight Buccaneers from Lossiemouth dropped 1,000lb bombs onto the ship, to burn off the remaining oil. Fires soon started and the smoke rose to 8,000 feet as twenty-six Hunters from 229 OCU, Chivenor, stoked up the fires by releasing 100-gallon drop tanks into the flames. Further strikes by Hunters and Buccaneers, together with Sea Vixens from Yeovilton, continued over the following two days until Shackletons from St Mawgan declared that the wreck was free of oil.

Press reporters travelled by air to St Mary's in the Islands and to Land's End, and camera-equipped helicopters were based at Penzance Heliport to televise events. Military helicopters based at the Heliport worked with Culdrose-based Wessex to support beach-clearing parties repairing the environmental damage. Thus it was that, just over twenty years after the end of the Second World War, aircraft were involved in operations off the coast of Cornwall again, working closely together from half a dozen South West airfields.

Two Culdrose-based Wessex HU5s fly over Torrey Canyon *aground on the Seven Stones in March 1967.*

One of the opposing armies can be seen in this photograph taken from a Bristol Boxkite during the Salisbury Plain Army manoeuvres of September 1910, in one of the earliest pictures to be taken from an aeroplane in flight. The Boxkite's shadow can be discerned in the right foreground.

Captain Percival Phillips pioneered aviation in the South West, giving joyrides, stunt flying and barnstorming with his Cornwall Aviation Company during the 1920s and '30s. He is shown flying his bright red Avro 504K G-EBIZ at Hanham, Bristol, in May 1931, with mechanic Frank Cradock on the top wing!

The Luftwaffe's interest in the South West is demonstrated by this target photograph of Penzance and Newlyn taken on 8 November 1940.

The first awakenings of interest in aviation can be traced to the South West when, in the 11th century, the first recorded attempted flight was made, at Malmesbury in Wiltshire. Brother Eilmer, a Benedictine monk, made a pair of wings and jumped off the roof of the Abbey. He travelled some 200 yards and the fact that, although he broke his legs, he wasn't killed, must have been due to the wings giving him some lift.

Other early pioneers included John Stringfellow and William Henson, who patented an aerial steam carriage and formed the Aerial Transit Company at Chard, Somerset, in 1842. They persevered with their ideas, and six years later built the first ever aeroplane to be flown under its own power. It was unmanned, had a wingspan of 10 feet and, incredibly, was powered by a lightweight steam engine! They received the Aeronautical Society's first Gold Medal for their pioneering achievements.

As Samuel Cody made the first powered flight in the UK in October 1908, Horatio Barber was having his own aeroplane built. It was delivered to his hanger at Larkhill in June 1909 and, having been joined there by fellow pioneers G. B. Cockburn and J. B. Fulton, the airfield became an important centre for British aviation. In June 1910 the British & Colonial Aeroplane Company opened a flying school there (together with one at Filton), and a couple of the company's Boxkites took part in Army manoeuvres that September. Military aviation had started in Britain in 1878 when the Royal Engineers started experimenting with balloons, and these were used for training on Salisbury Plain. The Royal Engineers also experimented with aeroplanes, forming the Air Battalion on 1 April 1911, with two companies, No 1 flying balloons from Farnborough and No 2 with aeroplanes at Larkhill, where they took delivery of six Boxkites.

With the formation of the RFC on 13 April 1912 it was realised that the training of pilots needed to be more formalised, and this resulted in a Central Flying School being established at

No 12 School of Technical Training, Melksham, in June 1942. It has eight large hangars, all containing aircraft, but no airfield from which to fly them!

Tiger Moth II DE709 of the AOP School, Middle Wallop, over Stonehenge in 1953.

Upavon in June 1912 to standardise the training of military flying instructors. Larkhill remained the powerhouse of British military aviation, and the Military Aircraft Trials were held there in August 1912 in an attempt to determine the aeroplane type best suited for Army aviation. However, the airfield had physical restrictions, and became gradually overshadowed by Upavon and Netheravon, both of which had more room for expansion up on the Plain.

By the outbreak of the First World War the RFC consisted of a mere seven squadrons, so maximum effort was put into building more aeroplanes and training pilots to fly them. The schools at Upavon and Netheravon were working at full tilt and, as the war went on, were joined by more at Lake Down, Lopcombe Corner, Stonehenge, Leighterton, Minchinhampton, Boscombe Down, Old Sarum and Yatesbury. Aircraft production was undertaken by Bristol & Colonial at Filton, which made Boxkites from 1910 (and went on to make fighters such as the Brisfit), at Yeovil, where Westland built seaplanes and bombers, and at Brockworth, then used for assembly and flight-testing. Although there was no need for Home Defence fighters in the South West, the seas around it were threatened by U-boats, which by 1916 were becoming a menace. A number of RNAS stations were created for use by airships and seaplanes, a major one being at Mullion, with a number of sub-stations. Further stations were opened in 1917 such as Tresco and Cattewater, and in 1918, to combat a renewed U-boat offensive, at Newlyn, Padstow and Torquay.

With the end of the war, most sites were closed, and the South West lost most of its airfields. A few remained, such as Upavon, Netheravon and Old Sarum, but only the marine base at Cattewater remained open west of Salisbury Plain. A number of civil operators, such as the Cornwall Aviation Co, used war-surplus aircraft to start services in the 1920s, and did joyriding tours to bring aviation to the public. In 1932 Sir Alan Cobham started his 'flying circus', which he took around the country to publicise aviation, and was a popular visitor to the South West. In the late 1930s airports of various sizes opened in the region, among them Bristol, Exeter, Plymouth, Land's End and St Mary's.

In the 1930s the rapid increase in size of the German forces, particularly its Air Force, prompted the British Government to build up its own armed services, and in 1934 the RAF Expansion Scheme was initiated. Starved of cash until then, the service had 850 aircraft, balancing the only other continental air force that up until then could pose a threat to Britain – which was France. The rapid rearmament of Germany came as an unpleasant shock, both in terms of size and capability. The fastest British aircraft in 1934 was the 207mph Hawker Fury biplane fighter; the Messerschmitt Me109 monoplane, which flew the following year, could reach 300mph.

Construction of new airfields was started, and orders placed for more aircraft. The South West's four main aircraft manufacturers, Bristol, Gloster, Parnall and Westland, had somehow managed to keep going, producing aeroplanes at their factory airfields, and were well placed to assist with the build-up of the RAF and FAA. Gloster was making Gladiators and later Hawker Hurricanes, Bristol was licence-building Hawker Audaxes as well as producing its new Blenheim bomber, and Westland was making Lysanders. The net result of this preparation was that on the outbreak of war the RAF had 2,000 aircraft in front-line service and 2,200 in reserve (many of them modern monoplanes such as the 300mph Hawker Hurricane and Supermarine Spitfire fighters, with bombers such as the Vickers Wellington and Handley Page Hampden). It faced a modern Luftwaffe of more than 4,000 front-line aircraft, with 1,000 in reserve. Although the airfield construction programme was concentrated more to the east, as the RAF wanted more operational bases closer to Germany, its effects were felt in the South West with the reopening of Boscombe Down in 1930 and later the establishment of South Cerney for flying training and Aston Down as an ASU/MU.

When war came in September 1939 four large airfields were under construction in the South West, three for the RAF and one for the FAA. Yeovilton was unusual in that it was being built with concrete runways, as the RAF was then still resisting such things being laid across its green turf except on heavy bomber stations. RAF airfields were nonetheless given tarmac perimeter tracks and their layout was excellent. A number of C-type hangars were generally provided, major buildings and messes were finished in tasteful brick or stone, and the airmen's quarters were of the popular H-block design. Middle Wallop was one of the last to be completed in this form, and remains an excellent example of its type today. However, St Eval, which was to become the major anti-submarine station in the South West, was hurriedly completed with wooden huts, which contrasted with the massive hangars being erected. Colerne, too, was still under construction when the war started, and many of the stone buildings planned for it were never completed.

Once again, as during the First World War, the South West was initially involved in flying training. Stations such as South Cerney, Aston Down, Lyneham, Castle Combe and Yatesbury trained thousands of aircrew, often having more than a hundred aircraft on strength, which meant using satellites and RLGs to avoid congesting the main base. Naval flying training also took place in the region, primarily at Yeovilton, Henstridge and St Merryn. The only operational station in the region at that time was Mount Batten, from where Sunderlands were already patrolling the Western Approaches and keeping convoys safe. The relative safety of the South West resulted in training expanding and experimental establishments such as A&AEE taking refuge there. However, with the fall of France in June 1940 this changed, and the whole region came within range of the Luftwaffe. Coastal patrols were made by Army Cooperation Lysanders and frantic efforts were immediately made to extend the fighter defences westwards, initially with detachments, then whole squadrons being posted as far west as St Eval which, together with Middle Wallop and Filton, became sector stations as part of 10 Group, Fighter Command. Formed under Air Vice-Marshal Sir Quinton Brand on 13 July 1940 with its HQ at Rudloe Manor, the Group's squadrons, despite being thinly spread, managed to break up almost every Luftwaffe attack that came its way during the Battle of Britain. As the raids built up, a number of dummy airfields were laid out to lure German bombers away from the real ones, and these diversionary tactics led to Q decoy sites, lit at night to simulate airfields, cities and ports.

Coastal Command's efforts were expanded and by 1941 Sunderlands were regularly making offensive patrols, and anti-submarine operations from St Eval were producing results. Nocturnal attacks by the Luftwaffe during 1940 had not met with very effective opposition, but in 1941 purpose-built night-fighters, particularly Beaufighters flying from Middle Wallop and Colerne, were proving their worth (being active during raids on Bristol, Southampton and Plymouth). Several Blenheim squadrons had made detachments to the region to make shipping strikes the previous year, but in 1941 the RAF really started moving over to the offensive. More Blenheim operations were made, and they were joined by Whirlwinds of 263 Squadron, a unit that took the prize for being the most nomadic, having seemingly operated from every major airfield in the region at some stage.

Forward airfields such as Portreath, Predannack, Harrowbeer and Bolt Head were also commissioned, enabling fighter squadrons to mount *Circuses*, *Rodeos*, *Rhubarbs* and *Ramrods* in taking the war to the enemy. The South West's airfields provided a convenient jumping-off point for ferrying aircraft overseas, especially Portreath, together with St Mawgan, which was also used as a reception airfield for aircraft arriving from the USA. Other activities included ASR and target facilities, peripatetic units such as 276 and 286 Squadrons moving around the region in order to provide their services.

As well as airfields there were many other establishments in the South West that supported RAF and FAA activities. These included Innsworth, Gloucestershire, which as No 7 School of Technical Training was responsible for the training of groundcrews, and later became a WAAF training depot and RAF Receiving and Training Centre for the South of England. No 12 School of Technical Training was opened at Melksham, Wiltshire, in June 1940, with eight hangars housing a variety of aircraft types for ground training, ranging from Spitfires and Ansons to Wellingtons and later Lancasters. Quedgeley in Gloucestershire was one of many MUs not located on an airfield; as 7 MU, it was dispersed over eight sites, and handled a wide range of essential stores and equipment. Pucklechurch in Gloucestershire was No 11 Balloon Centre, a holding unit and depot responsible for supporting barrage balloon units in the South West. No 11 MU at Chilmark, Wiltshire, was an ammunition depot storing aerial bombs of various weights in underground stone 'quarries' (technically mines, as they were completely underground). Browns Quarry near Bath housed the underground operations centre of 10 Group HQ, Rudloe Manor (the author's mother, Noreen, a WAAF teleprinter operator, was stationed there in 1943 before being posted to the Portreath Sector HQ). Monkton Farleigh Quarry nearby housed another ammunition depot, and in Spring Quarry, Corsham, Bristol set up an underground factory to manufacture Centaurus aero-engines, next door to another where British Small Arms produced Polsten cannon barrels. There were also RAF Hospitals at Wroughton near Swindon and Melksham, Wiltshire.

During 1942 the Leigh Light Wellingtons of Chivenor made a successful debut and airborne forces began to consolidate on the airfields of Salisbury Plain. US forces began to arrive, needing more airfields for their airborne forces and tactical support. While building up for the eventual invasion of Europe, some USAAF units took part in Operation *Torch*, using South West airfields as launch points. The Luftwaffe attacked several towns and cities in the region in 1942 as part of the 'Baedeker' revenge raids – starting with Bath in April, followed by Bristol and Weston-super-Mare, these resulted in night-fighter defences being strengthened. Operation *Jubilee* on 19 August involved many 10 Group squadrons in the support of the Dieppe raid, which, although unsuccessful, proved invaluable experience in preparation for D-Day.

More Luftwaffe attacks came in early 1943, when German fighter-bombers raided coastal towns, and more raids came in on Plymouth later in the year. Disruption caused by the disbandment of Army Cooperation Command and the formation of the Second Tactical Air Force in June was repeated in November, when Fighter Command became Air Defence of Great Britain, and with 2nd TAF became part of the Allied Expeditionary Air Force.

More airfields were needed to accommodate incoming US forces, as well as RAF squadrons that were being built up for offensive operations against occupied Europe. Airfield building became the largest single project in wartime Britain, and more than 1,000 airfields were in use or under construction in 1944. To build just one station was a considerable undertaking, requiring 40,000 square yards of concrete to be laid for a standard three-runway airfield, together with 50 miles of pipes and conduits. It took more than seven months to build with all its hangars and other buildings, and employed more than a thousand men.

In the autumn of 1943 the USN became operational from Dunkeswell. Preparations for the invasion were well under way with the steady build-up of airborne forces and the construction of a series of ALGs along the South Coast. Invasion preparations gathered momentum, and from early 1944 more squadrons arrived in the South West as part of this. Some attacks were made by the Luftwaffe on the invasion ports, but defensive fighters overwhelmed them. As the invasion fleet approached the French coast at midnight on 5 June paratroop aircraft tugs and gliders that had left the runways of Blakehill Farm, Keevil and Tarrant Rushton flew overhead, taking advance parties of airborne forces, followed by C-47s from Exeter, Merryfield, Weston Zoyland and Upottery taking paratroops and gliders. Further drops were made during the day, re-supply missions being flown over the next few days. Once airstrips were established on the beachhead, tactical squadrons moved forward, and casualties started arriving at West Country airfields aboard returning supply aircraft. Many of these airfields were back in action in September, for Operation *Market Garden*, and again in March 1945 for Operation *Varsity*.

The remainder of the war was somewhat of an anti-climax in the South West, although Warmwell was to see a procession of fighter squadrons passing back through on armament practice camps until the end of the war. The region was then a rest and re-equipment area, and the base for the long-range transport force. Training continued, as did aircraft production. The Westland plants at Yeovil and Ilchester were busy throughout the war, manufacturing the company's own designs and rebuilding and repairing those of other companies, especially Spitfires. Gloster not only produced standard types such as the Hurricane and Typhoon, but also developed Britain's first jet fighter, the Meteor. Bristol manufactured a series of twins, from the Blenheim and Beaufort to the Beaufighter, many of the latter at its Old Mixon works, while Supermarine manufactured Spitfires in Salisbury and Trowbridge, being assembled and flight-tested at High Post and Keevil respectively.

With the Japanese surrender in August 1945, the run-down of Britain's armed forces started, and many airfields were put onto C&M or closed. Others were retained on standby, and some of these, including Weston Zoyland, were reopened to give refresher training to aircrew during the Korean War. By the late 1950s the RAF and FAA had settled down to the Cold War. A few of the South West's airfields remained in operation, and continued to play an important role, such as monitoring Soviet naval activity from St Mawgan and St Eval, supporting deployed FAA squadrons from Culdrose and Yeovilton, mounting round-the-world transport operations from Lyneham, and training tactical support pilots at Chivenor, as well as providing R&D and experimental facilities at Boscombe Down.

St Eval soon succumbed, but the other airfields fulfilled important roles in support of Britain's defence interests at home and abroad. The *Torrey Canyon* episode was one of many in which their units have provided invaluable aid and assistance. SAR units based at Culdrose, St Mawgan and Chivenor have saved thousands of lives all over the South West and in the seas that surround it, as during the Fastnet Race of 1979 and the evacuation of Boscastle in 2004. Lyneham's transport aircraft have been flying humanitarian operations almost ever since the Berlin Airlift. In more recent times its Hercules have appeared at trouble spots, bringing supplies in the aftermath of mud slides in Chile, civil wars in Rwanda and Angola, flooding in Mozambique and earthquakes in Pakistan.

Yeovilton and Culdrose played a key role in the Falklands Campaign, in assault, communications, transport and logistics, including the sinking of an Argentinian submarine. Lyneham provided vital support in helping to maintain the airbridge to Ascension and later the Falklands, while Boscombe Down came up with important aircraft modifications to enable the aircrews to do their job. These activities were reprised during the Gulf War of 1991 in support of 1st Armoured Brigade, the air strike force and naval forces at sea. Further involvement by these stations has included Bosnia in the 1990s, Sierra Leone, Gulf 2003 and maintaining the peace in Iraq since, then Afghanistan. Lyneham's reward for this intense and sustained involvement is, like St Mawgan, to be closed, and its squadrons transferred. In the absence of a front-line RAF presence in the South West, Culdrose and Yeovilton fly the flag for the Royal Navy, and seem secure for some time to come, particularly in view of the proportion of warships that now carry helicopters, and the building of two new aircraft carriers. Boscombe Down, too, continues to play a vital role in supporting the three services by enhancing and improving the effectiveness of their aircraft and weapons.

The airfields of the South West have played an important part in Britain's history. Although the first of them was only constructed a few generations ago, much has been forgotten. It is hoped that this volume will remind or inform its readers of their eventful and fascinating stories.

A P47 of 404th FG at Winkton in June 1944.

Military Airfields of South-West England

001 Alton Barnes, Wiltshire
002 Aston Down, Gloucestershire
003 Babdown Farm, Gloucestershire
004 Barnsley Park, Gloucestershire
005 Barnstaple, Devon
006 Beaulieu, Hampshire
007 Bisterne, Hampshire
008 Blakehill Farm, Wiltshire
009 Bolt Head, Devon
010 Boscombe Down, Wiltshire
011 Brockworth, Gloucestershire
012 Bude, Cornwall
013 Calshot, Hampshire
014 Castle Combe, Wiltshire
015 Charlton Horethorne, Somerset
016 Charmy Down, Somerset
017 Chedworth, Gloucestershire
018 Chickerell, Dorset
019 Chivenor, Devon
020 Christchurch, Hampshire
021 Cleave, Cornwall
022 Clyffe Pypard, Wiltshire
023 Colerne, Wiltshire
024 Culdrose, Cornwall
025 Culmhead, Somerset
026 Davidstow Moor, Cornwall
027 Down Farm, Gloucestershire
028 Dunkeswell, Devon
029 Everleigh, Wiltshire
030 Exeter, Devon
031 Falmouth, Cornwall
032 Filton, Gloucestershire
033 Guernsey, Channel Islands
034 Haldon, Devon
035 Hamworthy, Dorset
035 Harrowbeer, Devon
037 Henstridge, Dorset
038 High Post, Wiltshire
039 Holmsley South, Hampshire

040 Hullavington, Wiltshire
041 Hurn, Hampshire
042 Ibsley, Hampshire
043 Jersey, Channel Islands
044 Keevil, Wiltshire
045 Kemble, Gloucestershire
046 Laira, Devon
047 Lake Down, Wiltshire
048 Lands End, Cornwall
049 Larkhill, Wiltshire
050 Leighterton, Gloucestershire
051 Long Newnton, Gloucestershire
052 Lopcombe Corner, Hampshire
053 Lulsgate Bottom, Gloucestershire
054 Lymington, Hampshire
055 Lyneham, Wiltshire
056 Manningford, Wiltshire
057 Marlborough, Wiltshire
058 Merrifield, Cornwall
059 Merryfield, Somerset
060 Middle Wallop, Hampshire
061 Moreton, Dorset
062 Moreton Valence, Gloucestershire
063 Mount Batten, Devon
064 Mullion, Cornwall
065 Needs Oar Point, Hampshire
066 Netheravon, Wiltshire
067 Newlyn, Cornwall
068 New Zealand Farm, Wiltshire
069 North Stoke, Gloucestershire
070 Oatlands Hill, Wiltshire
071 Okehampton, Devon
072 Old Sarum, Wiltshire
073 Overley, Gloucestershire
074 Padstow, Cornwall
075 Penzance, Cornwall
076 Perranporth, Cornwall
077 Portland, Dorset
078 Porton Down, Wiltshire

079 Portreath, Cornwall
080 Prawle Point, Devon
081 Predannack, Cornwall
082 Rendcombe, Gloucestershire
083 Roborough, Devon
084 Rollestone, Wiltshire
085 St.Eval, Cornwall
086 St.Mary's, Isles of Scilly
087 St.Mawgan, Cornwall
088 St.Merryn, Cornwall
089 Sandbanks, Dorset
090 Shrewton, Wiltshire
091 South Cerney, Gloucestershire
092 Staverton, Gloucestershire
093 Stoke Orchard, Gloucestershire
094 Stonehenge, Wiltshire
095 Stoney Cross, Hampshire
096 Sway, Hampshire
097 Tarrant Rushton, Dorset
098 Thruxton, Hampshire
099 Tilshead, Wiltshire
100 Toller, Dorset
101 Torquay, Devon
102 Townsend, Wiltshire
103 Treligga, Cornwall
104 Tresco, Isles of Scilly
105 Upavon, Wiltshire
106 Upottery, Devon
107 Upton, Dorset
108 Warmwell, Dorset
109 Watchet, Somerset
110 Weston-super-Mare, Somerset
111 Westonzoyland, Somerset
112 Westward Ho!, Devon
113 Whitchurch, Somerset
114. Winkleigh, Devon
115 Winkton, Hampshire
116 Worth Matravers, Dorset
117 Yate, Gloucestershire
118 Yatesbury, Wiltshire
119 Yeovil, Somerset
120 Yeovilton, Somerset
121 Zeals, Wiltshire

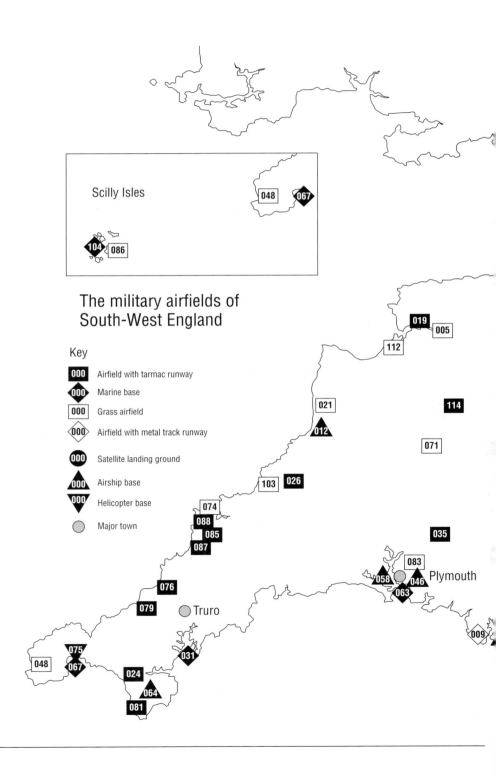

Scilly Isles

| 048 | 067 |

| 104 | 086 |

The military airfields of South-West England

Key

000	Airfield with tarmac runway
000	Marine base
000	Grass airfield
000	Airfield with metal track runway
000	Satellite landing ground
000	Airship base
000	Helicopter base
●	Major town

019
005
112
021
114
012
071
103 026
074
088
085
087
035
083
058 046 Plymouth
063
076
079 ● Truro
009
075
048 067
031
024
064
081

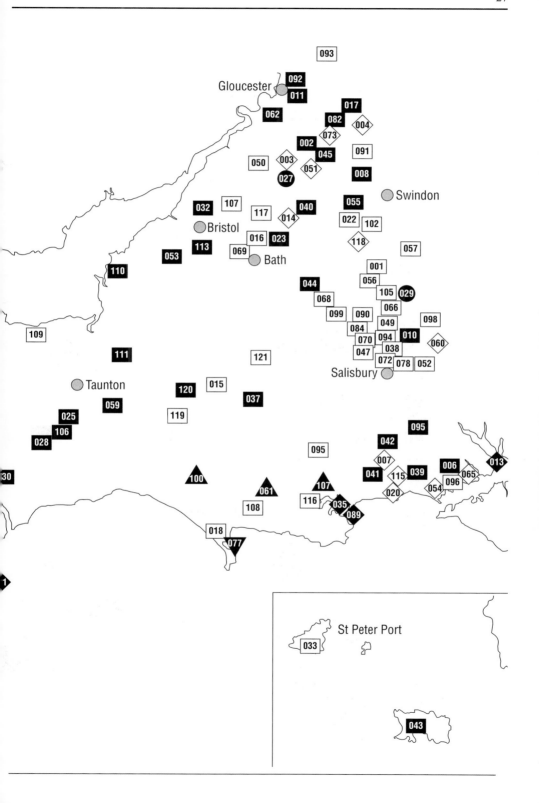

THE AIRFIELDS

ALTON BARNES, Wiltshire

SV100620, 4 miles NW of Upavon

Also known as Brown's Farm, Alton Barnes was first used as an airfield in 1936 by the CFS, based only a few miles away at Upavon. It was one of a number of practice landing grounds maintained in the area by the school to give student pilots a varied training environment. Originally used for circuit planning and forced-landing practice, Alton Barnes was, unlike many other such fields, easy to locate. From the Upavon direction pilots only needed to point the nose of their aircraft at the prominent White Horse cut into the side of Milk Hill, and it could be found below, sandwiched between the Kennet & Avon Canal and the Stanton St Bernard road to the north.

The first aircraft to use Alton Barnes were Avro 504N two-seat trainer biplanes, but these were soon replaced by the more powerful Avro Tutor, which used the airfield until 1941. Originally just a field with a windsock, facilities at Alton Barnes were gradually enhanced. Rudimentary ground defences constructed during the summer of 1940 were strengthened with more gun positions following an air raid on 14 September, when a German bomber dropped three bombs on the airfield.

The demand for flying instructors increased as the war went on, and this led to the increased use of Alton Barnes. Unfortunately courses were shortened to increase the output of graduate pilots, and this led to a decline in flying standards and a resulting increase in accidents. Several Tutors were damaged in accidents here and their replacement by even more powerful Masters and Oxfords exacerbated the situation. On 18 June 1941 Master III W8477 and Oxford II N6365 collided over the airfield, killing the occupants of both aircraft.

At the end of the year the airfield was transferred to 29 EFTS, based at Clyffe Pypard, newly opened 9 miles to the north. Work then began on upgrading Alton Barnes to RLG standard. Nissen and Maycrete buildings were built along the Honey Street/Alton Barnes road to provide teaching and support facilities, and ten Blister hangars were built around the airfield's perimeter. Night-flying facilities included the provision of rendezvous lights on Milk Hill. These, and goose-neck flares laid out for night-flying practice, attracted unwelcome attention during the night of 16/17 April 1942, when an aircraft from a bomber OTU dropped a number of flash bombs on the airfield, having mistaken the lights for a night-bombing range.

The EFTS flew DH Tiger Moths and Miles Magister trainers to give elementary flying training to budding RAF and RN pilots, but this changed in May 1942, when Army students arrived for pre-glider training. The school consisted of four training flights based on Clyffe Pypard, the students being trained at Alton Barnes travelling daily to the site. From 6 June the flights were increased to six, the extra two being based at Alton Barnes. The circuit at the RLG was by then becoming congested, so it was decided to set up a form of air traffic control. This was not as sophisticated as we are used to nowadays, consisting of an airfield controller, who maintained flying schedules and used an Aldiss lamp to signal aircraft when to take-off and land.

Pre-glider pilot training stopped at Alton Barnes in December 1942, when RAF grading courses were introduced. Because of its heavy usage, there had been concerns over the state of the airfield's surface. When the weather worsened during the winter of 1943/44 it was decided to lay metal Sommerfield tracking around the perimeter and in areas prone to waterlogging. This proved successful, and in October 1944 FAA students replaced RAF ones on the grading courses, which continued into 1945. However, with the end of the war the task of 29 EFTS was drastically reduced. On 7 July 1945 flying was stopped at Alton Barnes, and all aircraft were returned to Clyffe Pypard. Two days later the RLG was closed, and put onto a C&M footing.

Although Alton Barnes was used occasionally for forced-landing practice by aircraft from Clyffe Pypard over the next couple of years, it was de-requisitioned in 1947 and returned to farmland. Today little remains to show that there was an airfield here. The Blister hangars (including the one through which a disgruntled instructor flew a Tiger Moth in 1944) have all gone together with most of the buildings, save only for the link trainer building. A few concrete hut bases and air raid shelters have remained over the years in mute testimony of the mundane, but important, role that Alton Barnes played during the Second World War. The Wiltshire Historical & Military Society has erected a couple of monuments on the former airfield explaining its past to passers-by.

Main features:
Runways: N-S 2,460ft, NE-SW 3,300ft, E-W 2,460ft, NW-SE 2,460ft, grass.
Hangars: four EO-Blister, six Standard Blister. *Hardstandings:* none.
Accommodation: ORs 130.

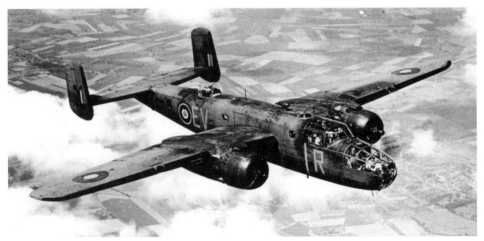

Mitchells were processed by 20 MU at Aston Down during 1942. This one, Mk II FL185 of 180 Squadron, returned in September 1943 on detachment to 52 OTU (Fighter Command School of Tactics).

ASTON DOWN, Gloucestershire

SO912010, 1½ miles SE of Chalford on A419

Flying first took place from this airfield during the First World War. Then known as Minchinhampton, it was established for flying training by the RFC. However, the first occupants were the AFC, which wanted to set up training elements in the UK to support its front-line squadrons in France. Coming under the control of HQ 1st Wing AFC at Tetbury, Minchinhampton was opened as No 1 Station of 1st Wing in early 1918. The first unit to arrive was 6 (Training) Squadron, which moved in with its Bristol Scouts, Sopwith 1½ Strutters and Pups, on transfer from Tern Hill, on 25 February 1918.

Built on 170 acres of relatively level downland, the new airfield was roughly rectangular, giving a landing run from NW to SE of 3,400 feet, and from SW to NE of 2,800 feet. The technical site was built in the south-western corner of the airfield, and consisted of four standard GS hangars for aircraft storage and maintenance (each of 170 x 100 feet), two workshops, three MT sheds and two general storage sheds. The domestic area was to the north of the airfield, across the main road.

The second AFC Squadron to arrive was 5 (Training) Squadron, from Shawbury, on 2 April 1918. Like 6 Squadron, its aeroplanes (Shorthorns, DH6s and Pups) soon carried the distinctive white kangaroo markings that were to distinguish the aircraft of No 1 Station. Soon both squadrons were hard at work, training fighter pilots for the Western Front. It was not long before Sopwith Camels (including a few two-seaters) joined 5 TS, while 6 TS received SE5As (eventually to re-equip with twenty-five of them). By August 1918 many of the earlier types had been withdrawn, at that time the station's establishment standing at twelve Camels, twelve SE5As and twenty-four Avro 504K trainers. The more advanced Sopwith Snipe single-seat fighter later supplemented the other types.

With the Armistice in November 1918, flying activity came to a sudden end at Minchinhampton. Both AFC squadrons were disbanded in January 1919, and the airfield cited for disposal. Following the auctioning off of the buildings in 1920, the site was cleared and returned to agriculture. However, in less than twenty years the former Minchinhampton airfield would once again reverberate to the sound of aero-engines. As part of the RAF's Expansion Scheme of the mid-1930s the site was selected for a new airfield to house an ASU, and work began in 1937. A compact administrative and technical site was constructed in the north-west corner of the airfield, and eight large storage hangars were dispersed at various points connected by a concrete taxiway.

When it opened as RAF Aston Down on 12 October 1938, the resident unit was 7 ASU, under the command of Sqn Ldr N. A. Tait. However, to conceal the unit's role, five days later it was re-titled 20 MU. At first the hangars were used for the storage of vehicles and aircraft bombs, the latter being stored in the more distant hangars! In February 1939 the first aircraft started to arrive. That summer Fighter Command surveyed Aston Down and decided that it would make a good training base for fighter pilots. It formed 12 Group Pool on 23 August 1939 using Harvards, Gladiators and Blenheims to provide advanced training to fighter pilots that had been allocated to the Group, but were awaiting postings to squadrons.

The outbreak of war made itself felt at Aston Down when, on 3 September, twelve Wellington bombers of 214 Squadron landed, having flown from their base at Feltwell; the unit had been dispersed for fear of air attacks. However, it became apparent that the Luftwaffe was not about to go on the offensive, so after a few days the Wellingtons returned home. Civil flying was stopped at this time, save for limited authorised cargo and passenger services. All privately owned aircraft not used on those services were requisitioned for the war effort, and ferried to collection centres. One of these was 20 MU, where the aircraft were inspected for potential RAF use. More aircraft arrived during late 1939, filling up the hangars. Aircraft were then stored in the open, and fields adjoining the airfield were requisitioned so that new arrivals could be dispersed safely in case of air attack. The majority of the MU's staff were civilian, and by the end of 1939 more than 600 were employed by the unit. More than 400 aircraft were then in store, including Hawker Audaxes, Harts and Henleys, Bristol Beauforts and Blenheims, and Fairey Battles.

No 12 Group Pool took on a new role in January 1940, of aircraft delivery. The first ferry flights started in 10 January, when Blenheims left for Aden. Flights were later made to Egypt. Other Blenheims left during this time for Yugoslavia, but they were flown by Yugoslav pilots. Wg Cdr Dragic Hinco commanded the first flight of four aircraft, which left on 1 March; more Yugoslav aircraft followed two weeks later. From spring 1940 Vickers Ltd had the use of one of the hangars on D Site, in the south-east corner of the airfield, where it repaired Wellingtons that had been badly damaged on operations or in accidents. MU staff were impressed with the achievements of the Vickers engineers, who bought many 'basket-cases' back as serviceable aircraft. This was made possible by the revolutionary geodetic construction devised by the Wellington's designer, Barnes Wallis, which meant that whole sections of damaged fuselage and wing could be cut out and replaced with new.

The pool was re-titled on 15 March 1940, becoming 5 OTU, and was by then flying Spitfires, Hurricanes, Blenheims, Defiants, Masters and Battles. Its role had become one of operational training – the rapid output of new crews for Hurricane day and Blenheim night-fighter squadrons. Although training, many of the fighters flew fully armed, as there were German intruders in the area, and there had been several incidents of unarmed RAF trainers being shot down near their airfields. On 25 July one of the OTU Spitfires intercepted a Ju 88 of KG9 and shot it down near Oakridge, 2 miles from the airfield. Aston Down became an important facility during the Battle of Britain, when 20 MU's priorities centred on the preparation of fighter aircraft for front-line squadrons. The majority were Spitfires and Hurricanes newly delivered from their manufacturers, but also included aircraft that had been returned to 20 MU for repair or salvage following accidents or battle damage. Between July and October 1940 the MU repaired 257 Hurricanes, a critical addition to front-line fighter strength.

Construction work had continued at Aston Down throughout the autumn of 1940 and into the following winter. The site contractors, Walter Lawrence & Son, worked busily on accommodation, lecture rooms, stores, fuel compounds, MT sheds, messes and station headquarters. In early 1941 construction of runways commenced, but progress was slow due to bad weather and the high level of flying activity. However, flying was dramatically reduced in the spring when orders came through for the transfer of 55 OTU (as 5 OTU had become in November 1940) to Usworth. The weather improved, and good progress on runway building was made. Interruptions from 20 MU arrivals and departures continued, but more unwelcome disruptions also occurred during the spring of 1941. Several air raid warnings were received, during which time the workforce prepared to take cover, but fortunately no actual raids on Aston Down resulted. The only attack came in on 29 March, when one of the airfield's decoy sites was bombed; this was the 'Q' site at Horsley, $3^{1}/2$ miles to the south-west.

The runways were barely completed when another unit arrived to take residence in August 1941. This was 52 OTU, which transferred from Debden with Tomahawks, Blenheims, Masters and Hurricanes. These were flown hard, and became involved in a number of spectacular accidents, both on and off the airfield. The unit accounted for most of the twenty-one flying accidents that occurred at Aston Down during 1941. Spitfires supplemented the Hurricanes and by the spring of 1942 the circuit at Aston Down was very busy. It was decided to open a satellite at Chedworth, near Cirencester, and this was used from April onwards. In August 1942 two of the OTU's flights moved to Chedworth and on 15 January 1943 these became the Fighter Leaders School. On 9 February the school left for Charmy Down, and Chedworth became a satellite of South Cerney.

Aircraft processed by 20 MU during 1942 included bombers such as the Avro Lancaster and North American Mitchell. The ferrying of such aircraft by then had become almost solely undertaken by pilots of the ATA. These were experienced civilian pilots, and included a number of women, such as the pioneering long-distance pilot Amy Johnson. Despite some initial reservations, the ATA pilots soon proved their worth. Other aircraft to arrive at Aston Down that year were Airspeed Horsa gliders. However, these were not flown in, but arrived in several large sections by road, and were assembled and flight-tested at the MU before being put into store. By April 1942 Aston Down had been nominated as one of the main glider storage sites in preparation for the Allied invasion of the continent.

Despite the gliders and bombers that appeared at 20 MU for preparation and/or storage, the main types dealt with by the MU during 1942 and 1943 were fighters, mainly the Supermarine Spitfire and Hawker Typhoon. Many of these did not have far to travel, as they had been manufactured in the Vickers-Supermarine Castle Bromwich shadow factory, or those in Hampshire and Wiltshire. Most of the Typhoons came from the Gloster factory, not far away at Brockworth.

No 52 OTU had continued its training role at Aston Down and in early August 1943 was rejoined by its Fighter Leader School, returning from Charmy Down. Shortly afterwards, on 16 August, the parent unit itself was renamed as 52 OTU (Fighter Leader School). A few months later, in October, it was again re-titled, as 52 OTU (Fighter Command School of Tactics), although throughout this time its role remained much the same. Towards the end of January the unit moved to Millfield, Northumberland, where on 26 January 1944 it was disbanded to form part of a new Fighter Leader's School. In the meantime, more gliders arrived at the MU, and with them a new type that was to play a decisive part in the forthcoming fighting – the Hawker Tempest.

The move of the OTU coincided with a build-up of units and equipment at Aston Down in preparation for the invasion. One of these was 84 Group Support Unit, formed at Aston Down on 14 February 1944. This was a mobile unit whose role was to provide a reserve of pilots and aircraft for 84 Group squadrons, with an establishment of 110 Mustangs, Spitfires and Typhoons. Ferrying of pilots and aircraft for the GSU was undertaken by 1311 Transport Flight, which moved to Aston Down from Llandow on 21 May. It was joined by eight field squadrons of the RAF Regiment, swelling the population of the station to 3,500, (2,500 of whom were under canvas). As the field squadrons moved to their ports of embarkation, they were replaced by other units, such as 8 General Hospital, a forward RAF field hospital. Following the D-Day landings, most of these units moved forward to the continent, although 84 GSU/1311 Transport Flight remained until 10 July, when they moved to Thruxton.

In their place, on 17 July, came 3 Tactical Exercise Unit from Annan. Consisting of two squadrons flying Typhoon IBs and Hurricane IIAs, this unit's role was the training of fighter-bomber pilots for ground-attack squadrons. Student pilots were trained in the use of rocket projectiles and other weapons to destroy ground targets by strafing and dive-bombing. By the end of August the unit had sixty-four Typhoons on strength, alongside a few Hurricanes, Mustangs, Masters and Martinets. A familiar title reappeared at Aston Down on 18 December when 3 TEU was disbanded, doubled in size and reconstituted as 55 OTU.

New aircraft continued to arrive at 20 MU, which by early 1945 was working to support the squadrons that were fighting across Europe and in the Far East. Later versions of established designs, such as the Griffon-engined Spitfires, appeared at the MU, as did new types, such as the Avro Lincoln. No 55 OTU continued its training, inevitably with the occasionally accident. For example, on 25 March 1945 a Typhoon crashed into a dispersal hut on the north-east side of the airfield, injuring fifteen personnel and killing three, including the pilot.

VE Day was celebrated at Aston Down, and although lights could come back on again without blackout shielding, the war continued in the Far East. However, as more Spitfires and Lincolns were prepared for Tiger Force, the RAF formation to attack the Japanese home islands, it had already been decided that the Service had more trained pilots than it needed. Therefore on 14 June 1945 No 55 OTU was disbanded and control of Aston Down reverted to 20 MU. Changes were also felt at the MU as, with the reduction in aircraft numbers, outlying storage sites and dispersals were closed, the aircraft being brought back to the main site. Although more than 1,000 aircraft were then stored on the airfield, the majority of these were already being stripped of their equipment and put aside for disposal, the newer ones being stored inside.

With the end of the war against the Japanese, front-line units were disbanded and their aircraft returned to 20 MU. Towards the end of 1945 the ATA, too, was disbanded. In its place 2 Ferry Pool was formed at Aston Down with Ansons, Oxfords, Tiger Moths, Proctors, Spitfires and Mosquitoes. No 41 Group Training Flight also formed at Aston Down in November 1945, flying Harvards and Mosquitoes to train ferry pilots. The unit disbanded on March 1946 to become 1689 (Ferry Pilot Training) Flight, using a variety of aircraft including Lancasters, Hornets and Meteors. No 83 Gliding School arrived in October 1946 from Moreton Valence to train Air Cadets.

Apart from air movements to and from 20 MU, post-war flying at Aston Down was maintained at a modest level, with air movements to and from 20 MU, ferrying by 2 Ferry Pool (which became 2 (Home) Ferry Unit on 7 February 1952), and training by 1689 (FPT) Flight and 83 GS. On 1 February 1953 No 2 (Home) Ferry Unit was re-titled as 187 Squadron, its role being to ferry aircraft within the UK and to RAF Germany. A few months later, on 9 April 1953, No 1689 (FPT) Flight moved to Benson to become part of the Ferry Training Unit. In September 1955 No 83 GS closed,

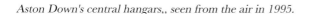

Aston Down's central hangars,, seen from the air in 1995.

and on 2 September 1957 the last RAF flying unit to operate from Aston Down, 187 Squadron, was disbanded. Although 20 MU remained in residence for a while, it was closed on 30 September 1960, following a rationalisation of the MUs. Although the airfield was still used by CFS Little Rissington for training, the closure of 20 MU ended Aston Down's viability as a RAF station.

Nonetheless a need was still seen for Aston Down, and on 1 April 1963 it was transferred to the Ministry of Aviation to become its depot for the storage of aircraft production jigs, tools and other equipment. This new lease of life was to become the airfield's longest in Government hands, for under the MoA and MoD it was to remain open for almost another forty years. In 2002 the hangars and storage sites were finally disposed of by the MoD for industrial storage. The airfield itself was sold to the Cotswold Gliding Club, which maintains it in daily use for glider training, general flying and competitions, and as such it is one of the premier gliding sites in Britain today.

Main features:
Runways: 036° 5,025ft x 150ft, 094° 3,300ft x 150ft, 164° 3,225ft x 150ft, concrete and tarmac. *Hangars:* fifty of various kinds. *Hardstandings:* forty-four. *Accommodation:* RAF Officers 84, SNCOs 96, ORs 1,734; WAAF Officers 11, SNCOs 10, ORs 389.

A T-type hangar still in use at Babdown Farm in March 2008.

BABDOWN FARM, Gloucestershire

ST845938, 3 miles W of Tetbury on A4135

This airfield was planned in 1939 as an RLG for 9 FTS Hullavington, and took its name from the farm that provided most of the land. Although it first officially came into use in July 1940, the first flying accident to occur there had taken place on 17 April, when Audax K7308 of the then 9 SFTS crashed on landing (presumably its pilot was trying out the new airfield!).

Babdown Farm was used initially for night-flying training by the student aircrews of 9 SFTS, flying Harts, Audaxes and Oxfords. The aircraft were flown over from Hullavington in the late afternoon when night-flying was scheduled, and were handled by a ground party detached especially for the purpose. The groundcrews would also deploy a flare-path of goose-neck oil lamps so that the pilots could find the field in the dark. Unfortunately the flare-path also attracted enemy aircraft, and the groundcrews had to be ready to douse the lamps should a hostile be heard in the area. They weren't quite quick enough to do this on 3 August 1940, when a German bomber dropped several HE bombs on the airfield, fortunately without injury or damage.

The RLG was used from time to time by other units, such as 16 OTU Upper Heyford and the Overseas Despatch Unit, Kemble. One of 16 OTU's Hampdens crash-landed at Babdown Farm on 1 August when its undercarriage collapsed. ODU crews flew Martin Marylands from the RLG during November for night-flying practice prior to delivering the aircraft to Malta.

The Luftwaffe made its second visit to Babdown Farm on 26 March 1941, when one of its bombers dived out of cloud and machine-gunned the airfield. Although several aircraft were on dispersal, no damage was sustained. By this time Masters and Hurricanes were regular visitors for night-flying training, and this was reflected in the large number of accidents that occurred. During March alone three aircraft crashed – one Hurricane and one Master spinning in, while another Master hit a shed while flying in the circuit! Between late April and late September twelve Hurricanes were seriously damaged in separate incidents.

In February 1942 No 9 SFTS was re-designated as 9 (P)AFU. Its role changed to that of advanced pilot training, and it was decided to make better use of Babdown Farm by upgrading its facilities. Three metal Sommerfield track runways were laid, connected by a concrete perimeter track. Blister hangars were erected, together with accommodation, technical and administration buildings. While the work took place 9 (P)AFU used Castle Combe for training. However, it was never to return to Babdown Farm; although the upgrade of the RLG was completed in August 1942, the unit had been transferred to Errol in Scotland the month before. In its place 3 FIS(A) came to Hullavington, and it was this unit's Masters, Magisters, Harvards and Oxfords that arrived at the reopened Babdown Farm. Two flights took up residence in the new accommodation at the airfield, and soon the circuit was busy once again with aircraft on training sorties, predominantly by night but also by day. The day users also included the Spitfires of 52 OTU based at Aston Down and Chedworth. On 26 January 1943 the airfield also played host to aircraft whose crews had become lost. These were an Oxford, a fully bombed-up Wellington and a Curtiss Cleveland. The latter (a US biplane carrier-borne torpedo bomber) was a mystery plane, as only a few had arrived in the UK on diversion from the French Navy, and were officially for ground instructional duties only, the type's in-service introductory trials having been cancelled in August 1940!

In the spring of 1943 a Standard Beam Approach was installed on the main runway. This was a radio instrument system that meant that student pilots did not have to rely on lighting to land on the airfield at night. In June 1532 (BAT) Flight arrived to provide training on the system with Oxfords, on transfer from Hullavington. Other improvements during this time included the construction of a new maintenance site on the south-east side of the airfield using three Teeside hangars. No 3 FIS(A) moved out of the area in September 1943, relocating its flights to Lulsgate. No 1532 (BAT) Flight then remained the sole residents until the end of October, when part of 15 (P)AFU arrived on transfer from Ramsbury, to make room for newly arrived USAAF units. By then Babdown Farm had become a satellite of Castle Combe, which had been taken over as 15 (P)AFU's main base. The unit's Ansons, Oxfords and Tiger Moths were soon active in the area.

Electric lighting was installed during early 1944 to aid night-flying, and it was undoubtedly this that attracted a German bomber to drop two bombs during the night of 15 May. Fortunately no damage resulted. More hazardous was flying training, and a series of accidents occurred throughout Babdown Farm's existence. One of the more serious occurred during night-flying on 29 August 1944 when the duty runway controller was killed by an Oxford that crashed into his caravan.

Bad weather during the autumn and winter of 1944/45 caused waterlogging and the runway matting to lift, and for three months the airfield was only partly usable. Similar problems at Castle Combe and 15 (P)AFU's other satellite at Long Newnton didn't help matters. However, as conditions improved during the late spring of 1945, so the need for more pilots reduced, and flying training was run down. In May 1945 all of the 15 (P)AFU flights transferred to Babdown Farm. On 15 June 1532 (BAT) Flight was disbanded, and this was followed by 15 (P)AFU itself four days later. The aircraft were ferried away to MUs, and the airfield was closed.

After a month or so Babdown Farm was taken over by 7 MU Quedgeley as a sub-site for storage, and this continued until January 1948 when the station was de-requisitioned and put up for disposal. It soon reverted to agriculture, and the buildings were put to new use as farm storage. Babdown Farm is still recognisable as an airfield today, although most of the buildings have now been demolished. The airfield itself remains unchanged: the perimeter track is still in place, and the three Teeside hangars and a Blister are well-maintained and in use by a number of trading and logistics companies.

Main features:
Runways: 045° 3,000ft, 123° 3,039ft, 343° 3,000ft, Sommerfield track. *Hangars:* three T1, five Blister, four Double-Blister. *Hardstandings:* none. *Accommodation:* RAF Officers 68, SNCOs 153, ORs 350; WAAF Officers 4, SNCOs 7, ORs 212.

BARNSLEY PARK, Gloucestershire

SP075075, 4 miles NE of Cirencester off A433

One of the satellite landing grounds allocated to 6 MU Brize Norton, Barnsley Park consisted of a number of clearings in a heavily wooded estate. Opened on 23 April 1941 by the Ministry of Aircraft Production as No 22 SLG, it was intended as a temporary storage area for new production aircraft pending the development of a much larger satellite at Woburn Abbey. Facilities at Barnsley Park were rudimentary, consisting of an administration office, guard posts and light AA defences.

It was intended that aircraft would land in fields adjacent to the woods and move into the clearings for storage. However, the surface proved unsuitable for repeated use by aircraft, and in November 1941 the site was closed for re-grading. Contractor W. G. Chivers & Son of Devizes was brought in to do the work, but bad weather impeded progress, and it was not until the spring of 1942 that work could be started. A test-landing by a Gloster Gladiator a few months later proved unsatisfactory, so work continued to bring the site up to a suitable standard. Eventually some 120,000 square yards of steel mesh were laid. The headquarters building was replaced by a brick one, built to resemble a domestic bungalow, and other buildings such as guard posts were reconstructed to resemble farm implement and machinery sheds.

Eventually reopened on 26 September 1942, 2 SLG was handed over to 5 MU Kemble. However, due to proposals for a larger airfield in the area, the SLG was not immediately used; although those proposals were shelved, it was not until November 1943 that the first aircraft, three Hurricanes, arrived at Barnsley Park for storage. Numbers soon increased due to the pressure on the main site at Kemble, and many aircraft were stored in the forest clearings under the trees. This activity continued throughout 1944 and into 1945, but with the end of the war in Europe the aircraft stored on site started to disappear just as quickly as they had appeared.

Barnsley Park was cleared of aircraft during the summer of 1945, and in September, no longer needed, the SLG was closed. The steel mesh was lifted and in early 1946 the area was returned to agriculture. Today little remains, apart from a few outbuildings and the administration building, which has been converted into a bungalow – just what it was designed to look like in 1943!

BARNSTAPLE, Devon

SU505345, 3 miles W of Barnstaple

North Devon Airport was opened on 13 June 1934 and consisted of two sheds and a clubhouse that had been built for the Barnstaple & North Devon Flying Club. Flying in the area had started the year before, when the newly-arrived Sussex aviators, Bob Boyd and Tommy Nash, started a joyriding and flying instruction business using a small field alongside the Taw estuary. Having opened the airport, Boyd and Nash started a passenger service to Lundy Island. Using a seven-seat DH Dragon, the business gradually built up, and by the summer up to ten flights per day were being made.

In April 1937 the company became Lundy & Atlantic Airlines, and had begun flying regular services to Cardiff and Plymouth with Short Scion four-engine monoplanes. The following year the company started flying training under the recently introduced Civil Air Guard Scheme, a Government initiative that offered flying training to civilian volunteers in return for a commitment to service in a state of emergency. Many people took up this offer, and by July 1939 well over 3,000 had gained their pilots licences nationwide; many went on to serve with the RAF and ATA. On 8 May 1939 the airport really appeared on the map when Western Airways started a service from Manchester to Penzance (Land's End) calling in at Barnstaple. However, this level of activity was not to continue for much longer: following the declaration of war in September 1939 the airfield was requisitioned by the Air Ministry and passenger services ceased.

Lundy & Atlantic Airlines continued trading for a while longer, overhauling light aircraft for the RAF and flying its Short Scions on army cooperation and searchlight training work. However, in May 1940 work started on a new airfield to the west to be known as Chivenor, and the airport was closed. The old airfield was used for dispersals as the new one developed, and after the war married quarters were built on the site.

A Typhoon IB of 486 Squadron formates with its replacement, a Tempest V, as the unit re-equipped at Beaulieu in February 1944.

BEAULIEU, Hampshire

SU350005, 4 miles NE of Lymington on B3055

The first airfield at Beaulieu was laid out to the east of the later one, close to the village of East Boldre. It was established in 1910 when William McArdle and J. Armstrong Drexel opened the New Forest Flying School on Bagshot Moor in three sheds on the edge of East Boldre village. However, the school was only active for just over a year before it went out of business, and in January 1912 its Bleriot monoplanes were put up for sale. The sheds remained, and were offered with the aerodrome for use by the RFC. Although the offer was not at first taken up, things changed with the outbreak of war, and the War Office took out a lease on one of the sheds.

East Boldre was little used until the autumn of 1915 when the increasing need for more flying schools resulted in the reopening of the old landing ground. A T-shaped area was marked out for a new airfield, and the first aeroplane arrived on 17 December 1915. This was the same day that the first squadron to be formed at Beaulieu, No 16 Reserve Squadron, came into being, equipped predominantly with the BE2C, two-seat Scout and the Avro 504K two-seat trainer.

The airfield was soon found to be too small, so was enlarged, with wooden and brick buildings mushrooming alongside to provide ground training facilities and accommodation. Three iron-framed hangars were erected, with galvanised-sheet coverings, and social facilities were later provided in the form of wooden huts and a brick-built YMCA institute.

In June 1916 No 23 RS was formed from a nucleus of No 16 RS personnel. Flying BE2Cs, the squadron left for Aboukir, Egypt, in August. In January 1917 No 84 Squadron, an operational scout unit, formed with BE2s at East Boldre, and started training before moving to Lilbourne near Rugby for final work-up. Re-equipped with SE5A single-seat fighters, the squadron moved to France that September.

In February 1917 another unit, No 87 RS, arrived from Gosport, but was in transit, and soon left aboard ship for Canada, leaving behind some Curtiss JN-4 Jenny trainers; these No 16 RS took on charge to fly alongside its BE2Cs, which had been supplemented by DH6s and RE8s. In late May 1917 the Reserve Squadrons were renamed Training Squadrons. No 79 Squadron arrived on 4 August to work up with its new Sopwith Dolphins, going to France in February 1918. No 103 Squadron was formed as a day-bomber squadron with a mix of types at Beaulieu on 1 September 1917, but only stayed a week before moving to Old Sarum (and later moving to France with DH9s). Then, on 30 November, No 16 TS swapped places with No 59 TS, moving to Yatesbury. (However, No 59 TS did not stay long, moving to Lilbourne early in 1918.)

No 117 Squadron, a day-bomber unit, formed at Beaulieu on New Year's Day 1918 with DH4s and RE8s. It was soon joined by Nos 1 and 70 TSs, which flew Sopwith Pup and Camel single-seat fighters as part of No 17 Wing, Southern Training Brigade. A further unit then joined them when No 73 TS brought its Avro 504s and Pups to Beaulieu in February 1918. By then the station was in the throes of a massive building programme, involving the construction of four 170ft x 100ft GS hangars on the western side. Additions were also made to the original technical site near East Boldre, and a new domestic site to the south-west of the airfield provided much-needed extra accommodation for personnel.

Following the formation of the RAF on 1 April 1918 there was considerable reorganisation to bring the former RFC and RNAS units together into the new third service. Training Squadrons in particular were reshuffled to form Training Depot Stations. No 1 and part of No 73 TS became No 29 TDS at Beaulieu on 27 July, while No 70 TS and the remainder of No 73 TS went to South Carlton to join No 28 TDS. The establishment of No 29 TDS was thirty-six Avro 504Ks and thirty-six Sopwith Dolphins, but Camels remained on strength until sufficient Dolphins became available.

The building programme was almost complete when the Great War came to an end. The inevitable run-down followed, although the airfield remained in use until 1919. No 29 TDS was disbanded, and by July most of the personnel and equipment had left the site. Two months later the buildings were put up for sale by the Aerodrome Disposal Board. The airfield was then cleared, although it was several years before most of the concrete foundations were lifted (a few are still in place – another survival is the YMCA building, which still exists today as the East Boldre Village Hall).

The former airfield was used by the occasional light aircraft during the 1920s and 1930s, but never on a regular basis. When war came again, however, Beaulieu was once again considered as a military flying base. Surveys were made, and it was decided to build a new airfield to the west of the former site, across the Beaulieu-Lymington road on Hatchet Moor. Mowlem & Co was brought in to start construction in 1941. Three runways were laid in the classic 'A' shape with a perimeter track encircling them, much of the brick-rubble hardcore foundations for which came from Southampton bomb-sites. Together with most of the airfields built in southern England in the early war period, pipe-mines were built into the runways; these were explosive-filled pipes laid in a herringbone pattern, so that should an invasion occur the mines could be detonated to render the runways useless to the Germans.

The new airfield was so urgently required for use by 19 Group, RAF Coastal Command, that it was opened early, on 8 August 1942. Although the runways were surfaced, most of the operational buildings were incomplete, a number of T5 hangars were yet to be roofed, and most personnel lived in tents while their accommodation was still being worked on. Eventually there were to be several living sites (consisting of brick-built and wood/steel Nissen huts) scattered near and in the trees, and three communal sites with messes, station HQ, sick quarters and stores.

No 224 Squadron was the first to operate from Beaulieu, its Liberator Mk II and IIIA aircraft starting to arrive from Tiree on 9 September 1942. They immediately began patrols over the Western Approaches and into the Bay of Biscay, in search of U-boats threatening Allied shipping. Success soon followed, for on 20 October Liberator 'H' captained by Fg Off David Sleep found U-216 on the surface, and went into the attack and sink the submarine with depth charges. The attack was at such a low level (some 30 feet) that the Liberator's elevators were damaged by the force of the explosions, but the crew were able to nurse the aircraft back to a force-landing at Predannack. Three days later came the first attack on Beaulieu, when a German bomber dived out of low cloud and dropped four bombs, but causing no casualties and little damage. The RAF's revenge followed the next day, when Liberator 'G' of 224 Squadron flown by Plt Off Liddington found U-599, sinking it with depth charges.

This period coincided with the build-up to the Allied landings in North Africa (Operation *Torch*), which required many convoys to pass through the Bay of Biscay. The desperate shortage of Coastal Command aircraft forced Bomber Command to lend it squadrons, and at Beaulieu this resulted in the arrival of fifteen Halifax B Mk 2s of 405 (RCAF) Squadron and five from 158 Squadron, on 25 October. They joined the Liberators on patrols, using St Eval as a forward base. The success of this strategy was proved when Flt Lt Palmer of 405 Squadron, flying Halifax 'J' on 27 November, caught U-263 running on the surface. Despite determined fire from escorts, Palmer made two runs and severely damaged the submarine. Unfortunately these operations did not come without cost, and during 405 Squadron's stay three of its aircraft crashed during take-offs or landings, with the loss of seventeen crew members. They were not alone, as a Liberator of 224 Squadron crashed near Lymington during this time, the crew being killed when the aircraft's depth charges exploded. The 158 Squadron detachments returned to the unit's base at Rufforth on 6 December, but 405 Squadron stayed, taking part in anti-shipping sweeps and convoy escorts as well as anti-submarine patrols. It eventually left Beaulieu on 3 March 1943, returning to Topcliffe.

As 224 Squadron began to receive the later Marks V and VIII of the Liberator during March, they were joined at Beaulieu by a detachment of 1 (Coastal) OCU, which specialised in converting crews to the Liberator. While training it also undertook patrol work, and gradually took over from 224 Squadron, which moved to St Eval on 25 April 1943. The Wellingtons of 311 (Czech) Squadron arrived at Beaulieu on 26 May, for replacement by the Liberator. Already a successful Coastal squadron, the Czechs maintained their success on the new type. Having started to receive these in July, they were declared operational on the Liberator the following month. Operating from Beaulieu, Liberator 'M' of 311 Squadron was attacked by a Ju 88 on 30 August; although the Liberator's tail gunner was killed, the remaining gunners managed to shoot down the German fighter, enabling the Liberator to return to base.

The Czechs were joined by 53 Squadron, which had converted to the Liberator Mk V at Thorney Island and arrived at Beaulieu on 25 September 1943. Both squadrons were then involved in operations in the Bay of Biscay, searching for enemy shipping. The Liberators were fitted with ASV radar, particularly useful for detecting surfaced U-boats. During their time at Beaulieu the Czechs claimed two U-boats destroyed, two damaged, and several Ju 88 fighters shot down. One successful action on 10 November employed rocket projectiles, which were fitted to some Liberators: U-966 was located and damaged by a Wellington of 612 Squadron in the Bay of Biscay, and further damaged by two US PB4Y-1 Liberators of the USN from Dunkeswell. The U-boat was escaping when it was attacked by a Liberator of 311 Squadron, whose rockets penetrated the submarine's hull, forcing its crew to beach the boat on the Spanish Coast, where they blew it up.

Some of the 53 Squadron aircraft also had the new Leigh Light, a powerful wing-mounted searchlight. Early on the morning of 13 December 1943 Liberator 'B' of the unit located a U-boat on its radar, then illuminated it with its Leigh Light. When the U-boat opened fire, the pilot, Sqn Ldr L. C. Crawford, switched off the light and, using available moonlight, straddled the U-boat with six depth charges. After the submarine disappeared, wreckage and bodies were seen in the water.

With the impending invasion of the European mainland, it was decided to move Coastal Command squadrons further west to Cornwall and Pembrokeshire in order to lock off the Western Approaches to U-boats. This would also leave bases in the south, such as Beaulieu, available for the build-up of the invasion forces. No 53 Squadron transferred to St Eval on 3 January 1944, followed to Cornwall by 311 Squadron on 23 February, which went to Predannack.

Nine weeks after 53 Squadron's departure, the servicing echelons of two Typhoon 1b units arrived to take over. These were from 257 Squadron, Warmwell, and 263 Squadron from Fairford Common. The Typhoons soon arrived, and eight aircraft of 257 took off on their first operation from Beaulieu on the 2nd, to attack targets on the Cherbourg peninsula. No 263 Squadron's aircraft soon followed suit, and both units went on to maintain a high level of fighter-bomber operations against targets in occupied France, as part of 2TAF. Towards the end of January Beaulieu was also used by the Ibsley Wing for mounting *Rodeos* (fighter sweeps over enemy territory). Typically, on the 29th two Typhoons of 266 Squadron, five of 193 and eight of 257 went on a sweep to the outskirts of Paris. One Do 217 bomber and two training aircraft were shot down for no loss, although three of the Typhoons were damaged by flak.

On 31 January 1944 No 257 swapped places with 486 Squadron, and moved to Tangmere. No 486 was another 2TAF fighter-bomber squadron flying the Typhoon, but starting to convert to the Tempest, an improved and faster development. As well as attacking the German defences, the Beaulieu Wing then became heavily involved in targeting V-1 flying bomb launch sites. The 2TAF units departed in early spring 1944, No 486 Squadron to Drem on 28 February and 263 to Warmwell on 6 March. Beaulieu was then handed over to the US 9th Air Force (the US equivalent of the 2nd TAF) and in came the 365th Fighter Group, 84th Fighter Wing, from Gosfield in Essex. The three Squadrons that made up the group, the 386th, 387th and 388th Fighter Squadrons, flew the P-47D Thunderbolt. Having arrived in the UK just before Christmas 1943, these squadrons were initially employed on escort work, flying with the bombers of the US 8th Air Force on daylight raids into Germany. Following the arrival of the longer-range P-51 Mustang, the Thunderbolt units were transferred to the 9th Air Force for use in the fighter-bomber role.

Arriving at Beaulieu on 4 March and having their aircraft fitted with bomb racks, the US pilots began fighter-bomber training, and flew their first mission from Beaulieu on 20 March, making dive-bombing attacks on an airfield in northern France. Some escort work for B-26 medium bombers followed, but the majority of their missions then involved dive-bombing and ground attack. On the day of the Allied landings, 6 June, Lieutenant-Colonel Robert Coffey (the group's Air Executive) led

NK530, an Anson X photo-chase aircraft, outside the AFEE hangars at Beaulieu after the war.

forty-seven Thunderbolts of the 365th, armed with 500lb and 1000lb bombs, on the first of several missions that day, to attack targets near the US landing beaches. The group lost three pilots that day, but flew five missions on D-Day+1 over Omaha Beach, and another three missions on D+2.

As well as attacking ground targets, the P-47s also intercepted Luftwaffe fighters, and were credited with twenty-nine aerial victories while operating from Beaulieu. One of its best days was 25 June, when eight enemy fighters were destroyed. On 2 July Robert Coffey became the 9th Air Force's third P-47 ace when he shot down a Bf 109. However, the group's losses mounted the more ground-attack missions it undertook, losing twenty-four P-47s in total during its four months at Beaulieu. Aircraft of the 365th FG had been using forward air strips in Normandy to refuel and rearm since 14 June, and it was decided that the time was right to move to the continent. The group therefore began moving to US Airfield A-7 at Azeville on 21 June, with the last members of the rear party leaving Beaulieu on 2 July.

The P-47s were in turn replaced by the B-26 Marauders of 323rd Bombardment Group, 98th Bomb Wing, which began to arrive from Earls Colne on 11 July. Over the ensuing five weeks more than sixty B-26s of the Group's units (the 453rd, 454th, and 455th Bomb Squadrons) moved in. Their crews flew twenty-eight missions from Beaulieu for the loss of only one aircraft, and that was not due to enemy action, having crashed after running out of fuel. Eventually, like the P-47s before them, the B-26s of the 323rd BG also started to move to the continent; the first aircraft left for A-20 Lessay in France on 16 August, the last leaving ten days later.

Beaulieu remained active as a useful staging post for aircraft moving to and returning from the continent, but was returned to RAF control on 27 September. Although plans were made to develop it into a bomber base, Beaulieu then became the new location for the Airborne Forces Experimental Establishment, which started to arrive in December 1944. The AFEE had been established at Ringway in 1942, having its origins in the Central Landing School. It later moved to Sherburn-in-Elmet, from where it relocated to Beaulieu. The AFEE's early work included the development of military parachutes, such as the X-type standard troop parachute, and other load-carrying and supply parachutes. It also developed the use of gliders, and made a major contribution to the effectiveness of the Allied airborne forces. One of the attractions of Beaulieu was its proximity to the old East Boldre airfield, which provided a ready-made DZ and range for parachute-dropping. Paratroopers could be returned to the airfield from their drops by jeep just as their aircraft was coming in to land.

Although the AFEE came under the MoS, it was staffed by civilian and military personnel. Airborne trials were undertaken using Stirlings, Halifaxes and Lancasters to tow Horsa, Hamilcar and Hadrian gliders. Other towing and chase duties were flown by a variety of types including Spitfires, Martinets, Tempests, Ansons, Mosquitoes and Beaufighters. A number of different types of helicopters were also flown by AFEE, to evaluate their potential and develop their role as military aircraft.

The AFEE continued its work at Beaulieu into the post-war years. As helicopters developed and parachuting techniques improved, the 'Plywood Air Force' of gliders was gradually phased out. By 1948 major activity concerned the use of Valettas and Hastings in paratroop trials, which eventually proved of great use during the last operational jump by British paratroops, on El Gamil airfield during the 1956 Suez campaign. A reorganisation of R&D establishments resulted in the transfer of the work of the AFEE to A&AEE Boscombe Down in September 1950, and the closure of Beaulieu as an airfield, exacerbated by the deterioration of its runways.

Beaulieu's outline could still be seen from the air in August 2008.

Beaulieu was placed on C&M, but held as a standby base at the request of the USAF. In 1953 the runways were duly repaired, and extended to take B-29 bombers. However, the airfield was never needed by the Americans, and in 1959 it was sold off to the Forestry Commission. Over the years most of the buildings have been removed, together with the majority of the concrete and tarmac runways and taxiways. A few buildings remain, including part of No 5 living site, which is now a campsite. Although the runways have long since gone, the soil allows only thin vegetation cover, and the outline of the old airfield is still clearly visible today.

Main features:
Runways: 088° 5,910ft x 150ft, 027° 4,110ft x 150ft, 151° 4,110ft x 150ft, concrete. *Hangars:* Two T2, one Blister. *Hardstandings:* Fifty concrete. *Accommodation:* RAF Officers 181, SNCOs 502, ORs 1,436; WAAF Officers 10, SNCOs 40, ORs 288.

BISTERNE, Dorset

SU155030, 1¹/₂ miles S of Ringwood on B3347

One of a number of locations surveyed for ALGs in the New Forest, construction at Bisterne started in June 1943. The airfield was to be one of a number of temporary airfields with basic facilities to be used as forward bases to accommodate some of the vast influx of aircraft that were to be built up prior to the Allied invasion of Europe.

Hedges were cleared from the selected area half a mile north of the village of Bisterne, trees were cut down, and the area levelled and graded. Most of this work was undertaken by a flight of 5005 Airfield Construction Squadron, RAF, whose personnel then laid two runways, taxiways and dispersals, all of steel Sommerfield tracking. Four Blister hangars were erected to the east of the main runway, with fuel and ammunition storage facilities to the west. Although completed by September 1943, the airfield was allocated to a US fighter group, which meant that additional marshalling areas and taxiways were needed; these were added in January 1944.

USAAF advance parties erected tents on the airfield the following month, and on 7 March the personnel of the 371st Fighter Group began to arrive, having travelled by sea to Liverpool aboard the liner *Mauretania*. The Group consisted of three squadrons, the 404th, 405th and 406th Fighter Squadrons. These were gradually equipped with P-47D Thunderbolts on delivery from the USAAF Base Aircraft Assembly Depot at Filton. Conditions at the ALG were very primitive, with facilities under canvas, apart from a few farm buildings (Brixey's Farm was commandeered as Group HQ). Servicing of aircraft was in the open or in the open-ended Blister hangars, until the Americans built a large portable hangar in the south-west corner of the site.

After a hectic period of training, the first combat mission was flown from Bisterne on 12 April when eighteen P-47s from each squadron took off on a fighter sweep. Further sweeps, escorts and fighter-bomber missions were flown during April and May, but the airfield surface gradually succumbed to the substantial pounding that the 8-ton P-47s gave it. When the first aircraft to land from a returning mission on 21 April nosed over on the subsiding runway and the second aircraft to land narrowly avoided it, the rest of the formation were diverted to nearby Ibsley, 3 miles to the north. They flew from there while runway repairs were undertaken, returning to resume operations from Bisterne on 14 May (having had their first encounter with the Luftwaffe on the 8th, shooting down two Bf 109s for the loss one of one P-47), and were soon busy usually flying two missions per day to attack communications, airfields and other targets in France.

A typical day was 21 May, when the 371st FG despatched fifty P-47s on a sweep to the Loire Valley. They attacked three trains, but two aircraft were hit by flak and were lucky to get back to land at Warmwell. On D-Day, one squadron, the 404th, flew a dive-bombing mission in support of forward troops. Further ground-attack operations followed. On 8 June the 406th Fighter Squadron, led by Major Rockford Gray, encountered a number of FW 190s. Gray shot down three of them, to become the 9th AF's first P-47 ace (having achieved five victories).

Preparations started for the group's move to France as soon as a suitable airfield became available, and on the 17th an advanced echelon moved out to A-6 Beuzeville. While the move took place (which took twelve days) the group operated from both airfields. During this time, on 18 June, it was tasked to support US ground troops on the Cherbourg peninsula. One of the 371st's most successful actions ensued that day, with all three squadrons attacking enemy gun emplacements, tanks and troops. In one attack alone the 404th caught a German armoured column and destroyed more than a hundred vehicles. Ground-attack work continued, and on the 19th, during an armed reconnaissance mission, four pilots of the 405th Fighter Squadron each shot down a Bf 109.

Most of the fighters had left Bisterne towards the end of June, and on the 29th the rear party saw off the last C-47 taking stores to A-6. No longer required, Bisterne was cleared of stores and equipment. In November 1944 the RAF's 5025 ACS started work on clearing the tracking, but some of it was so embedded in the ground that it was bulldozed into a ridgeline. It was not until some time after the war that three of the Blister hangars were removed. The fourth remained in place and was used for storage by Brixey's Farm until it was moved to Crow Farm; it is still in use today as part of the Crow Owl Sanctuary. Virtually nothing remains of the former ALG today, apart from the odd piece of tracking rusting away in the hedgerows.

Main features:
Runways: N-S 4,800ft, E-W 4,050ft, Sommerfield track. *Hangars:* four Blister.
Hardstandings: eighty Sommerfield track. *Accommodation:* tented camp.

BLAKEHILL FARM, Wiltshire

ST080915, 2¹/2 miles SW of Cricklade, SE of B4040

Although close to the village of Chelworth, Blakehill Farm took its name from the agricultural land that had been requisitioned for it in 1943. It was one of three new airfields to be constructed north of Swindon to house 46 Group, the Transport Command formation that brought together the RAF's tactical air transport squadrons in preparation for the invasion of Europe, the others being Down Ampney and Broadwell.

Blakehill Farm was opened on 9 February 1944, but was hardly ready for occupation as few buildings were finished. Nonetheless its first resident, 233 Squadron, arrived on 5 March 1944. Originally a Hudson unit within Coastal Command, the Squadron had been brought back from

Blakehill Farm seen under construction in August 1943.

Gibraltar to re-equip with Dakotas and re-role as an airborne forces squadron, to tow gliders and drop paratroops. It was followed by 92 and 93 Field Staging Posts, which prepared for the move to the continent – they trained in freight loading and casualty evacuation, and were joined by 91 and 94 FSPs, which stayed until 28 April. A Casualty Air Evacuation Centre was also established. Later in March HQ Wing Glider Pilot Regiment arrived, its task being to administer glider pilots at each of the three 46 Group stations.

Training for 233 Squadron aircrews started with paratroop-dropping, then glider-towing, and they were kept busy from mid-March. They participated in huge 46 Group exercises, many of which took place over Salisbury Plain, regularly flying more than twenty Dakotas, towing Horsas and dropping paratroops. With the expected invasion impending, these exercises increased in pace

A Dakota IV of 437 Squadron in May 1945.

and in number. On 24 April 1944 a Exercise *Mush* took place at Corps level to rehearse the airborne phase of the invasion. During this build-up period crews gained operational experience by being sent on *Nickel* raids, dropping propaganda leaflets over France.

On 1 June 233 Squadron's aircraft were brought up to a state of readiness for Operation *Tonga*, the airborne phase of *Overlord*, the overall D-Day operation. They were joined by some aircraft from 271 Squadron, which had been deployed to Blakehill because of congestion at its base at Down Ampney. Following a final briefing on 5 June, the crews of 271 and 233 Squadrons at Blakehill Farm were among those of the fifteen RAF transport squadrons who boarded 362 aircraft at eight airfields in the south of England that night. The first to take off from Blakehill at 2250 hours were four 233 Squadron Dakotas towing Horsas, followed by twenty-four carrying paratroops. They had the furthest to go, in order to deliver British paratroops to Toufreville, the most southerly of the DZs, and also to the east of the beachhead, to drop paratroops on the Merville Battery, which threatened the landing beaches.

All went well, the paratroops and gliders being successfully delivered. However, two of Blakehill's Dakotas were shot down. Once the beachhead had been established the Dakotas flew re-supply missions, including a series code-named Operation *Rob Roy*. On 8 June twenty-one Dakotas of 233 Squadron took off carrying 371 panniers containing food, ammunition, fuel and radios. As they approached the French coast the formations came under intense fire from 'friendly' naval vessels. Two aircraft (the leader and the number two) went down in flames, but the remainder dropped their supplies successfully. On 13 June a 233 Squadron Dakota became the first Allied transport aircraft to land in France after the invasion, touching down at a British-built airstrip to take in supplies and bring out casualties. With the establishment of airstrips on the continent from which the Dakotas could operate, regular transport flights took place. Soon an average of five daily services were being flown to France, delivering freight, food, spares, weapons, fuel, ammunition and personnel, returning with casualties. The Dakotas were not dedicated air ambulances, but Air Ambulance Nursing Orderlies were trained to supervise the loading and securing of the patients and look after them on the return flight to the CAEC. Each Dakota could carry eighteen stretcher cases and six sitting casualties.

These flights continued throughout July and August, their continental destinations gradually getting further from the coast as the Allied armies moved inland. In early September seventy-five USAAF C-47s used Blakehill to load fuel in jerry cans urgently needed by advancing US forces. By then the station's Dakota strength had doubled, with the formation of 437 (RCAF) Squadron on 4 September. The new unit began working up and soon it and 233 Squadron were making intensive preparations for another airborne operation, *Market Garden*, the capture of the bridges to Arnhem.

In the initial assault on 17 September, twenty-two Dakotas of 233 Squadron towing Horsas carried 308 troops and their equipment into battle from Blakehill Farm, while another dozen Dakotas of 437 Squadron took another 146 men. Next day 233 Squadron flew sixteen Dakota/Horsa combinations, and 437 Squadron flew six. German resistance was light during this time, but during the re-supply on 20 September flak units and FW 190 fighters took a heavy toll of the Allied transports. No 233 Squadron lost three out of eighteen Dakotas to FW 190s and 437 Squadron lost four. A further Dakota of 233 Squadron was shot down during a supply drop on the 23rd.

After Arnhem and into 1945 the station's aircraft returned to freight and casevac duties. These were interrupted by more glider-towing practice in the early spring, when the Allied armies were poised on the borders of Germany. It was decided to use airborne troops to secure the far bank of the Rhine while ground troops crossed the river. Operation *Varsity* was mounted during the night of 23/24 March 1945, and for this the Blakehill squadrons were moved forward to Birch in Essex in order to maximise the Dakotas' range. At dawn on 24 March twenty-four aircraft of 233 Squadron and another twenty-four of 437 Squadron took off for the bridgehead, taking troops of the Oxfordshire & Buckinghamshire Light Infantry. The troops landed, regrouped and successfully took their objectives. Both squadrons resumed transport duties following the Rhine crossing, flying at maximum effort to support the rapid advance of the Allied armies across northern Germany. The main commodity in demand was fuel, and daily flights were made to the forward airfields of Selle, Rheine and Luneburg. No 437 Squadron moved to the continent on 6 May to provide a shuttle service around Allied bases there, 233 Squadron continuing to operate from Blakehill until 8 June, when it moved to Odiham. Earmarked for service in the Far East, the unit began moving to India in August 1945.

The Dakotas were replaced at Blakehill Farm by the Hamilcar gliders and Albemarle tugs of 22 HGCU, but with diminished need for glider-towing the unit was disbanded on 15 November. A month later Dakotas reappeared when 575 Squadron arrived at Blakehill. It did not stay for long and at the end of January 1946 left for Bari in Italy. In December 1528 Radio Aids Training Flight arrived with its Oxfords to use the station's Blind Landing System, installed the year before, for training. Although this unit moved to Fairford in February 1946, it reformed as 1555 RATF and returned to Blakehill Farm in April 1946, but left again the following August.

Closed and put on C&M on 5 November 1946, the airfield had a brief resurgence in December 1948 when 2 FTS South Cerney used it as an RLG. This continued when the FTS became the Basic Element of the CFS in 1952. When in May 1957 the CFS moved this unit to Little Rissington, flying at Blakehill Farm finally came to an end.

The airfield remained in Government hands, and in 1967 GCHQ set up an experimental radio and monitoring station there, which entailed erecting a 200-foot wooden mast on the airfield. There was a partial site clearance in the 1970s, when the runways were torn up to provide hardcore for the M4 motorway. GCHQ moved out in the late 1990s and the MoD finally disposed of Blakehill Farm in 2000. Most of the land has since been returned to agriculture, or been acquired by the Wiltshire Wild Life Trust for reinstatement to meadowland. A few of the airfield buildings remain, some forming part of the Chelworth Industrial Estate. A memorial to the members of 437 (RCAF) Squadron stands near the site of the main entrance to the station.

Main features:
Runways: 240° 6,000ft x 150ft, 130° 4,200ft x 150ft, 190° 4,200ft x 150ft, tarmac. *Hangars:* two T2. *Hardstandings:* forty-six loop. *Accommodation:* RAF Officers 224, SNCOs 365, ORs 1,990; WAAF Officers 7, SNCOs 16, ORs 122.

Spitfire Mk XII of 41 Squadron is seen at Bolt Head in May 1944.

BOLT HEAD, Devon

SX713373, 1 1/2 miles SW of Salcombe

A number of rudimentary airfields with minimal facilities were built near the coast in late 1940 to extend the effective range of day-fighters, which then had a particularly short endurance. Originally for defence, they also became useful for bomber and convoy escort work. Bolt Head, built on the Devon headland of the same name, was a typical example of such a Forward Operating Base.

Originally little more than a grass field with a windsock and number of huts, Bolt Head was opened in the spring of 1941 for the fighters of 10 and 11 Groups, Fighter Command, when escorting the medium bombers of Bomber Command's 2 Group engaged on raids into western France. A permanent ground handling party was provided by the personnel of RAF Hope Cove, a nearby GCI Station. Although opened for fighters, the first users were the Lysanders of 16 Squadron, an Army Cooperation unit based at Weston Zoyland, detached to give chemical warfare defence training to locally-based troops.

The first aircraft to be actually based at Bolt Head were also Lysanders. In the autumn of 1941 two aircraft from 276 Squadron, an ASR unit based at Harrowbeer, began operations from the airfield. They proved their worth on the afternoon of 18 December, when called on to search for the crew of a Halifax II of 35 Squadron. The bomber had been hit by flak during a raid on Brest, and came down in the Channel some 60 miles off the English coast. The Lysanders located the aircraft's crew, who were rescued.

The airfield was upgraded during the winter of 1941/42 with the laying of two Sommerfield track runways, each originally 2,700 feet long, but later extended. Taxiways and parking areas were also laid out, two Blister hangars erected and bulk fuel storage tanks built, together with barrack huts, flight and administration offices. The first fighters to use the improved airfield were the Spitfire VBs of 317 (City of Wilno) Squadron, from the Polish Wing formed at Exeter in August 1941. However, the Luftwaffe had noticed this new activity in the area, and sent over two FW 190s on 7 March 1942 to attack the airfield. They strafed the area and hit a Spitfire that was just taking off (its pilot managed to return and land safely).

The Germans returned at the end of April to bomb the airfield, but no damage was sustained. The Spitfires continued with their escort work from Bolt Head, but tragedy occurred on 15 March when twelve 317 Squadron pilots were detailed to escort a Boston raid to northern France. On their return they found their base shrouded in sea mist. Short of fuel, only two pilots managed to land at Bolt Head, the others either force-landing or baling out. Five aircraft were destroyed, the CO being killed and two others injured. When the Poles moved to Northolt the following month they were replaced at Exeter by the Czechs, and 310 Squadron started using Bolt Head for mounting fighter sweeps, bomber escorts, convoy patrols and *Rhubarbs* (small-scale fighter attacks on targets of opportunity). Typical of these was the attack on St Malo on 3 July 1942. Twelve Bostons of 88 Squadron took off from Exeter, escorted by fighter wings from Ibsley and Portreath as well as Exeter, joining squadrons from Tangmere, totalling almost 100 aircraft. Two of the Exeter squadrons flew from Bolt Head, formating with the Bostons over the airfield and flying at low level until 30 miles from the French coast. They then climbed to 8,000 feet, bombed the target and, turning for Start Point, descended to sea level. Some of the fighters remained with the Bostons as close escort while the remainder attacked a nearby German airfield before returning.

The Czech Spitfires were replaced at Bolt Head in September 1942 by the Typhoons of 257 Squadron. Having only recently converted to the new type, their pilots were initially engaged in local area defence. They claimed their first success on 28 September, when they intercepted a Ju 88. On 3 November Teignmouth was bombed by FW 190s; the 257 Squadron pilots set off in pursuit, and caught up some 35 miles west of Guernsey. They shot down two into the sea and damaged several others.

On 26 September 1942 three squadrons used Bolt Head as an advanced base in order to escort B-17s of the 8th Air Force raiding U-boat pens at Brest. They were a North American Wing comprising 401 (RCAF) Squadron, based at Kenley, 412 (RCAF) Squadron, Redhill, and 133 (Eagle) Squadron, Great Sampford. All three were equipped with the latest Spitfire, the Mark IX, which could engage the FW 190 on equal terms. The Wing took off and climbed to 2,500 feet to meet the Fortresses. Unfortunately, instead of the forecast headwind, the bombers had met a strong tailwind, and to find them the fighters had to set off in pursuit. Because of bad weather the B-17s were recalled, and met the Spitfires coming back. Unfortunately by then the fighters' fuel state was getting critical and, having escorted the B-17s to a bomb-dumping area off the coast, most of the Spitfires only just managed to get back to Bolt Head. Unfortunately 133 Squadron wasn't so lucky: disorientated in the cloud, a formation of ten Spitfires descended and found themselves over the coast, not the Devon one as they thought, but the French coast. Nine Spitfires were then shot down, or captured when they landed at Luftwaffe airfields. The tenth managed to escape, and crash-landed near Kingsbridge in South Devon, just short of Bolt Head. No 133 Squadron was all but wiped out, a tragic end to its short life in Fighter Command. On 29 September the unit was transferred to the USAAF as the 336th Fighter Squadron of the 4th Fighter Group.

Various fighter squadrons continued to use Bolt Head as an FOB during the winter of 1942/43, and into the spring. The following summer, 610 (County of Chester) Squadron became the first to actually be based at Bolt Head when it flew in on 26 June from Perranporth. It flew Spitfire Mk VBs at this time, and was mainly involved in anti-*Rhubarb* patrols (as well as flying a few Rhubarbs themselves over France!). During one operation they located the dinghies of the crew of a B-17 downed in the Channel, and beat off attacks from German fighters. While at Bolt Head they claimed four Bf 110s during one ten-day period. The unit left for Fairwood Common in mid-December 1943.

Several fighter squadrons used Bolt Head from March to September 1944, most only briefly – for example, the Typhoons of 266 Squadron arrived from Harrowbeer on 7 March and returned five days later. They were followed by 234 Squadron on 18 March, which flew its Spitfire Vs in from Coltishall. The Squadron departed on 29 April for Deanland. More Spitfires arrived later that day, this time of the Griffon-powered variety, when the Spitfire Mk XIIs of 41 Squadron arrived from Fairwood Common, their aircraft having been modified for bombing.

Engaged on pre-invasion strike operations, 41 Squadron deployed to Fairwood Common on 16 May for a week, and while it was away 610 Squadron returned to Bolt Head from Culmhead. It brought with it another new version of the Spitfire – the Mk XIV, which was also Griffon-powered, and was the higher-altitude version of the Mk XII. The Squadron mounted coastal patrols before moving on to Harrowbeer, handing back to 41 Squadron, which then concentrated on patrolling the coast to the west of Portsmouth to prevent enemy aircraft reaching the D-Day invasion build-up areas. These patrols were extended to cover the assault convoys assembling in the Channel on 5 June, thirty-two sorties being flown that day. The Squadron mounted twenty-five sorties on D-Day itself, a mixture of shipping and ASR patrols. During the invasion period other residents at Bolt Head were the Spitfire LFVBs and Walrus IIs of B Flight 276 Squadron, an ASR unit, whose job was to patrol the Western Approaches for downed airmen. If the Spitfires, which operated in pairs for mutual protection, found anyone, they would orbit the area until one of the Walruses arrived on the scene to make the pick-up. Other brief D-Day residents were the Auster AOP IVs of 652 (AOP) Squadron. On D-Day+2 the Austers left Bolt Head with a Walrus escort for an ALG in Normandy, and became the first British aircraft to be based in France following the invasion.

When 41 Squadron departed for Westhampnett on 19 June it was replaced by the Typhoons of 263 Squadron, engaged on attacks on coastal shipping and radar sites in France. They moved to Hurn on 10 July. Mosquitoes of 151 Squadron then used Bolt Head occasionally, on detachment from their base at Predannack. The last fighter squadron to operate from the airfield was 611 Squadron, its Spitfire Mk IXs flying in from Predannack on 17 July. After a brief interlude on coastal and shipping patrols they departed on 30 August for Bradwell Bay.

Also in late August 276 Squadron moved to the continent, and its B Flight was replaced at Bolt Head by most of 275 Squadron, another similarly equipped ASR unit, which moved across from Warmwell. 275 Squadron departed for Exeter on 18 October, leaving a detachment behind. Its Walruses and Spitfires were the last residents at Bolt Head, and when the unit was disbanded on 15 February 1945 operational flying from the airfield came to an end. It was retained on C&M as an emergency landing ground for a while (a Wellington XIII suffered an undercarriage collapse following just such a landing on 1 May 1946), but Bolt Head finally closed in 1947, when the site was cleared of metal tracking and returned to farmland.

A radar station was built on the site in the 1950s and, although it too has since been closed, its large concrete bunker remains in place. Some private flying takes place from a small grass strip at the former airfield, but the remainder of the site is National Trust property and a memorial stone stands at the intersection of the two former runways.

Main features:
Runways: 237° 4,200ft, 293° 3,900ft, Sommerfield track. *Hangars:* two Blister. *Hardstandings:* five Sommerfield track. *Accommodation:* RAF Officers 39, SNCOs 60, ORs 375; WAAF Officers 1, SNCOs 12, ORs 120.

BOSCOMBE DOWN, Wiltshire

SU182398, 1 1/2 miles SE of Amesbury

Like Farnborough, Boscombe Down is one of the great names in the annals of British aviation. Unlike Farnborough, however, Boscombe Down is still active in the role that has been its forte for seventy years – aircraft research, trials and development. Originally known as Red House Farm airfield, Boscombe Down was first opened as a training airfield for the RFC in October 1917. Covering some 330 acres, it was established as No 6 Training Depot Station. With Avro 504K, BE2E, DH4 and DH9 aircraft, the station's role was to give advanced training to pilots in order to meet the demands of operations along the Western Front. As well as British pilots, pupils from Australia, New Zealand and the USA were trained at 6 TDS. The original accommodation for both

An aerial view of Boscombe Down in 1918, showing many tents and buildings including two General Storage Sheds with four more under construction and thirteen canvas Bessoneau hangars.

Mosquito VI HJ662 on trials at the A&AEE in the intruder role with four 20mm and .303-inch guns and two 250lb wing-mounted bombs.

troops and aeroplanes was in tents, but more permanent buildings were gradually constructed. Wooden-framed canvas Bessoneau hangars (a proven design still in use with the RAF sixty years later!) were erected, supplemented by six GS Aeroplane Sheds and an Aircraft Repair Shed. Other wood and brick buildings housed the operations and technical staff and provided living quarters.

The end of the Great War saw a massive reduction in the armed services and their bases. Although limited flying continued at Boscombe Down until May 1919, it was one of the many bases closed during the post-war euphoria. On 1 April 1920 the site was sold back to its former owners together with the buildings, and the aircraft were also disposed of. Sheep returned to the area, and the hangars were used for the storage of hay and feed. Nonetheless, the sheep's good fortune was not to last! During the mid-1920s the Air Ministry felt that Boscombe Down would be ideal for a new bomber station. The site was re-purchased, together with an additional 200 acres, and work started in October 1927 to make it into a permanent station. Hangars were renovated, and other buildings repaired or replaced, to provide sufficient accommodation for two bomber squadrons as part of the Wessex Bombing Area. This included a station headquarters, Officers' and Sergeants' Messes, accommodation blocks and married quarters.

The new station was officially opened on 1 September 1930, the first squadron to arrive being 9 (Bomber) Squadron, which transferred with Vickers Virginias from Manston on 26 November. It was joined in February 1931 by the Porton Experimental Flight, formed to support the Royal Engineers Experimental Station at Porton Down. Equipped with a Fairey Fox, two Hawker Horsleys and a Blackburn Dart, the flight had moved from Netheravon. The second bomber squadron, No 10, equipped with Handley Page Hinaidis, took up residence on 1 April 1931, having been previously based at Upper Heyford. Both squadrons played an important part in expanding the RAF's bombing force. No 9 Squadron retained the Virginia during its time at Boscombe Down, while 10 Squadron re-equipped, first also with the Virginia in 1933, then with the more advanced Heyford in 1935.

As their crews' proficiency on these types developed, it was decided to use them to establish and train more bomber squadrons. In September 1935 this resulted in the formation of 214 Squadron from B Flight of 9 Squadron, and 97 Squadron from B Flight of 10 Squadron. Both 9 and 214 Squadrons moved away to Andover a month later, but 10 Squadron remained and a repeat process resulted in the formation of 78 and 166 Squadrons in November 1936. By February 1937 all four units had moved to other stations.

With no squadrons, Boscombe Down went to 16 (Reconnaissance) Group, Coastal Command, becoming the base for a number of maritime reconnaissance squadrons, including 224 Squadron with Ansons, and 217 Squadron, which formed at the airfield (also with Ansons) on 15 March 1937. By July both units had moved on, and the airfield returned to Bomber Command. In fact, two bomber squadrons, 51 with Ansons and 58 with Whitleys, were already in residence, having been transferred from Driffield earlier in March. They were joined by 88 Squadron, which transferred from Waddington with Hawker Hinds.

With the opening of ranges on Salisbury Plain and at Porton Down, Boscombe Down became an important bomber squadron training base. Several units passed through on training exercises during 1936 and 1937. In January 1938 No 88 Squadron re-equipped with the Fairey Battle, which it was eventually to take to war. In April 51 and 58 Squadrons moved to Linton-on-Ouse, and were replaced shortly afterwards by 218 Squadron, which flew its Battles in from Upper Heyford. Another Battle unit appeared on 8 August 1938, when 150 Squadron formed.

The three Battle squadrons formed 75 Wing, and their role upon mobilisation was to form part of the Advanced Air Striking Force. With international tension mounting from 1938, this plan increasingly began to become reality. On 23 August 1939 orders came to partially mobilise the Wing. All personnel were recalled from leave and the squadrons put on a war footing. With the declaration of war ten days later, the squadrons of 75 Wing moved to France. A few weeks later Sergeant K. Letchford, the gunner aboard Battle K9243 of 88 Squadron flown by Fg Off L. H. Baker, scored Britain's first air combat kill of the Second World War when, on 20 September, he shot down a Messerschmitt Bf 109.

As 75 Wing departed for the continent, it was replaced by the advance parties of another organisation, the Aeroplane & Armament Experimental Establishment. Its role was to test and evaluate all land- and carrier-based aircraft proposed for use by the flying services, which involved the flight-testing of the prototype of a new design, or a new mark of an established design, together with their armaments. Originally formed as the Testing Flight of the RFC at Upavon in 1912, the unit later went to Martlesham Heath in Suffolk, but with the onset on war it was felt to be too vulnerable to attack there. The War Plan was therefore to evacuate the A&AEE to the safer location of Boscombe Down. Within a few days the sixty-two aircraft of the A&AEE fleet had arrived and work started on recreating the establishment's organisation at its new base. On 20 September 1939 the A&AEE was once again declared operational. Although commanded by Gp Capt B. McEntegart, the establishment was a civilian one, working to the Air Ministry. The two most senior civil servants were Mr E. T. Jones, the Chief Technical Officer, and Mr F. Rowarth, the Chief Engineer. It comprised two squadrons, the Performance Testing Squadron, with thirty-seven aircraft, and the Armament Testing Squadron, with twenty-five.

Although the A&AEE had become operational at its new base, technical and domestic accommodation was inadequate, and a programme of building started. However, problems were exacerbated on 30 September when the Whitleys of 58 Squadron returned to Boscombe Down. The unit had been temporarily transferred to Coastal Command and detached to its former base in order to boost southern defences. On 10 October the Whitleys began convoy patrols over the Channel, which continued until mid-February when they returned to Linton-on-Ouse. The building programme had continued in the meantime; extensive ground defences were constructed, together with improved facilities including a control tower and stop-butts for gun-testing. Later a blower tunnel was erected for exhaust flame-damping tests (which, subsequently powered by four Rolls-Royce Merlin engines, is still in use today).

Off-site facilities were also added. Initially the ranges on Salisbury Plain and Porton Down were used for armament testing, but restrictions meant that only small, inert or practice bombs could be used. By early 1940 other ranges had been acquired, at Crichel Down, near Blandford (bombing and gunnery), in Lyme Bay (bombing and later rocket-firing), and at Ashley Wood in the New Forest. The latter covered an area of $3^1/2$ miles by $1^1/2$, enclosed by a 10-mile fence. A variety of targets were built on the range to simulate various objectives, including ground defences, airfields, concrete fortifications and U-boat pens.

The Luftwaffe visited Boscombe Down for the first time on 26 June 1940, when a single raider dropped four bombs on the airfield, fortunately without damage. With the Battle of Britain developing, Luftwaffe aircraft were to be seen ranging all over southern England. Because Boscombe Down was felt to be particularly vulnerable, 249 Squadron's Hurricane Mk Is were transferred from Church Fenton, arriving on 14 August. At 1700 hours, as the pilots were still unpacking, they were scrambled to intercept two large formations of German bombers approaching the Hampshire coast. In ensuing dogfights south of Salisbury, the Hurricane pilots claimed three Bf 109s.

Two days later, as Red Section of 249 Squadron was on patrol at 18,000 feet over Southampton, it was bounced by enemy fighters (possibly Bf 109s, but probably Bf 110s). All three Hurricanes were hit; Sqn Ldr Eric King, Red 3, managed to evade the Messerschmitts and nurse his badly damaged aircraft back to base. Plt Off Martyn King (Red 2) bailed out of his critically damaged aircraft, but unfortunately died when he hit the ground after his parachute failed. Red 1, Flt Lt James Nicolson, was also preparing to bail out of his burning Hurricane when a Bf 110, possibly his attacker, overshot it. The incensed Nicolson got back into his cockpit, opened the throttle and gave chase. Ignoring the flames, he fired at the Messerschmitt until it dropped out of sight. Only then did he abandon his aircraft. However, Nicolson's trials and tribulations that day were not over. Thinking that the descending parachutist was German, an LDV Sergeant fired his shotgun and hit the pilot in the lower trunk. Taken off to the Royal Southampton Hospital, Nicolson later made a full recovery and returned to flying. For his exploits over Southampton he was awarded the VC, the only such award to a pilot of Fighter Command.

Patrols by 249 Squadron continued until the end of August, when it moved to North Weald, exchanging with 56 Squadron. The latter, also flying Hurricanes, had been in the thick of the fighting over London, and spent three months at Boscombe Down, defending the airfield and the local area. The squadron's Hurricanes intercepted many German raiders and were involved in several large dogfights during the period, before transferring to Middle Wallop on 29 November.

As the A&AEE gradually expanded to meet the requirements of the war effort, more personnel were employed (the workforce of 700 in 1939 was to expand to well over 2,000 by 1945) and new departments were formed. One of the latter was the Beam Approach Training & Development Unit, which had come into existence shortly after the A&AEE first arrived at Boscombe Down in September 1939. This unit was to get involved in another battle, the lesser known 'Battle of the Beams'. Boscombe Down was well equipped for night-flying from the war's beginning, having the Mk II night landing system and Lorenz

Liberator GRV FL927 flying from Boscombe Down in May 1943 while undertaking RP trials at the A&AEE.

Bill Beamont lands the prototype TSR2 XR219 after its first flight which took place from Boscombe Down on 27 September 1964. A Shackleton, a Victor, two Vulcans and several Canberras can be seen beside the Weighbridge Hangar in the background.

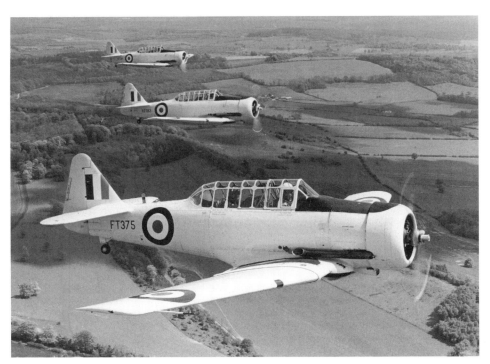

Seen in 1975, these three A&AEE Harvard chase-planes are KF314, KF183 (which still flies from Boscombe today) and FT375.

The third pre-production example of the Phantom FG1, XT597, was used for trials by the A&AEE from December 1969. It was photographed in June 1998.

Tornado GR1 ZA326 outside A Squadron hangars (which were originally at High Post), June 1998.

blind landing equipment. The latter was a widely used pre-war German system for the landing of aircraft using instruments only; the RAF had become aware of its importance in mounting and recovering operations in bad weather and at night, and was progressively installing the system at operational stations. The BATDU had been formed to train crews in the use of the Lorenz equipment and develop its applications for operations. Following examination of downed Luftwaffe bombers it was suspected that the Germans had modified the Lorenz system as a bombing aid, using electronic signals beamed to targets across Britain. The BATDU was asked to investigate, and embarked on some extremely hazardous research, which involved flying its Ansons and Whitleys into the German bomber streams to try to pick up signals on their finely tuned radio receivers. This work was dangerous, not only because the BATDU risked being shot at by the enemy bombers or their escorts, but also by 'friendly' AA guns.

The first German beams were picked up and identified by Flt Lt Hal Bufton and Corporal Denis Mackey in their Anson on 21 June 1940. Codenamed 'Knickebein' by the Germans, the frequencies were found and their point of origin noted on ensuing missions. This enabled jamming methods to be developed against the transmitters, and the 'bending' of beams away from their intended targets. The BATDU was re-titled as the Wireless Interception Development Unit in September 1940, a title that by then more accurately reflected its role. Flying from Wyton as well as Boscombe Down, the unit continued to monitor the beams, as by November the Germans had realised that they were being interfered with, and had started counter-measures. Direct action was then mounted by the WIDU, starting on 14 November when two of its Whitleys were sent out to attack the 'Knickebein' transmitter at Cherbourg. Following the success of its operations the WIDU was given squadron status on 10 December 1940, as 109 Squadron. Its Whitleys and Ansons were supplemented by Wellingtons in early 1941, which formed a new Strike Flight for attacking radio and radar stations. The Squadron remained essentially a research unit, and was divided into four flights. Three of these were moved to other stations in January 1942, while the Wireless Investigation Flight (Radio Countermeasures) remained at Boscombe Down. In April 1943 all four flights moved to Stradishall, where they were to develop the *Oboe* blind-bombing system, and later became one of the first units of 8 Group, the Pathfinder Force, responsible for pinpointing targets with Mosquitoes and Lancasters.

Other units formed at the A&AEE during the war years included 207 Squadron on 1 November 1940 to introduce the new Avro Manchester into service, and similarly, four days later, 35 Squadron for the new Handley Page Halifax. A High Altitude Flight was formed as part of the A&AEE on 30 December 1940 to carry out research work on the use of aeroplanes at heights above 30,000 feet. With Spitfires, Hurricanes, Wellingtons, Fortresses and Mosquitoes, the HAF devised new equipment, techniques and fuels during its existence.

It is surprising that Boscombe Down was never treated as a priority target by the Luftwaffe, even though it must have been aware of the A&AEE's role. A couple of light raids were made in

1940, and the heaviest came during March and April 1941, when five attacks were made on the airfield, each one involving the dropping of a dozen or so HE bombs. Hangars were hit and, although no one was injured, forty aircraft were damaged and another two destroyed.

More units were formed as the need occurred. Wellington Flight was formed in April 1941 to test high-altitude versions of the bomber. The Intensive Flying Development Unit came into existence seven months later, to pioneer the techniques of reliability and maintainability of combat aircraft. Another unit, which was to outlive the others, was formed in May 1943 – the Test Pilots Training Flight. Later to become the Empire Test Pilots' School, it was to pioneer the flight-testing of aircraft and develop techniques that were later to become standard throughout the world. Students attending the ETPS were originally from British Empire and Commonwealth countries, but were later accepted from many other nations. The school left Boscombe Down in October 1945 for Cranfield but was to return later. The students of the TPTF and ETPS were to be involved in the flight testing of new types, and established types in new roles, and their expertise enabled much more to be gained from the A&AEE's work. All trials were carefully documented and sometimes sound-recorded, enabling a mass of knowledge and information to be built up during the war years.

In addition to the ever-increasing test work on new prototypes (more than 1,500 prototypes or new marks were tested at the A&AEE during the Second World War), armament trials and intensive flying tests to replicate in-service conditions, a proportion of new production bombers manufactured in the shadow factories were tested to ensure that adequate production standards were achieved by MAP contractors. Armament work, too, varied tremendously, and ranged from the installation and trials of various types of guns, such as machine-guns and cannons, to rockets and bombs. The largest example of the former to be carried by an RAF aircraft was the 75mm cannon fitted to the Mitchell, while the latter included the complete ranges of aerial bombs, together with special weapons such as the dam-busting bouncing bomb, and the deep-penetration 12,000lb Tallboy and 22,000lb Grand Slam bombs. All were trial-fitted into A&AEE aircraft and tested on the A&AEE range at Ashley Walk.

Accidents were an ever-present risk where test flying was concerned. Air traffic control at busy airfields such as Boscombe Down was always challenging, particularly when such a wide variety of aircraft types was being flown. An added complication at Boscombe Down was the close proximity of another airfield, High Post, only 2 miles away. On the morning of 10 September 1943 Lancaster Mk III JA984 of 617 Squadron was carrying out low-level runs to measure Air Speed Indicator system pressure errors when it collided with Oxford EB981 from 7 FIS, which was approaching High Post. All occupants aboard both aircraft were killed. In total there were thirty-two aircraft accidents to Boscombe Down aircraft during the Second World War, resulting in the deaths of fifty-eight personnel, nine of whom were civilians.

Surprisingly, much of this intensive flying had taken place from grass runways, and it was not until January 1944 that construction started of the first hard runway at Boscombe. The airfield was also extended at this time, out to the west, which brought it even closer to High Post. To avoid disruption to flying, construction of the new runway took time, and it was not open for use until early 1945. In the meantime the first jets such as the Spider-Crab (renamed Vampire) had arrived, and were already scorching the airfield's grass with their jet-pipes.

In 1944 the A&AEE had been reorganised into three Assessment Divisions (Performance, Armament and Engineering), together with a Flying Division, which consisted of four squadrons – A (Fighter), B (Four engines), C (Naval) and D (Twins and miscellaneous), together with relevant servicing support. By the summer of 1945 the A&AEE had 176 aircraft on strength, and more than 2,000 personnel. Following the end of the war an immediate downturn in work resulted in reduced personnel and aircraft – by mid-1947 there were only fifty-one aircraft in use. Nonetheless, aeronautical R&D was given high priority by the post-war Government, and from its new headquarters (the Ministry of Supply from 1 April 1946) the A&AEE received a massive investment in new facilities and equipment. Work commenced on new accommodation blocks, headquarters building, workshops, ATC tower, bulk fuel storage and bomb store. Four large hangers were also planned, although only one was eventually completed – when it was finished, in 1954, it was fitted with an aircraft weighbridge, which gave its name to the building.

A Squadron was provided with a new hangar, moved from the then defunct High Post in 1947. Other hangars were added in the mid-1950s. Two additional concrete runways were laid between 1948 and 1950, when the main runway was also extended. Following the war the A&AEE was defined as the centre for 'conducting acceptance trials on aircraft and their associated equipment destined for use by the fighting services and the civil corporations'. A Civil Aircraft Testing Section was formed to

Andover C1 XS646 on finals for Boscombe Down in July 2008.

undertake the latter work (which continued until 1960). In September 1950 the A&AEE's work expanded when it absorbed the Airborne Forces Experimental Establishment, which moved from Beaulieu (this work continues today with the parachuting of troops and equipment, and the testing of helicopters). The ETPS returned to Boscombe Down in 1968; from Cranfield it had moved to Farnborough in 1947, and began a successful association with the RAE. It eventually returned to Boscombe Down because of increasing congestion and air traffic restrictions in the Farnborough area. The school continues to train Test Pilots and Flight Test Engineers using a variety of aircraft types.

In the late 1940s work on piston-engine fighters such as the Spitfire, Tempest and Hornet declined, as work on the new jet fighters such as the Meteor and Vampire increased. Jet flight brought with it new problems that challenged A&AEE staff. Work on the Canberra jet bomber, Meteor night-fighters and the Javelin all-weather fighter followed, and the three V-Bombers in the mid-1950s. This continued into the 1960s with further versions of the Victor and Vulcan, and, with the cancellation of the TSR2, trials continued with the Buccaneer.

A surprising number of aircraft types have performed their maiden flights from Boscombe over the years. These included the Lysander in June 1936, Attacker in July 1946, Victor in December 1952, English Electric P1 (later the Lightning) in August 1954, and the incomparable TSR2 in September 1964. The RAF Handling Squadron (which had been at Boscombe as the Handling Flight from 1940, before moving to Hullavington in 1942) is responsible for producing Pilots Notes. This publication is indispensable to all pilots as it gives vital information on each aircraft type, to enable it to be flown safely and effectively. The Squadron returned to Boscombe in 1954, and is still in residence today.

Trials on large aircraft included the Hastings, Shackleton, Beverley, Argosy, Belfast and VC10. Work was also undertaken in support of naval fixed-wing aircraft such as the Sea Vixen, Buccaneer and Phantom, but this decreased in the 1970s following the run-down of the fixed-wing element of the Fleet Air Arm. The RN instead expanded its use of helicopters, utilising the A&AEE, which had been involved in the development of the early Dragonfly, Sycamore and Skeeter designs, later followed by the Wasp/Scout, Wessex, Sea King and Merlin. Between 1946 and 1970 there was intense pressure to develop new aircraft for front-line service, a task made more difficult by the rapid advances in airframe and engine design, and later in avionics. Unfortunately this took a heavy toll on the A&AEE, which suffered the lost of forty-two aircrew and forty-five aircraft during the period.

A new spate of construction work started in 1979 when the airfield was nominated as a NATO dispersal base, and a quantity of Hardened Aircraft Shelters were erected. During re-surfacing of the runway at this time, a wartime German 500kg bomb was found and dealt with by RAF EOD technicians. In 1980 the new HASs were used by a detachment of USAF F-111 bombers flown from the USA, and several more such deployments followed during the 1980s.

The invasion of the Falkland Islands in 1982 caused a surge of activity at the A&AEE. Trials included fitting Sidewinder missiles to Harriers, Shrikes to Vulcans and air-to-air refuelling (AAR) equipment to Vulcans, Hercules and Nimrods. In 1983 the Tornado Operational Evaluation Unit was formed at Boscombe to evaluate the new Tornado GR1. This later became the Strike Attack Operational Evaluation Unit, undertaking trials using Tornado and Harrier aircraft. The SAOEU moved to Leeming in 2005. Units remaining at Boscombe Down include 2 AEF/SUAS, with Grob Tutors.

The A&AEE found itself heavily involved in trials of aircraft and weapons during Operation *Desert Storm* in 1993. As well as AAR and missile installations, work included missile approach warning systems, flare dispensers, Thermal Imaging and Laser-Designating equipment. The success of British air operations during that operation was in no small part due to the work undertaken at Boscombe Down. History was to be repeated some ten years later, with the second Gulf War, when once again the scientists, technicians and test pilots of Boscombe Down played their part to ensure that British servicemen had the best equipment that could be provided within the timescales available.

The aircraft types flown from Boscombe Down have always been unusual. Although they reflect those used by the three services, some have found a home at the establishment even after their peers have been withdrawn from service. Examples are many, but include a Javelin flown as a chase aircraft in an eye-catching red and white colour scheme (until withdrawn and donated to the Imperial War Museum at Duxford in the 1990s), Phantom XT597, the last to fly in British service (now withdrawn to the Boscombe Down Museum), and three Harvard trainers, all painted bright yellow, one of which is still flown as a chase aircraft.

Following a reorganisation of defence research establishments in the early 1990s, familiar titles such as RAE and A&AEE were trashed, replaced by the Defence Trials & Evaluation Organisation (DTEO) and in 1997 by the Defence Evaluation & Research Agency (DERA). In 2001 this changed again to Qinetiq, which took most of the DERA, including Boscombe Down, into a science and technology company. Despite the name changes, Boscombe Down's work continues, and it is just as vital in support of British military aviation today as it has been during its eventful past.

Main features:
Runways: 240° 9,000ft x 300ft, concrete, WNW-ESE 4,200ft, SSE-NNW 4,200ft.
Hangars: sixteen of various types. *Hardstandings:* seventeen of various kinds.
Accommodation: RAF Officers 111, SNCOs 202, ORs 1,768; WAAF Officers 7, SNCOs 9, ORs 550.

BROCKWORTH (HUCCLECOTE), Gloucestershire

SO882160, half a mile S of Brockworth on A417

Forever to be linked with the Gloster Aircraft Company, Brockworth was home to the company for many years. The airfield originated in 1915 when a field near the village of Hucclecote was selected as an Aircraft Acceptance Park by the Air Board, the Government authority for aircraft production during the Great War. Aircraft received there included Bristol F2Bs and Nieuport Nighthawks manufactured under sub-contract by the Gloucestershire Aircraft Company at Sunningend in Cheltenham. The AAP consisted of five hangars for aircraft assembly. Storage sheds were subsequently added, and by the time of the Armistice were twenty-one in number. In 1919 the AAP was closed, but the Air Board retained the airfield.

The Gloucestershire Aircraft Company remained in business despite the downturn at the end of the war, initially by completing production orders for F2Bs and Nighthawks. When the Nieuport and General Aircraft Company closed towards the end of 1920, its design rights were purchased by the Gloucestershire Aircraft Company, which also took on Nieuport's chief designer, Harry Folland, famous for his SE5 fighter. The following year the company rented a hangar at Hucclecote for servicing and maintenance. Limited production in another hangar followed in 1925, and eventually it was decided to move the company's entire production across from Cheltenham. In 1928 the

Javelins being produced in Brockworth's 450-yard-long erecting shop, in which more than 7,000 aircraft were built between 1939 and 1959.

Hucclecote site, covering 200 acres, including hangars and office accommodation, was purchased for £15,000. Three years earlier the company had changed its name to the 'Gloster Aircraft Company', which was simpler for its overseas customers to pronounce!

Although Gloster built a series of successful racing aircraft and fighters, supplemented by subcontract work, it was struggling to survive by the early 1930s, and even an initial order for the Gauntlet fighter in 1933 failed to guarantee its financial stability. In 1934 the Hawker Aircraft Company made a successful take-over bid as it was looking for more production capacity for its successful range of Hart-type biplanes. Hawker retained the Gloster name, and invested in improved production facilities at Hucclecote. Gloster designs continued in production alongside Hawker types, such as the Gladiator, which replaced the Gauntlet in RAF service.

Work on a new factory beside the airfield began in 1938, under orders from the MAP. This was a shadow factory primarily for the production of Hurricanes, and was built on land on the eastern side of the airfield, at Brockworth. The new factory was completed in November 1940, covering 24 acres of floor space. Production of the Henley, a target tug using Hurricane components, was started at the new factory, alongside the Hurricanes. The roof of the new factory was camouflaged to blend in with the local countryside, and the airfield itself had simulated hedgerows printed across it, which were surprisingly effective. A concrete runway was built at this time, to provide a good all-weather surface from which to fly.

Hurricane production had in fact started in another part of the factory while the Brockworth factory was being constructed, the first Gloster-built Hurricane having been completed on 27 October 1939. Components for the aircraft were supplied by forty-three local manufacturers, and in 1940 a total of 1,211 Hurricanes were turned out from Brockworth. This had been achieved despite German raids on the factory in 4 October 1940 when No 7 Machine Shop and the toolroom were damaged by two bombs. As well as Hurricanes, the Brockworth shadow factory also housed production of Armstrong Whitworth Albemarles. After completion of the initial thirty-two aircraft as bombers, the design was modified as a glider tug and airborne forces transport, and more than 600 Albemarles were eventually produced at the factory.

Typhoons replaced Hurricanes in production at Hucclecote during 1941 and, despite a false start due to engine and structural problems, the aircraft entered volume production. The next

Finished Albemarles outside the factory at Brockworth in 1943, with Typhoons in the background.

Typhoon IB EK286 runs up on the airfield, having just left the finishing shop in 1943.

The second prototype Javelin FAW4, XA630, just before its first flight from Brockworth in March 1956.

Luftwaffe raid was made during this time when, on 4 April 1942, more bombs were dropped. Although no damage was sustained by the factory, thirteen workers were killed. By December 1942 160 Typhoons were being produced per month. When the last one rolled off the line in 1945 the total production stood at 3,330 aircraft, all produced at Hucclecote.

Gloster continued to produce its own designs as well as manufacturing those of other companies. On 1 February 1940 the company received an Air Ministry contract for two prototypes of the revolutionary E28/39, built to prove the practicability of the gas turbine. On 8 April 1941, during taxying trials at Brockworth, the aircraft actually left the ground but its first official flight was made at Cranwell on 15 May. Four months later the Air Ministry placed a contract for an operational successor to the E28/39.

Frenzied activities at Gloster over the next two years resulted in the completion of the Meteor, which first flew on 5 March 1943. Production started soon afterwards, and the Meteor was to keep Gloster afloat during the post-war years. However, with the advent of jet aircraft the short runway, with its difficult approach over houses, meant the transfer of flight testing to Moreton Valence. Production continued at Brockworth (which the airfield had by then been officially named), and although many Meteors, and later Javelins, took off from there, they were flown to Moreton Valence to complete their test programmes before delivery. Others were taken by lorry to Moreton Valence as major components for assembly there before flight test. This continued until 8 April 1960, when the last production aircraft was flown out of Brockworth. This was a Javelin FAW8, which Gloster's Chief Test Pilot Dicky Martin flew to Moreton Valence. Although Gloster's aeronautical work continued at Moreton Valence, the company's Brockworth factory went over to non-aviation activities, such as the production of fire appliances, road tankers and refuellers, under a new company, Gloster Saro Ltd, which became part of the Hawker Siddeley Group.

The airfield was no longer in use when in April 1964 Hawker Siddeley sold the site to Gloster Trading Estates. The former Hucclecote and Brockworth factories then became industrial units, and were in constant use until the site was redeveloped from 2000 onwards. Plans to preserve the control tower and hangars were put aside, and today the only indication of Brockworth's place in aeronautical history is the presence of a full-scale replica of a Gloster E28/39 placed on a roundabout at the entrance to the former factory's location.

BUDE, Cornwall

SS238012, 4 miles SSE of Bude, off minor road

A sub-station of the large airship station at Mullion was set up near Bude early in 1918. Situated in a heavily wooded valley near the hamlet of Langford Barton, the mooring-out site was sheltered from the prevailing south-westerlies, with the added advantage of being close to good roads and the railway. It was established to act as a refuge for airships operating off the north Cornish coast when bad weather closed the main base. It also acted as a forward base in order to cut down on transit time for airships to reach their operating areas.

Groundcrews to handle the airships were detached from RNAS Mullion. The officers were quartered in Langford Barton House, while the ratings lived in tents, replaced by wooden huts in the autumn of 1918. The site was capable of accommodating two Coastal-type airships, which were moored to large concrete blocks and kept fully inflated and serviced daily by the groundcrews. When any maintenance was required the aircraft were returned to Mullion.

Operational patrols were flown from Bude over the St George's and Bristol Channels, under the command of the RN C-in-C Devonport. When in April 1918 the RAF was formed, the unit became part of 9 Group, RAF. Flying continued from Bude until the end of 1918, one of the airships based there at this time being SSZ75, which was diverted to Padstow late in December due to gale force winds preventing its mooring in the confined space at Bude.

Non-rigid airship operations ceased early in 1919, and the Bude sub-station was closed. Its wooden buildings were used for agricultural storage for some years afterwards, but today nothing remains of the former base.

Fairey IIID N9495 on the slipway beside Calshot Castle in the 1920s.

CALSHOT, Hampshire

SU489205, 2 miles SE of Fawley

R NAS Calshot was opened as a seaplane base on 29 March 1913. Built on Calshot Spit, which projected into the western edge of the Solent, the original station consisted of three sheds housing twelve seaplanes. These were erected at the end of the spit, not far from Calshot Castle, a

Tudor artillery fort. Accommodation was initially provided by the castle and a few coastguard cottages nearby. The station's main function was experimental, and armament trials there included the first launch of a torpedo by a British aircraft, during the summer of 1914. Calshot took on a training role in August 1914, but with the outbreak of war later that year became a base for RNAS Channel patrols using seaplanes and later flying boats.

This activity continued through the war years. The station gradually expanded along the spit, but to provide living accommodation a new camp was built near the landward end at Eaglehurst. To aid construction, a narrow-gauge railway was laid from there to the end of the spit, and this was later retained as the main camp transport. Two large aircraft sheds, timber-framed and clad in corrugated iron, known as F and G Sheds, were erected in 1917 to provide extra storage for aircraft. Ground was cleared for a much larger building, H Shed, in 1918, and this enormous building still stands; it is 120 feet wide, with three sets of doors on its 625-foot-long landward side.

Many thousand of hours were flown by RNAS Calshot's aircraft during the First World War, ranging from 3,400 flying hours during 1916 to 9,000 hours in just three months in early 1918. Many U-boats were sighted during these patrols, some of which were attacked, and at least five of which were sunk. With the formation of the RAF in April 1918 Calshot became the HQ of 10 Group, and the flying units became 345 and 346 Flights with Felixstowe F2A and Curtiss H12B flying boats, and 410 Flight with Short 184, 320 and Campania seaplanes. These flights were combined to form 240 Squadron, whose aircraft sighted twelve U-boats during the last three months of the war, eight of which were attacked.

Calshot remained open following the war's end, 240 Squadron continuing to fly from there. Although disbanded on 15 May 1919 it was replaced by the School of Aerial Navigation, which formed on 13 February 1920 with Short 184 and Fairey IIID floatplanes. This unit was merged with the School of Naval Cooperation, formerly at Lee-on-Solent, on 1 April 1920, to form the School of Naval Cooperation & Aerial Navigation, with Felixstowe F5 flying boats added to its fleet. A large marine craft unit was also housed by the station at this time, to provide rescue and support facilities for the flying units. On 5 February 1922 No 480 (Coastal Reconnaissance) Flight formed at Calshot with Felixstowe F5s; in August these were replaced by Southamptons. The station was expanded during the 1920s with more hangars and sheds built.

Calshot became famous in the late 1920s due to the activities of the RAF High Speed Flight, formed for the Schneider Trophy Competitions. The Flight had trained at Calshot prior to winning the 1927 Schneider Cup Competition in Venice, when Flt Lt Webster had achieved a speed of 281.65mph in his Supermarine S5. The flight returned to Calshot, and it was there that Flt Lt Sam Kinkhead was flying the Supermarine S5 on 12 March 1928 when it crashed into the Solent, killing him. Nonetheless, the 1929 Schneider Trophy Race was held at Calshot with the RAF team flying a new aircraft, the Supermarine S6 designed by R. J. Mitchell around the new Rolls-Royce 'R' Engine. Flt Lt Waghorn raced the S6 around the seven laps at an average speed of 328.63mph to take the prize for Britain on 7 September. Five days later, while flying from Calshot, Sqn Ldr Orlebar broke the world airspeed record in an S6 at 365.1mph.

Calshot was the centre for the 1931 Schneider Trophy Race and the RAF High Speed Flight was again victorious. This time, with Flt Lt Boothman winning the race in the much-improved Supermarine S6B at a speed of 340mph on 13 September, the Schneider Trophy was retained for Britain. The S6B was largely financed by Lady Houston, who donated £100,000 to the project. As if to emphasise this outcome, two weeks later Flt Lt Stainforth smashed the world airspeed record flying the S6B to 407mph.

On 1 January 1929 No 480 Flight, still flying Southamptons, had become 201 Squadron. Primarily a training unit, the squadron was later re-equipped with a variety of types and was to be the sole operational unit at Calshot for the ensuing eight years. The unit's C Flight became the nucleus of 240 Squadron, which reformed at Calshot on 31 March 1937. Following the Munich Crisis of September 1938, a number of defensive measures were taken at Calshot. The spit was cleared of beach huts, replaced by shelter trenches and machine-gun posts. The Flying Boat Training Squadron formed at the station on 2 January 1939 with a variety of types including the Supermarine Stranraer, Short Scapa and Short Singapore, and began training crews in earnest, as hostilities could not be far away.

Nos 201 and 240 Squadrons (by then both flying Saro Londons and Supermarine Stranraer flying boats) left Calshot in August 1939 for their war-stations at Invergordon in Scotland. When war came the following month four major functions were retained at Calshot. These included the major servicing of flying boats (including Londons, Stranraers, Lerwicks and later Sunderlands and Catalinas), the service and maintenance of RAF marine craft, and the training of their crews. Flying training by the FBTS also continued at the station. To cope with the extra personnel Eagleshurst camp was increased in size.

Supermarine Schneider Trophy-winning S6B S1596 flown by Flt Lt John Boothman, seen at Calshot just before the race in 1931.

During the summer of 1940 the station took part in Operation *Dynamo*, the evacuation of the British Expeditionary Force from France. On 31 May five of its seaplane tenders crossed the Channel and succeeded in rescuing 500 men from the Dunkirk beaches, despite being attacked by German aircraft. Following the fall of France, the Luftwaffe's attention was turned on Britain, and Calshot found itself very much in the front line. On 23 June the FBTS was withdrawn to Stranraer (where it later formed part of 4 (C)OTU). Meanwhile, the station's defences were strengthened, a number of 3-inch AA guns being installed. Barrage balloons were also brought in, and these undoubtedly prevented a number of low-level attacks. Calshot did not remain untouched however, as on 27 August 1940 and again on the 30th German bombs were dropped on the spit, fortunately without much damage. The AA guns soon proved their worth, shooting down an He 111 on 24 September.

Unusual aircraft appeared at Calshot during the summer of 1940. These were four Heinkel He 115 floatplanes that had served with the Royal Norwegian Air Force until flying to Britain following the Norwegian surrender. The aircraft were given RAF markings and serials (one being BV184), and operated from Calshot on clandestine operations, dropping off and picking up agents and equipment. They worked along the coast of occupied Europe, and were detached to Scotland and Malta, but continued to use Calshot as a base until November 1942, when the last aircraft crashed.

On 21 May 1942 all marine craft training was transferred to Corewall, Galloway, but the Calshot facilities were then used for a succession of marine craft units. They provided vital support for flying boat operations, but also high-speed launches as part of the ASR organisations that patrolled the Channel for downed aircrew. Marine craft repairs continued at Calshot, as did the maintenance and repair of flying boats. In September 1943 the aircraft repair organisation became 6 Flying Boat Servicing Unit and began to concentrate on the Sunderland. The capabilities of the unit and its throughput increased, so that by April 1944 twenty-two aircraft per month were being repaired and modified there.

In May 1944 a mobile ASR unit consisting of fourteen high-speed launches was formed at Calshot. This was to cover the D-Day landings, and at first light on 6 June six of them sailed to appointed positions alongside Fighter Direction Tenders off the beachhead, ready to respond to any Mayday calls. RAF Calshot also took part in the operation, as its slipways were used for the embarkation of tanks and troops aboard landing craft headed for Normandy. Although the front line moved away from the Channel following D-Day, Calshot was no less vital; its work with flying boats and marine craft continued, well after the end of hostilities.

In March 1946 Calshot once more became a flying station when 201 Squadron arrived from Pembroke Dock with its Sunderlands. It was joined that September by 230 Squadron, also with

Five Sunderland Vs at Calshot in 1946; ML819 is in the foreground, with a Catalina behind it.

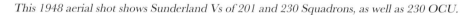

This 1948 aerial shot shows Sunderland Vs of 201 and 230 Squadrons, as well as 230 OCU.

Sunderlands, from Castle Archdale. A third Sunderland unit, 4 (Coastal) OTU, also transferred from Pembroke Dock on 31 July 1947, and immediately on its arrival was re-designated 235 OCU. All three units were detached to Germany in July 1948 to take part in Operation *Plainfare*, the Berlin Airlift. Although the OCU element was withdrawn after a few weeks, for five months the two squadrons flew more than a thousand sorties, taking vital supplies from Hamburg to Lake Havel in Berlin, and returning with evacuees from the city.

The return of the squadrons to Calshot in December 1948 was tinged with sadness, as they were detailed to transfer to Pembroke Dock. No 201 Squadron moved in January 1949, joined by 230 Squadron the following month. The Sunderlands of 235 OCU soldiered on at Calshot for a few more years, together with another two aircraft operated from Calshot by the Air Sea Warfare Development Unit, detached from its main base at Thorney Island. Flying finally came to an end in 1952 when, on 17 October, the Sunderlands moved to Pembroke Dock, and RAF Calshot was transferred from Coastal Command to Maintenance Command. The station then became the base of 238 MU, which continued with the repair and maintenance of RAF marine craft. A bomb disposal flight was added in 1956, followed by the Equipment, Explosives & Fuels Training Unit later that year. In 1957 the Maintenance Command Ground Defence School was formed there.

Calshot had changed little after the end of the war. However, in 1947 the railway was closed and the lines lifted. One of its locomotives escaped the cutter's torch, and today is still operated on the Talyllyn Railway in North Wales. Before the Sunderlands had moved out they were joined by two of the elegant but ill-fated Saro Princess flying boats. These 140-ton machines were designed to carry 100 passengers for 5,000 miles, but the project was shelved, and two of the uncompleted aircraft were put into cocooned storage at Calshot to await better times. The Princesses remained after the closure of RAF Calshot on 1 April 1961, until they were removed eight years later.

For two years the former RAF station remained empty, its forty buildings gradually decaying. In the summer of 1963, however, moves were made to establish an educational use of the site. Sailing training courses were started, and in November 1963 the Crown Estate agreed to lease the spit to Hampshire County Council. Since then an imaginative development of the site has taken place, as an adventure training centre. This has included the refurbishment of the hangars, and the conversion of the main hangar to include three ski-slopes, a climbing wall, archery and shooting ranges, and a world-class velodrome with stands for more than 400 spectators.

Calshot's flying boat legacy did not end with the Princess. In 1981 Sandringham (a civilianised Sunderland) *Southern Cross* landed at Calshot after an epic journey from the Pacific. It was refurbished and became an exhibit in the Hall of Aviation in Southampton. In 1984 the last flying Sunderland, ML814 *Excalibur*, came ashore at Calshot for storage and eventual sale. After an extensive refit, on 20 July 1994 it took off from Calshot on delivery to the Kermit Weeks Collection in Florida. The RAF Marine Craft connection with Calshot has also been maintained, with the refurbishment of ASR launch No 102, which was officially re-launched from the spit by HM The Queen Mother on 5 July 1996.

Calshot remains today a hive of activity and its aviation heritage is kept alive by Hampshire County Council, which maintains an exhibition in the reception area within the Calshot Activity Centre's main building, now named the Sunderland Hangar.

CASTLE COMBE, Wiltshire

ST854767, half a mile SE of village

Close to the picturesque village of Castle Combe is a motor racing circuit that erupts noisily into action during the season, utilising the old perimeter track of an airfield built for the RAF. Racing Control occupies its control tower, and other airfield buildings are used for engineering and administration.

Castle Combe first saw regular use during the spring of 1941 when it started operating as a practice landing ground for the Harts and Audaxes of 9 SFTS based at RAF Hullavington. Upgraded to RLG status in May 1941, it was used for day and night circuit flying by the school, which then also flew Masters and Hurricanes. Although satisfactory during the summer, the grass surface became waterlogged during wintertime, a problem that would bedevil flying operations.

On 14 February 1942 No 9 SFTS became 9 (P)AFU, its role changing to that of advanced flying training of newly qualified pilots. As well as RAF and Commonwealth pilots, these included FAA ones, so naval aircraft such as Albacores, Swordfish, Rocs and Walruses were added to the

Castle Combe circuit's Race Control utilises the old control tower, seen here in 2007.

This September 2008 view clearly shows the Castle Combe circuit, based on the airfield's perimeter track.

fleet. Harvards and Oxfords were also taken on strength to increase experience for the students. Due to pressure on the facilities at Hullavington, it was decided to move all of 9 (P)AFU's flying to Castle Combe, so work began to upgrade its facilities. Flying operations and ground instruction buildings were erected, together with domestic accommodation, some of which were on dispersed sites in the surrounding countryside. However, the unit was hardly to benefit from this work before it was moved on; at the end of July 1942 No 9 (P)AFU transferred to Errol in Scotland.

No 3 FIS(A) formed at Hullavington on 1 August 1942 and took over Castle Combe. Hardly had it started training with its Masters, Magisters, Harvards and Oxfords than poor weather and waterlogging caused delays to courses. Conditions became so bad that staff and students had to travel daily to Hullavington, Colerne and Charmy Down for flying. More work that winter resulted in the construction of a Teeside and seven Blister hangars, and with the laying of two Sommerfield track runways and a 50-foot-wide concrete perimeter track the airfield once again became usable. Flying training was in full swing by May 1943, and 3 FIS(A) had a good summer's flying before being told that it had to move on. This followed the decision to relocate 15 (P)AFU to Castle Combe to make room for the USAAF at Ramsbury. The aircraft and staff of 3 FIS(A) moved to Lulsgate Bottom in early October 1943, but before their replacements arrived at the end of the month the airfield surface was given more treatment to combat waterlogging.

Flying recommenced with the arrival of 15 (P)AFU's Oxfords, but bad weather interrupted training. Waterlogging at Long Newnton, a unit satellite, increased the pressure on the facilities at Castle Combe during January 1944, and the AFU was still struggling to catch up on its backlog during the spring when, on 13 March, a Stirling force-landed. Its weapons load exploded, causing substantial damage to the airfield buildings, and it was three days before flying training could recommence.

Problems with the airfield surface persisted throughout the remainder of 1944, and flying continued to be disrupted by bad ground conditions. More repairs took place, and by March 1945 the runways were just about serviceable again. It was about this time that Long Newnton was closed, and its flying transferred to Castle Combe. The resulting high level of activity did not carry on for long, as the end of the war in Europe in mid-May saw a reduction in the need for pilots. Later that month 15 (P)AFU transferred to Babdown Farm, where it disbanded in June. All flying then ceased at Castle Combe and the airfield was put on C&M, pending a decision on its future.

In July 1946 the station was taken over by 27 Group Technical Training Command, as 2 (Polish) Resettlement Unit, for the accommodation of Polish ex-service personnel. Closed again in June 1948 Castle Combe was finally disposed of. Much of the former airfield remains in place today, and as a motor racing circuit it sees the links with its past re-established when the occasional light aircraft drops in over the hedge to bring personnel to the track.

Main features:
Runways: 313° 2,790ft, Sommerfield track, NE-SW, 3,255ft, grass. *Hangars:* one T1, five O-Blister, two EO-Blister. *Hardstandings:* none. *Accommodation:* RAF Officers 105, SNCOs 247, ORs 454; WAAF Officers 4, SNCOs 8, ORs 144.

CHARLTON HORETHORNE, Somerset

ST643244, 2 miles NW of Charlton Horethorne

The attractively named Charlton Horethorne, situated on an escarpment to the west of Blackmoor Vale, was anything but a pleasant place from which to fly. Envisaged as a satellite for Exeter, construction started during the summer of 1941. By the following spring, contractor Costain Ltd had completed most of its work, but the airfield was then more of a landing ground than a fully developed airfield, as it had a good grass surface but few buildings (two Blister hangars a watch office and a number of blast-pens). The living sites were widely dispersed to the east and were, like the airfield itself, carefully camouflaged.

An advance party from RAF Exeter arrived at the new airfield on 1 June 1942, but it was not until the 30th that the NAAFI opened! By the time the station itself opened, it was in fact no longer required by 10 Group, and was made available to the FAA. Two days later the Fulmars of 886 and 887 Squadrons arrived from Yeovilton. No 887 Squadron soon moved on to St Mawgan, but 886 was joined by 790 Squadron on 27 July. The latter reformed at Charlton Horethorne as part of the Fighter Direction School based 8 miles away at Yeovilton. With Oxfords and Fulmars, its role was that of fighter interception training, and it was to remain at Charlton Horethorne for most of the rest of the war.

On 10 August 1942 the Fulmars of 886 Squadron moved to Turnhouse, and were replaced the following day by the Sea Hurricanes of 891 Squadron. This unit had been earmarked for front-line service, and spent its time at Charlton Horethorne working up in preparation for carrier operations, including air interception training with 790 Squadron. After a month 891 moved on to St Merryn, later taking part in Operation *Torch*, the North African landings. It was replaced by 893 Squadron, which flew its Martlet fighters in as the Hurricanes left on 9 September. After almost a month of training, 893 also moved (on 6 October), and was later to embark aboard HMS *Formidable*, also destined for Operation *Torch*. Similarly, 879 Squadron, then 809, both with Fulmars, trained briefly at Charlton Horethorne before going on to operations in the Mediterranean.

On 1 December 1942 the station was formally transferred from 10 Group to the Admiralty and was commissioned as HMS *Heron II*, a satellite of Yeovilton. As the resident unit, 790 Squadron continued as part of the Fighter Direction School. Ground training was undertaken at Yeovilton, before students moved on to the flying phase at less-congested Charlton Horethorne. On 790 Squadron they gained practical experience of fighter direction, using Oxfords to simulate bombers and Fulmars the intercepting fighters. Other units continued to pass through, such as 897 Squadron, which, with Sea Hurricanes, arrived on 11 January 1943 and moved on to St Merryn on 22 March, later taking part in the Salerno landings.

Work started at HMS *Heron II* in early 1943 to improve what was then still a rudimentary airfield. Watch tower, stores, administration and living accommodation were constructed, as well as four Blister hangars. The airfield itself was improved and re-graded, with five runways being laid out, mown into the grass surface. On 6 April 1943 No 804 Squadron with Sea Hurricanes arrived for training. Leaving on 20 June, it was later to re-equip with Hellcats and take part in the Atlantic convoys. It was replaced on 10 July by 887 Squadron with Fulmars; re-equipped with Seafires, this unit later flew from escort carriers in the Mediterranean.

Seventy-one aircraft can be seen dispersed at Charleton Horethorne in this October 1944 photograph.

A longer-term resident appeared in 9 October 1943. This was 780 Squadron, a pilot refresher training unit. Flying a variety of aircraft including Tiger Moths, Masters and Harvards, it had previously been based at Eastleigh, and was joined on 1 December by 794 Squadron on transfer from Henstridge. This was a target-towing and air firing training unit supporting the Fighter School at Yeovilton, and flew from its new base until 30 June the following year, when it disbanded.

Meanwhile, on 10 February 1944 No 765 Squadron came into being. It was reformed at HMS *Heron II* as the Travelling Recording Unit, its main purpose being to check and calibrate naval radar units. The unit also had the secondary role of maritime reconnaissance, and was one of the few FAA squadrons to fly the Wellington. However, 765 didn't stay long at Charleton Horethorne, possibly because its Wellingtons couldn't fly from the airfield unless lightly loaded and in perfect weather conditions. It moved to Lee-on-Solent on 18 March, later moving to the Mediterranean.

No 790 Squadron was still flying Oxfords in the summer of 1944, but in June its Fulmars were replaced with Fireflies. Detached to Culmhead on 10 August, the Squadron returned to its home base on 26 September, and became sole resident at Charlton Horethorne when 780 Squadron moved to Lee-on-Solent at the end of November. Receiving Spitfire VBs in February 1945, followed by early Seafires the following month, the unit didn't remain much longer at Charlton Horethorne, as it had been agreed that the airfield would be taken over by the RAF, in exchange for Zeals in Wiltshire. On 1 April 1945 No 790 Squadron started leaving for Zeals.

Charlton Horethorne was taken over by 42 Group, Maintenance Command, and used as a sub-depot of 11 MU Chilmark for the storage of ammunition. This continued until June 1948 when the airfield became a satellite of Old Sarum, having been cleared of munitions. Later held on C&M, it was eventually de-requisitioned and returned to farmland. Today there are few signs of the former airfield, apart from a small number of buildings that have been incorporated into Charlton Hill Farm, and the remains of fighter pens in the fields.

Main features:
Runways: NE-SW 3,600ft, NW-SE 2,700ft, grass. *Hangars:* two EO-Blister, four Blister. *Hardstandings:* six double pens, five stands. *Accommodation:* RN Officers 62, ORs 457.

CHARMY DOWN, Somerset

ST764700, 3 miles W of Bath on A46

Selected as a site for 10 MU Colerne on a plateau in the hills above Bath, work on Charmy Down started in 1940. By then it had been decided to complete the airfield as a sector station for 10 Group, so it was laid out as a fighter base, its grass surface encircled by a tarmac perimeter track with thirty-nine dispersals. Accommodation for aircraft and equipment included twelve Blister hangars erected around the airfield, and a Bellman hangar on the technical site to the east. The runways were originally marked out on the grass, but in 1941 were replaced by three tarmac runways.

The airfield was opened by Fighter Command in November 1940 as a satellite of Colerne, and a flight of Hurricanes from 87 Squadron was detached from there. These were joined by more aircraft the following month, when the whole squadron moved in on the 18th. The unit operated in the night-fighting role, defending the Bristol and Bath area, and from its new base it started flying nightly standing patrols.

In the New Year 87 Squadron started sending detachments to St Mary's to defend the Isles of Scilly and shipping in the area. With the spring came increased German activity and more intensive night-flying by the defending fighters. The Hurricane was not an ideal night-fighter, as it depended on visibility, its pilot usually only seeing a target when silhouetted against cloud. It was not until early May, therefore, that the first success came while flying from Charmy Down – a Dornier Do 17 was shot down by the CO, Sqn Ldr 'Widge' Gleed. The Squadron then mounted intruder operations of its own, sending patrols over Luftwaffe night-fighter bases in the Caen area. These continued until the Squadron moved to Colerne on 7 August.

The following day two more squadrons arrived at Charmy Down – 125 with Defiant Mk Is from Colerne and 263, the first squadron to fly the new Westland Whirlwind Mk I, on transfer from Filton. The Defiants mounted night patrols, while the Whirlwinds flew intruder missions against enemy airfields, also providing escorts for bomber missions. In September 1941 a second Whirlwind

An 87 Squadron pilot sits on the exhaust blanking plate of Hurricane IIc HL864 at Charmy Down in October 1944.

Charmy Down, seen in September 1958.

Squadron, 137, was formed at Charmy Down from a cadre of 263's personnel. Within a month one flight was operational, and on the 24th it flew its first mission, a *Ramrod* on railway marshalling yards in Brittany. However, a spate of bad luck followed when the unit's CO, Sqn Ldr J. Sample, was killed in a mid-air collision, and a pilot flew into the sea on an operation two days later. The squadron reverted to non-operational status for a short period until it moved to Coltishall in November. A new unit, 417 (RCAF) Squadron, formed on 27 November 1941 with Spitfire IIAs. It worked up before moving to Colerne on 26 January 1942, where it received the Mk VB, becoming operational on 17 February. Meanwhile 263 Squadron had resumed operations with its Whirlwinds and remained at Charmy Down flying convoy escort missions. These continued throughout December and into the New Year until, on 28 January 1942, it moved to Colerne.

With the persistent night offensive by the Luftwaffe over Britain during the winter of 1941/42, many ideas were trialled in order to intercept German bombers. One of the more promising of these was the Turbinlite, an aircraft-mounted searchlight. Devised by Wg Cdr Helmore, this called for a twin-engine aircraft to carry AI radar and a Turbinlite in the nose. Douglas Havocs and Bostons were used, each accompanied by a Hurricane. When the twin found a target on its radar, illuminated it with its searchlight and positively identified it, the Hurricane moved in to shoot down the enemy aircraft. No 1454 Flight was formed at Colerne in June 1941 to work with 87 Squadron, and on 27 January 1942 both units moved to Charmy Down to mount operations from there. Standing patrols were often flown, but few contacts were made and no interceptions.

Meanwhile No 87 Squadron continued to fly its own night patrols, but with limited success. In May 1942 it recommenced offensive operations over the continent. This continued throughout that summer and included, on 19 August, Operation *Jubilee*, the commando raid on Dieppe, when the Hurricanes flew ground-attack missions against German airfields and installations. Despite being formed into squadrons for ease of operation (1454 Flight became 533 Squadron on 8 September), the lack of success of the Turbinlite units led to their withdrawal in early 1943, No 533 Squadron being disbanded on 25 January 1943. The Hurricanes of 87 Squadron had already left Charmy Down by this time, and by early November 1942 were en route for North Africa.

Charmy Down was used for forward deployments by various units during the latter part of 1942. These included 234 Squadron, which flew in on detachment from Portreath on 23 August for a couple of weeks while flying offensive sweeps over France. RAF bombers were also deployed during this time, such as the Bostons of 88 Squadron, which in mid-September mounted several raids from Charmy Down on shipping in Cherbourg and Le Havre harbours.

The Fighter Leader School formed at Chedworth on 15 January 1943, but moved to Charmy Down after having completed its first course on 9 February. The school was part of 62 OTU, and used thirty-six Spitfire Vs to give short, sharp courses in tactics to fighter flight and squadron commanders. It also devised new tactics, including bomber defence, when the Boston crews of 88 Squadron flew sorties against FLS students in April 1943.

However, with the expansion of the USAAF in Britain during the summer of 1943, Charmy Down was made available to the Americans. In early August the FLS was evicted to Aston Down, joining its parent unit, 52 OTU. It was not until November 1943 that the US 9th AF took over the airfield. The first unit to arrive was the 4th Tactical Air Depot, which received, stored and maintained P-38s and P-51s. It moved to Kingston Bagpuize early in 1944, and was replaced in March by a unit whose personnel were to have an unhappy time at the station. Apart from the living conditions 'on a windy hilltop with no heating', they had few aeroplanes to fly. They were with the 422nd Night Fighter Squadron of the 474th Night Fighter Group, and had been moved to Charmy Down to train on the new Northrop P-61. However, the P-61s hadn't arrived, and the crews had to keep up their flying hours on Oxfords and Cessna Bobcats. They were joined by personnel of the 423rd NFS on 18 April, also awaiting P-61s.

During the spring of 1944 a 9th Air Force Troop Carrier Service Wing (Provisional) was established at Charmy Down to provide maintenance and servicing for the USAAF troop-carrier units in the South West. Limited flying took place during this time by detachments, including clandestine missions to the continent in support of the OSS and French Resistance groups as part of the invasion preparations.

The personnel of 422nd NFS moved to Scorton on 6 May, where they received their P-61s. Due to the limited number of the type available, it was decided to re-role the 423rd NFS as a night photographic unit on F-3A Havocs. With their new aircraft the unit moved to Chalgrove on 10 May.

Charmy Down's control tower, still well-preserved in November 1980.

They were replaced by the personnel of the third squadron of the original 474th NFG, the 425th NFS, who arrived on 26 May, but only had to wait until 12 June, when they joined the 422nd at Scorton. The USAAF retained storage and maintenance facilities until October 1944, when they handed Charmy Down over to 23 Group RAF Flying Training Command, as a satellite for South Cerney.

No 15 (P)AFU used the airfield due to waterlogging at Castle Combe. Its Oxfords were joined by more of the type when B Flight of 3 (P)AFU moved in following the closure of Bibury. The aircraft of 15 (P)AFU returned to Castle Combe early in 1945, but 3 (P)AFU continued to use Charmy Down into the spring of 1945. With the end of the war in Europe all flying training stopped at the airfield, and 3 (P)AFU moved out. Between January and October 1946 it was used for Air Cadet glider training by 92 Gliding School, its accommodation sites used as a Personnel Resettlement Centre. The latter was then closed, and 92 GS moved to Colerne.

De-requisitioned in 1949, Charmy Down stood more or less intact for many years. However, the runways were eventually broken up, and most of the buildings gradually deteriorated and were demolished. Today parts of the taxiway remain and the control tower still stands, together with a few other buildings to bear witness to the airfield's short but exciting past.

Main features:
Runways: 310° 4,350ft x 150ft, 250° 4,050ft x 150ft, 012° 2,799ft x 150ft, tarmac. *Hangars:* twelve Blister. *Hardstandings:* forty-five dispersals. *Accommodation:* temporary.

Chedworth's armoury in May 2002.

CHEDWORTH, Gloucestershire

SP042131, 1 1/2 miles NW of Chedworth village

Chedworth airfield lies on a plateau with splendid views to the north and east over the Cotswold Hills. It was constructed during the winter of 1941/42 in an unusual layout of two runways almost at right angles to each other, of 1,400 and 1,300 yards. A taxiway, punctuated by twenty-four dispersals, ran around the perimeter. Two Blister hangars were later built, together with control tower, administrative offices and battle HQ. A number of living sites provided accommodation for the station's staff, in and around Withington Woods to the north-west.

Chedworth opened in April 1942 as a satellite of Aston Down. The first user was 52 OTU, which flew its Spitfires and Masters in on detachment from the main base. It was decided to permanently base two of the OTU's flights at Chedworth, and these took up residence in August 1942. Towards the end of the year Fighter Command decided to form a new training organisation to teach combat tactics to fighter squadron and flight commanders. This resulted in the formation of the Fighter Leaders School within 52 OTU, utilising the two flights at Chedworth, which dealt with the more advanced training. On 15 January 1943 the first FLS course started at Chedworth, lasting for three weeks. It dealt during the first week with section tactics, then during the second week squadron and wing tactics, followed by Army support for the third week. The first course was successful, but it was found that Chedworth as too small for the new school, so shortly afterwards, on 9 February 1943, it moved to Charmy Down.

Ten days later Chedworth came under the control of South Cerney, and was used by the Oxfords of 3 and 6 (P)AFUs for flying training. Both units used the airfield for approach and landing training and a detachment of 6 (P)AFU was based there for a few months. In October 1943 control of the airfield changed again, to that of Honiley. No 2 (Air Gunnery) Squadron of 63 OTU moved in from there, and was joined by the Air Gunnery Squadron of 60 OTU, from High Ercall in Shropshire. A combined 60/63 OTU Gunnery Squadron formed, flying Mosquitoes, Beaufighters and Masters from the airfield. After a period of intensive flying the two units returned to their home bases in January 1944.

Chedworth was next used by the Oxfords of 3 (P)AFU, which returned in the spring of 1944 for flying practice. This was due to South Cerney's airspace becoming congested due to its close proximity to Fairford, Down Ampney, Blakehill Farm and Broadwell, airborne forces support bases heavily involved in training and preparation for the impending invasion. Following the successful landings, Chedworth was used briefly by the USAAF, when the HQ squadron of 9th AF was based there between 19 June and 9 July 1944. L-4 Cubs and L-5 Sentinels of 125th Liaison Squadron flew from the airfield during this period.

On 17 July 1944 control of Chedworth returned to Aston Down, then the base of 3 Tactical Exercise Unit, which trained RAF pilots in the close support of the Army. The Mustangs of its C Flight moved in, but Hurricanes and Typhoons of the unit's other flights also used Chedworth. The TEU was re-titled 55 OTU on 18 December 1944 and given more aircraft, eventually having 120 on complement. This period was probably the busiest for Chedworth, supporting an intensive flying training programme to hone the ground-attack skills of RAF pilots, particularly important during the final phases of the war in Europe.

Following VE Day, flying ran down, then ceased at Chedworth on 29 May 1945, when all aircraft and personnel returned to Aston Down. The airfield was then placed on C&M. The Admiralty took an interest and reopened Chedworth in December 1945 for storage, and the airfield was also later used as an ELG by CFS Little Rissington. A gliding club was opened in the later 1960s, and during the 1970s Chedworth was used for tactical exercises by RAF helicopters. However, by the mid-1980s agriculture was the sole activity at the former airfield. There are nonetheless a number of remnants of its past still in place, including one of the hangars, the battle HQ and a few barrack buildings.

Main features:
Runways: 035° 4,200ft x 150ft, 115° 3,900ft x 150ft, tarmac. Hangars: two EO-Blister. Hardstandings: twenty-five. Accommodation: RAF Officers 21, SNCOs 120, ORs 465; WAAF Officers 1, SNCOs 5, ORs 60.

CHICKERELL, Dorset

SY655796, 1½ miles NW of Weymouth

Originally established in the spring of 1918 as one of a series of small aerodromes strategically placed along the British coast for use by short-range anti-submarine and patrol aircraft, Chickerell has had a lengthy but intermittent career. The first user was D Flight of 253 Squadron, operating three DH6 patrol aircraft at the end of June 1918. In August the Flight was replaced by 513 (Special Duty) Flight of 241 Squadron, also flying the DH6.

The RAF left Chickerell at the end of 1918, and the site was earmarked as a civil aerodrome for Weymouth, one of a number that were then planned to cover the county. For a short period Handley Page Air Transport flew 0/400 passenger aircraft to Chickerell as part of a network of services from its base at Cricklewood, but these were not a financial success and were abandoned. For three years from 1927 Chickerell was used as a temporary base by the RAF, for FAA units exercising with ships from Portland. Facilities were limited to a windsock and landing circle painted on the roughly square grass field, each unit having to provide its own tentage on arrival. During the 1930s Sir Alan Cobham appeared regularly at Chickerell with his 'circus' to give flying demonstrations and passenger flights.

In 1937 the Air Ministry leased the field as a forward base for armament training on the Chesil Bank Ranges, and this started a phase in the airfield's life that was to last throughout the wartime period. It was used by 6 Armament Training Station, based at Warmwell (then known as Woodsford) for the rearming of aircraft using the ranges, and also as an ELG should an emergency occur. There followed a procession of RAF squadrons that used Chickerell for training while on detachment to Warmwell for Armament Practice Camps. These were usually fighter squadrons flying single-engine aircraft such as the Spitfire and Hurricane, but units flying the Blenheim also appeared. FAA squadrons used Chickerell occasionally, such as 793 Squadron with Rocs in August 1940 and 794 Squadron, which, as an Air Firing Unit, based its Skuas, Defiants and Blenheims at Warmwell and Chickerell between March and July 1943. The airfield was used continuously throughout the wartime period until the summer of 1945, when range use rapidly diminished. The last RAF APC closed at Warmwell in November 1945.

The FAA continued to use the ranges, and a detachment of 771 Squadron used Chickerell. The airfield was also used for communications flights for Portland. Dragonfly helicopters of 705 Squadron spent three months at Chickerell in early 1953, but with the withdrawal of 771 Squadron in August the airfield fell into disuse. Chickerell was finally decommissioned in 1959, and today nothing can be seen of its former use as the area is covered by housing and industrial estates.

Wellington GRXIV NB829, NX-O, of 14 Squadron at Chivenor in September 1944.

CHIVENOR, Devon

SS492344, 5 miles W of Barnstaple

As the 1,076-ton Italian submarine *Luigi Torelli* was charging its batteries on the surface in the Bay of Biscay in the early hours of 4 June 1942, its lookouts were suddenly blinded by a brilliant white light. The Officer of the Watch ordered a hard turn to port, whereupon the light went out as an aircraft flew overhead. The crew of the aircraft, a Wellington of 172 Squadron, realised that they had glimpsed a submarine, but too late to attack it. The pilot, Sqn Ldr Greswell, turned the aircraft back towards the sighting position, was surprised to re-establish the contact on radar, and delighted when the Italians fired recognition flares. At a height of 250 feet, and three-quarters of a mile away from it, the submarine was again picked up in the light's beam. At 50 feet the pilot released his 250lb depth charges. It was the perfect straddle, but though the boat was badly damaged it was able to limp into Bordeaux. This was the first time that the Leigh Light had been used operationally, and it was to become virtually synonymous with Chivenor.

The airfield had its origins in North Devon Airport, opened in June 1934 as a base of the North Devon Flying Club and Atlantic Coast Air Services (later Lundy & Atlantic Coast Air Services), which flew services to Lundy Island. In 1939 Western Airways added a Manchester-Penzance route using the airport. With the outbreak of war later that year most civil flying was stopped, but Lundy & Atlantic Coast Airlines started war work by operating as a Civilian Repair Unit, repairing crashed and damaged military training aircraft such as Tiger Moths. Some 500 acres of land had been requisitioned to the west of the airport for a new airfield, and work on the construction of this was started in May 1940 by George Wimpey & Co Ltd. Three 3,000-foot runways were laid, and eight hangars constructed, together with extensive hutted accommodation.

Opened as RAF Chivenor on 1 October 1940 under 17 (Training) Group, Coastal Command, it was to remain a Coastal station for six years. The first unit to take up residency was 3 (Coastal) OTU, which formed on 27 November with Blenheims, Ansons, Beauforts and Lysanders to train new Coastal crews. This included night-flying, and on the evening of 26 November an unusual shape joined the circuit for landing. As the aircraft taxied in to refuel, it looked like a Beaufort, but when the MT driver realised that it was a Ju 88, he blocked the aircraft's path, and its crew were arrested. The German bomber (M2+HK) had been on an anti-shipping patrol over the Irish Sea when the crew had been confused by British 'Meacon' radio countermeasures. They mistook the Bristol Channel for the English Channel, and thought that they had landed in France. The aircraft was later put into service by the RAF with 1426 (Enemy Aircraft) Flight.

On 1 December 1940 No 252 Squadron arrived from Bircham Newton to convert from the Blenheim to the new Beaufighter. However, because Fighter Command had priority on the type, this took a little while. The Squadron finally departed on 3 April and was replaced by 272 Squadron to undertake the same task. No 252 Squadron made its first operational sortie from Aldergrove on 6 April, and scored its first victory, an FW 200, ten days later.

From 24 December 1940 until February 1944, when Hurn became Britain's main international airport, Chivenor was used by KLM as a staging post for its flights from Whitchurch to Lisbon, Portugal. These aircraft were usually Douglas DC2s or DC3s, which topped up their tanks before crossing the Bay of Biscay. Any fighter escorts available would also rendezvous at Chivenor. Although not a frequent occurrence, the odd aircraft was attacked by the Luftwaffe, the best-known being DC3 G-AGBB, shot down in June 1943 by a Ju 88; all aboard the airliner were lost, including film actor Leslie Howard.

In early 1941 Chivenor's main runway and its taxiways were extended, and additional dispersals were laid. As if this had attracted their attention, the Luftwaffe raided the improved airfield in March, causing little damage, but returned with a vengeance on 16 April, severely damaging parked aircraft, the runways and control tower, putting the station out of action for several days.

In July 1941 No 3 (C)OTU moved on, and was replaced by 5 (C)OTU, which formed at Chivenor on 1 August 1941. Its equipment was similar to that of its predecessor, but also included Battles and Hudsons. Although Coastal squadrons made detachments to Chivenor, it was not until the spring of 1942 that complete squadrons were based there, the first being 172 Squadron.

During 1940 Sqn Ldr Humphrey de Vere Leigh developed the Leigh Light, a powerful searchlight that could illuminate a potential target submarine once it had been located on radar. After some delay it was decided to form, on 18 January 1942, No 1417 (Leigh Light Trials) Flight at Chivenor to evaluate the equipment. With service trials complete, 1417 Flight was expanded, then disbanded and reformed as 172 Squadron on 4 April 1942, with a complement of twenty Wellingtons.

Increasing U-boat activity in the Bay of Biscay during this time resulted in the deployment of the Whitleys of 51 and 77 Squadrons to Chivenor, on detachment from Bomber Command, to join 172 Squadron on patrols. Relief for the overcrowded airfield was provided in May when 5 (C)OTU left, and Chivenor was proclaimed as a fully operational airfield by being transferred to Coastal Command's Mount Batten-based 19 Group. In June more than 190 anti-submarine patrols were mounted from Chivenor, but six of its aircraft (one Wellington and five Whitleys) were lost, mostly to Ju 88 fighters. To combat this menace 235 Squadron was moved to Chivenor to mount patrols over the Bay with its Beaufighters. These arrived in May, as 5 (C)OTU was moving out. Locating and attacking the *Luigi Tirelli* had seen the first operational use of the Leigh Light, but the first kill using the device was achieved on 6 July 1942. Wellington 'H' of 172 Squadron, commanded by Plt Off Wily Howell, an American, made a Leigh Light attack on the U-502, a type IX U-boat returning from the Caribbean on its fourth war cruise. The submarine had sunk sixteen ships, but fell victim itself as it was straddled by four depth-charges as it attempted to crash dive.

In October the Whitley squadrons, whose aircraft had been useful in keeping the submarines' heads down, returned to Bomber Command so that Chivenor could then provide refuelling facilities for aircraft flying to Gibraltar and North Africa to take part in Operation *Torch*.

No 404 (RCAF) Squadron replaced 235 Squadron in January 1943 (and stayed until early April to fly escorts and shipping patrols), just as 172 Squadron began to receive the new Wellington GRXII. These aircraft were fitted with the Leigh Light and the more advanced ASR Mk III radar, which the U-boat receivers could not detect. The result was disastrous for the Kriegsmarine. U-665 was the first victim, sunk by Fg Off P. H. Sternbridge and his crew in G/MP539 of 179 Squadron on 22 February 1943. In March alone twelve sightings resulted in seven attacks by the squadron. They were joined by Chivenor's first four-engine aircraft in February, when the Fortresses of 59 Squadron arrived. However, Chivenor was not really big enough, so after a few weeks they returned to Thorney Island. In their place two more Wellington squadrons, 407 (RCAF) and 547, moved in. No 547 left in June and was replaced by 612 Squadron, which made the last operational sortie by a Coastal Whitley on 5 June before converting to Wellingtons.

The three Wellington squadrons moved to St Eval in November when Chivenor's runways needed resurfacing, but returned the following month. With the arrival of 304 (Polish) Squadron from Davidstow Moor in February 1944, Chivenor was able to field four Wellington units in time to combat the expected spring U-boat offensive. In May the submarines began to concentrate in the Biscay ports ready to attack the expected allied invasion of Europe and sightings were few. The Chivenor squadrons were then engaged in the effort to ensure that enemy vessels were unable to interfere with the vast gathering Allied armada. Operation *Cork* called for an area of 20,000 square

*Spitfire LF16
TE441, HX-C,
of 203 AFS at
Chivenor in
1948.*

miles of sea to be patrolled every 30 minutes round the clock. No 19 Group coordinated the thirty-one RAF, FAA and USN squadrons involved, with Chivenor's Wellington units bearing the brunt of the night operations. Although more than 350 patrols were mounted from Chivenor during June, only one U-boat was sunk, but very few attacks on Allied vessels by the Germans were recorded.

On the night of 27 August a posthumous George Cross was won by Fg Off R. B. Gray, a navigator with 172 Squadron. His aircraft detected a U-boat on radar and confirmed this by Leigh Light. On the run-in to attack, the U-boat's flak set fire to the Wellington's port engine, and as the aircraft dropped its depth charges, its starboard engine was also hit. The Wellington ditched and four of the crew escaped from it, but had only one small dinghy between them. Gray helped the wounded pilot and another survivor into it, and with the fourth man, clung to the outside. With the dawn, Gray was found to be dead from loss of blood; his leg had been shot away, but he had not mentioned it. Fifteen hours after the ditching, a Sunderland of 10 (RAAF) Squadron landed and picked up the survivors.

With the Biscay ports in Allied hands, the U-boats moved away. During September 172, 304 and 612 Squadrons moved out and were replaced by 36 and 14 Squadrons, the latter converting from Marauders to Wellingtons. All three Chivenor squadrons then converted to the later mark of Leigh Light Wellington, the GRXIV. With these they flew long and often fruitless patrols over the English Channel, sometimes in terrible weather. In February 1945 Chivenor was under a foot of snow, and it took all available station personnel to clear the runway. After the aircraft took off a thaw set in and the airfield was flooded! The runways had been extended during 1944 and new dispersals were added, some on the original North Devon Airport. By the spring of 1945, however, the U-boat war was out of range. The last wartime U-boat attack by a Chivenor-based aircraft had occurred on 30 December 1944 when Wellington GRXIV L/NB855 of 407 Squadron commanded by Sqn Ldr C. W. Taylor spotted the schnorkel wake of U-772, a type VIIC in the Channel south of Portland. Six depth charges were dropped and the U-boat sank. On 9 March 36 Squadron moved to Benbecula in the Hebrides, 14 Squadron disbanded on 25 May, and the last Chivenor Wellington squadron, 407, disbanded at the station on 4 June 1945.

During the wartime period Chivenor's aircraft were responsible for sinking fifteen U-boats and damaging fourteen. However, the price paid was high – twenty-one Whitleys and twenty-eight Wellingtons were lost on operations from the station. For their courage and gallantry Chivenor crews were awarded one George Cross, three DSOs, twenty-five DFCs, five DFMs, one AFC and seventy-four Mentions in Despatches.

The first year of peace saw the end of Chivenor's tenure under Coastal Command. A strike wing, of 248 and 254 Squadrons with Mosquitoes, briefly occupied the station, followed by the Halifax Met Vs of 517 Squadron on meteorological duties. By 1 April 1946, however, 21 Aircrew Holding Unit was in sole occupancy of the station. Fighter Command took it over on 1 October 1946 to house 691 Squadron, an anti-aircraft cooperation unit flying Spitfire XVIs, Oxfords and Martinets. No 203 AFS from Keevil arrived eleven months later, remaining until 1950, when

Hunter F6 XJ634/34 of 229 OCU taxies by in August 1970.

Meteor F8, WK941/E, 229 OCU, Chivenor, in August 1971.

Hawks of 7 FTS lined up at Chivenor in August 1992.

Chivenor was taken over by Transport Command for 1 Overseas Ferry Unit. This unit's duties included the delivery of Mosquitoes, Meteors and Vampires to the Middle and Far East.

However, the unit did not stay long, for on 28 March 1951 No 229 OCU arrived from Leuchars to start what would become a twenty-four-year association with Chivenor. Equipped with Vampire FB5s and Meteor T7s, the unit had only formed three months before, to train pilots for the Korean War. The OCU's role was to provide tactical training for pilots in the day-fighter role. Air-to-air firing was carried out on ranges off the North Devon and South Wales coasts, at targets towed by Tempests, Beaufighters and later Mosquitoes and Meteors. The Vampires were replaced briefly by Sabres in April 1954, but just over a year later the first Hunters arrived. Extensive alterations to the runways and taxiways were made during this time and a large hardstanding laid in front of the hangars, but the RAF was strangely reluctant to consider Chivenor as a permanent station, and wartime wooden huts remained as accommodation and offices.

In 1957 the first helicopters, Sycamore HR14s, arrived with E Flight of 275 Squadron to provide ASR cover for the station. Some eighteen months later they were replaced by Whirlwinds of 22 Squadron, another unit that has since had a long association with Chivenor, carrying on to this day. In October 1965 No 624 Gliding School moved to Chivenor from Exeter with Sedbergh and Kirby gliders to provide training at weekends for Air Cadets. The three units shared the airfield until the end of August 1974 when 229 OCU was moved to Brawdy to become 1 Tactical Weapons Unit. Chivenor was then put on C&M, pending its possible disposal, although 22 Squadron and 624 GS continued to fly from the airfield.

In 1980, however, a £17 million refurbishment programme was started when Chivenor's runways were upgraded, its hangars re-clad and the wartime-vintage technical site rebuilt. On 1 August a detachment of 1 TWU with Hawk T1s moved in from Brawdy, and on 1 April 1981 this became 2 TWU. The unit trained fast-jet pilots in the art of air-to-air combat, weaponry and tactical low flying. Under 'Options for Change', 2 TWU became 7 FTS on 1 April 1992 and Chivenor transferred from Strike Command to Support Command. A further £12 million rebuilding programme was then initiated, entailing new engineering facilities, simulators, hangarage and messes. It was during this time that the last of the wartime wooden huts were demolished.

However, despite the massive expenditure on the station, the following year it was decided to disband 7 FTS, and this took place on 30 September 1994. The last Hawks, from 4 FTS, which had used Chivenor as a detachment base, left the airfield on 17 March 1995, bringing to a close an important chapter in RAF history.

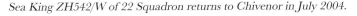

Sea King ZH542/W of 22 Squadron returns to Chivenor in July 2004.

On 1 October 1995 Chivenor was transferred to the Royal Marines, for use by 3 Commando Logistics Regiment and 59 Independent Commando Squadron, Royal Engineers. The airfield is still maintained, and is used by A Flight of 22 Squadron, which now flies Sea Kings, and the gliders of 624 Volunteer Gliding Squadron.

Main features:
Runways: 102° 6,000ft x 150ft, 242° 4,380ft x 150ft, 162° 3,510ft x 150ft, concrete and tarmac. *Hangars:* four Bellman, four Hinaidi, one EO-Blister. *Hardstandings:* forty-five spectacle, five 150ft diameter. *Accommodation:* RAF Officers 266, SNCOs 506, ORs 1,906; WAAF Officers 2, SNCOs nil, ORs 331.

The factory at Christchurch can be seen at the top left in this 1948 shot, the main airfield below it, and the runway built for the USAAF to the right.

CHRISTCHURCH, Dorset (previously Hampshire)

SZ185932, half a mile NE of Christchurch

Initially a minor pre-war aerodrome, Christchurch developed into an important wartime airfield due to its use for research work, by the Airspeed Company as the site for an aircraft factory, and its later use by the USAAF.

Opened in 1935 as a small flying club airfield on meadowland beside the River Mude, Christchurch attracted summer scheduled services by a number of small airlines. However, all found it difficult to make their routes viable and it was not until 1939 that Great Western & Southern Airlines started to make the airfield pay.

In September 1939, with the outbreak of war, civil flying was curtailed and the airfield was closed. However, in April 1940 it was requisitioned by the Air Ministry for the use of its Telecommunications Research Establishment at Gosport. The TRE had a Special Duty Flight, which operated a number of Battles, Blenheims, Ansons and Harrows, previously flown from St Athan.

The capitulation of France during the summer of 1940 put the South Coast in the front line, and there was anxiety about the vulnerability of aircraft parked at Christchurch. An ELG was therefore established at Sway, some 6½ miles to the east. Three of the SDF's Hurricanes were allocated to defence duties, and it was in one of these, L1562, that Flt Lt D. L. Rayment intercepted and shot down a Ju 88 off St Catherine's Point on 19 September. A week earlier the pilot had attacked another Ju 88 while flying a trials Blenheim. One SDF Hurricane, L1592, later flew during the Battle of Britain, survived the war, and is preserved at the Science Museum in London. In October 1940 H Flight of 1 AACU arrived from Gosport, its Battles then working with the SDF on trials for the Air Defence Experimental Establishment at Swanage. By the end of the month there were more than thirty aircraft at Christchurch, straining accommodation for equipment and personnel. No.420 Flight had formed at Christchurch on 25 September with Harrows and Battles, but soon moved to Middle Wallop.

Work on the erection of a shadow factory had started during the summer of 1940 alongside the western boundary of the airfield. Completed towards the end of the year, it was taken over by Airspeed Ltd for the production of Oxfords, and eventually 550 of the type were to be built there. Because of the vulnerability of the site, the factory was well camouflaged, as was the airfield. 'Hedges' were painted across the grass with creosote, and roads were simulated by light-coloured stone chippings. The effect was so convincing that the pilot of a visiting Hampden circled the field several times but did not land because he thought it too small. In January 1941 the first of three retractable ground defence pillboxes was installed. Twin dispersal pens were also constructed around the airfield.

Plans were made to move the SDF to Hurn in early 1941, but the flight was still in residence when Sway was bombed on 9 April, followed by Christchurch itself a month later. A He 111 attacked at low level, dropping thirteen bombs that damaged huts on the airfield, as well as some houses on its edge. Another He 111 attacked during the early morning two days later, but flew off when the defences opened fire. A stir was caused on 30 April 1941 when a Luftwaffe Bucker Jungman biplane trainer landed. It was flown in by two French Air Force pilots who had stolen it from Caen airfield and flown at low level across the Channel. Both pilots went on to serve with the RAF. Another arrival was a Boeing 247 for trials on AI radar in August 1941. Just before this, on 1 July, H Flight, 1 AACU, was disbanded and absorbed into the SDF, which then did move to Hurn as originally planned, in August. A detachment remained behind at Christchurch until November.

Christchurch was transferred to the control of 10 Group on 1 August as a satellite of Hurn, but from November it was used almost exclusively by Airspeed. The company expanded its activities, building Horsa gliders, the first of which was collected by a Whitley and towed away in February 1942. Another 694 Horsas followed. In 1943 came a contract for the conversion of Spitfire Mk Vs into Seafires, involving the fitting of arrester hooks, catapult spools and other minor modifications; some 160 such conversions were undertaken at the factory.

In 1943 the Air Ministry reviewed the New Forest area for suitable sites as forward airfields for the USAAF in preparation for the planned invasion of France. Although Christchurch was too small as it stood, it was decided to enlarge the landing area across nearby fields by piping the River Bure underground. After preliminary excavation and levelling by 5055 Construction Squadron, RAF, the US Army laid a fabric-supported Square-Mesh Track main runway of 4,800 feet. It was opened for flying on 18 January 1944 and at the end of February the advance party of the 405th Fighter Group of the US 9th AF arrived. Part of the 84th Fighter Wing, the group was made up of 509th, 510th and 511th Fighter Squadrons, each flying the P-47 Thunderbolt. The Americans roughed it at Christchurch, living in tents and working on their aircraft in the open. They flew their first mission on 11 April, when fifty-four P-47s took part in a sweep over north-west France. Over the following months the US fighters attacked bridges, railways, airfields and other targets of interest, but experienced several flying accidents during this time. Three aircraft crashed on take-off one day, and on 29 June a P-47 crashed into a bungalow just off the airfield, one of its bombs exploding. This killed the pilot and three people inside the building, but also brought down another P-47 (although its pilot managed to escape with burns). When a crash tender and people gathered to rescue the injured, the second bomb exploded, killing another ten and seriously inuring twenty-three. The Americans were kept busy following the D-Day landings, and from 22 June began to use the strip at A-8 Picaville as a forward landing ground. The group used both bases for a period until 18 July, when the last aircraft moved to A-8, followed by the rear echelon. Twenty P-47s were lost on operations while operating from Christchurch.

With the departure of the USAAF the airfield returned to relative peace, its sole users being Airspeed Ltd. Despite being transferred to 11 Group Fighter Command, no further RAF units were based there. Instead, Airspeed had decided that its factory at Christchurch was easier to develop

An early-production Ambassador for BEA climbs out over Christchurch Priory in 1952.

Venom NF3 WX737, one of the first for the RAF, on test from de Havilland's Christchurch factory in early 1954.

than that at Portsmouth, and expanded its facilities there. Design and drawing offices, research facilities and a technical block were constructed and the design team moved in to concentrate their efforts on a new project, the A557 (later named Ambassador). Control of Christchurch went to 46 Group, Transport Command, in March 1945, and on 10 January 1946 was taken over by the MAP as a factory airfield. That year assembly of the prototype Ambassador started, its maiden flight taking place from the airfield on 10 July 1947. The last British passenger aircraft to be equipped with piston engines, the Ambassador flew with BEA until 1958. Airspeed was given the task of developing the trainer version of the Vampire on subcontract from de Havilland, and a tarmac runway was laid in 1950 to allow the flight-testing of the prototypes.

In July 1951 Airspeed was absorbed by de Havilland and, with a strengthened design team, developed the Venom for naval use as the Sea Venom, and later completed an 80 per cent re-design of the DH110 to produce the Sea Vixen. A reduction in military contracts eventually led to the ending of production at Christchurch in 1962, with the closure of the airfield five years later. Housing estates then started to encroach from the south-west and the de Havilland works was taken over by various industrial concerns. In 1979 the main airfield site was sold to Barratt Developments Ltd for an extension of the industrial estate and for housing. Nothing of the airfield itself remains today, although road names in the area such as de Havilland Way and Ambassador Close recall the site's aviation heritage.

Main features:
Runways: 245° 4,950ft x 150ft, concrete and grass, N-S 3,000ft, NE-SW 3,000ft, E-W 3,000ft, NW-SE 2,850ft, steel mesh. *Hangars:* one Bellman, three EO-Blister, one Bessoneau. *Hardstandings:* none. *Accommodation:* RAF Officers 4, SNCOs 9, ORs 236.

Cleave's cliff-top position can clearly be seen here in 1938, with canvas accommodation of various types for both men and aircraft.

CLEAVE, Cornwall

SS205125, 4 miles N of Bude

Planned as a landing ground for summer anti-aircraft cooperation camps, work on the cliff-top site at Cleave was started in February 1939, the first military airfield to be built in Cornwall. Initially two, later three, wood and canvas Bessoneau hangars were erected for the maintenance and storage of aircraft, the airmen being accommodated in tents.

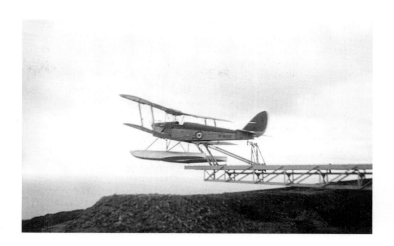

*Queen Bee being
launched off the
catapult in 1938.*

The first to use the new airfield, opened by Army Cooperation Command in May 1939, were the personnel of 1 AACU, which had its headquarters at Biggin Hill. G Flight, formed at Usworth shortly before, flew in on the 15th with its Westland Wallace target tugs, while V Flight was formed at Cleave the day before to operate the Queen Bee (a pilot-less target version of the Tiger Moth). Initially equipped with floats, this was intended to be catapulted off the cliffs and flown under radio control, to be fired at by AA batteries along the coast or by ships at sea. If damaged or unscathed, the aircraft would then be landed on the water for recovery by lighter. The catapult and crane were erected on the cliff-top and ready for use in June. However, a few flights proved the equipment to be too cumbersome, and it was found far easier to fit the Queen Bees with undercarriages and fly them off the field as normal aircraft.

V Flight flew predominantly for the gunners of 6 Heavy Anti-Aircraft Practice Camp, Cleave, while G Flight flew mainly for 12 Light AAPC at Penhale. Just after the outbreak of war, on 6 September, D Flight, with Henleys, arrived from Bircham Newton to work with 10 LAAPC, St Agnes Head. All three flights steadily increased their sortie levels, so it was decided to develop Cleave into more of a permanent airfield. In October construction started on proper living quarters, messes, administration and operational buildings. Two steel Bellman hangars were erected and a 2,700-foot runway was laid out on the grass. By the end of July 1940 Cleave began to look more like a normal RAF station. However, this activity drew the attention of the Luftwaffe and on 26 August two Ju 88s dropped a dozen bombs, damaging two Wallaces and injuring a civilian worker. In a further attack on 2 October a 500kg bomb hit one of the hangars, but fortunately failed to explode.

*Wallace II K6015,
following a heavy
landing at Cleave in
1939.*

Henley L3245 on the beach after force-landing near Cleave.

On 5 November 1940 O Flight was formed at Cleave with Henleys and Wallaces, also to work with 12 LAAPC. The thin soil and impervious rock on the cliff-top made water absorption and drainage very slow, and waterlogging was a constant problem during the winter. Flying was interrupted because of this and a couple of Beauforts that landed in March 1941 were lucky to get down safely. Despite this, diversions by operational aircraft were regular occurrences and during 1942 included Spitfires, Whirlwinds and at least one Mosquito.

No 1 AACU was reorganised during the winter of 1942 and on 1 November its flights were given numbers. D Flight became 1602 (AAC) Flight, G Flight became 1603 (AAC) Flight, O Flight became 1604 (AAC) Flight, and V Flight became 1618 (AAC) Flight. Despite this, they soldiered on as before, with Henleys having by then replaced the Wallaces. Waterlogging again caused problems, and in mid-December all three Henley flights moved out while repairs were made, 1602 and 1604 to Trebelzue (returning on 28 February and 23 March 1943), while 1603 went to Davidstow Moor, returning on 27 January. Diversions continued, and in April a USAAF B-17 landed without difficulty, probably because it was lightly loaded, having spent 13 hours flying from North Africa. Its VIP passengers, led by Major General Edwards, US Army, were probably relieved to reach terra firma.

Army Cooperation Command disbanded in June 1943 and was absorbed into Fighter Command, but the work of the Cleave units continued unchanged. On 1 December all four flights were amalgamated to form 639 Squadron, although Queen Bee flying by the former 1618 Flight was coming to an end. The large Army camp on the northern edge of the airfield was by then partially occupied by the Americans for gunnery training and even attracted full US Army stage shows – one had Bob Hope and the Glenn Miller Band appearing on the same bill!

In August 1944 No 639 Squadron received Hurricane IVs for gun-laying training, enabling the Henleys to concentrate on towing live-firing targets. AAPCs continued into 1945 but, with the war in Europe coming to an end, started to wind down. Cleave's closure came soon after VE Day when, on 16 May, it was reduced to C&M. No 639 Squadron had in fact by then already disbanded (on 30 April) and the airfield was closed in November. Nonetheless, the site remained in Government hands and has more recently become the Combined Signals Organisation Station Morwenstow. Nearly all of the old brick buildings have been replaced and two large dish aerials now dominate the area. The small village of Cleave disappeared when the airfield was enlarged, and today the only use of the name is in Cleave Crescent, part of the married quarters since built to the east of the old airfield.

Main features:
Runways: ENE-WSW 2,700ft, N-S 2,250ft, grass. *Hangars:* two Bellman, one Blister. *Hardstandings:* none. *Accommodation:* RAF Officers 11, SNCOs 28, ORs 380; WAAF Officers 2, SNCOs 4, ORs 74.

The surviving Bellman hangar and Maycrete building at Clyffe Pypard in October 2008.

CLYFFE PYPARD, Wiltshire

SU070755, 3¹/₂ miles S of Wootton Bassett

Situated on flat farmland to the north of the Marlborough Downs, Clyffe Pypard's four runways were of grass, with a concrete perimeter track running round. Accommodation for personnel was situated to the north-west and a technical site alongside the airfield consisted of four Bellman hangars and various Maycrete buildings. A number of Blister hangars were later added.

No 29 EFTS was formed at the new airfield on 13 September 1941, operated by Marshall's Flying Schools of Cambridge and employing civilian staff as flying instructors and maintenance engineers. With seventy-two Tiger Moths and thirty-six Magisters, its role was to teach students to fly to solo standard. No 1 Course opened on 15 September with seventy students from 7 ITW Newquay, and one from Duxford. The airfield was soon very busy and in order to relieve the congestion the SLG at Alton Barnes was transferred to 29 EFTS at the end of the year.

FAA pilots were being trained at 29 EFTS during early 1942, and in May the school's courses were expanded to include the training of Army gilder pilots. On 3 June the school was increased in size by one-third, its four flights being increased by two, including two at Alton Barnes. Battles and Ansons appeared to supplement the Tiger Moths and Magisters. Another new type arrived on the night of 18 October 1942 when the ferry pilot of Liberator AL538 from Prestwick mistook Clyffe Pypard for Lyneham. The aircraft landed too fast for the small airfield and crashed through the eastern boundary fence, catching fire; it was written off, but the crew survived unscathed.

From 21 November 1942 29 EFTS began to use another RLG to increase its flying training capacity; this was Manningford, transferred from CFS Upavon. Courses were added to the school's syllabus to assess the flying standards of pilots and instructors, to identify any further training needs.

Flying was interrupted in January 1943 when snow fell heavily, and 4-foot drifts covered the area. A snowplough was used to clear road access and cut a 900-yard emergency runway.

Another unexpected arrival at Clyffe Pypard was Stirling BK667 of 15 Squadron, which overshot and crashed into trees on the north-east side of the airfield on 22 March 1943. The aircraft had returned from an aborted raid on St Nazaire and, although its bomb-load of incendiaries exploded, the crew escaped with only one injury.

The work of 29 EFTS continued throughout 1943 and into the following year. In October 1944 Grading Courses were introduced to assess candidate pilots for the FAA. Pilots who reached a satisfactory standard then went on to a naval flying school for further training. Heavy snow and melt-water rendered Clyffe Pypard unserviceable towards the end of January 1945, and in February more snow, strong winds and low clouds restricted flying even further. Despite widespread closures elsewhere with the end of the war in Europe, 29 EFTS remained open; its RLG at Alton Barnes closed on 9 July 1945, but Manningford was used for a further year. The training of RAF and FAA pilots continued at Clyffe Pypard until late 1947 when, on 5 November, 29 EFTS was disbanded and absorbed by 21 EFTS at Booker.

The airfield remained in RAF hands for some years, its buildings being used as transit accommodation for Lyneham. This continued until main-base trooping facilities were eventually provided, and RAF Clyffe Pypard finally closed in June 1961. Following disposal the airfield returned to agriculture and several of its buildings remain in farm use, including one of the Bellman hangars and some of the Maycrete huts. The station's battle headquarters and several mushroom pillboxes also remain in position.

Main features:
Runways: N-S 3,300ft, NE-SW 3,480ft, E-W 4,000ft, NW-SE 3,150ft, grass.
Hangars: four Bellman, one O-Blister, fourteen Standard Blister. *Accommodation:*
RAF Officers 48, SNCOs 98, ORs 482.

A change of pilots for Spitfire IA X4381 SD-J of 501 Squadron at Colerne in June 1941.

COLERNE, Wiltshire

ST803715, 4 miles NE of Bath, of Fosse Way

Perched on a plateau just inside the Wiltshire border with Somerset, Colerne was one of the last Expansion Scheme airfields to be completed. Laid out as an MU, it was still under construction as war came in September 1939. Many of its buildings were incomplete when the station was opened by 41 Group, Maintenance Command, on 1 January 1940. No 39 MU was formed on 18 May and, as an Aircraft Storage Unit, was sole occupant of the new station. However, in September Fighter Command took an interest, as

Hastings C2, WD495, of 36 Squadron flown in by the author as an Air Cadet from Colerne, August 1966.

it needed a new Sector Station within 10 Group, its HQ being at nearby Rudloe Manor. On 27 November 87 Squadron arrived, with its black-painted Hurricane night-fighters, but found the runways incomplete and moved on to the satellite at Charmy Down.

Colerne was then used for fighter squadron training, 256 Squadron staying for a few weeks before exchanging with another Defiant unit, 307 (Polish) Squadron. Flying the odd patrol from Colerne, the Poles claimed their (and the station's) first confirmed victory when a German bomber fell to their guns on 12 April 1941. No 501 Squadron arrived on 9 April to exchange its Hurricanes at 39 MU for Spitfires. Having worked up with the new type, the Squadron left for Chilbolton.

The first fully operational unit to arrive at Colerne was 600 Squadron, which flew in its Blenheim I and Beaufighter II night-fighters on 27 April and started patrols to cover Bristol, extending these south-westwards. They scored regularly, bringing down a Ju 88 and He 111 before the end of the month, and two more He 111s on 7 May. The next night a Ju 88 was damaged, but on the evening of 9 May a Beaufighter was lost, shot down by another British night-fighter. It was difficult to tell friend from foe at night, and this incident showed just what a risky business night-fighting was. A BOAC repair facility was established in early 1941, using hangars erected to the north of the airfield. Although intended to repair aircraft operated by the airline, it also started assembling fighter aircraft. The RAF later (in March 1942) took over the facility and, as 218 MU, it undertook special installation work such as that of AI radar.

Poles reappeared at Colerne on 18 June when 316 Squadron transferred from Pembrey with Hurricanes. They spent a couple of months flying convoy patrols, but little happened until, escorting Hampdens on Operation *Sunrise*, they claimed a Bf 109. A string of other units passed through during 1941, including 125 Squadron, which reformed at the station on 16 June, drawing its new Defiants from 39 MU. On 4 July 1454 Flight formed with Turbinlite Havocs. Partnered with 87 Squadron, it later moved to Charmy Down and was followed by 1457 Flight on 15 September, which paired with 247 Squadron and moved to Predannack. On 22 December 1941 No 286 Squadron arrived at Colerne, and was to be much in evidence at the station during the ensuing 3¹/₂ years. This was an anti-aircraft cooperation unit, formed the month before at Filton. Equipped with Lysanders, and later expanded with Oxfords, Defiants, Martinets and Hurricanes, the unit provided target facilities (ie target-towing and target simulation) for units of all three services throughout the South West.

The Spitfires of 407 (RCAF) Squadron arrived from Charmy Down in January 1942. They were joined by 125 Squadron, which returned to replace 600 on night patrol work gained one of its last victories with Defiants on 26 April, just before converting to Beaufighter IIFs, courtesy of 39 MU. No 264 Squadron also converted to the Beaufighter in May 1942, exchanging its Defiants at the MU, and was soon operational again, damaging a Do 217 over Weston-super-Mare. The unit's first kill with the Mosquito was a Ju 88 on the night of 30/31 July. Little night action followed, so in December the Squadron went over to day operations, mounting shipping patrols over the Bay of Biscay, and occasional *Rangers* over France. The unit remained at Colerne until the end of April 1943.

Hercules C1 XV188, 24 Squadron, at Hercules Engineering Wing, Colerne, July 1970.

Unusual visitors in September 1942 were the Lockheed P38F Lightnings of the 27th FS, 1st FG, 12th AF, USAAF, which spent nearly two months at Colerne before leaving for North Africa. In December 1942 No 184 Squadron formed at Colerne with Hurricane IID tank busters, and later also the rocket projectile-equipped Hurricane Mk IV. In March 1943 it moved to Chilbolton. Other units to appear during the spring of 1943 included 175 and 183 Squadrons, converting from Hurricanes to Typhoons.

Having transferred from Wittering at the end of April, 151 Squadron flew intruder operations with Mosquito NFIIs from Colerne. Exchanging these for NFXIIs in July, the unit moved to Middle Wallop the following month. It was replaced by 456 Squadron, which had operated a detachment of Mosquito NFIIs from Colerne in mid-March 1943, and was based there from mid-August. Flying night intruder operations over Luftwaffe fighter bases and day *Ranger* patrols, the unit found eight Ju 88s on 21 September and went into the attack, downing one and damaging two more. Moving on in November the unit was replaced by 151 Squadron, returning to Colerne for re-equipping at 39 MU with the Mosquito NFXIII. It claimed an Me 410 with its new mount and shot down an He 177 during one of the first 'Baby Blitz' raids during the night of 21 January 1944. Another successful night followed six weeks later, when one Ju 88 and four Ju 188s were claimed. The unit moved to Predannack in March, replaced by a detachment of 219 Squadron's Mosquito NFXVIIIs, which scored almost immediately when, on 27 March, Sqn Ldr Ellis destroyed a Ju 88 of 3/JG54 over Yeovil.

No 488 (RNZAF) Squadron, another Mosquito unit (flying the NFXII and NFXIII), part of 2TAF, arrived from Hunsdon on 3 May. After a short period it moved to Zeals, and another Mosquito unit, 604 Squadron, took its place on 13 June 1944. It and the two Zeals squadrons (488 was joined by 410 on 18 June) then made up 147 Wing, a specialist night-fighter formation designed to protect 2TAF units moving to the continent. When 410 and 488 moved to Colerne on 28 and 29 July, the Wing was able to fly together more effectively. Their aircraft took off at dusk to roam nightly over France, with great success. The highlight of this activity was undoubtedly the sortie by Flt Lt G. E. Jamieson (Pilot) and Fg Off N. E. Crooks (Radar Operator/Navigator) of 488 Squadron on the night of 29/30 July. Flying MM466 on patrol over Normandy between Caen and Lisieux, they intercepted and destroyed four German night-fighters (three Ju 88s and one Do 217), all in the space of 20 minutes, using only 360 rounds of cannon ammunition.

Colerne, seen from 25,500 feet in May 1998.

Spring/summer 1944 was a busy time for 39 and 218 MUs as both prepared aircraft for the build-up to the invasion. New aircraft were received from the manufacturers, equipped to service standards and incorporated with any modifications that were necessary. Other aircraft were returned from units for modifications and updating before reissue. Stocks of front-line aircraft were built up by 39 MU to replace expected heavy losses, but in the event these were not that heavy and the MUs were fairly quiet during the invasion period itself.

No 604 Squadron moved to the continent on 6 August, but the rest of 147 Wing remained to fly night patrols to counter enemy raiders, and *Anti-Diver* patrols by night and day. The crews of 410 received the more powerful Mosquito NFXXX in August, achieving their first success with it during the night of August 19/20, when they shot down two Ju 88s. The unit moved to Hunsdon on 9 September. NFXXXs were also issued to 488 Squadron, before it followed 410 on 9 October. No 604 Squadron returned briefly in November and was joined by 264 on shipping reconnaissance over the Western Approaches. They both left in December, and the following month Colerne entered a new era when the Meteors of 616 Squadron arrived, and it became the RAF's first permanent jet fighter base. Having already added thirteen V-1 flying bombs to its score-card, the unit prepared for operational deployment to the continent, its first detachment departing for Melsbroek/B58 on 4 February. To assist with the establishment of Meteor squadrons, 1335 (Meteor) Conversion Unit was set up at Colerne on 8 March, flying Oxfords and early Meteor variants. Its first job was to train 504 Squadron, which was joined by 74 Squadron in May to form the first jet fighter wing in the RAF. Although 1335 (M)CU went to Molesworth in August, the Wing stayed until September 1946 as part of ADGB.

Colerne then transferred from Fighter Command to 41 Group Maintenance Command, with 39 and 218 MUs still in residence, its airfield then being used for test flying and ferrying, as well as by the gliders of 62 GS, which had transferred from Charmy Down. No 218 MU was disbanded in 1948, but replaced in May by 49 MU, which arrived from Lasham and was retained when the original Colerne MU, No 39, was closed in October 1953. Two flights of 662 Squadron, a RAuxAF unit flying Auster AOPs, were formed in February 1949, but it was not until 12 June 1952 that the station regained some of its former glory when a Fighter Command unit returned to Colerne.

This was the Airborne Interception School, which trained night-fighter radar operators in locating and tracking hostile aircraft. Three days after arrival from Leeming, it was re-designated 238 OCU, which formed on 15 June. It flew students in Brigands, using Balliols as targets, replacing these with Valettas and Meteor NF12s in 1956. The unit moved to North Luffenham on 1 January 1957, by which time Colerne had been transferred to Transport Command, and on the day that 238 OCU left, 24 Squadron arrived from Abingdon. On 1 May another Hastings unit, 511 Squadron, transferred from Lyneham. From Colerne the aircraft of both units flew throughout the world on Transport Command scheduled routes and performed various special tasks. No 511 Squadron was renumbered 36 Squadron on 1 September 1958, and the following spring a third Hastings unit appeared with the reforming of 114 Squadron on 13 April 1959.

No 49 MU continued to use the hangars at the northern end of the airfield until 1962, when it too was closed, having spent its last years on Shackleton modifications. No 114 Squadron was disbanded on 30 September 1961, but the other squadrons flew on. In the spring of 1967 Colerne started gearing up to be the RAF's centre for the Hercules; an engineering base was opened up in April, and conversion courses started for the new type. No 36 Squadron became the first unit to operate the Hercules, moving to Lyneham in August 1967. It was followed by 48 Squadron, which took its Hercules to Changi in October 1967. No 24 Squadron received its aircraft in January 1968 and soon it too moved to Lyneham. Colerne continued as the Hercules engineering base until there was sufficient room at Lyneham for both squadrons and technical organisations.

Colerne was among the airfields listed as being no longer required in the 1975 Defence White Paper, and closure followed on 31 March 1976. The thriving museum, formed there in 1964, was closed, and its aircraft sent to other museums or scrapped. The station was then taken over by the Army, which still occupies it as Azimghur Barracks, currently the home of 21 Signal Regiment, Royal Signals. Much of the aerodrome and its buildings are complete, the MoD using one or two of the hangars for storage. The airfield itself is still operational and is used regularly by Bristol UAS/3 AEF. Flying Grob Tutor aircraft, the unit trains university students to solo standard and provides flying experience for Air Cadets.

Main features:
Runways: 196° 3,600ft x 150ft, 256° 5,850ft x 150ft, 302° 3,450ft x 150ft, concrete and tarmac. *Hangars:* one Type J, three Type K, five Type L, one O-Blister, six Robins. *Hardstandings:* sixteen TE, one Fortress. *Accommodation:* RAF Officers 143, SNCOs 266, ORs 2,646; WAAF Officers 24, SNCOs 19, ORs 242.

CULDROSE, Cornwall

SW675258, 2 miles SE of Helston on A3083

The largest naval air station in Europe, RNAS Culdrose's principal role today is to support the Anti-Submarine and Airborne Early Warning helicopter squadrons of the Fleet Air Arm. However, more familiar to the thousands of holidaymakers who visit Cornwall every year are the light grey and red Sea King helicopters they see along the coast. These are also based at Culdrose, providing 24-hour all-year-round Search and Rescue coverage for the whole of the South West. Often operating in extreme weather and to the limits of endurance, thousands of people owe their lives to the brave crews of these helicopters.

Many military airfields have been rebuilt since having been originally laid out during the Second World War, but Culdrose is the only one opened in the UK after the war on a site that had not previously been used for flying. The airfield's gestation period had been long, the initial survey for a new flying training station having been started in 1942 and the 750-acre site being purchased by the Admiralty in 1944. Three farms were absorbed by the new development, which consisted of

Sea Hornet NF21 VW949/485 of 809 Squadron, formed at Culdrose in January 1949.

Culdrose-based Whirlwind HAS7 XL898/X of 847 Squadron in June 1963.

a barracks area and technical site as well as the airfield itself. Three runways were laid and eventually twenty-seven hangars erected, as well as a three-storey control tower. Some 1,500 personnel and nine squadrons were to be accommodated.

Construction of the station, provisionally called RNAS Helston (HMS *Chough*), proceeded through 1945 and 1946, but when opened on 17 April 1947 its title had changed to RNAS Culdrose (HMS *Seahawk*). The station's initial role was to house 780 Squadron, the Naval Instrument Flying School; the unit moved in from Donibristle on 27 May 1947 with Oxfords and Harvards. It was joined by 807 Squadron on 19 August, then in the process of exchanging its Seafire FXVIIs for Sea Furies, and by 813 Squadron, with Firebrands, in December. Later that month 790 Squadron arrived, with Mosquitoes, Sea Mosquitoes and Seafires, to form the Fighter Direction Training Unit. A Station Flight was formed in December 1947 using Harvards, later adding Sea Otters to provide an SAR capability. During January 1948 No 792 Squadron reformed at Culdrose as a Night Fighter Training Unit, with Fireflies, Oxfords and Ansons. On 8 January 810 Squadron arrived with its Sea Hornets to form the 1st Carrier Air Group with 813 Squadron; the Group left Culdrose for HMS *Implacable* in early March 1948.

Later that month the School of Naval Air Warfare moved in from St Merryn. This was followed by 762 Squadron from Ford, which flew Ansons, Oxfords and Mosquitoes on twin-engine conversion training. Together with 792 Squadron, 762 started work to aid the introduction into service of the first specialised night-fighter to enter service with the FAA, the Sea Hornet NF21. No 809 Squadron formed on 20 January 1949 with four (later eight) Sea Hornets, and a prolonged work-up followed, for the unit not only had to evolve operational night-fighter tactics, but also to train in the strike/fighter role. It embarked aboard HMS *Vengeance* in May 1951.

Meanwhile, in February 1950 Culdrose had become No 1 Naval Air Fighter School, which comprised 736 Squadron that had moved from St Merryn, and a reformed 738 Squadron. The school had sixty Sea Furies and twelve Seafires on strength, later supplemented with Sea Hornets. The day of the piston-engined naval fighter was drawing to a close, however, for the Naval Jet Evaluation & Training Unit (702 Squadron) had been at Culdrose since April 1949. Flying Attackers and Meteors, it merged with 736 Squadron in August 1952 as the phase-out of the Sea Fury was under way. Trials at

Wessex HAS3 XM876/66 of 706 Squadron, seen at Culdrose in October 1970.

Culdrose were undertaken by 778 Squadron using four Douglas Skyraiders that had been fitted with AN/APS-20 AEW radar. With the successful completion of the trials, on 6 July 1952 No 778 Squadron was disbanded and reformed as 849 Squadron. This unit consisted of an HQ Flight based at Culdrose, and four self-contained operational flights embarked on carriers as required.

During the autumn of 1953 a reshuffle took place, with No 1 Naval Air Fighter School moving to Lossiemouth and Firefly-equipped units from St Merryn (796 Squadron) and Lossiemouth (766 Squadron) arriving to form the Naval Observer & Air Signals School. They were joined by 750 Squadron with Sea Princes in March 1954, and HMS *Seahawk* then got down to a new task of producing naval observers for anti-submarine and all-weather fighter squadrons. A married quarters estate had been built on the outskirts of Helston, and this was extended from 1953, when more accommodation was built on the station. No 766 Squadron was disbanded during November 1954, but its place was taken by 815 Squadron, which arrived from Eglington with Avengers. It worked up in the anti-submarine role before leaving the following summer. In February 1955 No 765 Squadron reformed at Culdrose as a Piston Engine Pilot Pool squadron. Flying Fireflies, Oxfords and Sea Balliols, the unit disbanded in March 1957, when its tasks were taken over by 750 and 796 Squadrons.

The first Gannet squadron to form at Culdrose, No 825, did so on 4 July 1955, closely followed by 816 and 817 Squadrons of the Royal Australian Navy, also with the type. In November the Skyraiders of 849 Squadron embarked aboard both HMS *Albion* and HMS *Eagle* to participate in Operation *Musketeer*, the Anglo/French landings in the Suez Canal Zone. More Gannet squadrons were formed during 1956 – No 814 in January and 825 in May. The Aircraft Torpedo Development Unit had often deployed to Culdrose from its base at Gosport to use the torpedo ranges off Cornwall and the Isles of Scilly, and on 1 June 1956 it transferred from Gosport. Although part of 81 Group, RAF, it was responsible for the development of air-delivered torpedoes and mines for both the RN and RAF. It moved into a new site on the Lizard road with a variety of aircraft, including examples of the Lincoln, Seamew, Wyvern, Canberra, Whirlwind and Brigand. Although control of the unit passed to the Ministry of Supply at the end of October 1958, it remained at Culdrose, using ranges off Scilly and east of the Lizard, utilising the Falmouth-based RAF Marine Craft Unit for weapons recoveries.

Another specialised unit, 751 Squadron, arrived in September 1957. Flying Avengers and Sea Venoms, it was engaged in various electronic trials, including countermeasures. In March 1958 it was re-designated the Electronic Warfare Unit, and in May became 831 Squadron. Gannets and Sea Vampires were added to its strength in 1959. It spent a lot of time on detachment, but with the move of 750 Squadron to Hal Far in October 1959 it maintained the fixed-wing presence at Culdrose with 849 Squadron, until leaving for Watton in 1963.

Helicopters had first appeared at Culdrose during the summer of 1953, when Dragonflies had replaced Sea Otters in the *Seahawk* SAR Flight. The first recorded rescue of a civilian by a Service helicopter took place that year when a teenager who had been injured in a fall was taken by Dragonfly to Truro's Treliske Hospital. In January 1953 705 Squadron had arrived from Lee-on-Solent with Dragonflies, Whirlwinds and Hiller HT.1s, and a few months later it was announced that Culdrose had been selected as the main helicopter training base for the FAA. Predannack was taken on as a satellite during this time, to extend Culdrose's facilities. Other training units arrived during 1959, including the School of Aircraft Handling, which formed at the station in January, tasked with training ratings in the intricate business of moving aircraft about the flight deck of an aircraft carrier. The school used time-expired airframes on a dummy deck that had been marked out on the airfield with simulated angled deck, catapults and lifts to provide realistic training. It also undertook fire and rescue training using airframes battered from dummy deck training.

No 700H Squadron formed at Culdrose on 1 June 1959 as the Intensive Flying Trials Unit to introduce the Whirlwind HAS7 into service. Having solved engine problems, and its job done, the squadron was disbanded at the end of August. Later that month 700G Squadron was formed as the IFTU for the Gannet AEW3, the replacement for the Skyraider. By February 1960 the unit's work had been completed, and 700G became 849 Squadron. In April 700H Squadron was reformed as the IFTU for the Wessex HAS1, and this provided the Royal Navy with its first purpose-built anti-submarine helicopter.

Meanwhile, Whirlwind HAS7 squadrons were being formed, 814 Squadron in May and 825 Squadron in August 1960. It was not long before the Wessex HAS1 entered service, with 815

Squadron in July 1961 and 814 Squadron in November. In January 1962 700H became 706 Squadron, remaining at Culdrose as a training unit. A new role was found for the Wessex in April 1962 when 845 Squadron reformed at Culdrose for Commando operations. A further Commando Squadron, 846, was formed in June, but with Whirlwinds. This was followed eleven months later by 847 Squadron, also using Whirlwinds, for Commando helicopter pilot training.

New helicopter types were being introduced at a rapid rate during this time, resulting in the formation of 700W Squadron as IFTU for the Wasp in June 1963, and 700V for the twin-engine Wessex HU5 for Commando use in December 1963. Both types were introduced into the Culdrose training set-up during 1963, the Wasp with 706 Squadron and the Wessex HU5 with 707 Squadron. 700V was reformed as 848 Squadron in May 1964, introducing the Wessex HU5 into service. With some sixty-five helicopters then on strength, increasing to more than 110 when the front-line squadrons were disembarked, Culdrose could justly claim to be the largest helicopter base in Europe. On 5 December 1964 849 Squadron left Culdrose for Brawdy, marking its departure with a formation flypast of eight Gannet AEW3s and six T.5s. A further anti-submarine squadron, 826, recommissioned at Culdrose in March 1966 with the Wessex HAS1. In June of the following year the Wessex HAS3, following a period of work-up with a reformed 700H Squadron, entered service with 706 Squadron, and in August with 814.

On 18 March 1967 one of the world's largest tankers, *Torrey Canyon*, hit the Seven Stones Reef off Land's End, and its cargo of almost 120,000 tons of crude oil began to leak from its damaged hull. Two Wessex helicopters from Culdrose were the first on the scene to give a comprehensive appraisal of the situation. The tanker was later bombed in an effort to destroy the oil, but massive pollution of the Cornish coastline occurred despite this. The helicopters of both 707 and 848 Squadrons were kept busy over the ensuing weeks, ferrying detergent and equipment to the beach-cleansing parties.

In October 1968 a new round of construction work started to make Culdrose more suitable for helicopter operations. New landing areas were laid, hangars rebuilt, new training facilities added and a flyover constructed to join the airfield with the domestic and administration side of the station. This work was partly in preparation for the arrival of a new helicopter type, the Sea King, which was received by a newly formed 700S Squadron on 1 July 1969. The new aircraft had twice the range of

Sea Venom FAW21 WW217/736, ex-FRU, on the SAH flight-deck at Culdrose in October 1970.

Sea Princes of 750 Squadron lined up beside Culdrose's tower ready for a day's flying in April 1975. WM739/574 is nearest the camera.

the Wessex and could carry much more powerful weapons. No 706 Squadron was the first to receive the new type, in January 1970, followed by 824 in February and 826 Squadron in June. In 1971 a further development programme started, with the rebuilding of domestic accommodation, messes and the addition of a social centre, cinema and theatre. In a second phase a new Helicopter Ground School, Engineering School and Observer School were added, the latter to accommodate 750 Squadron, which returned with its Sea Princes in 1972. May 1972 saw the departure of 707 and 846 Commando Squadrons to Yeovilton, followed by 845 and 848 Squadrons in the autumn.

Due to its success with the introduction of the Sea King into service, Culdrose was able to provide training to other air arms that had bought the type from Westland. Between 1972 and 1976 Sea King crews from the Indian, West German, Pakistani, Royal Australian and Egyptian navies were trained at Culdrose, together with those of the Norwegian and Belgian air forces. Because of its range, the Sea Kings were often used for some of the longer-distance rescue operations, trainee aircrews often taking part in these. After the sinking of the 480-ton *Merck Enterprise* in appalling weather on 16 January 1974, five Sea Kings from 706, 824 and the German Squadron went to the rescue. Eleven survivors and several bodies were recovered by the helicopters, aided by the Russian trawler *Leningrad* – truly international cooperation at its best!

No 705 Squadron gradually replaced its Hillers and Whirlwinds with Gazelles from March 1974, and in September 771 Squadron arrived from Portland with Wessex HAS1s to provide SAR training (the unit later took over inshore SAR from *Seahawk* Station Flight's Whirlwinds). A further Sea King unit, 814 Squadron, arrived at Culdrose on 9 April, having transferred from Prestwick. As with many other front-line squadrons, it was based at Culdrose while not deployed aboard the carriers or RFAs. When the RAF ordered the Sea King, Culdrose hosted its Sea King Training Unit, formed on 17 February 1978 with six Sea King HAR3s. When the unit disbanded on 4 October 1979 training continued with the RAF Sea King Training Flight formed within 706 Squadron, using two RAF Sea Kings for the purpose.

From October 1978 the Sea Princes of 750 Squadron were progressively replaced by Jetstreams, which continued in the role of training Observers, the final Sea Prince leaving on 1 May 1979. No 771 Squadron re-equipped with the Wessex HU5 in the SAR role later that year, and in August flew non-stop for three days during the Fastnet Races. The competing yachts had been caught in sudden gales, and the helicopters eventually rescued a total of seventy-five yacht crewmembers, while flying more than 200 hours. The much improved Sea King HAS5 entered service with 706 and 826 Squadrons in January and March 1981 respectively. A year later Culdrose became heavily involved in events thousands of miles away, when Argentine forces invaded the Falklands. The Falklands Task Force Air Group included more than fifty helicopters, mostly from Culdrose, and sailing with it were contingents from 814, 820, 824 and a reformed 825 Squadron.

Sea King AEW2 XV650/88, newly delivered to 849 Squadron in November 1984.

The Culdrose Station Flight was disbanded in January 1983, its two Sea Devons and two Chipmunks being transferred to 771 Squadron. The Devons were eventually retired in 1989, the Chipmunks soldiering on until 1993. In February 1983 No 810 Squadron reformed at Culdrose with ten Sea Kings to take over advanced and operational Sea King training from 706 Squadron, as well as observer and aircrewman training from 737 Squadron at Portland, and in November the following year 849 Squadron also reformed, to operate an AEW version of the Sea King. Work on a new control tower started in 1986, to replace the original one, forty years old. A year later 771 Squadron exchanged its Wessex for Sea King HAR5s, which gave far greater range and endurances for SAR operations. The new control tower opened in 1989 and another major SAR mission in October involved the rescue of forty crewmen from the Pakistani container ship *Murree*, sinking off Start Point.

The Gulf War of 1991 saw the deployment of a flight of 826 Squadron for the support of, and long-range stores delivery to, warships in the region. It was later involved in the detection and destruction of mines. However, in July 1993 the Squadron was disbanded as part of the 'Options for Change' cuts, together with the ATDU the following month (which had been operating at Culdrose for some years as Test & Evaluation Establishment Helston). Despite this, there were always more operations that the station's units were needed for, and as 826 Squadron was running down others were preparing to deploy to Bosnia. Nos 814, 820 and 849 Squadrons took part in IFOR and SFOR operations in the former Yugoslavia from 1993.

After a thirty-two-year gap, jets returned to Culdrose in 1996 when the Fleet Requirements & Air Direction Unit (FRADU) moved from Yeovilton with thirteen Hawk T1s in support of Flag Officer Sea Training, who had moved from Portsmouth to Devonport. Operated under contract by Serco Defence & Aerospace, the unit's Hawks, leased from the RAF, are flown by civilian pilots with military fast-jet experience. FRADU's role is threat simulation to add realism to training exercises for naval aircrew and ships' crews. Working with Falcon 20s flown by FRA from Hurn, the Hawks can simulate missiles being launched from an aircraft by breaking formation with the Falcon and heading at high speed for a 'target' warship, while its Falcon simulates a missile's target-seeking radar and 'lights up' the ship. The Falcons also carry jammers and chaff to disrupt the ship's radar. The Hawks also provide radar targets for fighter pilot training and give fighter evasion training to helicopter pilots. To maintain surprise during exercises the Hawk pilots often observe radio silence, even before leaving Culdrose, communication with the tower for taxi and take-off approval being by visual light signals.

Merlin HM1 ZH847/13 of 824 Squadron, Culdrose, June 2008.

The RAF SKTF within 706 Squadron was disbanded on 1 April 1996, and a Sea King OCU was formed the same day by the RAF at St Mawgan, becoming 203 (Reserve) Squadron on 1 November. With the formation of the Defence Helicopter Flying School in April 1997, all helicopter flying training was moved to RAF Shawbury. This included 705 Squadron, which retired its Gazelle HT1s and moved from Culdrose to Shawbury to become the naval element of the new school. The School of Aircraft Handling became the School of Flight Deck Operations in 1998, having absorbed the Flight Deck Training Unit from Portland, which trained groundcrews in the operation of helicopters from the flight decks of small ships. Another transferee from Portland was the Fleet Target Group, which arrived in July with its Northrop MQM-74C Chukar aerial targets for gunnery and missile-operator training. The Chukars were replaced by Mirach 100/5s during 2001, and on 29 November that year the unit was re-designated 792 Squadron.

A new shape appeared in the skies over Culdrose in November 1998 when the first Merlins arrived to enter service with 700(M) Squadron, formed on 1 December as the Merlin IFTU. No 824 Squadron recommissioned in 2000 as the Merlin Training Squadron utilising the purpose-built Merlin Training Facility to undertake all aspects of aircrew and maintenance training on the type. As more Merlins arrived to replace Sea Kings in the front-line squadrons in June 2001, 814 Squadron re-equipped with four of the new type, followed by 820 Squadron, also with four Merlins, in December 2003. With the reduction in Sea King activity, 810 Squadron disbanded in July 2001, its training tasks being taken on by 771 Squadron, which continues to maintain Culdrose's SAR capabilities. Merlin Ships Flights for Type 23 frigates were formed within 824 Squadron, HMS *Lancaster* being the first, deploying to the South Atlantic in 2002. HMS *Monmouth* followed later that year, HMS *Westminster* in 2004 and HMS *Northumberland* in 2005. All flights transferred to 829 Squadron when it was recommissioned on 21 October 2004, resuming its former role.

Culdrose squadrons were deployed to the Gulf in 2003 for Operation *Telic*, with 814 and 849 Squadrons embarked aboard HMS *Invincible* and 820 aboard HMS *Illustrious*. Their operations were very successful, marred only by the loss of two Sea Kings of 849 Squadron that collided in mid-air on 22 March while operating from HMS *Ark Royal*, with the loss of seven crew.

The station was selected to become the Merlin Main Servicing Base in 2004, to undertake the major servicing of all RN and RAF Merlins, and this became the Merlin Depth Maintenance Facility in

June 2005 following the introduction of pulse-line working. More jets arrived at Culdrose in March 2006, when six Sea Harrier FA2s and two T8s transferred from Yeovilton. Their delivery flights were their last, however, as they were to be used by the SFDO for deck training. As with many of the ground training aircraft, their engines were to be kept serviceable so that they could be taxied under their own power. With the accent being on expeditionary forces, for the ease of their deployment on operations as autonomous units, A and B Flights of 849 Squadron were re-designated in mid-December 2006 as 854 and 857 Squadrons, leaving 849 Squadron responsible for training and evaluation.

Culdrose continues to play an important role for the Fleet Air Arm. It is a busy airfield, with 26,000 rotary and 9,000 fixed-wing movements per year. Having some 1,800 military personnel, 300 civil servants and 500 contractors working on the station, it is the major employer in Cornwall, contributing more than £1 million per week to the local economy. RNAS Culdrose is well worth as visit. It has an annual air-day, and a public viewing enclosure, shop and café; coach tours are also run around the air station during summer months for visitors.

Main features:
Runways: ESE-WNW 6,000ft x 150ft, N-S 3,300ft x 150ft, ENE-WSW 3,300ft x 150ft, concrete and tarmac. *Hangars:* six Mainhills, twenty-one Pentad Portables. *Accommodation:* RN Officers 300, ORs 1,200.

CULMHEAD (CHURCH STANTON), Somerset

ST208154, 5 miles SE of Wellington

Seafires joining the Culmhead circuit on 20 April 1944 caused little interest, but the sudden influx of naval uniforms at the station was noticed. They caused quite a stir in the nearby villages of Church Stanton and Churchingford, for this compact airfield was high up in Somerset's Blackdown Hills, far away from the sea. No 24 Naval Fighter Wing, led by Lieutenant Commander N. G. 'Buster' Hallett, had been formed at Henstridge for service in HMS *Indefatigable*. The two squadrons that made up the Wing, Nos 887 and 894, brought their Seafire Mk IIIs to Culmhead to work up with 10 Group, RAF, to support Typhoons on anti-shipping strikes. During the ensuing three weeks they flew 400 sorties along the French coast, and although they saw no enemy aircraft they saw lots of action. When no Typhoon operations were scheduled the Seafires went on *Rodeos*, visiting St Nazaire on 7 May, but fuel was always a problem and they were forced to hold off during an attack on a destroyer four days later. The last full-wing sorties were flown on 12 May, the Typhoons bombing a merchant ship off St Malo, while the Seafires shot up shipping before strafing the radio station at Cherbourg. Having received their baptism of fire, the Seafires embarked a week later for operations off Norway.

Originally intended as an ELG as a satellite of Exeter, RAF Church Stanton was opened as a typical fighter station on 1 August 1941, under the control of 10 Group, Fighter Command. It had three runways, a dozen twin-bay fighter pens off its dispersals, ten Blister hangars and later a larger Teeside hangar. Its single-storey watch office was later superseded by a two-storey version.

The first aircraft to land at the new airfield did so when it was unfinished, arriving early one morning. Its pilot approached Mr Long, a roller driver, who was just getting up steam, but neither could understand one another, and when the pilot sprinted back to his aircraft and took off, Long realised that it was probably a German bomber that had landed in error. The first official arrivals, Hurricane IIBs of 302 and 316 Squadrons, came on 2 August. Both units, formed with Polish personnel, were declared operational on 1 September. After four days, however, 302 Squadron was moved to Warmwell. Intended for the defence of Bristol and Exeter, 316 Squadron initially flew convoy patrols, as Luftwaffe activity over the UK was low. From early November the unit converted to the Spitfire VB, and on the morning of 9 November took part in its first sweep over northern France. The aircraft returned later with two badly shot up, minus their CO, Sqn Ldr Wilczewki, who had been shot down and taken prisoner. The unit flew Channel sweeps and the occasional bomber escort until 12 December, when it moved to Northolt, being replaced by another Polish Spitfire squadron, 306. The new unit started flying air defence patrols, and on 28 December operated from Bolt Head. On the 30th, flying their first sweep over France, the Polish pilots shot down four enemy fighters for the loss of one of their own.

On 15 February 1942 O2 Detachment of RAE Farnborough arrived at Church Stanton from Exeter to undertaken special trials. These included the testing of balloon-cutting devices fitted to

The Spitfire XIIs of 610 Squadron spent April and May 1944 on operations from Culmhead.

trials aircraft that were deliberately flown into the cables of tethered balloons to test their effectiveness. When the detachment OC flew Wellington P9210 into a cable on 24 March the aircraft started breaking up, forcing the pilot to bail out.

The Poles left Church Stanton in May 1942, and were replaced by 154 Squadron, also with Spitfires, from Duxford, which spent its brief time at the station on training and convoy escort duties before moving on 7 June. It was replaced the following day by the Czechs of 313 Squadron, flying in Spitfire VBs from Fairlop. They too went onto convoy escort duties, and were joined in this rather mundane activity by another Czech Spitfire VB unit, 312 Squadron, arriving on 9 October. Both flew their first operation together, a *Rhubarb* over France, on 14 October, during which they destroyed several ground targets. The Czech Wing, as they were known, then went onto the offensive, mounting sweeps along the French coast and over Brittany and Normandy, together with the occasional bomber escort mission. On one of these, on 6 December, the Wing escorted a diversionary raid on Abbeville, while a large 2 Group raid was made on the Philips valve factory at Eindhoven. More escort operations were flown from January 1943, together with *Ramrods* and *Circuses*. These were interspersed with Air Defence Patrols along the South Devon and Dorset coast, to counter hit-and-run raids being made by FW 190s.

The Czechs left in June 1943 and were replaced by 66 and 504 Squadrons, Spitfire VB units that continued the pattern of activity of their predecessors, with convoy patrols, sweeps, *Circuses* and *Ramrods*. However, they were also called in to assist with the occasional ASR search, as on 13 July when they searched for a Lancaster that had come down in the Channel. Unfortunately the aircraft's crew, captained by Wg Cdr John Nettleton VC, were never found. Both squadrons moved out in mid-August and were replaced by 131 and 165 Squadrons, from Redhill and Kenley respectively. Both had just re-equipped with the latest Spitfire, the Mark IX, designed to counter the FW 190. Although they flew sweeps and *Ramrods*, it was not until 26 November that they came up against their intended foe. Following a massive dogfight two FW 190s were claimed as shot down, three more as probables, and six damaged. One Spitfire was lost.

On 22 December 1943, to avoid confusion with others prefixed with 'Church', the station was re-named RAF Culmhead. Its wing celebrated the New Year while covering the withdrawal of a large force of USAAF B-17 and B-24 bombers that had attacked targets in the Bordeaux area on 31 December. Pilots of 165 Squadron intercepted five rocket-armed enemy fighters that were about to attack a box of B-17s over the Breton town of Paimpol, shooting down four of the enemy (three FW 190s and a Bf 109). The Wing flew more escort missions and *Ramrods* into 1944 using 45-gallon long-range tanks for the first time, before moving to Colerne on 10 February. No 165 returned to Culmhead on 10 March for a short period to provide fighter cover for a US disembarkation exercise taking place in South Devon.

The next squadron to fly from Culmhead was 610, which transferred with its Griffon-powered Spitfire XIVs from Exeter on 7 April. This unit was joined three days later by two target-facilities squadrons, 286 and 587, which flew in from Weston Zoyland with a variety of aircraft, including Oxfords, Defiants, Hurricanes, Masters and Martinets. On 20 May No 286 moved again, to Colerne, but 587 stayed on.

No 610 Squadron attempted to fly its first operation from Culmhead on 17 April, but was recalled shortly after take-off because of bad weather. Three days later the unit met with success, taking part in a 10 Group *Rodeo*. On its return to base, it found that the Seafires of 24 Naval Fighter Wing had arrived for shipping strikes and *Rodeos*, as described above.

With the departure of 610 Squadron to Harrowbeer towards the end of May, 616 Squadron (Spitfire VIIs), then 126 and 131, both with the Spitfire IXs, arrived at Culmhead. All three spent the next few weeks on intensive operations leading up to and following D-Day, weather permitting. They mounted shipping recces, escorted bombers, and flew *Rhubarbs*, attacking locomotives, marshalling yards, convoys, bridges, batteries and airfields. On the day itself, carrying D-Day stripes, the Culmhead Wing attacked goods trains and vehicle convoys to prevent German reinforcements moving forward. This pattern of operations continued after D-Day, together with the odd airfield attack, such as on 12 June when Le Mans and Laval were attacked. Several aircraft on the ground were destroyed, and more in air combat.

On 13 July Meteors arrived at Culmhead. It had been decided that 616 should be the RAF's first jet fighter squadron and that Culmhead, isolated in the Somerset Hills, was an ideal location for their training to proceed in secret. However, within just over a week 616 Squadron had gone, on transfer to Manston. With 126 Squadron having departed for Harrowbeer early in July, 131 was left as sole occupant of Culmhead. It continued *Rhubarbs*, *Rodeos* and *Ramrods* into August, together with the occasional bomber escort missions, formations of 250 Lancasters being not uncommon. ASR aircraft, such as Warwicks, used Culmhead as a forward base in June, July and August, because of heavy traffic over the Channel during this period.

On 10 August 1944 No 790 Squadron FAA arrived, having brought its Fireflies and Oxfords over from Charlton Horethorne for a six-week detachment. Meanwhile, the resident Spitfires continued operations, flying from their quiet Somerset base into intense combat over France. On 11 August 131 Squadron flew its longest operation, escorting Lancasters to attack U-boat pens at La Pallice, the 690-mile round trip taking almost 4 hours. The unit continued flying such operations from Culmhead until the end of August, when, on the 28th, it started to move out, to Friston.

Spitfire VII NX-B of 131 Squadron flying from Culmhead in August 1944.

Culmhead's control tower in April 2005.

No 790 Squadron returned to Charlton Horethorne on 6 September and, following 587 Squadron's departure for Weston Zoyland on 1 October, Culmhead started to run down. It was transferred to 23 Group Transport Command in December 1944, becoming a satellite of Stoke Orchard, and was then used by a detachment of 3 GTS, with Hotspur gliders and Master II tugs. Although the school moved to Exeter in January 1945, it continued to use Culmhead until July, when it moved again, to Wellesbourne Mountford. Reverting to C&M, the airfield was used for storage by Maintenance Command for a few months, but closed in August 1946.

However, Culmhead did not leave Government service. It was taken over by the Composite Signals Organisation of GCHQ, which built a radio listening station in the centre of the airfield. This closed in 2000, and its buildings are now utilised as the Culmhead Business Centre. The airfield is now privately owned, but still retains substantial reminders of its wartime past, including parts of the runways and taxiways. Some of the fighter pens remain, and several of the airfield buildings, including a Blister hangar and the two control towers, still stand.

Main features:
Runways: 216° 4,230ft x 150ft, 276° 3,390ft x 150ft, 330° 3,450ft x 150ft, concrete and asphalt. *Hangars:* one T2, four O-Blister, six EO-Blister. *Hardstandings:* nine TE, twenty-seven SE. *Accommodation:* RAF Officers 13, SNCOs 100, ORs 1,023; WAAF Officers 10, ORs 291.

DAVIDSTOW MOOR, Cornwall

SX150850, 2 miles NE of Camelford off A39

The name itself suggests isolation and bleakness, and at 970 feet (296 metres) above sea level Davidstow Moor was the highest operational airfield in the UK. At such a height on Bodmin Moor, it was exposed to Atlantic gales and suffered from rapid changes in weather and persistent low cloud. It was a difficult place from which to operate, and was rarely used for anything other than a relief base.

Davidstow was laid out as a standard Class A Bomber airfield, one of the few built in the South West during the Second World War. Intended as a Coastal Command station to cover the East Atlantic and Western Approaches, it was opened by 19 Group on 1 October 1942. This was somewhat premature, however, as the accommodation was not ready, and there was no water supply. The airfield's three runways were nonetheless complete, three T2 hangars were up and from the taxiways

*Beaufighter TFXs of
404 Squadron await
another operation at
Davidstow Moor in
June 1944.*

sprouted fifty dispersals. The opening had been brought forward due to the onset of Operation *Torch*, as every airfield in the South West was in demand as a springboard for the Allied landings in North Africa. On 12 October a ninety-eight-vehicle convoy of US Army vehicles arrived, and the Americans set up a supply base. Nothing then happened until 8 November, when eighteen B-24 Liberators of the 44th and 93rd Bombardment Groups arrived, part of the US 8th Air Force, then a relatively small force. The aircraft were refuelled and bombed up before leaving again the following day to join B-17s in an attack on the U-boat pens at St Nazaire. Having crossed the Channel at low level, the US aircraft climbed to 18,000 feet before running in on the target. The defensive flak was intensive, but all aircraft returned safely to Davidstow. Similar missions were flown by B-17s of the 8th AF later in the month, and more US aircraft appeared in December, when Bell Aircobras of 360th Fighter Group staged through on their way to join the US 12th AF in North Africa.

The first British aircraft to use Davidstow Moor were Henleys of 1603 (AAC) Flight due to waterlogging at Cleave during December 1942, but with the departure of the Americans a number of Hudsons arrived. These aircraft belonged to 53 Squadron and had been operating in the Caribbean until their return to the UK. The aircraft started arriving on 31 December, and once reassembled the Squadron departed for Docking on 17 February 1943. More Hudsons arrived that month from Bircham Newton; these were from 279 Squadron, an ASR unit, its aircraft being fitted with airborne lifeboats, and stayed on detachment for a few weeks, covering the Western Approaches.

Detachments from other units followed, mainly anti-submarine squadrons, including 304 (Polish) Squadron from Docking. On 18 April 1943 No 612 Squadron arrived from Wick with Whitleys and Wellingtons and flew patrols over the Bay of Biscay before moving to Chivenor on 23 May. A week before this, on 16 May, the Liberators of the 44th and 93rd BGs returned. Early on the 17th the B-24s took off to attack Bordeaux. They flew a 700-mile arc out into the Atlantic to mislead the German radar, before returning at 22,000 feet to bomb their target. The ruse worked, with only light opposition being met. The dock, pier and an aero-engine works were hit.

On 31 May No 547 Squadron arrived from Chivenor to resume the work that 612 Squadron had started from Davidstow, anti-submarine patrols over the Bay of Biscay. Its Wellingtons were joined by those of 304 (Polish) Squadron, which flew in from Docking on 7 June. The squadrons found and attacked a number of U-boats, damaging several and forcing others to return to base for repairs. However, the submarines started crossing the Bay in packs, and stayed on the surface to fight it out with aircraft, making them a dangerous foe. In July 304 Squadron lost two aircraft in combat, and two more in August, as did 547 Squadron. Several of them were victims of Ju 88 fighters, an added hazard for Coastal crews.

In August the squadrons started dropping flares to catch surfaced U-boats at night, but it was obvious that the Leigh Light was far more effective. As soon as Wellington XIVs became available, 304 Squadron started training on them, handing over its Mark XIIIs to 547 Squadron, which left for Thorney Island towards the end of October. The poor weather at Davidstow prompted the Air Ministry to install GCA radar; trials started in September, but the very reason for it being installed

Warwick I HF944 of 282 Squadron on patrol from Davidstow Moor in June 1944.

prevented its calibration, and it was eventually transferred to St Eval. As 547 Squadron left Davidstow, 192 flew in a detachment of four Wellington Xs and a Halifax III from its base at Feltwell. The unit was engaged in electronic intelligence duties, and used Davidstow to fly out over the Bay of Biscay in order to monitor U-boat radio traffic. The unit stayed until the following May, flying fifty sorties per month, but losing three aircraft during its stay.

Meanwhile 304 Squadron, having worked up on its new Leigh Light Wellingtons, was ready for operations, and on 13 December moved to Predannack. Shortly after its departure a detachment of 280 Squadron arrived, with ASR Warwick Mk Is. This unit was soon able to notch up a success, for on 8 January 1944 280/E, escorted by six Beaufighters, dropped a lifeboat to a Mosquito crew that had ditched 95 miles south-west of Brest, and the two survivors were soon heading for home. Later that day the Hudsons of 267 Squadron arrived from Reykjavik; this coastal patrol unit had returned to the UK to convert to the ASR role, and over the following weeks it also received Spitfires and Walruses. Having re-equipped and worked up, the unit left in March for Lagens in the Azores; the Hudsons flew out via Gibraltar, while the remaining aircraft were ferried out by the aircraft carrier HMS *Premier*. Another ASR unit, 282 Squadron, appeared on 1 February, when it reformed at Davidstow with Warwicks. It flew regular patrols from the station as well as taking on the role of training new Warwick crews. By D-Day there would be twenty-two Warwicks at Davidstow.

Meanwhile, on 11 March nine Wellingtons of 172, 304 and 612 Squadrons used Davidstow as a forward base to fly a concentrated anti-submarine patrol. All landed back at their home base of Chivenor, except 612/R, which was lost, and 612/C, which landed short of fuel at Portreath, having attacked a U-boat well out into the Bay. This operation seemed to remind Coastal Command of the airfield's original purpose for, on 7 April, No 524 Squadron was reformed at Davidstow, having previously operated Martin Mariner flying boats from Oban. Equipped with the Wellington GRXIII, fitted with ASV radar, its role was to seek out the Kriegsmarine's fast torpedo boats, the E-

Davidstow Moor in June 1951.

and R-boats, as well as U-boats, mainly at night. Its first operation was on 30 April, and the unit carried out forty E-boat patrols during May. Some of these were with the Beaufighter Xs of 144 and 404 Squadrons, which transferred from Wick on 10 May and really brought Davidstow to life with dozens of noisy Bristol Hercules engines. Making up 154 Wing with 524 Squadron, the Beaufighter squadrons made their first major strike from Davidstow on 19 May, when twenty-two Beaufighters escorted by twenty-eight Spitfires, attacked two destroyers and two escorts near Brest. Although none of the vessels was sunk, they were forced back into port.

The Davidstow squadrons' operations then focused on clearing the Western Approaches of enemy naval forces in the lead-up to D-Day. On 6 June, with fifty Beaufighters on strength, 154

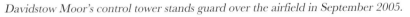

Davidstow Moor's control tower stands guard over the airfield in September 2005.

Wing was kept busy. Early in the evening thirty-one Beaufighters took off from Davidstow, rendezvoused with their escort of eight Mosquito VIs of Portreath-based 248 Squadron, and headed for Bordeaux. There they caught three German destroyers leaving the Gironde estuary, engaged them with rocket projectiles, and sank all three. One Beaufighter went down shortly after the attack, but its crew were dropped a lifeboat by an ASR Warwick. Several other Beaufighters were badly damaged, one force-landing at Predannack.

On 1 July, with the immediate threat over, 154 Wing moved out, 524 Squadron going to Docking, the others to Strubby, although 404 Squadron left a large detachment at Davidstow. On 6 August the latter was joined by the Beaufighter TFXs of 236 Squadron, moved from North Coates in response to increased German naval activity in the Bay of Biscay. In a series of attacks over the following few weeks they sank or severely damaged destroyers, minesweepers, armed trawlers and a floating dock. During their final attack on 24 August, twenty Beaufighters sank a destroyer and torpedo boat in the port of Le Verdon. Three aircraft, badly damaged by flak, put down at Vannes airfield, which was unoccupied. Another Beaufighter landed and rescued the crews, after they had set fire to their damaged aircraft. This was the swansong of the strike wings in the Bay, as the Beaufighter detachments then returned to their Lincolnshire bases, and on 17 September 282 Squadron's Warwicks departed. The station was then used as a training camp by the RAF Regiment, which built up to eight squadrons by November 1944. Running down again the following year, they left on 5 October 1945. Two months later Davidstow Moor was closed.

The airfield has since been occasionally used for motor racing, for Commando helicopter training, and for powered gliding. Davidstow Moor is remarkably intact today: the runways and taxiways are still in place, as is the shell of the control tower that stands guard over it. Although the hangars have gone, many Maycrete buildings remain in various states of repair, and one barrack block on the old domestic sites has been refurbished as a museum. Davidstow is well-known nowadays as the brand name for a variety of Cheddar cheese, produced by the modern creamery constructed on the western side of the old airfield.

Main features:
Runways: 304° 6,000ft x 150ft, 248° 4,200ft x 150ft, 210° 4,200ft x 150ft, concrete and tarmac. *Hangars:* three T2. *Hardstandings:* fifty 150ft diameter concrete. *Accommodation:* RAF Officers 298, SNCOs 718, ORs 1,732; WAAF Officers 4, SNCOs 22, ORs 486.

DOWN FARM, Gloucestershire

ST 855906, 3 miles SW of Tetbury off A433

Down Farm proved to be one of the most successful aircraft dispersal and storage sites. Located in woods on the Westonbirt Park estate with an airstrip laid out alongside, work on the site began during 1940, as 23 Satellite Landing Ground of 10 MU Hullavington.

However, the site's opening date of 1 April 1941 had to be postponed due to waterlogging, following an inspection by 10 MU. Within a couple of weeks the situation had improved and, following a test landing, the SLG was opened on 15 April. Four Defiants then landed and were picketed out, followed by three Hampdens. Many more soon followed. The aircraft were parked in clearings under the trees, well camouflaged from above. Security was a problem at such sites, and RAF guards were provided from August 1941, later replaced by Army personnel, supplemented by guard dogs in July 1942.

Additional dispersals and a secondary runway were proposed by the Air Ministry early in 1942 as part of a plan to develop the site into a full-scale airfield for the USAAF, but this was blocked by the MAP as Down Farm was one of its most successful storage sites.

Following a survey Down Farm was cleared for the handling and storage of four-engine aircraft, and the dispersals were reinforced by the laying of Sommerfield track. This was completed during August 1943, when 110 aircraft were in storage. Stirlings were brought in, and further aircraft arrived during 1944 with the build-up to D-Day. From October 1944, with the need for concealment reduced, the Oxfords of 15 (P)AFU South Cerney started to use the airfield for training, due to waterlogging at its SLG at Babdown Farm. Night-flying took place with the aid of a sodium-light flare-path from March 1945, but, with Babdown Farm back in commission, the

Oxfords stopped using Down Farm early in April.

The end of the war in Europe brought more aircraft to Down Farm as units started to disband, peaking at 182 aircraft in July 1945. This number reduced as aircraft were drawn back to Hullavington, and it was decided to clear the site; all of the aircraft had left by the end of January 1946. A working party then laboured to move the 146 tons of Sommerfield tracking that had been laid! The land was handed back to its owners in February 1946, and today there is little sign of the former airfield, which forms part of Westonbirt Arboretum.

A PB4Y-1 Liberator takes off from Dunkeswell in 1943.

DUNKESWELL, Devon

ST 134078, 4 miles N of Honiton

The United States Navy used Dunkeswell as its only operational air base in the UK during the Second World War. For eighteen months it flew PB4Y-1 Liberators on operations, the only ones to be mounted from the airfield during three years of war.

Dunkeswell was built in the hills above Honiton by George Wimpey & Co during 1941-42 as a standard Class A three-runway airfield. Originally planned as a fighter airfield, it was opened on 26 June 1943 by 19 Group Coastal Command. The RAF then had no immediate use for the new airfield, so it was allocated to Fleet Air Wing 7 of the USN, its HQ newly set up at Plymouth.

The first US anti-submarine aircraft to arrive at Dunkeswell, on 6 August, were in fact from the USAAF. The 4th and 19th Squadrons of the 479th Anti-submarine Group of the US 8th Air Force had been assigned to fly B-24D Liberators on maritime patrol and anti-shipping operations, and first flew these from St Eval in July 1943. They had accrued some experience, having shared in the destruction of three U-boats with RAF squadrons. The group's first operation from its new base was on 7 August, when a B-24D took off for a 10-hour patrol. Later joined by the 6th and 22nd

Four PB4Y-1s stand on Dunkeswell's dispersals in 1943.

Squadrons direct from the USA, the USAAF flew regular patrols throughout the following month and into October. Crews located few U-boats and only one was attacked, inconclusively, on 7 September. They did, however, see some combat, in the form of attacks from Ju 88 and Me 410 fighters sent out to intercept them; the air battles resulted in three B-24Ds being lost. The last action was on 17 October when C/22 was attacked by twelve Ju 88s, which disabled one engine. Despite this, the pilot, Captain Estes, managed to evade his attackers and return safely. At the end of October 1943 the 479th AG stood down, handing over maritime air operations to the USN.

VP103 was the first USN anti-submarine squadron to move to Dunkeswell, having flown from St Eval the month before. It was joined by VP105 and VP110 in October, under the Command of FAW7. They flew the PB4Y-1 anti-submarine version of the Liberator, with a ball-turret replaced by a retractable radar scanner, some carrying a Leigh Light beneath the starboard wing. As the USN built up its operation, Dunkeswell developed into a major base, with a large number of dispersals, five large T2 hangars and two canvas hangars. Large dispersed accommodation sites were in wooded countryside to the south-east.

The winter of 1943-44 was particularly severe in the West Country, and the USN found it difficult to maintain operations form Dunkeswell. Its first loss occurred on 8 November, when a PB4Y-1 of VP110 failed to return from a patrol over the Bay of Biscay, probably a victim of Ju 88s. On the 10th three aircraft, one from each squadron, attacked U-966, located by a Wellington of 612 Squadron. The submarine was also attacked by RP-armed Liberators of 311 (Czech) Squadron and was severely damaged. It was later beached on the north Spanish coast and blown up by its crew. Two days later Lieutenant Brownell of VP103 and his crew located and attacked U-508 in the Bay of Biscay; both U-boat and PB4Y-1 failed to return, but it was the first unassisted U-boat kill by USN aircraft.

The Dunkeswell squadrons were also engaged on shipping strikes, and during December attacked blockade runners, enemy merchant vessels and warships. U-boats were still hunted, and on 28 January 1944 Lieutenant Enloe and his crew sank U-271 off the west coast of Ireland. In February a total of 253 sorties were flown by the Liberators, despite appalling weather conditions, which may have contributed to the loss of three aircraft that month.

PB4Y-1 of VP103 in late 1943.

By May the three squadrons were capable of flying eighteen aircraft per day, though crew shortages meant each had to fly every other day. This intensive flying rate continued during early June and resulted in many U-boat sightings and the first operational use of the schnorkel device being reported. On 22 June eight contacts were made, followed up by four attacks. During the month of June the squadrons flew 470 sorties, made twenty-four sightings and seventeen attacks, but with no confirmed sinkings. No aircraft were lost during this period, despite having flown more than 4,680 hours.

A special unit, Project Anvil, was set up at Dunkeswell in June to carry out attacks on V-weapons sites using war-weary Liberators converted into radio-controlled drones. The aircraft were packed with explosives, but required a pilot and co-pilot/radio engineer to take-off and fly it until radio-contact could be established with a guide aircraft. The crew would then bale out and the guide would take the drone to its target. On 31 July the unit moved to a forward base at Fersfield in Norfolk. Lieutenant Joseph Kennedy was serving with VP110 at Dunkeswell at this time and, having completed a combat tour of thirty missions, volunteered to fly the first Anvil operation, targeting the V-3 site at Mimoyecques near Calais. He took off from Fersfield on 12 August, but as the B-24 was heading towards the Suffolk coast at 2,000 feet it exploded, killing Kennedy and his co-pilot, Lieutenant Wilford Willy.

Other aircraft based at Dunkeswell at this time included a detachment of PBY-5A Catalina amphibians, two Vengeances and a single N3N biplane for training. Six Seafire IIs were loaned to the Americans in August; they retained their British markings but were fitted with US VHF radios and used for air combat training with the P4BY-1 crews. With western France in Allied hands, enemy activity in the Bay of Biscay declined rapidly, and there were few sightings during the autumn of 1944 and the spring of 1945.

The two final U-boat sinkings by Dunkeswell squadrons took place on 11 March 1945 when U-681 was sunk by Lieutenant R. N. Field and his crew of VP103, and on 25 April when U-326 was sunk with the aid of a homing torpedo dropped by the PB4Y-1 flown by Lieutenant Nett and his crew of VP103. The squadrons kept up their patrols, and were rewarded with the first surrender of a U-boat after the cessation of hostilities, when U-249 raised a black flag off the Isles of Scilly on 9 May 1945. With the end of the war in Europe, the rundown of Dunkeswell airfield was rapid, the Liberators leaving for the USA in June. The HQ of FAW7 moved from Plymouth to Dunkeswell on 11 July, then went to the USA at the end of the month.

On 6 August Dunkeswell was transferred to 46 Group, RAF Transport Command. No 3 OAPU moved in from Llandow, becoming 16 Ferry Unit when it absorbed 11 FU, Talbenny, on 15 August. Used for ferrying aircraft to the Middle East and to foreign air forces, one of its major customers was the French Air Force, which received large numbers of surplus airframes from British stocks, ranging from Tiger Moths to Halifaxes. When 16 FU moved to St Mawgan in March 1946, Dunkeswell became an equipment disposal centre for 265 MU, Cliffs Norton (having already opened a sub-site there in August 1945), and 267 MU, Croughton, from November 1946. Flying

A Catalina flies past Dunkeswell's control tower again in 2006, as preserved G-PBYA gives a flying display in August that year.

continued during this time, a Lancaster of 16 FU overrunning following an aborted take-off while visiting on 7 May 1946, and being scrapped on site. Both MUs disbanded on 31 December 1948.

After the RAF disposed of the airfield in February 1949 it was used by the Devon & Somerset Gliding Club until they moved to nearby North Hill. The airfield was then purchased by Westward Aviation Ltd, and the Dunkeswell Aero Club started in 1967. Flying and skydiving continue on the airfield, which today is very active. The control tower has survived together with other airfield buildings, including the command centre and several hangars. A memorial and museum commemorates wartime USAAF and USN operations from the airfield.

Main features:
Runways: 230° 6,000ft x 150ft, 360° 4,410ft x 150ft, 270° 3,810ft x 150ft, concrete and asphalt. *Hangars:* five T2, two US Canvas. *Hardstandings:* forty-four 125ft diameter tarmac-covered concrete, forty-four spectacle. *Accommodation:* USN Officers 252, Enlisted Men 2,320.

EVERLEIGH, Wiltshire

SV186556, 4 miles E of Upavon

Everleigh spent most of the Second World War as an MU dispersal airfield, but differed from most as having started as a relief landing ground, utilising a grass field to the north of the village of Everleigh on Salisbury Plain. Being relatively flat and almost surrounded by trees, it was used for circuit training and as a practice force-landing ground by Masters of CFS Upavon during 1940/41. One aircraft, N7426, was overturned by an unfortunate student on 13 May 1941, but by this time Everleigh had been identified by 15 MU Wroughton as the potential location for an SLG. Its main attractions were a suitable landing area and good natural camouflage for dispersed aircraft in the surrounding woods.

Opened as 31 SLG on 22 November 1941, the airfield consisted of little more than a Detachment HQ and guard hut, but a grass strip orientated NW/SE was completed the following month, and the first aircraft landed shortly afterwards. Hardcore tracks were added for access to hides under the trees. Security was provided by a twenty-man Defence Flight, and by April fourteen aircraft were in store. That same month Everleigh was chosen as the venue for an airborne forces exercise organised by 38 Wing, laid on by 1st Airlanding Brigade for Sir Winston Churchill and a number of high-ranking Allied and Commonwealth observers. A Whitley flew over to drop paratroops ahead of a glider landing, but it experienced a problem and had to circle. Unfortunately

Everleigh's Super Robin hangar in June 2002.

when the paratroops did drop, they landed as eight troop-carrying Hotspur gliders were approaching. The glider pilots did what they could to land on a field full of paratroops, but unfortunately one soldier was killed by a glider, which then cartwheeled into a hedge and broke up, fortunately without further injury. Another swerved into a bank. The escorting officers tried to divert the Prime Minister's attention to troops deploying from successfully landed gliders, but he was clearly not impressed.

Tree-lopping in May 1942 provided the approach to a new NE/SW grass strip, but further cutting was kept to a minimum to preserve the natural camouflage of the site. The SLG was then able to accommodate thirty-seven aircraft, which included Blenheims, Hurricanes, Lysanders, Oxfords, Spitfires, Wellingtons and Hotspurs. On 30 September 1942 Everleigh was transferred to 33 MU Lyneham, the guards replaced by five guard dogs and handlers. More access tracks were laid into the woods, and dispersals were constructed to the north-west of the airfield in Everleigh Ashes, to the north at Cow Down and to the east in Hog Down Wood. A Super Robin hangar was erected in 1943 and, following an inspection, Everleigh was cleared for the landing and storage of four-engine aircraft. In December it became one of several SLGs used by 10 MU, Hullavington, for the storage of Stirlings, the numbers of which built up as D-Day approached. The number of aircraft stored reached a peak of eighty-seven in July 1944, but by the end of the war this number had reduced to seventeen and in November 1945 the site was cleared and closed down shortly afterwards.

Today little remains to indicate that Everleigh was once a large aircraft storage area, although the farm shed in use on the site is probably the Super Robin put there in 1943. Aircraft do still appear there, as the Army Air Corps uses a strip in the field next to the former landing ground, and the area is used as a parachute DZ for exercises on Salisbury Plain.

Hurricane I P3886 of 601 Squadron at its Exeter dispersal in July 1940.

EXETER, Devon

SY002948, 1 mile E of Clyst Honiton alongside A30

On the night of 12/13 May 1941 RAF Exeter was attacked by a large force of Luftwaffe bombers. They scattered HE and incendiary bombs across the airfield, and a number of the station's buildings were set alight. Although both the Officers' and Sergeants' Messes were destroyed and much equipment lost (including one Defiant), amazingly there were no casualties. Sector Control was caught out by this surprise attack, and the only night-fighter to get airborne was a Defiant of 307 (Polish) Squadron, which went on its crew's initiative. Dodging the bomb craters, the two Sergeants took off and caught up with the raider, claiming an He 111. This was typical of the Poles, and although this indiscipline earned them a mild reproof, the mechanic who started the engine and guided the aircraft onto the runway into the air raid got a richly deserved Polish Cross of Honour!

Built as a municipal airport to the east of the city, Exeter was opened on 31 May 1937. Its inaugural service was by Jersey Airlines to the Channel Islands. The aerodrome was operated on behalf of the local authority by the Straight Corporation, which also ran the Aero Club and gained a contract from the Air Ministry to operate a flying school for RAF reservists. This was 37 E&RFTS, which formed on 3 July 1939 with Tiger Moths; it was not to last for long, however, as with the outbreak of war in early September it was closed down, together with the flying club, and Exeter Airport came under the jurisdiction of the National Air Communications organisation. NAC, established to coordinate the effects of the civil airlines in wartime, nominated Exeter as the English terminal for the Channel Islands, and, with its aircraft camouflaged, Jersey Airlines continued services to the islands.

The first RAF personnel to arrive at Exeter came on 14 September 1939 with a unit from RAE Farnborough, known as O2 Detachment. Flying a mixed bag of types, including Battles, Harrows and the Fairey P4/34 prototype, they occupied a hangar recently built near the passenger terminal. The detachment undertook trials work on various techniques and equipment, such as the protection of bombers from balloon cables. They remained at Exeter until February 1942, when accommodation became available at Church Stanton. The unit had been joined at Exeter by the Gunnery Research Unit, which formed on 3 June 1940 from a nucleus of personnel from A Flight, Armament Testing Squadron, A&AEE. The GRU was to remain for nearly four years, testing guns, turrets and gunsights for a large variety of aircraft types.

With the fall of France the demand for seats on Jersey Airlines flights to the Channel Island fell, but return flights were fully booked! Evacuation of the islands by the airlines continued until the Germans arrived in early July. The occupation of France forced Fighter Command to spread its forces further west, and on 18 June 1940 the Hurricanes of 213 Squadron arrived at Exeter on transfer from

A Whirlwind of 263 Squadron taxying at Exeter in January 1941.

Biggin Hill. They were joined by 87 Squadron on 6 July, the day that the airport was taken over by the Air Ministry to become RAF Exeter. Over the following months it was developed by 10 Group into one of its main fighter stations. Ten hangars were erected on the north and south sides of the airfield, together with large dispersed accommodation sites. Fighter pens were also built, and the airfield itself extended to the east and north-west, with the laying of three concrete and tarmac runways.

The Exeter squadrons were tasked with the defence of Exeter and Plymouth (with its naval dockyard), but their first contact with the enemy on 11 August was further east. Fourteen Hurricanes were scrambled that morning as a large enemy force, estimated at 165 aircraft, was detected heading for the South Coast. The Hurricanes arrived over Portland at the same time as the main formations of Ju 88s and He 111s, and went into the attack. They shot down two Junkers before getting mixed up with the fighter escort and an intensive dogfight ensued. The final tally at the end of the day was eighteen enemy aircraft claimed for the loss of five. More raids followed, and the Hurricanes were kept busy. By the end of August the Exeter squadrons had claimed more than eighty enemy aircraft, but had lost nineteen Hurricanes, with fifteen pilots killed. Among 87 Squadron's leading pilots were Flt Lt Ian Gleed and Fg Off Roland Beamont.

From the beginning of September A and B Flights of 87 Squadron started night-flying rotas to Bibury, and by the end of the year the unit would be almost exclusively engaged on night operations. On 7 September 213 Squadron moved off to Tangmere, exchanging places with another Hurricane unit, 601 Squadron. By this time the air war in the west had slackened, and the Hurricane squadrons had few contacts, although one on 12 December resulted in an He 111 being claimed by 601's Flt Lt Whitney Straight, pre-war pilot, racing-driver and wealthy founder of the Straight Corporation, former operator of Exeter Airport!

When 87 Squadron left for Colerne on 28 November it was replaced by 263 Squadron from Drem, which brought a new shape to Exeter with the Westland Whirlwind. From its new base the unit started flying *Chameleon* patrols, searching the Channel for E-boats that were known to be loitering to pick up ditched bomber aircrews after night raids on the West Country. It was joined by the Hurricanes of 504 Squadron from Filton on 18 December (replacing 601 Squadron, which went to Northolt), and when 263 moved on to St Eval on 25 February 1941, the unit was replaced that day by 66 Squadron, flying Spitfire IIs, from Biggin Hill.

A succession of Hurricane and Spitfire squadrons spent short periods at Exeter during 1941, using the airfield to carry out coastal and shipping patrols, while officially resting. RAF Exeter was attacked by the Luftwaffe five times during the early part of the year, the most serious being on 5 April when a low-level attack by three bombers wrecked the main hangar, damaged sixteen aircraft and destroyed a Wellington. The arrival of 307 (Polish) Squadron on 26 April with its Defiant Is meant that day and night defence for the area was available for the first time. No 307 was the first

Polish squadron to appear at Exeter, and would be followed by others. Apart from the 'unauthorised' attack by one of the unit's Defiants in May described above, the Poles had little contact with the Luftwaffe until 1 November, when a sudden burst of German activity enabled them to claim two Do 17s destroyed, and three other aircraft damaged. Three weeks later they destroyed a Ju 88 over Plymouth. These victories were gained on the Beaufighter IIF, the Squadron having traded its Defiants during September.

In the meantime 2 Polish Fighter Wing had been formed with three Hurricane Squadrons, Nos 302 and 316 at Church Stanton, and 317, which had arrived at Exeter on 21 July to defend the local area. Exeter UAS was formed on 21 August with Tiger Moths, operating until August 1943 when it was disbanded. On 12 February 1942 the airfield was attacked by three Do 217s, and in April the 'Baedeker' reprisal raids started, with forty bombers from KG2 (Do 217s), KG100 (He111s) and KG106 (Ju88s) targeting Exeter on the 23rd. The night was cloudy and only one aircraft hit the target, but the next night they returned and caused much more damage. The Beaufighters of 307 Squadron managed some interceptions, damaging several enemy aircraft, and during a further raid on 3 May destroyed four Ju 88s over Exeter.

No 317 Squadron had moved to Northolt on 1 April, and was replaced by another Polish unit, 308 Squadron, which stayed until 7 May when it too moved on and 310 (Czech) Squadron arrived from Redhill. It was joined by 247 Squadron, one of the last night-fighter squadrons still flying the Hurricane. It had in fact made Exeter detachments from December 1941, and on 17 May 1942 the main squadron joined the detachment. The unit brought with it a flight of Havocs of 536 Squadron, with which they had been paired for Turbinlite patrols. As well as these, fitted with long-range tanks, the unit's Hurricane IIBs mounted intruder missions over north-west France, targeting Luftwaffe bases. In August they also started night *Roadsteads*.

In mid-August No 310 Squadron detached to Redhill, and from there on 19 August took part in Operation *Jubilee*, the Commando raid on Dieppe. First covering anti-E-boat Hurricane sorties, the Squadron's Spitfires flew top cover over the beaches later in the day, claiming one destroyed, three probables and six damaged. No 247 Squadron departed for High Ercall on 21 September, and later that day a type new to Exeter arrived – the Typhoon, flown in by 257 Squadron. The unit flew anti-*Rhubarb* patrols in an attempt to catch coastal raids by FW 190s.

Towards the end of 1942 naval uniforms were seen for the first time at Exeter when a detachment of 825 Squadron arrived on 30 December with Swordfish IIs. The black-painted aircraft were fitted with ASV radar and flew from Exeter to seek out E-boats operating in the Channel at night. The detachment stayed until 1 February 1943, and was replaced by 834 Squadron, also with the Swordfish, a week later. Several contacts were made and most were followed up by attacks, but it was difficult to ascertain whether they were successful or not. The patrols continued throughout most of the year, a detachment of 841 Squadron taking over on 9 July, this time with Albacores. Detachments from this unit stayed at Exeter until the end of November.

When 257 Squadron departed in January 1943 it was replaced by another Typhoon unit, 266 Squadron, which took on the anti-*Rhubarb* defence role, with some success: three Typhoons caught two FW 190s in January, another two in February and a further two in March. During its nine-month stay at Exeter it also operated from Warmwell as a forward airfield and later flew escorts to other Typhoons on *Roadsteads*. No 310 (Czech) Squadron had resumed the offensive in January, mounting sweeps across the Channel. On 29 January its pilots were involved in a dogfight over Morlaix airfield during which it claimed one FW 190 destroyed, another probable, and two damaged, for the loss of two Spitfires and their pilots. The Squadron then went over mainly to shipping patrols, with the occasional offensive operation.

No 307 Squadron left on 15 April 1943, after a two-year stay at Exeter, the longest of any of the operational squadrons. It swapped places at Fairwood Common with 125 Squadron, also flying the Beaufighter. The latter had a successful night on 13 June, successfully intercepting seven enemy bombers during a raid on Plymouth; four were destroyed, the others damaged. However, this activity was unusual, night combats at this time being few and far between, but the crews were also sent out on ASR night patrols.

On 26 June 1943 No 310 (Czech) Squadron left for Castletown. The Typhoons of 266 Squadron carried on with their bomber escort missions and sweeps until that unit also moved away, to Harrowbeer, in September. An exchange of Beaufighter squadrons took place on 14 November, when 125 Squadron went to Valley, in place of 406 (RCAF) Squadron. The Canadians spent the spring of

Mosquito TT35 VP181/54 of 3 CAACU over the North Devon countryside in the early 1960s.

1944 patrolling southern England and keeping German aircraft away from the invasion build-up areas. They had been joined by 616 Squadron, flying Spitfire VIIs, in December 1943, and by 610, with Spitfire XIVs, in January 1944, which patrolled the South Coast by day. However, in April the RAF squadrons were moved out of Exeter to make way for the USAAF, which took it over as Station 463.

On 1 April 1944 the four squadrons of the 440th Troop Carrier Group of the US 9th Air Force arrived, but there were insufficient hardstandings for their seventy C-47s and many had to be parked on the grass, together with their CG-4A gliders. The group then resumed training exercises, working up for D-Day. They dropped paratroops near Carentan in the early hours of 6 June, and on the following day dropped supplies into the same area. Three C-47s were shot down by flak on D-Day and another three were lost on the re-supply missions, although one of the latter was struck by bombs from a P-47. The group then operated casualty evacuation flights from the beachhead. It sent three of its squadrons (the 95th, 96th and 97th TCS) to Italy in mid-July, where they flew supplies to Rome and took part in Operation *Dragoon*, the landings in southern France, on 15 August. The 98th TCS, remaining behind, moved to Ramsbury on 7 August, from where it dropped supplies to encircled US troops at Mortain. It returned to Exeter on 23 August, and the other squadrons returned from the Mediterranean the following day. The 440th TCG established a new base at Reims in September, and started moving there. The last of the air echelon left Exeter on 13 September, the USAAF retained the airfield for the air evacuation of wounded, and a US base squadron remained until November.

With Exeter returned to RAF control, a Flight of 275 Squadron moved its six Walruses in from Bolt Head. It remained until 10 January 1945, when Exeter was transferred to 23 (Training) Group and 3 GTS arrived, bringing with it Master II tugs and Hotspur gliders. ASR presence was retained in the form of a Walrus detachment from 282 Squadron based at St Eval.

In June 1945 Exeter returned to Fighter Command, this time as part of 11 Group, with Cleave and Bolt Head as satellites. The Tempests of 222 Squadron arrived from Boxted on 12 June before leaving again on 25 June for B155/Dedelstorf. The Oxfords, Hurricanes and Vengeances of 691 Squadron then moved in from Harrowbeer for target-towing duties on 1 August, followed by the Spitfire XVIs of 329 (Free French) Squadron nine days later from Fairwood Common. The latter was disbanded in November 1945, and 691 Squadron became Exeter's sole resident until 15 April 1946, when 222 Squadron returned, this time with Meteor F3s. They were joined by the Mosquito Mk XXXs of 151 Squadron on 1 June; however, their stay was not to last long, and both departed for Weston Zoyland on 8 July. When 691 Squadron left in October 1946, the station was closed down.

Exeter was transferred to the Ministry of Civil Aviation on 1 January 1947 and reopened for civil operations. Chrislea Aviation moved in from Heston to manufacture its Super Ace and Skyjeep light aircraft, until taken over in 1952. The Aero Club also restarted, but there was then no interest in the resumption of scheduled services.

Flybe Dash 8 G-JEDR at Exeter Airport in April 2009.

Military flying resumed from Exeter in May 1949, when 10 RFS opened to train reservists on Tiger Moths, Chipmunks and Ansons, but was closed again in June 1954. No 3 CAACU was formed in March 1951 and started calibration and target-towing operations in support of Service units in the South West, using Spitfires and Beaufighters; managed by Exeter Airport Ltd, the unit later received Vampires, Meteors, Mosquitoes and Hunters before it, too, was disbanded in late 1971, its duties having been taken over by 7 Squadron at St Mawgan. The last RAF unit to form at Exeter was 4 AEF in September 1958; it flew Chipmunks to give flying experience to Air Cadets in the South West (including the author, from St Mawgan) until disbanding in December 1995.

Scheduled services from Exeter were resumed in 1952, initially to the Channel Islands by Jersey Airlines (subsequently British United (CI), British Island Airways and Air UK). Other operators have come and gone, such as Airways Union, North-South Airlines, Westpoint and British Eagle. A number of companies have run the airport, but when Devon County Council took over in April 1974 its situation stabilised.

In 1981 the wartime control tower was replaced and improvements included the extension of the main runway to 6,250 feet, an installation of a Racal-Decca ILS and new approach and runway lighting. The following year came a new fire station and upgraded passenger terminal. Facilities have been steadily improved over the years and in 1999 a new arrivals building was opened, followed by a new departures building in June 2003, capable of accommodating 400 passengers.

Nowadays, as well as Flybe's scheduled series with Dash 8s, all-inclusive charters are also flown from Exeter to the Mediterranean by First Choice with Boeing 757s and Airbus 320s, Air Malta with Boeing 737s and Airbus 320s, Britannia with Boeing 767s, and Globespan to Canada. Although Exeter Airport has been substantially redeveloped, a number of buildings from its RAF days are still in place, including several hangars and a number of former administrative and technical buildings.

Main features:
Runways: 200° 2,700ft x 150ft, 266° 6,000ft x 150ft, 312° 4,350ft x 150ft, concrete and asphalt. *Hangars:* seven Hinaidi, six O-Blister, four EO-Blister. *Hardstandings:* nineteen TE, five SE. *Accommodation:* RAF Officers 210, SNCOs 544, ORs 1,594; WAAF Officers 14, SNCOs 8, ORs 631.

Southampton S1044 visiting Falmouth in the late 1920s.

FALMOUTH, Cornwall

SW 815334, in outer harbour, N of town

Falmouth's natural harbour had long been considered as a seaplane base, being ideally placed for Atlantic operations. However, it suffered from poor approaches by air, and was only occasionally used by detachments of floatplanes during the First World War. Squadron cruises by flying boats during the 1920s and '30s used moorings between Trefusis Point and the village of Flushing, and the area was earmarked as an emergency base.

With the declaration of war in September 1939, 204 Squadron soon found itself overwhelmed with operational commitments as it tried to carry out anti-submarine patrols and merchant shipping escorts from its base at Mount Batten. A detachment of three London flying boats was therefore sent

London II K5260 of 201 Squadron, detached to Falmouth from Calshot in 1939.

by 240 Squadron from Invergordon, and on 20 September they were moved to Falmouth. From there they mounted convoy escorts until 4 October, when they were relieved by three Stranraers of 209 Squadron, which had arrived from Invergordon on 1 October. These good-looking, but antiquated, biplanes continued the work for another month before rejoining their squadron. During the detachment one Stranraer, K7294, crashed near Falmouth on 3 November, but otherwise their operations were uneventful.

A C&M party remained at Falmouth and the moorings were occasionally used by Sunderlands visiting or on detachment from Mount Batten and Pembroke Dock. During one such visit in March 1940 Sunderland N9021 of 204 Squadron was damaged when it ran aground. From February 1941 the C&M party operated from Mount Batten, but the base was finally closed on 1 December 1942 when other diversion bases became available. No 42 Marine Craft Unit, established at Falmouth to service visiting flying boats, later ran ASR launches and, renumbered after the war as 1102 MCU, continued in service until the 1970s.

Filton aerodrome in July 1931.

FILTON, Gloucestershire

ST 595802, 4 miles N of Bristol alongside A38

On the morning of 25 September 1940, a formation of Bf 110 fighters and He 111 bombers appeared over the Channel and crossed the South Coast, apparently heading for Yeovil. 10 Group ordered three fighter squadrons to the area, but the bombers passed well to the east and reached their target unopposed, the Bristol Aeroplane works at Filton. The pathfinders, the Bf 110s of Erprobungsgruppe 210, dropped markers, closely followed by fifty-eight He 111s of KG55, which then dropped more than 100 tons of bombs onto the factory roofs and the airfield. Substantial damage caused production to be halted, eight Beaufighters being totally destroyed and another twelve aircraft badly damaged. Of the 238 casualties among the factory workers, ninety-one had been fatally injured. Three of the enemy bombers were shot down by local AA defences, and four more intercepted on their return leg, together with four German fighters.

The airfield at Filton is one of the oldest in Britain, dating back to February 1910 when the British & Colonial Aeroplane Company was formed, starting production in two sheds leased from Bristol Tramways at its Filton depot. The company started by licence-building Zodiac aeroplanes

Blenheim Is in production at Filton in early 1938; K7072 is nearest the camera.

before developing its own design, the Boxkite, which started to sell, and in March 1911 a War Office order was received for a quantity of the type. Land to the north of the sheds was acquired for an airfield and in August Filton House was added to provide offices as the works expanded. Following the declaration of war in August 1914 the company expanded enormously, increasing its staff from less than a hundred to more than 3,000 by the time of the Armistice. In the intervening period it built thousands of aeroplanes for the RFC and RNAS in enlarged works at Filton and at the Bristol Tramways works in Brislington, which was also leased. These included the BE2 under licence, followed by the Bristol Scout, the M1 monoplane and the F2 Bristol Fighter, or Brisfit. All were test-flown from the airfield, which was also used by the RFC from December 1915 to work up new squadrons before they left for France. The South West Aircraft Acceptance Park was also set up during this time to accept new aircraft that had been completed by factories in the area, using eighteen large hangars built on the airfield.

After the war activities at Filton were reduced. In March 1920 the company's title was changed to the Bristol Aeroplane Company, and on 28 May 1923 it opened a Reserve Flying School under RAF contract. Instruction was given on Bristol types, such as Bristol Fighters and the Bristol PTM (Primary Training Machine). A variety of others followed until 1933, when Tiger Moths were standardised. On 14 June 1929 No 501 (County of Gloucester) Squadron was formed as a bomber unit within the Special Reserve. It started flying Avro 504Ns, and received its first operational type, the DH9A, in March 1930. That same year work started on improvements to the RAF site on the north side of the airfield; existing buildings were altered and new ones erected, to accommodate one regular and one reserve squadron. The Reserve Flying School became 2 E&RFTS in 1935, still operated by Bristol.

With the adoption of the Blenheim as the RAF's standard light bomber, production capacity was expanded and the workforce increased. New manufacturing methods such as monocoque construction also required new tool rooms, machine shops and erecting shops to be added. A new aero-engine factory was built in 1936 to produce the Bristol Mercury, Pegasus, Taurus and Hercules engines that were in demand. These developments resulted in the Filton works being the largest single aircraft manufacturing unit in the world in the late 1930s. To deliver completed aircraft a Ferry Pilots Pool was formed at Filton on 16 January 1939; ATA pilots joined the unit later in the year, and eventually took over all ferrying from Filton during the war years.

No 501 Squadron had become part of the Auxiliary Air Force in May 1936, and a fighter unit in December 1938, receiving Hurricanes in March 1939. It was on its summer camp at Manston in September 1939 when war was declared, and was embodied into the RAF for the duration. It immediately returned to Filton ready to repel raiders, and was joined by 25 Squadron on 15 September, which flew in its Blenheim Mk IF fighters to boost the area's defences. However, there was little action, and the Blenheims returned to Northolt after a couple of weeks. Another squadron that had appeared at Filton was No 263, which was formed there on 2 October with Gloster Gladiators.

Having been scrambled only three times without success since its return, 501 Squadron moved on 28 November to Tangmere (later moving to France). No 263 Squadron then took on local air defence until April 1940, when it was given notice to move to Norway. There in June, it took part in the short campaign that resulted in the withdrawal of British forces, the squadron subsequently being lost aboard HMS *Glorious* when the carrier was sunk by German surface ships.

No.8 CAACU arrived from Ringway towards the end of April 1940, but after a few months moved to Weston Zoyland. On 23 May No 236 Squadron moved to Filton from Speke. A Coastal Command Squadron flying the Blenheim IVF, it stayed for a few weeks flying convoy patrols over the Bristol and English Channels before moving to Middle Wallop on 14 June. Filton's defences were boosted on 1 June when 935 (Balloon Barrage) Squadron arrived. However, the flying of a balloon barrage interfered with flying training by the resident flying school, which had been re-designated 2 EFTS with the outbreak of war. On 4 August it moved to Staverton, where conditions were far more conducive for training.

The Luftwaffe's interest in Bristol and Filton, with its docks and factories, became apparent on 24 June, when the first night raid was made on the city, and this was followed by several day and night attacks during July and August. Damage and casualties added to the disruptions caused by the air raid warnings themselves. The Hurricanes of 504 Squadron had been sent to Filton following the heavy raid of 25 September and they continued standing patrols until moving to Exeter on 18 December. They were replaced by 501 Squadron from Kenley with a one-day overlap. A slack period followed, during which the Hurricane pilots spent most of their time on convoy patrols over the Bristol Channel. On 9 April 1941 263 Squadron returned, this time with the deadly Whirlwind twin-engined fighter. It too spent much of its time on convoy patrols, together with 501 Squadron, until the latter left for Colerne on 22 April. The Whirlwinds also flew the occasional *Rhubarb* over the French coast, and found time to engage in some anti-tank trials. In August they mounted a series of *Rhubarbs* against targets in Normandy under Operation *Warehead*, targeting airfields and E-boats. On 6 August Maupertus airfield was attacked, and in the ensuing dogfight three Bf 109s were shot down and a further one damaged. The Whirlwinds returned unscathed to Filton, and on a triumphant note moved to Charmy Down the following day, the last operational squadron to be based at Filton during the wartime period.

On 5 May 1941 a new unit formed at Filton. This was 10 Group Anti-Aircraft Cooperation Flight, with a varied fleet of aircraft including the Lysander, Blenheim and Hurricane. The Flight's role was to provide training and practice for AA units in the local area, and having later been expanded and reformed as 286 Squadron, would provide target facilities for units all over the South West. The author's father, Geoffrey Berryman, served with this unit from 9 July, when it was still a flight, as a Corporal Fitter II (Airframes). Promoted to Sergeant, he later travelled with the Squadron on detachments to Colerne, Lulsgate, Zeals, Weston-super-Mare, Weston Zoyland and Culmhead, until December 1944 when he was posted to Italy.

Towards the end of 1941 a secondary runway was built to supplement the main one laid during the summer of 1940, and Filton was transferred from 10 to 44 Group. On 20 December 3 and 4 Flights of the Overseas Aircraft Preparation Unit were formed (1 and 2 having been formed at Kemble). For the next two years the unit would prepare Beauforts and Beaufighters for ferrying to overseas theatres, including the fitting of extra fuel tanks to give the required range.

During 1942 Bristols reached its peak, employing 52,095 people. Blenheims in production before the war had been replaced by Beauforts, and these in turn gave way to Beaufighters, which rolled off the production lines in their hundreds. The majority of their engines were also produced at the Filton site. The last major night attack on Bristols took place on 11 April 1942, the Luftwaffe hitting the main Filton works with one bomb, which demolished a wind tunnel and the office building alongside, but caused no casualties.

The OAPU detachment at Filton became 2 OAPU on 1 December 1942. On 15 June 1943 No 528 Squadron was formed as a radar calibration unit with Blenheims and Hornet Moths. It stayed at Filton until mid-May 1944, then moved to Digby. To support its build-up in Britain, the USAAF formed IX Base Aircraft Assembly Depot at Filton in November 1943, on the north-west side of the airfield. This was near Avonmouth Docks, where aircraft arrived from the USA by sea; they were then taken to the BAAD for assembly and preparation for flight before delivery by air to units. Aircraft received included P-47s, P-51s, A-20s and CG-4A gliders. Following D-Day the depot was closed and remnant flights moved to Chilbolton and Membury.

On 6 June 1944 two USAAF P-51s landed for refuelling following operations over the beachhead, but little other operational activity was evident until 23 June, when RAF Ansons started a transport service to distribute medical supplies from the Army Blood Plasma Depot at Southmead in Bristol. On 25 June USAAF C-47s arrived from Normandy bringing casualties. USAAF Courier Service and USN liaison aircraft also used the airfield during this period.

Filton remained busy throughout the rest of the year, with, at times, some 2,000 movements per month (both visiting aircraft and local aircraft on test flights). A Centaurus Test Flight was set up during September 1944 with Bristol Buckinghams. New Year 1945 brought with it fog, gales and frost, but USAAF C-47s still brought in casualties from Europe, continuing into the spring. Production flight testing also carried on, maintaining the flow of aircraft to RAF units during the closing months of the war. This work continued after VE Day on 8 May, as Beaufighters were still required for the Far East.

Signs of near-peacetime normality occurred on 15 September 1945 when RAF Filton held an 'At Home' flying display to commemorate the Battle of Britain. In November Bristol UAS started flying from Filton with Tiger Moths, and on 10 May 1946 No 504 Squadron was reformed as a Royal Auxiliary Air Force Squadron with Spitfire LF16s. It was joined by 12 RFS in 1948, flying Tiger Moths and Ansons, operated by the Bristol Aircraft Company.

The company's contribution to the war effort was enormous, with some 10,700 aircraft, mainly Blenheims, Beauforts and Beaufighters, and tens of thousands of engines being produced. Its planned place in peacetime aviation had already been mapped out, by the Brabazon Committee during 1944. The decision to build the mighty airliner proposed by the Committee, and named after it, resulted in major changes to the post-war airfield. The main runway was widened and extended over the demolished village of Charlton, and the works was enlarged to include a huge new assembly hall for the new airliner. The Brabazon had eight engines, a wingspan of 230 feet and

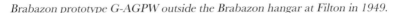

Brabazon prototype G-AGPW outside the Brabazon hangar at Filton in 1949.

Concordes in production in the Brabazon hangar at Filton in 1972. A Britannia is overhauled alongside.

weighed 290,000lb. It could carry 100 passengers over 5,000 miles. The aircraft first flew on 4 September 1949 and was demonstrated at the 1950 Farnborough Air Show. However, by then the Government had lost interest, and without its financial assistance the project ended. The Brabazon was an aeroplane ahead of its time, but that didn't save it from the cutter's torch in 1953.

With the cutback in reserve forces 12 RFS was disbanded in March 1953, followed by 501 Squadron in February 1957. The UAS was joined by 3 AEF in 1958, also with Chipmunks. The AEF moved to Hullavington in June 1989, and was joined there by Bristol UAS in March 1992, having been the last RAF unit at Filton.

Work on the Buckingham, Brigand and Freighter kept Bristol going in the 1950s, but knowledge gained in the research, development and construction of the Brabazon helped it produce the smaller but commercially successful Britannia, of which eighty-five were built at Filton. A number of other new projects were proposed, but few were produced. However, experience with the Bloodhound air defence missile and the Bristol 188 high-speed research aircraft put the successor to the Bristol Aeroplane Company, the British Aircraft Corporation, in a good position to produce the Concorde, in cooperation with the French, using the facilities at Filton. Further reorganisation followed, but the legacy of Bristol lives on with the British element of Airbus Industries based at Filton.

Main features:
Runways: 101° 4,500ft x 150ft, 030° 4,014ft x 150ft, concrete and tarmac. *Hangars:* twenty-three of various types, one one-bay Type B, one four-bay Type B. *Hardstandings:* aprons and hardstandings for up to sixty-three aircraft. *Accommodation:* RAF Officers 73, SNCOs 82, ORs 592; WAAF Officers 4, SNCOs 6, ORs 164.

A Bf 109E of JG53 being refuelled at Guernsey in August 1940. This aircraft was shot down by Spitfires of 234 Squadron, Middle Wallop, on 3 September.

GUERNSEY, Channel Islands

3 miles SW of St Peter Port

Military aircraft were first based in Guernsey during the First World War, when a French seaplane base was built on the southern side of St Peter Port Harbour in July 1917. Consisting of huts built by the RN and a Bessoneau hangar sent from France, two seaplanes initially operated from the base, but these gradually increased and by the end of the year eleven Tellier and ten FBA flying boats were on strength. Despite operational difficulties (the restricted landing and take-off runs being very tricky in strong winter winds), operations continued until December 1919, when the unit transferred to Cherbourg and the base closed.

Aeroplanes reappeared at St Peter Port when flying boat services were started in 1923. These continued for another sixteen years, when it was decided to build an airport for land-planes 3 miles away. Guernsey airport was opened by Sir Kingsley Wood, Secretary of State for Air, on 1 May 1939, and new scheduled services started four days later to Alderney, Jersey, Southampton and London. The airfield was originally of grass, with four runways varying in length from 2,040 to 3,060 feet, hangars and a terminal building.

Guernsey provided an excellent forward base for coastal patrol squadrons to cover the Channel, so with the deteriorating international situation in August ground personnel were sent to prepare the airport for use by the RAF. With the declaration of war, civil flying was stopped (with the exception of essential services), and A Flight of 48 Squadron moved its five Ansons across on 6 September 1939. Convoy escorts were started six days later, followed by anti-submarine patrols, which continued until the unit returned to Thorney Island on 8 October.

Guernsey Airways resumed limited services on 24 October to Shoreham and Tangmere. Visits by RAF aircraft were intermittent during the following months, but on 24 April 1940 the Ansons of the School of General Reconnaissance arrived from Thorney Island. With twenty-seven aircraft and ninety-five pupils, the school soon started training from its new base. However, the German offensive in France and the entry of Italy into the war altered the situation dramatically. The school was given instructions to withdraw on 11 June, and following the refusal of the French Government to allow RAF aircraft to bomb Italy from southern France, the Channel Islands were used as a refuelling stop for thirty-six Whitleys from 4 Group. Half of the force used Guernsey Airport, taking off during the night of 11 June to attack the Fiat aero-engine works in Turin, and the Ansaldo aircraft factory in Genoa.

Dragon Rapides of BEA await their passengers at Guernsey's terminal in September 1947.

On 16 June the Ansons of the SGR moved out, with the exception of the unserviceable K8825, which was later destroyed. The ground echelon left aboard the SS *Brittany* on the 18th, having detached two parties on Guernsey to service RAF fighters that were to operate as a rearguard. No 17 Squadron operated a detachment of Hurricanes for a short period, but on the 19th the servicing parties left on a train ferry and rejoined the school at Hooton Park.

Both Jersey Airlines and Guernsey Airways operated evacuation services to Exeter between 19 and 21 June, carrying 319 people in their DH86s. Then came a lull until 28 June when three Luftwaffe aircraft reconnoitred the island, followed by He 111s of KG27, which bombed St Peter Port, killing thirty-three and wounding many more. White flags were displayed in the town square and at the airport to deter any further aggression, and on 1 July an advance party of the Wehrmacht arrived at the airport in Ju 52s. The Luftwaffe was soon using Guernsey as a forward base for fighters and reconnaissance aircraft. During the Battle of Britain the Bf 109Es of JG27 and JG53 operated from the grass airfield, but not without problems. On 9 August a fighter of 1/JG53 made an emergency landing following an engine failure and collided with a flak emplacement, killing three men and injuring three more. 4/JG53 flew from Guernsey to support bombing raids on the West Country, such as that on 25 September by KG55 on Filton, but the German fighters could only provide cover to the English coast. After the Battle the Luftwaffe continued to use the airport, but only for communications and transport aircraft.

The Germans evacuated Guernsey on 9 May 1945, and were replaced by 160 Staging Post, which moved from Ibsley to prepare the airport for RAF use. Among the first visitors were Their Majesties the King and Queen, who landed from Jersey in Dakota KN386 on 6 June. Jersey Airlines resumed services to London (Croydon) on 21 June, followed by inter-island services on 18 July.

The airport was still grass-surfaced during the 1950s, but often suffered from waterlogging. As part of a major development programme in 1960 a 4,800-foot tarmac runway was laid, which remains in operation. A more recent development scheme included the construction of a new passenger terminal, opened on 19 April 2004 (its predecessor, built in 1939, being demolished a few weeks later). Traffic through the airport has steadily increased over the years, and today it is one of the main gateways to the Channel Islands. Current operators include Aurigny Air Services, Flybe, Blue Islands, Lufthansa and VLM, flying to a variety of destinations in the UK, France, Germany, the Netherlands and Switzerland. Cargo operators include Atlantic Airlines and Channel Island Traders. In 2007 Guernsey Airport handled 892,360 passengers, 77% from/to the UK, 21% inter-island and 2% to/from the continent.

The RAF association with the island continues with the annual RAFA flying display and with the adoption of 201 Squadron as 'Guernsey's Own', which dates back to the opening of the airport, when the unit was flying Saro London flying boats. A unit museum and display in Castle Cornet, St Peter Port, keeps this alive today.

Flybe BAe146 G-JEAT arrives at Guernsey in August 2002.

Aurigny Trislander G-BEVT on finals at Guernsey in June 2005.

DH60G Moth G-ACCW beside the Haldon clubhouse in 1933.

HALDON, Devon

SX915765, 2 miles NW of Teignmouth

Haldon airfield was developed by Mr Parkhouse of the Agra Engineering Company, a Teignmouth motor firm, on rough moorland just north of the golf course at Little Haldon. With grass planted on its prepared surface and a hangar erected, flying started with an air meeting on 21 September 1929. Such meetings became popular at Haldon during the 1930s, the Teignmouth Air Race Cup being strongly contested by many well-known British pilots. Alan Cobham also brought his 'circus' to Haldon. In April 1933 the Great Western Railway inaugurated an air service between Cardiff and Plymouth by Westland Wessex tri-motor, which called in at Haldon, and the following year Railway Air Services and Provincial Airways both started DH Dragon services via Teignmouth Airport, as it became known.

The Straight Corporation took over management on 1 January 1937 and regular summer services continued on a request-stop basis. However, this ended with the outbreak of war in September 1939, when civil flying largely ceased. Haldon was later requisitioned by the Air Ministry and used by aircraft from the A&AEE during armament trials on ranges in Lyme Bay. Transferred to the Admiralty and commissioned on 18 August 1941 as HMS *Heron II*, a satellite of Yeovilton, Haldon was used by detachments from 794 Squadron flying Skua target tugs and 761 Squadron with Masters. The aircraft towed targets for Yeovilton-based units and RN warships, but operation from the airfield proved difficult, despite having been extended north and south. During 1942 operating conditions were improved by land drainage and the laying of Sommerfield track, together with a tarmac apron. Haldon Tea-House had been requisitioned to house military guards, and billets were found for other personnel in Teignmouth until April, when Haldon Camp was taken over from the War Office to provide accommodation nearer the airfield.

Defiants and Martinets were able to use Haldon following these improvements, but high winds and low cloud often curtailed flying. In January 1943 the Admiralty transferred the name HMS *Heron II* to Charlton Horethorne and in May reduced Haldon to C&M. The airfield was used occasionally by visiting aircraft, and ATC gliders were flown from the site. Efforts were made to re-establish civil flying from Haldon in 1946, but the airfield eventually fell into disuse. It has since reverted to moorland, with only a few concrete building foundations remaining.

Main features:
Runways: 002° 2,700ft x 435ft, 047° 2,082ft x 450ft, 137° 1,500ft x 450ft, grass.

Sunderland III G-AGIA Haslemere *at Hamworthy in September 1943.*

HAMWORTHY (POOLE), Dorset

SZ035900, 1 mile S of Parkstone (Technical Base SY986903)

Even today flying to the USA is an adventure for most people, but consider what it must have been like in the dark days of 1940. Passengers were taken by Pullman train to Poole, where they would alight at a windswept platform at the eastern side of the harbour to be shepherded into a passenger reception masquerading as a pottery factory. After security checks they went by marine craft out to a Short C Class flying boat that was swinging at its mooring in the open harbour. Once all of its passengers were aboard, the aircraft's engines would be started and, after taxying into position, it would take off across Poole's splendid natural harbour, which had been cleared for the occasion. The C flying boats could not cross the Atlantic direct, but would go via Foynes in Eire, Botwood in Newfoundland and Montreal, before going on to the blazing night lights of unrationed and neutral New York. The change from blacked-out Britain must have been spectacular, but it was only for the few priority passengers, the five return flights made between August and November being mainly mail and freight services for the Government.

Poole Harbour had been earmarked by Imperial Airways in 1938 as a likely base for its flying boat operations should war come, as its terminal at Hythe would be vulnerable to enemy air attack. With hostilities the airline came under the control of the National Air Communications organisation, and its flying boats were indeed moved from Hythe to Poole. Only basic shore facilities were initially set up, maintenance being carried out at designated moorings just off the main channel on the north side of Brownsea Island, or, for more involved work, at Hythe, where engineering facilities were retained. In Poole Harbour the RAF had marked out four water runways with buoys and rubber tyres.

In April 1940 BOAC, formed from British Airways and Imperial Airways, took over the Atlantic services and flights to Africa. Others, by C Class flying boats, went on from Cairo to Lagos, Durban, Karachi, Singapore and Sydney. When the French capitulated the eastabout flights were initially suspended, but resumed with Blenheim fighter escorts across the Channel and into the Bay of Biscay. These services then became established as regular routes, and continued into 1941. In February a new shape was seen at Poole in the shape of a Catalina, acquired by BOAC for services to Lisbon. It was later joined by another, which operated a West African service.

However, these operations were not without their problems, as on 11 May 1941, when an He 111 dropped several bombs over Poole Harbour. Although the Heinkel was brought down by AA fire, one of its bombs hit Short S21 *Maia*, which was destroyed. This aeroplane had been designed to carry a floatplane, the *Mercury*, to extend its range (although successful, war brought the project to an end and *Maia* was converted into a standard Short S30 Empire flying boat). A few days later

Sandringham V G-AHZB Portland *of BOAC takes off from Hamworthy in 1946.*

the first of three Boeing 314A flying boats arrived in Poole; these had entered service with BOAC and were flown to Foynes, then via Bathurst and Bermuda to the USA.

The summer of 1942 saw heavy engagement by Coastal Command in the Battle of the Atlantic, its main bases at Mount Batten and Pembroke Dock being kept very busy. It was therefore decided to use Poole Harbour, and an operating base was set up about $1\frac{1}{2}$ miles west of Poole in the northern end of the Wareham Channel. A slipway was started at the end of June 1942, but there was little room for hangars or other buildings. A number of houses were therefore requisitioned for workshops, administrative, domestic and operational purposes. RAF Hamworthy opened on 1 August, but when the nine Sunderlands of 461(RAAF) Squadron arrived from Mount Batten on 5 September the station's operational base had been moved to Saltern Pier.

Sunderland crews flying from Hamworthy were mainly engaged on daylight anti-submarine patrols over the Bay of Biscay, the crews travelling to Mount Batten for the occasional night take-off. Unfortunately the Luftwaffe was also active in the area, and during September 1942 three of 461's Sunderlands were intercepted by Ju 88 fighters, one being shot down on the 1st. Nonetheless, eight attacks were made on U-boats and a blockade-runner seriously damaged. In October the Squadron was also engaged in the build-up to Operation *Torch*, escorting convoys heading south across the Bay, additionally flying supplies and personnel to Gibraltar in support of 210 Squadron's operations from the Rock.

In January 1943 squadron HQ moved to the Harbour Yacht Club; accommodation was taken up in Parkstone, Lilliput and Sandbanks, and the Harbour Heights Hotel was taken over as an officers' mess. Although the Squadron's complement had been increased to twelve, it lost T9085, which failed to return on 21 January. Intensive activity followed during February and March 1943, hunting U-boats inbound and outbound from their bases on the French coast. Although fifteen attacks were made, only one submarine was sunk. On 21 March Sunderland T9111 was written off following a crash on the mudflats, its crew managing to escape unhurt.

The Sunderlands of 461 Squadron moved to Pembroke Dock on 21 April, exchanging places with the Catalinas of 210 Squadron. They too started operations over the Bay of Biscay, with 'Enclose 2', a Coastal Command offensive operation. Strengthened by crews from 119 Squadron, the Catalinas flew patrol lines across the Bay, designed to force U-boats to transit submerged and exhaust their batteries. When the submariners changed their routes, the RAF's patrol lines changed, Catalinas flying round-the-clock patrols along the north-west coast of Spain.

However, by late 1943 Hamworthy's limitations as an operational base resulted in a 19 Group decision to move out, re-establishing Calshot as a main diversion base. On 1 January 1944 No 210 Squadron moved to Sullom Voe, and on the 13th Hamworthy was transferred to Transport

Command for the use of M Flight (BOAC) in running its services to Portugal and India – for these the aircraft were flown in RAF markings. On 1 May 1944 RAF Hamworthy was closed, and a few weeks later BOAC was forced to temporarily move its operations to Pembroke Dock to make way for hundreds of landing craft brought to Poole for the invasion of Europe. RN and US Coastguard vessels were amongst the 300 craft that left the Harbour for Normandy on 5 June 1944.

Resuming operations from Poole in September, BOAC used the harbour as a base for some of its forty-two flying boats during the ensuing four years. Post-war flying boat routes were pioneered from Poole, using Hythe Class G-AGJM to make a survey flight to Australia, New Zealand, Hong Kong, China and Japan from February to April 1946. The airline finally left on 31 March 1948, transferring operations to Southampton.

A Spitfire VB of 312 Squadron being readied at its Harrowbeer dispersal in June 1942.

HARROWBEER, Devon

SX513680, half a mile W of Yelverton on A386

Constructed during late 1940/early 1941, Harrowbeer was designed as a satellite for Exeter, within 10 Group, Fighter Command. It was located on the edge of Dartmoor, some 6 miles from Plymouth, and was provided with three tarmac runways, ten hangars, a control tower (later repositioned) and a number of fighter pens. Opened on 1 August 1941, Harrowbeer's first residents a fortnight later were a detachment of Blenheim IVs of 500 Squadron, Coastal Command, briefly deployed from Bircham Newton for intruder missions over Luftwaffe airfields in France.

The first unit to be based at the new airfield was 302 (Polish) Squadron, which moved from Warmwell on 6 October 1941 to convert from Hurricane IIBs to Spitfire Vs. A few weeks later 276 Squadron formed at Harrowbeer on 21 October from ASR detachments at Roborough, Warmwell, Perranporth and Fairwood Common. With Lysanders for search and dinghy dropping and Walruses for rescue, the Squadron covered the western English Channel and Bristol Channel. A and HQ Flights soon moved to Portreath, but B Flight with two Walrus and three Lysanders remained to cover the Exeter sector. On 25 October 130 Squadron arrived from Portreath with Spitfire IIAs to convert to Mk Vs. It had flown convoy patrols and bomber escorts and, having worked up on its new mounts, resumed operations from Harrowbeer, joined by 302 Squadron. Both also flew sweeps over northern France until 30 November, when 130 Squadron moved to Warmwell. The Poles continued operations from Harrowbeer, flying some of their *Circuses* from the airfield, but often having to fly eastwards to 11 Group stations for briefings before rendezvous with the bombers.

A Bf 109 was claimed during a raid on Cherbourg Docks on 17 April 1942, followed a week later by a probable FW 190. On 26 April the Poles moved to Warmwell, replaced by 312 (Czech) Squadron from Fairwood Common on 2 May. They took up the fighter escort role in their Spitfire Vs, also mounting sweeps over France. On 3 June they encountered thirty FW 190s near Cherbourg, claiming one during the ensuing dogfight with a further four damaged, but lost two of their own. The Czechs moved to Redhill on 19 August to take part in Operation *Jubilee*, the largest air operation mounted up to that time, covering the Commando raid on Dieppe. Led by Sqn Ldr Cernak, 312 flew three missions that day, sinking one E-boat, damaging another and claiming two Do 217s and two FW 190s as probables. The unit was soon back and remained at Harrowbeer until 10 October, when it moved on to Church Stanton.

Hurricanes replaced Spitfires that day, when 175 Squadron arrived from Warmwell in the fighter-bomber role. It had mixed local and convoy escort patrols with attacks on enemy shipping, including E-boats, which were unpleasant adversaries. The station was enlivened by a visit from 1426 (Enemy Aircraft) Flight on 24 October, several captured enemy aircraft being demonstrated to the fighter pilots.

No 175 Squadron moved to Gatwick on 6 December and the airfield was relatively quiet until the 18th when 193 Squadron formed. Scheduled to receive Typhoons, with insufficient numbers available the unit got Hurricane IIBs, but these were gradually phased out as Typhoons arrived during January and February 1943. The unit began operations on 1 April, with shipping patrols and MTB escorts, but soon took the offensive with a dive-bombing attack on Guipavas airfield and anti-*Rhubarb* sorties against Bf 109 and FW 190 fighter-bombers raiding towns on the South Coast. During February and March the Typhoons had shared the airfield with the Whirlwinds of 263 Squadron, which were busy with night *Rhubarbs* on French airfields.

The arrival of 183 Squadron's 'Tiffies' on 5 June 1943 meant that the Harrowbeer units could operate as a wing for the first time. Attacks were made on road and rail communications, and airfields in France. Both squadrons left in August for 11 Group stations, but 193 returned in September to pair up with 266 Squadron from Duxford in a reformed Harrowbeer Wing. Targets remained mainly railways and airfields, but in November 1943 they began to concentrate on V-1 launch sites, code-named *Noball* operations. A typical day was 5 December, when a sweep in appalling weather forced the Typhoons to return on the deck for a quick refuel, followed by another sweep providing cover for a USAAF B-17 formation, on the return trip giving close escort to sixty B-24s picked up north of Lorient.

Movements in the spring of 1944 saw 193 Squadron off to Fairlop on 20 February, 266 to Acklington on 15 March, 263 returning on 19 March, this time with Typhoons, and 131 Squadron appearing with Spitfire Mark VIIs. 263 carried on with tactical strikes, and 131 flew high-altitude patrols, fighter sweeps and bomber escorts. More arrivals on 20 April looked rather incongruous among the high-speed fighters, when twelve Swordfish of 835 Squadron, FAA, flew in. These were equipped with ASV radar and rocket projectiles for anti-submarine operations as part of 156 (GR) Wing, RAF Coastal Command. On their first operation from Harrowbeer on the night of 30 April/1 May one Swordfish was shot down by coastal batteries, and another two aircraft failed to return. When 131 Squadron left for Culmhead on 24 May it was replaced that day by 610 Squadron, flying in its Spitfire XIVs from Bolt Head.

In early June, with the approach of D-Day, Harrowbeer was buzzing with activity – more than fifty Typhoons, Spitfires and Swordfish were operating as part of the build-up. Typhoons swept the Western Approaches, searching for enemy vessels, Spitfires mounted patrols, usually in pairs, looking for enemy reconnaissance aircraft or intruders, while Swordfish maintained nightly patrols for enemy shipping.

Just prior to the invasion, the airfield was also used by the Typhoons of 124 Wing (193, 197 and 257 Squadrons) for operations against German communications. Following the landings a number of Spitfire IX units, including 1 and 611 Squadrons, briefly used Harrowbeer for beachhead sweeps. On 23 June No 64 Squadron, another Spitfire IX unit, arrived from Deanland for a two-month stay. The Typhoons of 263 Squadron departed for Bolt Head on 19 July, and 1 Squadron's Spitfires briefly reappeared a few days later to provide close support for the Army. The Spitfire XIVs of 610

Spitfire IX MK126 of 126 Squadron at Harrowbeer in August 1944.

Squadron left for Friston on 2 July, replaced the following day by the Mark IXs of 126 Squadron. Together with 64 Squadron, they flew escorts, patrols and shipping strikes. Success was varied, but on 1 August the Wing Leader, Wg Cdr 'Bird' Wilson, destroyed two Bf 109s while escorting Mosquitoes. On 14 August No 126 Squadron swept over a Luftwaffe airfield just as its aircraft were landing, shooting down six and claiming another probable.

With the outstanding success of the Normandy landings and follow-up operations, units began to move away from Harrowbeer, starting with the Swordfish of 838 Squadron, which left for Worthy Down on 8 August 1944. They were followed by the Spitfire squadrons, departing for Bradwell Bay at the end of the month. Although Harrowbeer was then put on C&M, it was used occasionally by USN communications aircraft visiting Fleet Air Wing 7 Headquarters in Plymouth. They were not the first US aircraft to use the airfield, as two C-47s of the USAAF had arrived on 28 August, bringing in Major Glenn Miller and the American Band of the ETO to play for US forces in the Plymouth area.

When Exeter was transferred to Flying Training Command in January 1945, Harrowbeer was reopened as a self-accounting station within 10 Group with parenting responsibilities for Bolt Head and the GCI Stations at Exminster and Hope Cove. ASR Walruses of 275 Squadron arrived from Exeter on 10 January, staying until 15 February, when they moved to Linton-on-Ouse. The mixed fleet operated by 691 Squadron on target facilities work, including Defiants, Oxfords, Hurricanes and even Barracudas, flew in from Roborough on 21 February, and Vengeances were also received shortly afterwards.

The Mustangs of 26 Squadron passed through on 14 January, staying for a week, and returned again for training with 691 Squadron on 1 May 1945. This time they stayed until 23 May, when

Harrowbeer in 1946, with fighter pens evident on the southern side of the airfield.

Harrowbeer's fighter pens are still evident in August 2005, with the original control tower, now a tearoom, across the taxiways.

they left for Chilbolton, then Belgium. The last unit to visit Harrowbeer was 329 (Free French) Squadron, arriving from Skaebrae with Spitfire XVIs on 25 May, to take part in a flypast over Paris on 17 June celebrating the end of the war. The French Spitfires returned two days later and remained until leaving for Fairwood Common on 14 July. When 691 Squadron departed for Exeter on 1 August 1945, there was little remaining air activity at Harrowbeer, and the airfield reverted to C&M. No 229 MU used the site for storage, but it was finally closed on 13 May 1946.

The Ministry of Civil Aviation then took possession of the airfield, as there was a proposal to develop it as Plymouth Airport in preference to Roborough. Strong local opposition developed, while in December 1947 19 Group Communications Flight started using the airfield, having moved its Dominies and Ansons from Roborough. The flight stayed until August 1948, by which time plans to develop an airport had been dropped. Harrowbeer's accommodation was then used by the personnel of the radar unit at RAF Sharpitor until the early 1950s, when the latter closed. The station was then closed and cleared, but large portions of the taxiways remain, together with several fighter pens, and the original control tower is now a tearoom. On 15 August 1981 the first Station Commander, Gp Capt E. F. Ward, unveiled a memorial to those who had served at RAF Harrowbeer.

Main features:
Runways: 110° 3,900ft x 150ft, 166° 3,300ft x 150ft, 229° 2,700ft x 150ft, concrete and asphalt. *Hangars:* two Bellman, eight O-Blister. *Hardstandings:* eighteen TE. *Accommodation:* RAF Officers 69, SNCOs 139, ORs 1,260; WAAF Officers 7, ORs 224.

HENSTRIDGE, Dorset

ST752205, 1 1/2 miles E of Henstridge off A30

Travel along the A30 today and you will easily miss the airfield, but in 1943 Henstridge was swarming with fighter planes. These were Seafires, as it was one of the Navy's main flying training bases. The origins of Henstridge date back to the summer of 1939, when the Air Ministry Aerodromes Board offered the Admiralty several airfield sites for its newly regained Fleet Air Arm. These included Styles Farm in west Dorset, bordering Somerset, and when work started on 355 acres of farmland in August 1941 the site had become known as Henstridge, after the nearby village. Five runways were laid, one later being configured as an aircraft carrier's flight deck, complete with arrestor wires. Drem lighting was installed and numerous hangars and dispersals were built, but it was not until 1 April 1943 that the station was commissioned as HMS *Dipper*. The first unit to arrive was 761 Squadron, which was also 2 Naval Air Fighter School, training newly qualified pilots to fly fighters on its fleet of more than a hundred Fulmars, Seafire 1Bs, Spitfire Mk Vs and Masters. Later in the year an additional 18 acres were requisitioned at Gibb's Marsh Farm for an Aircraft Rectification Hangar site, and more land was obtained at nearby Fifehead Magdalen and Priors Down to provide extra living accommodation.

Seafire IBs, including NX957, of Henstridge-based 761 Squadron, in 1943.

When 894 Squadron disembarked from HMS *Illustrious* on 18 October 1943, it moved in to receive the new Seafire III. Together with 887 Squadron, arriving on 18 December, also with the new type, they made up 24 Naval Fighter Wing, and stayed until January 1944, transferring to Burscough. Another arrival in November 1943 was 794 Squadron, a naval air-firing unit, which brought Sea Hurricanes, Masters, Defiants and Martinets for a brief stay; it departed the following month for Charlton Horethorne. In February 1944 No 748 Squadron flew in from St Merryn, having formed there as part of the School of Air Combat the previous September, with the Barracuda. Other residents in early March 1944 were the forty-two aircraft of 3 Naval Fighter Wing. Consisting of 885 and 886 Squadrons with Seafire IIIs, and 808 and 897 with Spitfire Vs, it had formed at Lee-on-Solent as the naval contribution to 34 Reconnaissance Wing of the 2nd TAF, and used Henstridge for its pilots to practise low-level flying and spotting.

Sea Fury F10 TF908, 767 Squadron, Henstridge, 1952.

Henstridge from the air in June 2008, the outline of its five runways remaining clearly visible.

Spring 1944 was to be the busiest period during Henstridge's history, with almost 150 aircraft crowding its hardstandings, runways and airspace. At the end of March No 3 NAFWg returned to Lee, from where in June it was to take part in Operation *Neptune*, the naval phase of *Overlord*, the role being to spot for the guns of RN warships bombarding Normandy coastal defences. Henstridge was then left to the Naval Air Fighter School until early June, when it was joined by 718 Squadron. Formed at Henstridge on 5 June with Seafires and Spitfire PR XIIIs, the unit's role was to train pilots in reconnaissance and ground support, later assuming the title of the Naval School of Army Cooperation.

By October Henstridge had become the major training base for Seafire pilots and the only naval fighter school flying the type. It began training on the new Griffon-engined Seafires when they were introduced into service during 1945. Most graduating pilots were then posted to the Pacific, where the Far East Fleet was operating eight Seafire squadrons from its six in-theatre carriers.

The Naval School of Army Cooperation moved to Ballyherbert in August 1945, leaving 761 Squadron as sole resident until it disbanded in March 1946. Henstridge then became a satellite of Yeovilton, and was little used until August 1949 when Yeovilton-based 767 Squadron began to use the dummy deck for the training of deck landing control officers, using Seafire F15s. By 1951 the squadron was flying Firefly Is and Sea Fury FB11s, and was also using Henstridge to train pilots. The Squadron also trained at sea, using the carriers *Triumph* and *Illustrious*. At the end of December 1951 it relocated to Henstridge. Firefly Mk 4s started arriving to re-equip 767 in March 1952, and the unit went to sea several times during that year. On 20 September 1952, the final day of Exercise *Mainbrace* with HMS *Triumph*, the Squadron disembarked to Stretton. Reduced to inactive status, the station was reopened as a satellite of Yeovilton in 1954 and used for night deck-landing practice until it was finally closed in June 1957.

Air Whaling Ltd was formed by ex-FAA pilot Alan Bristow in 1953, using Henstridge as the base for Dragonfly, and later Whirlwind helicopter, maintenance and operations. He formed Bristow Helicopters at the airfield in 1955, initially operating four Widgeons for oil exploration in the Persian Gulf on behalf of Shell, but in 1958, with the company starting to prosper, it moved to new premises at Redhill. Shortly afterwards the Admiralty sold off the hangars and a part of the site nearest the A30, which later became Henstridge Trading Estate. The airfield itself was later sold to local farmers, one of whom reopened part of it for private flying. A number of light and executive aircraft were

Dorset & Somerset Air Ambulance EC135 G-DORS returns to its Henstridge base in August 2008.

flown from the airfield, and the PFA mounted fly-ins during the 1970s. A proposal to take over the airfield as a broadcasting relay station by the BBC was fought off in the early 1980s, and flying has continued from Henstridge ever since. Today a thriving flying club maintains the one remaining runway (which includes the dummy deck), and regularly uses it for club flying meetings and fly-ins.

A number of former airfield buildings remain on site, including the control tower and a number of hangars. Some of these house resident aircraft, including the Somerset & Dorset Air Ambulance EC135, maintained at Henstridge on constant readiness.

Main features:
Runways: 029° 3,000ft x 90ft, 075° 3,000ft x 90ft, 114° 3,600ft x 90ft, 160° 3,000ft x 90ft, 075° 3,000ft x 90ft, concrete and asphalt. *Hangars:* sixty 70-foot, sixteen Squadron, twelve Storage. *Hardstandings:* three *Accommodation:* RN Officers 211, ORs 1,232; WRNS Officers 13, ORs 440.

HIGH POST, Wiltshire

SU145372, 4 miles N of Salisbury on A345

Situated at the highest point on the road between Salisbury and Amesbury, High Post was established as an aerodrome by local businessman Sqn Ldr J. E. Dorian-Webb. It was opened in May 1931 as the Wiltshire Light Aeroplane & Country Club, initially with one Redwing light aircraft, an ex-Army hut as clubhouse and a galvanised shed as a hangar, on 40 acres of rough pasture. In October a more modern clubhouse and two hangars were built. One of the hangars was erected on the main A345 road, where the C292 crossed it, and the other, which had been moved from the former Stonehenge airfield, was located beside the clubhouse, which was a quarter of a mile along the C292 towards Middle Woodford.

The Wiltshire Flying Club was formed as a registered company in 1932 at the airfield, and set up the Wiltshire Flying School to train pilots under Air Ministry subsidy. Another 110 acres were

Spitfire Is being prepared in the High Post assembly hangar in 1941.

purchased, and in October 1936 a new building was constructed along the main road, which comprised offices, an observation tower, radio-room and fully licensed residential hotel with restaurant. The Wiltshire Flying School was by then flying the Cirrus Moth, Spartan Arrow, Gypsy Moth, and Desoutter Monoplane. Together with the Royal Artillery Aero Club, it also flew the Piper Cub from High Post, and from 1938 both participated in the Government's Civil Air Guard scheme, which encouraged civilians to qualify as pilots. The Wiltshire Flying School was the first to operate the Taylorcraft Auster, two being delivered in early 1939.

With the outbreak of war in September 1939 all non-essential civil flying was stopped, and the Wiltshire Flying School ceased operation. Its whole staff then volunteered, and many of the school's 150 former pupils went on to fly with the RAF, some flying during the Battle of Britain, others becoming flying instructors. The school's aircraft were stored away in the hangars at High Post, and the airfield was deserted until February 1940 when members of D Flight, which had been formed at Larkhill on the 1st, arrived. They surveyed the stored aircraft, which had been requisitioned, and were particularly interested in the Cubs and Austers for operational use.

The first unit to actually be based at High Post was 112 (RCAF) Squadron, the advance party of which arrived from Old Sarum on 6 June 1940. With a German invasion imminently expected, the Canadians immediately started defensive work, digging slit trenches and camouflaging airfield buildings. Although the hotel was taken over as operations centre and mess, accommodation for the majority of personnel was under canvas. The squadron's first aircraft, three Lysanders, arrived on 13 June, followed shortly afterwards by three Tiger Moths for training and communication, then four more Lysanders. Flying started with training in artillery observation during live shoots on the Larkhill ranges. Following the loss of a Hart Trainer from nearby Netheravon to a German fighter on 21 July, all aircraft were flown fully armed.

Several aircraft from the Special Duty Flight based at Christchurch used High Post in early August. They flew two Scott Viking sailplanes for towing trials, but unfortunately on 3 August one crashed while trying to avoid the other. A further crash a month later involved one of 112 Squadron's Tiger Moths, which came down to the north-west of the airfield. Following the squadron's departure for Digby on 13 November, other units began to use High Post for training. Soon Harts, Hinds, Harvards and Battles of 1 FTS, Netheravon, and Masters and Oxfords of CFS, Upavon, were seen in the airfield's circuits.

The Seafire F45 prototype, TM379, being test-flown from High Post by Jeffrey Quill in October 1944.

On 20 November 1940 the former Wiltshire Flying Club hangars were requisitioned for the Supermarine Company, for the assembly of Spitfires manufactured down the hill in Salisbury. This activity had started virtually overnight, following the bombing of the company's factory at Woolston on 26 September. Production and assembly work was dispersed to several sites in Hampshire and Wiltshire, including Salisbury, where garages and motor showrooms were requisitioned. Fuselages were manufactured at Wessex Motors in New Street, wings and other main assemblies were produced at the Wilts & Dorset Bus Company garage in Castle Street, while further along the road at Anna Valley Motors sub-assemblies such as tail units and wing leading edges, and components including fuel tanks and undercarriage doors, were fabricated. On completion the fuselages and wings were taken by low-loader up Castle Hill and on to High Post, where they were assembled and prepared for flight test. The first Salisbury-produced Spitfire to be flown in this way was Mk I X4497, on 12 January 1941, which was only two and a half months after production started in the city. Later, to meet increased demand, two purpose-built factories were erected in Castle Road.

While the main activity at High Post during 1941 and 1942 was Spitfire assembly and flight testing, the airfield continued to be used for training by nearby flying schools. The proximity of Boscombe Down was always a potential hazard, and this was tragically illustrated on 10 September 1943 when Lancaster BIII JA894 of 617 Squadron in Boscombe's circuit collided with Oxford EB981 from 7 FIS Upavon, making a touch-and-go at High Post. All six crew aboard both aircraft were killed.

Spitfire Mks I, V, IX, XII and XIV were manufactured in Salisbury, together with Seafires, most of which were assembled and test-flown at High Post. After clearance they were delivered by ferry pilots to the RAF MUs. Due to its increased usage, the original grass airfield was enlarged in the spring of 1942, the diversion of the road to Woodford enabling a runway of some 7,500 feet to be laid out on the grass, together with two others of 5,280 and 4,500 feet. Facilities were also improved at this time with the building of a new two-bay hangar. High Post gradually took over from Worthy Down as the home of Supermarine's Experimental Flight Test Department. Chief Test Pilot Jeffrey Quill moved his office there, and had a dozen test pilots on his staff, including Mike Lithgow, Les Colquhoun, Guy Morgan and later John Derry. Together they undertook development flying on new variants and types as well as flight-testing production aircraft. This included the projected Spitfire replacement, the Spiteful, which made its maiden flight from High Post on 30 June 1944 in the hands of Jeffrey Quill. Types from other company factories were also often seen at the airfield, including the Walrus and its replacement the Sea Otter.

Spiteful F14 RB520, which first flew from High Post on 22 September 1945, is seen after having been fitted with a sting arrestor hook for Seafang trials.

After the war High Post remained the test centre for Supermarine as production of the Spitfire continued, with the final variants, the Mk 22s and 24s, appearing, followed by the naval version, the Seafire FR47. Variety came with Sea Otter flight-testing and work with the Supermarine S24/37, otherwise known as 'Dumbo', an experimental high-wing monoplane with a variable-incidence wing. Supermarine's two-seat Spitfire VIII G-AIDN also appeared from time to time, which John Derry often flew as company demonstration pilot. Although the Spiteful had been cancelled in favour of other, jet-powered, types, some examples were retained for trials, and one of these, RB518, with a three-stage booster fitted to its Griffon, laid claim to being the fastest piston-engined aircraft in the world, officially attaining a speed of 494mph. The Spiteful's naval counterpart, the Seafang, became a useful test bed for the E/10/44, Supermarine's first jet. The Attacker, as it became known, was effectively a jet-powered version of the Seafang, with the latter's laminar-flow

The Attacker prototype TS409 during test-flying from High Post in July 1946.

wing being incorporated into its design. The Attacker prototype was assembled at High Post before being taken along the road to Boscombe Down for its maiden flight. This took place on 27 July 1946, with Jeffrey Quill at the controls, landing back at High Post. The jet flew from the airfield until Supermarine's flight test operations transferred to Chilbolton on 31 May 1947, prompted by the expansion of Boscombe Down, which had already extended its main runway towards High Post.

As the Wiltshire School of Flying, the pre-war residents re-established themselves at High Post in early 1946 with Austers and a Magister, joined by a reformed Royal Artillery Flying Club. However, with the expansion of Boscombe Down, they too decided that High Post was untenable, and transferred to Thruxton in March. Shortly after the closure of the airfield, Supermarine's flight test hangar was dismantled and moved to Boscombe Down, and there it still stands today, having been in use as A Squadron's main hangar for many years. Other buildings at High Post have been demolished or moved, but the original flying club hangar remains in place on the crossroads alongside the High Post Hotel, currently utilised by Apsley Engineering Ltd.

Adjoining the airfield site to the north is a pyrotechnics factory, established as the Wessex Aircraft Engineering Company in 1933 for the manufacture of aerial flares. The company merged with James Pain & Company in 1965 to form Pains Wessex, and for a while made fireworks for the domestic market as well as defence products. Nowadays, as part of the Chemring Group, the company develops, manufactures and proof-tests missile decoys and chaff for the RAF and RN at High Post.

HOLMSLEY SOUTH, Hampshire

SZ215988, 5 miles NE of Christchurch on A38

Carved out of the New Forest, Holmsley South was constructed as a standard Class A airfield during 1941/42. Like Beaulieu, it was urgently required for Coastal Command squadrons covering convoys heading to North Africa for Operation *Torch*, the landings in North Africa. In the haste to open the airfield on 1 September 1942, the domestic sites (which had been dispersed in nearby woodland) were incomplete, and living conditions were chaotic. The first aircraft to appear were the Wellington GRVIIIs of 547 Squadron, which reformed at Holmsley on 21 October. Surprisingly they were joined a few days later by B-24Ds of the USAAF. The Liberators were from the 330th Bombardment Squadron, 93 Bombardment Wing, diverted from the 8th AF to provide *Torch* convoy escorts.

As well as three runways, the new airfield was initially provided with two T2 hangars, followed by three more in 1943. Thirty-eight dispersals were eventually to be laid, but only two of these were in place in October 1942, and as more aircraft arrived they had to be parked on the secondary runways. Operations started on 28 October, and as the sortie rate gradually increased, so did U-boat sightings, but few attacks resulted. Luftwaffe fighters were a constant threat, and a B-24 was attacked by five Ju 88s on 21 November; its gunners managed to shoot down two of the enemy and claim a third before reaching cloud.

The Americans returned to Alconbury on the completion of *Torch*, and 547 Squadron moved to Chivenor on 10 December, being replaced by 58 Squadron, which flew in its Whitley VIIs from Stornoway eight days earlier. At Holmsley 58 Squadron re-equipped with the Halifax GRII, flying its first operations with the new type on 23 February 1943 – anti-submarine patrols over the Western Approaches. The following month it was joined by 502 Squadron, newly converted from Whitleys to Halifaxes at St Eval.

Another unit arrived in May, also in the process of converting from Whitleys to Halifaxes. However, this one, 295 Squadron, was part of 28 Wing in the airborne forces role. Crew conversion was completed as more Halifaxes arrived and, despite three serious crashes (including the loss of one crew), the unit was ready for its first operation, towing thirty-six Horsas to Morocco for subsequent airborne landings in Sicily.

After a spell of detachment to St Eval, both 58 and 502 Squadrons returned during July 1943 to continue anti-submarine patrols from Holmsley. They were soon in action, for on 20 July Halifax 'E' of 58 Squadron joined with a US Liberator to sink U-558. On 30 July two of 502's Halifaxes, together with a Sunderland, caught and attacked a pack of three U-boats, sinking U-462, then three days later another of the Squadron's aircraft severely damaged a German destroyer. However, 58 Squadron lost three of its aircraft to Ju 88 fighters over the Bay of Biscay during this period. One of the last messages received from one of them was, 'Have just made contact with fourteen Ju 88s.' Two Halifaxes lost in accidents meant a total of five losses during a nine-day period. On 27

September B/58 Squadron failed to return, with the Station Commander, Gp Capt Mead DFC, a member of the crew. The Halifax had found, attacked and sunk U-221, but was hit by return fire and forced to ditch. Six of the crew, including the Group Captain, managed to scramble into a dinghy and after eleven days at sea were picked up by an Allied destroyer. On 11 December 1943 two aircraft of 58 Squadron, and two of 502, took off on their last patrol from Holmsley, subsequently landing at St David's where they rejoined the remainder of their squadrons, which had in the meantime moved there from the New Forest.

The plan for Holmsley was that it should then be used, together with other airfields in southern England, for the build-up to the invasion of France. The south Hampshire airfields were to become the forward bases for the 2nd TAF and, with Holmsley allocated to 10 Group, the first of these units arrived at Holmsley in March 1944. These were three Canadian Squadrons – 441, 442 and 443 – which flew in their Spitfire IXs from Digby. Working up as 144 Wing, the Canadians began flying fighter sweeps over western France on 15 March. They did not stay long, however, and on 1 April moved to Westhampnett, exchanging places with 121 Wing, comprising 174, 175 and 242 Squadrons flying the rocket-armed Typhoon IB, which spent the following weeks attacking ground targets in France. On the eve of D-Day they attacked and destroyed the key radar site at Cap de la Hague, which obscured the Germans' view of the invasion fleet. The Typhoons spent the next few weeks disrupting enemy communications and harassing enemy transport to the rear of the invasion beaches.

A week after its arrival, 121 Wing had been joined by 418 (RCAF) Squadron's Mosquito FBVIs. Flying intruder missions over the continent both by day and night, they targeted Luftwaffe bases, and while at Holmsley brought down some fifty enemy aircraft in combat, destroying many more on the ground. It was during one of these missions on 14 June that a crew spotted one of the first V-1 flying bombs in flight, which marked the onset of the German V-1 offensive on southern England. The squadron then concentrated on fighting this new menace, and started flying *Anti-Diver* patrols at night. During the first of these, its Mosquitoes shot down three V-1s and claimed a further probable. By the end of July a further thirty were added to the score. Not all of these were from Holmsley, for on 14 July the Squadron moved to Hurn.

Meanwhile, 121 Wing had moved to the continent in mid-June, replaced by the Mustangs of 133 Wing from Coolham. This was an Anglo-Polish wing, consisting of 129, 306 and 315 Squadrons. Employed mainly on ground attack, while supporting US troops on 22 June they lost

Typhoon IB JR142 HH-D of 175 Squadron being recovered after turning over at Holmsley South in May 1944.

Mustangs of 129 Squadron being rearmed at Holmsley South in June 1944.

two Mustangs from 315 Squadron. The OC, Sqn Ldr Herbaczewski, saw that one of the downed pilots, W/O Tamowicz, had landed in a swamp and was injured. The OC landed at an airstrip just behind the US front line, and in a borrowed jeep drove out to the swamp. Having waded in to rescue the injured pilot, he drove him back to the strip, loaded him into the Mustang and, sitting on his lap, returned to base! Two days later twenty Mustangs from 306 and 315 Squadrons encountered forty German fighters on a fighter sweep and shot down nine for the loss of only one Mustang. Towards the end of June the squadrons of 133 Wing started moving out, 129 being the last to leave, on 9 July, for Brenzett.

This left Holmsley South to the USAAF, which needed a forward base to extend the range of its medium bombers. On 24 July the B-26 Marauders of the 394th Bomb Group (which consisted of the 84th, 585th, 586th and 587th Bomb Squadrons), 9th AF, arrived. Their role at this time was to assist the breakout of General Patton's 3rd Army in the St Lo area. Attacks were made against bridges, railway depots and ammunition dumps, many of which were heavily defended. The group flew twenty-four missions during its time at Holmsley, losing six B-26s in the process. It moved to A13/Tour-en-Bessin on 31 August.

Armourers of 586th BS prepare ordnance for the next B-26 operation at Holmsley South in July 1944.

Holmsley remained quiet until 116 Wing, RAF Transport Command, took over, and 167 Squadron reformed there on 21 October 1944 to fly Warwick transports. These began arriving the following month, and by December the Squadron was flying regular services to various Allied bases in Europe and West Africa. No 246 Squadron arrived from Lyneham on 1 December, flying Liberators and Halifaxes on schedules to the Middle and Far East. It also received Yorks at Holmsley, and used these to take on the duties of the VIP Flight of the Northolt-based Metropolitan Communications Squadron in February 1945. Skymasters were received in April, replacing Halifaxes.

No 167 Squadron moved to Blackbushe on 27 March 1945, leaving 246 as sole occupant of Holmsley, flying long-distance passenger services to India. A Battle of Britain display was held in mid-September 1946, but this was the airfield's last big event, as 246 Squadron departed a month later, the unit having been merged with 511 Squadron at Lyneham on 15 October.

The airfield was then closed, its living sites being taken by local councils as temporary housing. In 1950 the land was returned to its previous owners. Parts of the runways remain today at the privately owned western end, but the rest of the airfield has been excavated by the Forestry Commission, apart from the northern taxiways and dispersals, now used as a public road and campsite.

Main features:
Runways: 247° 5,910ft x 150ft, 302° 4,200ft x 150ft, 358° 4,110ft x 150ft, concrete and asphalt. *Hangars:* five T2. *Hardstandings:* thirty-five pan-handle, three loop. *Accommodation:* RAF Officers 177, SNCOs 522, ORs 1,926; WAAF Officers 10, SNCOs 16, ORs 312.

Anson Is N9765, N9561 and N9570 of 9 FTS near Hullavington in September 1939.

HULLAVINGTON, Wiltshire

ST900810, 5 miles N of Chippenham

Construction of Hullavington started in 1936 as one of eleven new stations under the second phase of the RAF Expansion Scheme. Opened on 14 June 1937 as a flying training station with a co-located Aircraft Storage Unit, its technical and domestic buildings were of attractive local Cotswold stone that blended in with the landscape.

The first resident of the new station was 9 MU, formed on 8 July 1938 to administer the ASU, which was located on five sites dispersed around the airfield, each centred on two hangars. The following day 9 FTS arrived from Thornaby, with Harts, Audaxes and Hinds, supplemented by Oxfords and Battles shortly after arrival. In February 1939 the ASU was renumbered as 10 MU, probably to avoid confusion with the FTS. By then aircraft were arriving in ever-increasing numbers, and all-metal types such as the Harvard had to stored outside.

Audaxes K7425, K3711 and K3695 in formation over the Wiltshire countryside not far from their base at Hullavington on 17 April 1940.

Mobilisation brought an influx of personnel, and on the day that war was declared, 3 September 1939, ten Blenheims of 114 Squadron arrived from Wyton, under the Bomber Command *Scatter* plan. They were joined six days later by a further seven Blenheims from 139 Squadron, also from Wyton. However, once it was realised that the Luftwaffe was not raiding East Anglian airfields, the Blenheims returned to their bases.

Becoming 9 SFTS on 3 September, the school also received Harvards. The MU became busier, and as the numbers of arriving aircraft increased rapidly, fields near the dispersal sites had to be used for storage. Flying training and maintenance continued into the winter of 1939/40, but activities on the airfield were severely curtailed by the weather, which got progressively wetter and colder. Courses had to be extended by 9 SFTS, and the backlog was not cleared until April.

In the spring of 1940 invasion was a very real threat, and at Hullavington trenches and gun-pits were dug and concrete pillboxes constructed. On 14 May Training Command gave orders for eight Ansons and twelve Audaxes to be fitted with bomb racks as an anti-invasion force. The airfield was used for camouflage trials, to devise ways of blending it into local surroundings. Hangars and other buildings were painted in brown, black and green shading, while the landing ground's shape was disrupted by the marking of hedgerows in black bitumen to simulate field patterns. The shine from concrete and tarmac surfaces was toned down by the use of stone chippings and bitumen.

This did not, however, prevent the Luftwaffe from calling, its first raid being on 25 June, during night-flying. Bombs were dropped, but no damage was done. However, a further raid by a single He 111 on 14 August resulted in four dead, ten wounded, and damage to a hangar and sixteen aircraft, including two Hurricanes used by the SFTS instructors for local defence. Fighter detachments had earlier been sent to Hullavington – Spitfires of 92 Squadron from Pembrey in early July, followed by Hurricanes of 87 Squadron, which used Hullavington as one of many bases for night patrols over the region.

To free up the main airfield, 9 SFTS used Leighterton as an RLG from March 1940, Babdown Farm from July and Long Newnton from September. By July 9 SFTS had become a single-engined school, and the following February had eighty-four Masters and twenty-four Hurricanes on strength. On 27 February 1941 a low-level daylight raid resulted in damage to a Hurricane and Hampden, but the He 111 had not caught the defences entirely by surprise, and AA guns claimed three hits on it. The only other raid during 1941 was unintentional, a German bomber jettisoning its load over the airfield while being chased by a night-fighter, causing slight damage to dispersed aircraft. During October work started on laying two concrete and tarmac runways.

Hurricane I Z479(?) and Spitfire IIA P7882 of ECFS near Devizes in 1943.

On 14 February 1942 No 9 SFTS was re-titled 9 (P)AFU, to reflect its new role of advanced training for pilots newly qualified from the Empire Air Training Scheme in the blue skies of Canada and South Africa, acclimatising them to British weather and flying conditions. Another change came on 1 April, when the Empire Central Flying School formed, from a nucleus of the CFS, transferred from Upavon. The ECFS was formed to pool the vast experience that existed within the worldwide RAF flying training organisation and to achieve standardised training procedures for flying instructors. It had an initial establishment of fifteen Oxfords, seven Blenheim Vs, fifteen Masters, fifteen Magisters, three Ansons and seven Hurricanes.

To make room for the ECFS, 9 (P)AFU transferred its aircraft to Castle Combe, leaving its HQ Flight at Hullavington until 31 July, when the whole unit relocated to Errol. The Luftwaffe gave them a send-off, a Do 217 dropping four 500kg bombs between two of the MU hangars on 27 July, causing much blast damage. No 3 FIS(A) formed at Hullavington on 1 August 1942, and most of its flying, on Oxfords and Masters, also took place at Castle Combe. On 15 October No 1532 (BAT) Flight at Hullavington with Oxfords to work with 3 FIS(A), and by mid-May 1943 had also moved out to Babdown Farm.

Having been busy on a variety of different types of aircraft until then, 10 MU lost its cosmopolitan appearance in May 1943 when it began to concentrate on Mosquito and Stirling work as part of a 41 Group rationalisation. Non-operational types such as the Hart, Harvard, Martinet and Defiant continued to be processed nonetheless. The work of both 10 MU and the ECFS continued throughout the rest of the wartime period without incident, the latter increasing its fleet to include such types as Hotspur, Proctor, Harvard, Spitfire, Lancaster, Wellington, Havoc, Ventura and Mosquito. Towards the end of the war 10 MU had become a long-term storage unit with more than 1,000 aircraft of various types on charge, being one of twenty-two MUs that were in operation as ASUs. With hostilities over, these units had to deal with the vast numbers of aircraft in storage. Those declared obsolete, such as Defiants, were dismantled and sent to one of the 'reduce-to-produce' plants that had been set up. Other types were put aside to be put up for sale, or retained in store.

No 3 FIS(A) had moved on within a few months of the war's end, but the ECFS remained (having become the Empire Flying School on 7 May 1946) until 31 July 1949, when it was absorbed into the RAF Flying College, Manby. The EFS was replaced by 1 ANS, which moved in from Topcliffe on 7 July 1949 with Anson T21s and Wellington T10s, later replaced by Valettas, Varsities and Marathons. It stayed until being disbanded on 1 May 1954 due to the transfer of navigator training to Canada,

Viking T1 ZE503 of 625 VGS alights at Hullavington in April 2005.

and was replaced that day by 2 FTS on transfer from Cluntoe, using Provost T1s and Chipmunks for elementary training. It also pioneered ab initio jet training when, in September 1955, a number of trainee pilots went solo using Jet Provost T1s without previous piston-engine experience. The unit moved to Syerston on 18 November 1957. Varsities returned on 23 December when No 1 Air Electronics School moved in from Swanton Morley; becoming the AES in 1961, it moved to Topcliffe on 14 January 1962. Meanwhile, 10 MU continued to store aircraft until December 1959, when it closed. No 2 ANS had taken over the station from the AES on 15 January 1962, but when its Varsities left for Gaydon on 15 September 1965, active flying largely ceased at Hullavington.

However, it remained an RAF station for a further twenty-eight years, accommodating a number of non-flying units, including the NATO Codification Centre, RAF Balloon Unit, No 1 Parachute Training School and 3, 11, and 15 Squadrons of 5 Wing RAF Regiment. The last was 4626 (County of Wiltshire) Aero Medical Evacuation Squadron, RAuxAF, which moved to Lyneham when RAF Hullavington finally closed in 1993. The station was transferred to the Army, to become Buckley Barracks, the home of 9 Supply Regiment, Royal Logistic Corps.

The airfield is still maintained, and RAF aircraft still fly from it in support of the Air Cadet Organisation. No 3 AEF had arrived from Filton with Chipmunks in July 1979, providing air experience flying for Air Cadets, and remained until August 1993, when it moved to Colerne. The Bristol UAS had arrived on 6 March 1992, also with Chipmunks, and it too relocated to Colerne in November 1993. No 625 VGS arrived in late 1992 from South Cerney, and was joined by 621 VGS from Locking in June 1993. These two units are still resident, and their Viking T1 gliders can be regularly seen in the circuit at the weekends. Hullavington has hosted many events in its time, including the World Aerobatic Championship in 1970. It continues to do so, and has in recent years been the venue for the Great Vintage Flying Weekend, a nostalgic gathering of vintage aeroplanes.

Main features:
Runways: 235° 4,050ft x 150ft, 140° 3,390ft x 150ft, concrete and tarmac. *Hangars:* four Type C, one Bellman, one ARS, six Type E, two Type L, two Type D, one B1, eleven Blister. *Accommodation:* RAF Officers 178, SNCOs 98, ORs 853; WAAF Officers 14, SNCOs 8, ORs 340.

HURN, Hampshire (now Dorset)

SZ115980, 4 miles NE of Bournemouth

All of the available airfields in the South of England were swamped with aircraft in early June 1944, due to the imminent invasion of Europe, but none more so than Hurn. In addition to its resident night-fighter unit, a second Mosquito squadron was temporarily based there, together with two Typhoon fighter-bomber wings. Each Typhoon wing had three squadrons, with thirty aircraft apiece, and the Mosquito Squadrons had eighteen aircraft each, so even Hurn's generous dispersal area must have been packed out!

Some of the earliest flights in Britain took place near Bournemouth, and the first purpose-built airfield in the area was established at Southbourne for the 1910 International Aviation Meeting. This drew a number of aeronautical pioneers such as Bleriot and Graham-White, but was marred for being the occasion of the first fatal accident to an aviator in England when the Wright Biplane flown by the Hon Charles Royce broke up and crashed, killing him instantly. Aerodromes also appeared soon afterwards at Talbot Village and Moordown (also known as Ensbury Park), but none lasted for long. When Sir Alan Cobham visited Bournemouth in 1929 he saw the potential of Parley as the site for a municipal airport and recommended this to the Corporation. However, nothing was done about it, and it was the Air Ministry that proved the reliability of his advice some ten years later.

Work began on the construction of a Fighter Command airfield at Hurn during the winter of 1940, and by the following March it was well advanced, despite a raid by the Luftwaffe on 3 December. By then the runways were complete, together with some dispersal pens. The airfield was eventually opened as a satellite of Ibsley in July 1941, and on its completion became one of the best-equipped wartime airfields in the UK, with seventy-six dispersals and seventeen hangars, the majority being Blisters. However, its first unit did not arrive until 10 November; this was Special Duty Flight, which transferred from Christchurch to be re-designated Telecommunications Flying Unit. Operating more than fifty aircraft of various types, including Tiger Moths, Whitleys, Halifaxes, Defiants, Mosquitoes and Bostons, it flew radar and radio trials on behalf of the TRE at Worth Matravers. One of the most important of these during early 1942 involved H2S, a ground position radar that was to become invaluable to Bomber Command from January 1943.

A detachment of Liberators from 1425 (Communications) Flight arrived from Honeybourne in December 1941, flying courier services, but after a few months departed for Lyneham. By the end of May 1942 the TFU had also gone, to Defford, as the TRE had been withdrawn to the more secure location of Great Malvern. This had the effect of making way for 297 Squadron (part of the newly formed 38 Group), which flew Whitleys in the airborne forces role. Having moved from Netheravon, it resumed training from Hurn during June, participating in paratroop exercises. It was joined later in June by 170 (Army Cooperation) Squadron, which had formed earlier in the month at Weston Zoyland with Mustang Is, and two months later by 296 Squadron, which also flew Whitleys, transferred from Netheravon. Both Whitley squadrons later flew leaflet-dropping (*Nickel*) operations over France. By 25 October all three 38 Group squadrons had left Hurn, 170 and 297 for Thruxton and 296 for Andover, as Hurn had been earmarked as a jumping-off point for Operation *Torch*. During November the airfield was inundated with USAAF aircraft, some taking cargo and personnel, others positioning for operations. By December more than a hundred C-47s and fifty-seven B-17s had transited through for Gibraltar and North Africa.

With the departure of the Americans, RAF Lysanders and Martinets appeared at Hurn, 1493 (Target Towing) Flight having formed early in December. They were joined by Whitleys of 296 Squadron, which returned on 19 December, together with some Horsa gliders, and the Mustangs of 239 Squadron (which had taken part in the Dieppe raid during August) from Odiham. The Mustangs left for Stoney Cross in January 1943, leaving 296 Squadron to continue glider-training, including night tows. The first Albemarles arrived during February, and by the end of May had replaced the Squadron's Whitleys. The first Albemarle operations were made from Hurn on 9 February, *Nickelling* over Lisieux, Normandy, followed on the 17th by a bombing raid.

Preparations then took place for Operation *Husky*, the invasion of Sicily, and 1 Heavy Glider Maintenance Unit was formed to prepare Horsas for long ferry flights. A detachment from 13 MU arrived to work on the Halifaxes of 295 Squadron, which had been brought to Hurn to be converted into glider tugs. In early June the Albemarles left for Portreath, on the first stage of their journey to Sicily, accompanied by the Halifaxes of 295 Squadron, which began a ferry service from Hurn taking Horsas out to the Mediterranean for the impending operations.

With the end of Operation *Husky*, 295 Squadron handed its Halifaxes over to 298 Squadron at Tarrant Rushton, and began converting to Albemarles in October 1943. Later that month it was joined by 296 Squadron, which returned from Goubine in Italy. A third Albemarle unit appeared on 15 November, when 570 Squadron formed. All three squadrons undertook an intensive training programme during the winter, and also flew operations, dropping supplies and equipment to SOE forces in France.

For Operation *Overlord* the 38 Group Squadrons moved inland (295 and 570 to Harwell and 296 to Brize Norton), leaving Hurn to the 2nd TAF in mid-March 1944. No 438 Squadron was the first to arrive, on 18 March, joined shortly afterwards by the two other squadrons of 143 (RCAF) Wing, Nos 439 and 440. All three had been initially equipped with the Hurricane IV, and were in the process of converting to the Typhoon IB. Once operational, towards the end of the month, the

Wing began sweeps over the Channel and Cherbourg peninsula. The Mosquito NFXVIIs of 125 Squadron flew in on 25 March to join coastal night-fighter defences, and were put to work on Operation *Eric*, dropping *Window* in support of night decoy bombing raids.

No 143 Wing went to Funtington for dive-bombing training in early April, just after 124 Wing (191, 182 and 247 Squadrons) arrived at Hurn with rocket-firing Typhoons. The Canadians returned two weeks later, when all six Hurn-based Typhoon squadrons began full-scale operations, attacking pre-invasion targets such as strongpoints and radar stations, during which 438 Squadron became the first unit to drop 1,000lb bombs operationally from its Typhoons.

Meanwhile 604 Squadron had brought Mosquito NFXIIIs to Hurn on 3 May, to bolster 85 Group night-fighter defences prior to D-Day. On the night of 15/16 May, during the last major nocturnal raid on Britain, they shot down a Ju 188, while 125 got a Ju 88 near Cherbourg. A week later, during spasmodic activity by the Luftwaffe, 125 Squadron claimed another Ju 88 and a Ju188 in the Southampton area. Hurn's Mosquitoes were airborne at dusk on 5 June, covering the Allied invasion fleet as it crossed the Channel for Normandy. The following night 604 Squadron shot down five enemy aircraft and another five on the 8th (including two He 177s). Although enemy night activity over the UK then tailed off, standing patrols over the invasion beachheads netted four enemy destroyed and one damaged for 125 Squadron on three nights towards the end of June.

The period leading up to D-Day was a busy time for Hurn's Typhoon squadrons. Attacking ground targets was dangerous work, and a number of aircraft were lost. They flew eighty-eight sorties on the day itself and, following the invasion attacks on German tanks, vehicles, railways and airfields, were pursued without respite. By 10 June more than 150 sorties were being flown daily. As the momentum carried the Allied forces forward, 2nd TAF units followed, and on 20 June 124 Wing moved to the continent, to airstrip B6 at Coulombs in Normandy. As it moved forward, it was replaced two days later by the first squadron from 123 Wing (198 Squadron), although the remainder (183 and 609 Squadrons) did not arrive until 1 July. By then the Wing had already started moving to B9 strip at Lantheuil.

The four squadrons of 146 Wing (193, 197, 257 and 266) were the next Typhoon units to use Hurn. They flew in from Needs Oar Point on 3 July and stayed for eight days. Remaining UK-based Typhoon units gradually moved to the continent, the last one to use Hurn being 263 Squadron, the only Typhoon unit operating in 10 Group, which arrived on 10 July and left for Normandy via Eastchurch on the 23rd.

During July six P-61 Black Widows of the USAAF were based at Hurn. Detached from the 422nd Fighter Squadron at Scorton, they worked with 125 Squadron to gain experience of radar-guided night interceptions, using Sopley radar. On 13 July the Mosquitoes of 604 Squadron left for Colerne, and were replaced the following day by 418 (RCAF) Squadron, another Mosquito unit. However, the Canadians were not to stay long, for at the end of the month they departed with 125 Squadron for Middle Wallop. Both units' last mission from Hurn was to provide cover for a bombing raid on the V-3 weapons site near Calais.

The reason for the Mosquitoes' sudden departure was that Hurn had been allocated for the use of the USAAF, and it became Station 492 of the US 9th Air Force. This heralded the arrival of the B-26 Marauders of 397th Bombardment Group, which flew in from Rivenhall on 4/5 August, continuing bombing operations without interruption, such as on the rail marshalling yards at Corbiel. The group consisted of the 596th, 597th, 598th and 599th Bombardment Squadrons, with more than sixty B-26s. It flew twenty-two missions from Hurn, losing three Marauders, before moving south at the end of August to A26/Gorges. Hurn was a forward airfield for a number of Allied units moving to the continent until 18 October.

The airfield was then taken over by BOAC, which transferred its main landplane operation from Whitchurch. The airline had had an interest in Hurn since January 1944, when it formed a Development Flight there to evaluate potential new aircraft types for post-war use. These included the Lancaster and its civil variants, the Lancastrian and York. It was a York that left Hurn in April 1944 on an inaugural service to Morocco, then Cairo. Once Hurn was transferred to the Ministry of Civil Aviation, other airlines joined BOAC, such as KLM, Sabena and Pan American Airways. It was not long after VE Day that the first eastbound England to Australia service was flown, Lancastrian G-AGLV of BOAC leaving Hurn on 31 May 1945. More international services followed and in October American Overseas Airways started flying DC4s to the USA.

Hurn was the centre of post-war pioneering civil flights, and became Britain's main

Lancastrian G-AGMG Nicosia of BOAC leaves Hurn for Australia in 1946.

international airport until it was gradually overshadowed by Heathrow, opened in May 1946. Although services were gradually transferred there, BOAC continued to use Hurn for crew training. It moved out of its hangars in 1950, and these were taken over by Vickers-Armstrong for aircraft manufacturing. Varsity trainers and Viscount airliners were produced there and, with the establishment of the British Aircraft Corporation, One-Elevens. The plant was taken over by British Aerospace and closed in 1984. Other manufacturers to use Hurn in the 1950s were Airspeed, which had a flight-test hangar for fighters built nearby at Christchurch, and Portsmouth Aviation, which undertook overhaul and modification work.

Meteor TT20 WD652 of FRU refuelled in the early 1950s.

Hurn seen from 10,900 feet in September 1960.

Another resident during this period was the Fleet Requirements Unit, which had been formed at Hurn by Airwork Services in the early 1950s, providing target facilities for naval guns and radar in the UK and overseas. To provide realistic targets it flew aircraft types that had only just left front-line service, working through the succession of Mosquito, Sea Hornet, Sea Fury, Attacker, Sea Hawk, Scimitar and Hunter. It flew from Hurn until October 1972, when, merged with the Air Direction Unit to become the Fleet Requirements & Air Direction Unit, it moved to Yeovilton. However, Airwork continued to maintain the aircraft as part of its repair and overhaul operation at Hurn until the contract was taken over by FR Aviation in 1983. Airwork itself was taken over by Shorts-Bombardier in October 1993. FR Aviation, re-branded as Cobham Aviation Services in

Viscount G-AVIW of Channel Airways taxies in at Hurn on 27 July 1970.

*Falcon 20 G-FRAF of
FRA lands at Hurn in
February 2007.*

2009, continues to support the RN fleet requirements contract from Hurn, and operates a fleet of more than twenty Dassault Falcon 20s to provide airborne warfare training for the armed forces of the UK and other nations. It also overhauls and modifies a variety of civil and military aircraft, including VC10s and Nimrods, for the RAF.

During the mid-1950s there was a gradual increase in airline services at Hurn. Jersey Airlines operated a fleet of seven Dragon Rapides to the Channel Islands, replaced by Herons during the summer of 1954. Silver City moved its car ferry operations to Hurn from Eastleigh in March 1959, using Bristol Superfreighters. Airlines operating Viscounts from Hurn during the 1960s included BEA, British United, Cambrian and Dan Air. With a downturn in traffic during the mid-1960s Hurn faced closure, but in April 1969 its future was assured when it was purchased by Bournemouth and Dorset Councils. In addition to One-Eleven services by Channel Airways, freight and flower flights by South West Aviation were introduced on Dakotas and Skyvans, and passenger and freight services by BIA with Heralds and Dakotas. Other operators during the 1970s included Westward Airways with Islanders, British Air Ferries with Carvairs, and Dan Air with HS748s.

Operators came and some went during the 1980s and 1990s, including Metropolitan Airways, Air Metro, Channel Express and Jersey European, and, with improvements to the airport's runways and facilities, traffic gradually increased in volume. Hurn's wartime past revisited it in 1991, with the discovery of pipe-mines that had been laid as denial charges when the runways had originally been constructed; fortunately they were dealt with by the Royal Engineers. In April 1995 National Express purchased the airport and immediately invested £10 million in improved facilities, including an extension to the main runway. This enabled charters to include transatlantic flights, but also attracted Ryanair, which introduced a regular service to Dublin.

Ryanair Boeing 737 EI-DPE at Hurn on 21 January 2009.

Vintage jet fighters were seen again at Bournemouth in 1981 when a Hunter arrived as the first in a collection that later became Jet Heritage. Warbirds of Great Britain and Source Classic Jets also operated from Hurn. Although these concerns have now gone, some of their aeroplanes remain at Hurn in the Bournemouth Aviation Museum.

In September 2000 the Manchester Airports Group purchased Hurn. It entered the record books in 2006 when, on 11 February, Steve Fossett made a landing there in his Global Flyer. He had taken off from Florida three and a half days beforehand and established a new world record for a solo flight when he landed at Hurn after 75 hours 45 minutes in the air, covering 26,380 miles.

Now Bournemouth Airport, its main services are currently operated by Ryanair within the UK and Europe, Thomson to the Mediterranean (both airlines flying the Boeing 737), and Easyjet (Airbus A319) to Switzerland. Charter flight operators currently include Palmair, Eurocypria and Lauda Air. With an airport terminal and infrastructure redeveloped to cater for passenger numbers of some 1.2 million per annum, Bournemouth Airport is looking confidently to the future.

Main features:
Runways: 265° 6,000ft x 150ft, 174° 4,800ft x 150ft, 309° 3,390ft x 150ft, concrete and tarmac. *Hangars:* four T2, three Bellman, ten Blister. *Hardstandings:* twenty 90ft frying pan, ten 100ft, forty-six loop. *Accommodation:* RAF Officers 166, SNCOs 273, ORs 1,549; WAAF Officers 8, SNCOs 10, ORs 444.

Spitfire IIA P8088 Spirit of Lambeth *was flown by 118 Squadron from Ibsley in the spring of 1941.*

IBSLEY, Hampshire

SU155090, 2 miles N of Ringwood on A338

Opened as a satellite of Middle Wallop on 15 February 1941, Ibsley airfield was built on low ground on the western edge of the New Forest. The Hurricane Is of 32 Squadron flew in from the parent station two days later and began convoy patrols along the Channel. However, within a few weeks the Luftwaffe had noticed this activity and visited the new station on the night of 13 March, dropping thirty-one bombs, nine of which hit the main runway, but luckily only one Hurricane was damaged.

Despite this, construction work continued, and three tarmac runways were eventually laid. Spitfires replaced Hurricanes when 32 Squadron moved to Pembrey, and 118 arrived from Warmwell on 18 April with Mk IIAs. Coastal patrols started badly when they shot down a Whitley on 4 May, but success soon followed with the mounting of escorts for Beauforts on anti-shipping strikes. Night patrols were also flown, and during one of these the OC shot down an He 111. The Squadron received the Spitfire IIB during July, and when similarly equipped 501 Squadron arrived

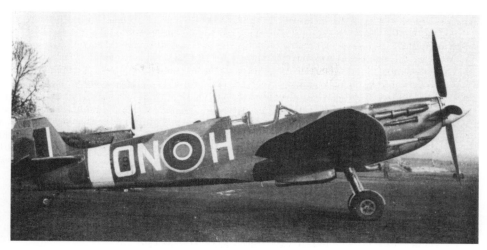

Spitfire HFVI BR579 of 124 Squadron was flown from Ibsley on detachment during the summer of 1943.

on 5 August, the two units supplemented convoy patrols with *Rhubarbs*, *Roadsteads* and *Ramrods*. Both received the more capable Mark VB in September.

Several units used Ibsley as a forward base for operations over France during the autumn of 1941, but when a third Spitfire VB squadron, 234, arrived from Warmwell in early November, the three Ibsley-based units began operating as a wing, under the dynamic leadership of Wg Cdr 'Widge' Gleed. As well as making sweeps they provided escorts for the fighter-bomber and medium bombers of 2 Group and the heavies of Bomber Command. Most of these operations were very successful, but a 300-mile long-range sweep on 16 March nearly ended in disaster due to bad weather; short on fuel, twenty-eight Spitfires managed to land at Exeter, four scraped into Bolt Head, but four more crash-landed with one fatality.

Airfield facilities had been improved during this time, with double fighter pens being provided around the perimeter and nine oversize Blister hangars erected. No 234 Squadron moved to Portreath on 27 April, exchanging with 66 Squadron, which immediately joined wing operations. These included, on 15 May, escorting eight 'Hurribombers' of 175 Squadron against three minesweepers off Cherbourg. As the attackers left the area, leaving one ship listing badly, another blew and the third burst into flames. Despite this and heavy flak, all of the aircraft returned to base successfully with only two of the Spitfires incurring slight damage. Operations continued that summer around a film unit and film stars Leslie Howard and David Niven, making *The First of the Few*. The crews and aircraft of the Ibsley Wing provide a fitting backdrop for this ageless film about Mitchell and the Spitfire.

On 18 August the Wing used Tangmere to fly operations in support of the Dieppe landings, and to take part in one of the largest aerial battles of the war. Most of the Ibsley pilots flew three missions that day, the Wing losing eight aircraft and three pilots. They did not return to their home base for long, as on 24 August No 501 Squadron left for Middle Wallop, and 66 and 118 for Zeals. Ibsley was then handed over to 1st Fighter Group of the USAAF as a forward operating base. P38F Lightnings of the 71st and 94th Fighter Squadrons arrived on 27 August from Kirton-in-Lindsay, and flew their first air defence sortie two days later. The units flew fighter sweeps and escort mission (273 in all) before departing for operations in North Africa on 14 November.

Following Ibsley's reversion to 10 Group control, on 23 December both 66 and 118 Squadrons returned from Zeals. They were joined by a third squadron at the end of December, 504 with the Spitfire VC. However, the two former units did not stay long, 118 leaving for Wittering on 3 January 1943 (having been replaced the day before by 616 Squadron from West Hampnett with high-altitude Spitfire VIs) and 66 departing for Skaebrae on 9 February, exchanging with the Mark VIs of 129 Squadron. The reformed Ibsley Wing was soon heavily engaged in sweeps, *Circuses*, *Ramrods* and *Rhubarbs*, including top cover for murderous daylight USAAF B-17 raids over

France. However, heavy rain during this time revealed one of Ibsley's main problems – poor drainage, causing extensive flooding. The Wing participated in Army Cooperation Exercise *Spartan* in March 1943, and escort work for 616 Squadron included the Prime Minister's Liberator on his return from Casablanca, and for HM the King returning from North Africa.

At the end of June 1943 No 504 Squadron moved to Church Stanton and 129 to Hornchurch, leaving 616 Squadron to provide high-level escorts until mid-September, when it moved to Exeter. Nos 310, 312 and 313 Squadrons then arrived between 18 and 21 September to take up residence as the Ibsley Czech Wing. Flying Spitfire Vs (310 having the Mk VI high-altitude version), the Wing concentrated on bomber escort operations, but saw little action. On 5 December Whirwinds arrived, from 263 Squadron, but were not to stay long as the unit was converting to the Typhoon 1b, leaving a month later for Fairwood Common. Other new equipment during this period at Ibsley was the Spitfire IX for the Czech squadrons; having converted onto the new type, the unit stayed until 19 February 1944, then moved to Mendlesham.

By this time Ibsley had once again been earmarked for the use of the USAAF, and advance parties were already upgrading the airfield, together with its dispersals, hardstanding and hangars. Personnel of the 48th FG (492, 493 and 494 FS) arrived at Ibsley on 29 March, and flew the first missions in its P-47Ds three weeks later. The unit was joined by the 371st FG in April while repairs were carried out on its base at Bisterne, and for three weeks more than 150 P-47s flew from Ibsley. Intensive training using the bombing range just to the east of the airfield enabled the 48th FG to reach operational status, and it carried out numerous sweeps in the lead-up to D-Day. Trains, marshalling yards, bridges, airfields, coastal batteries and radar stations were attacked, but D-Day itself was an anti-climax as the Group was given convoy escort and beach cover. It soon resumed its destructive sweeps, giving close support to Allied ground forces. The 48th FG became one of the first P-47 groups to move to the Normandy beachhead, and started using A-4/Deux Juneaux on 18 June, also operating from Ibsley until 4 July. During its time in Hampshire the 48th FG flew sixty-nine missions, including 1,956 individual sorties, and shot down four Bf 109s, losing eight P-47s.

L-8 Sentinels and UC-78 Expeditors of 14th Liaison Squadron arrived in early July, but only stayed until the 11th, when they flew to Normandy. In the meantime another USAAF P-38 unit arrived, the 367th Fighter Group, which transferred from Stoney Cross on 6 July. The Group lost six P-38s while flying twenty missions from Ibsley, and on 22 July it too moved to Normandy.

Then transferred back to 11 Group, Ibsley was used for a while by the Oxfords of 7 FIS, Upavon. In March 1945 it came under 46 Group, Transport Command, but only as a satellite for other local airfields. The Glider Pick-up Training Flight then moved in from Zeals and trained there for a few months with its Dakotas and Hadrian Gliders. A number of non-flying units then passed through, such as 160 Staging Post on its way to Guernsey, and 200 and 201 Signals Units, which assembled in

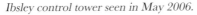

Ibsley control tower seen in May 2006.

readiness for Tiger Force. On 15 August 1945 a victory dance was held, but with the departure of the GPTF to Ramsbury in October, flying came to an end at Ibsley and the station started to run down, with its strength reduced from a peak of 3,000 to 350. Although some of the hangars were used for storage by 49 MU during 1946, it became inactive the following year and was de-requisitioned.

The airfield returned to agriculture, the runways being removed during the 1960s. Because of the valuable aggregate underlying its surface, Ibsley was purchased by Amey Roadstone in the early 1970s, and extraction has since resulted in the virtual disappearance of the airfield. The only remnant of this short-lived but important airfield is the control tower, which overlooks the large landscaped lakes that now occupy the site.

Main features:
Runways: 010° 4,800ft x 150ft, 050° 4,050ft x 150ft, 320° 4,200ft x 150ft, concrete and tarmac. *Hangars:* two Bellman, twelve Blister. *Hardstandings:* thirty-six circular and pen-type. *Accommodation:* RAF Officers 170, SNCOs 149, ORs 1,492; WAAF Officers 7, SNCOs 16, ORs 365.

Jersey Airport, seen from a Rapide on opening day, 10 March 1937.

JERSEY, Channel Islands

4 miles WNW of St Helier

The flying boats that provided the first air services to Jersey in the 1920s were replaced by landplanes, including DH Dragons, flying from the sandy beach at West Park in St Aubyn's Bay. The length of available runways depended on the tides, so in 1934 the States of Jersey Government agreed to build an airport, and purchased 218 vergees (acres) in St Peter. Jersey Airport opened on 10 March 1937, with a 2,940-foot grass runway. There were two hangars and the terminal building; the latter included a central control tower, had two wings, for arrivals and departures, and a restaurant and terraces on the second floor. Jersey Airways immediately transferred its operations there, joined by Air France the following year.

More than 20,000 passengers flew to Jersey during the first twelve months of the new airport's operation, and services were expanded to meet the demand, which included freight when growers

*A DH Flamingo of Jersey
Airways over Portelet
Bay in July 1939.*

realised that they had speedy access to new markets. In July 1939 Jersey Airways put Flamingos on its routes, but with the outbreak of war two months later all civil flying was suspended. Because of the importance of the air link to the islands, Jersey Airways resumed limited services between them and to Shoreham on 24 October.

The RN requisitioned the airport in early March 1940 for training, and on the 11th No 755 Squadron moved in from Worthy Down with its Sharks. The unit flew navigational exercises over the Western Approaches and was joined by the Albacores of 826 Squadron on 21 May. However, with the German breakthrough getting closer to the French coast, both squadrons evacuated to Lee-on-Solent on 31 May. Limited operations were made from the islands by the RAF, a major one being on 11 June 1940, when thirty-six Whitleys from 4 Group used Jersey and Guernsey Airports to refuel before flying across France to bomb targets in Italy. Although many were forced to turn back because of severe icing, at least two of the Jersey-based bombers hit their targets.

As the Germans advanced across France during June 1940, RAF squadrons were forced to withdraw. Nos 17 and 501 Squadrons moved their Hurricanes from Le Mans to Dinard in mid-June, then to Jersey, 17 Squadron arriving on the 18th, and No 501 the following day. They flew sorties to cover troop evacuations before being ordered to withdraw, 17 Squadron to Debden on 19 June and 501 to Croydon on the 21st. The airport was also used as a staging post for passenger aircraft leaving France during this time, including one carrying a Colonel Charles de Gaulle, which passed through on 17 June. With the declaration that the Channel Islands could not be defended, evacuations started, Jersey and Guernsey Airways carrying 319 people away to safety between 19 and 21 June. The undefended town of St Helier was bombed by the He 111s of KG27 on 28 June, killing eleven people,

Messerschmitt Bf 110 DE+UG photographed by a brave Jerseyman in 1942.

Jersey Airport terminal seen at close quarters from a passing Dakota in November 1947.

and the Germans threatened more raids unless white flags were displayed. On 1 July 1940 the advance elements of the German occupation forces arrived at Jersey Airport in Ju 52s, escorted by Do 17s.

A taxying accident on 22 August damaged a Bf 110C that was being flown from Jersey by ZG76 during the Battle of Britain, but otherwise the airfield was little used for operations as it offered no real advantage over French bases and quickly became congested. It also received the occasional attentions of the RAF, such as on 9 August, when two attacks by Blenheims damaged several aircraft, vehicles and buildings. Nonetheless Jersey Airport provided an important link for the German garrison and was used for the transport of supplies, equipment and personnel, and for communications with France throughout the wartime period. During their tenure the Germans erected another hangar and extended the airfield to the south, giving a 3,000-foot landing run NW/SE. The Channel Islands were liberated on 9 May 1945, and on 26 May Jersey Airways officials arrived by Rapide for the resumption of air services, which began on 21 June. One of the first flights delivered 20,000 chicks to re-stock island farms. Their Majesties the King and Queen paid a visit to Jersey in the meantime, arriving by air on 6 June.

The RAF operated the airport, finding it useful for transit to the continent. Visitors included an Me 262, which landed to refuel on its way to the UK for assessment. The airfield was handed back to the States of Jersey in October 1945. Scheduled services were gradually extended, and in the immediate post-war years passengers flying to and from the island doubled, from 65,059 in 1946 to 113,333 in 1947. In 1948 the States sanctioned £300,000 for new landing aids, hangar and tarmac runway. Jersey Airways had reopened as Channel Island Airways after the war, but was bought by BEA in 1947. Jersey Airlines formed the following year, and in 1951 was permitted to open up routes to Exeter and Paris with DH Herons. The tarmac runway was extended in 1953 to 4,550 feet, capable of taking BEA Ambassadors and Viscounts. By 1957 the airport was contributing more than £5 million per annum to the island's economy.

By the early 1960s Jersey Airlines was running a fleet of Dakotas and Heralds, not only to Paris and Exeter, but also to Amsterdam and the Canaries (via Gatwick). It became part of British United Airways (Channel Islands) in 1962. New radar and navigation systems installed in 1959 had made Jersey one of the safest airports to fly into, but tragedy came on 14 April 1965 when a Dakota of BUA(CI) crashed in fog on the approach, with only a stewardess surviving.

Cessna 421C N9AY takes off from Jersey, past taxying Boeing 737 G-GFFG of British Airways, in July 2008.

British Midland, flying services to Castle Donington in the mid-1960s, was one of several airlines then flying to Jersey, but BUA(CI) had been running into difficulties, and was wound up in October 1968. Jet operations had started in June 1967, with Channel Airways BAC One-Eleven services from Southend, followed by BEA with Tridents from Stansted. By the 1970s Jersey had become the sixth busiest airport in Europe. In August 1970 a new control tower was built and improvements were made to the passenger terminal, and in 1976 the runway was extended to 6,000 feet, with a 500-foot overrun. This was used on 22 August the following year, when a Viscount with seventy-seven people aboard left the end of the runway and used 495 feet of the extra tarmac, coming to a rest overlooking St Ouen's Bay.

Aurigny Air Services, which had begun daily services to Alderney, Guernsey and Granville in the late 1960s with BN2 Islanders, opened its own passenger terminal in 1972. Channel Airways collapsed in 1973, but Intra had started services to Jersey in 1971, becoming Jersey European Airways in 1979. BEA had become part of British Airways in 1973, replacing Tridents with One-Elevens, which in turn made way for Boeing 737s in 1981.

Improvements in the mid-1980s included new ILS and upgrading of ATC and communications systems, but the limited facilities, particularly at peak times, prompted plans for expansion. A modern extension to the terminal, which complemented its 1937 design, was opened in 1997. British Airways was by then operating to Gatwick and Heathrow from Jersey, and began a route to Paris. Air UK provided flights to the South Coast and other airports further north, while Jersey European added services to Ireland, and Crossair started a daily flight to Zurich.

Passengers board Flybe Dash 8 G-JECW at Jersey in July 2008.

The airport nowadays has more than 80,000 aircraft movements per year, with almost 1.6 million passengers passing through. Currently airlines serving Jersey include Aer Lingus, Aurigny, Blue Islands, BMI, BMI Baby, British Airways, Flybe, Easyjet and Jet2. Numerous charter and cargo airlines also use the airport, as do hundreds of privately owned aircraft. A major redevelopment scheme started in September 2008, resurfacing the main runway between then and April 2009. This was followed by demolition of the 1937 Jersey Airlines hangar, together with the terminal building and its control tower, replaced by completely new facilities.

Stirling IVs of 299 Squadron lined up at Keevil on 5 June 1944.

KEEVIL, Wiltshire

ST 922571, 5 miles E of Trowbridge

Planned in the early 1940s as a fighter training station, Keevil was built to bomber standards, but when it opened on 15 July 1942 it found itself in Army Cooperation Command! It was to be utilised for the build-up of British airborne forces, but the first user, in September 1942, was the USAAF.

The 62nd Troop Carrier Group, equipped with Douglas C-47 Skytrains, had come to Britain to take part in Operation *Torch*, the invasion of North Africa. Based at Keevil, the Group trained with US and British paratroops before moving to Cornwall in early November 1942, then heading for Gibraltar and North Africa. The Group's part in Operation *Torch* was a great success, in no small part due to its training at Keevil.

Three weeks after the 62nd TCG's departure, another USAAF unit, the 67th Observation Group, based at Membury, took over Keevil as a satellite. Providing low-level armed visual and photographic reconnaissance, that part of the Group to use Keevil was the 153rd Observation Squadron, flying Havocs and Bostons, as well as L-4 Grasshoppers. The unit also flew a number of Spitfire Vs transferred from the RAF – a type that was to become a familiar sight at Keevil over the years. From the spring of 1943 it started mounting reconnaissance missions over occupied France.

Following the bombing of the Supermarine's Woolston factory, production of the Spitfire was dispersed to several locations in Berkshire and Wiltshire, including Salisbury and Trowbridge. The new airfield at Keevil was seen as an ideal location at which to assemble and flight-test the Spitfires manufactured in Trowbridge, rather than High Post. In the spring of 1943 the MAP started a

Two Spitfire XVIIIs are being completed at Supermarine's Keevil works in 1946.

purpose-built hangar at Keevil for the final assembly of airframes and rigging for flight, and when completed that summer it could accommodate a dozen Spitfires. Forty experienced employees started at the Keevil works in August 1943, joined by more than a hundred lesser-skilled workers. Once assembled and flight-tested, Spitfires were collected by ferry pilots, usually of the ATA, many of whom were women. They would fly the aircraft to one of the Spitfire MUs (often Wroughton or Lyneham) to be taken on charge by the RAF, for eventual issue. The first aircraft to be delivered from Keevil was Spitfire VIII JF900, on 21 August 1943.

The 363rd Fighter Group, with P-51B Mustangs, arrived on 20 December 1943, but its stay was short, moving out to Rivenhall on 22 January 1944. The 153rd OS also left a few weeks later, due to a reshuffle of bases, and on 10 March the RAF ensign flew at Keevil. The first RAF squadrons arrived four days later – 196 Squadron from Tarrant Rushton, and 299 from Stoney Cross, both flying Stirlings. These units were in the airborne forces role, and were accompanied by Nos 1 and 2 (Horsa) Glider Servicing Echelons.

Training resumed from Keevil, the Stirlings towing gliders on cross-country navigation exercises and dropping paratroops. They also started operations, with supply drops to members of the SOE in occupied Europe. Ceaseless training came to an end on 3 June 1944, when all operational aircraft were painted in black and white identification stripes, and the crews were briefed on the imminent invasion of Normandy. After a weather delay of 24 hours, forty-six Stirlings lined up on Keevil's main runway to take 806 paratroops of the 6th Airborne Division to Normandy. Having dropped their paratroops during the night of 5/6 June, the Stirlings returned to Keevil, and that afternoon took the reinforcement troops of the 6th Airlanding Brigade to the LZs in thirty-six Horsas. Two aircraft were lost on D-Day operations.

Following the outstanding success of the landings, Keevil's Stirlings maintained regular operations in support of the SOE and SAS behind enemy lines. These continued until September, when another operation was tabled for them – Operation *Market Garden*. Both Keevil squadrons were initially to tow Horsa gliders to Arnhem, with 196 Squadron taking twenty-three, and 299 Squadron twenty-five. The first day of the operation, 17 September, went well – opposition was light, and the Horsas were released successfully over the LZs. A re-supply on the next day also went well, with twenty-two Horsas being successfully delivered. On the third day, however, German resistance stiffened, and their fighters attacked the British formations; three Stirlings were lost from 299 Squadron, and one from 196. More re-supply missions followed, but eventually it was realised that the troops in Arnhem were in an untenable position, and had to be withdrawn, which was achieved on the night of 25 September. In the operation to re-supply the bridgehead, the RAF lost forty-four Stirlings, with 105 aircrew killed – 196 Squadron lost eleven Stirlings and 299 fifteen.

Spitfire LF16 of 203 AFS lands at Keevil in July 1947.

C17 ZZ172 of 99 Squadron, Brize Norton, at Keevil during an exercise in August 2008.

The Stirling squadrons left on 9 October for Wethersfield, to continue their operations from there. They were replaced by 22 HGCU, which formed at Keevil on 20 October 1944 for the advanced training of glider pilots. With forty-six Horsa and Hadrian gliders, together with fifty-eight Albemarle tugs, the unit filled Keevil with aircraft! Training continued into 1945, until the end of the war in Europe. In June 1945 No 22 HGCU transferred to Blakehill Farm, and Keevil's circuit was left to the Spitfires flight-tested by Supermarine. It was not long before they were joined by RAF-flown Spitfires, when 61 OTU moved in. This was a fighter-pilot training unit, with Spitfire Vs and LFXVIs, together with Mustangs, Harvards, Martinets and Tiger Moths. Re-titled as 203 AFS in July 1947, it proved to be the last flying unit to be based at Keevil, and moved to Chivenor, Devon, a couple of months later.

Once again Supermarine remained the sole user of Keevil, but this was not to last. The final Spitfire work at Keevil was the conversion of a batch of South Marston-built Mark 22s to take them up to Mark 24 standard, and the works closed on 30 January 1948. More than 600 Spitfires of various marks were assembled and flight-tested at Keevil; they took part in fighter sweeps over occupied Europe, saw action in North Africa and Malta, and flew on operations in the Far East. There are at least eight Keevil-built Spitfires still in existence, four of them airworthy.

Although Keevil was put on C&M following the closure of the Supermarine factory in December 1955, it was handed over to the USAF as a standby base for the 3rd AF, was used for training by US airborne forces. Since being handed back to the Air Ministry in 1964, Keevil has continued to be used for training. It is retained by the MoD and many of the successful operations mounted by British Forces in recent years owe their success to the training and exercises undertaken at Keevil. The control tower and one T2 hangar still stand on the main airfield; the MAP hangar site also still exists, having been sold off and used for storage.

Main features:
Runways: 075° 6,000ft x 150ft, 132° 4,200ft x 150ft, 204° 4,200ft x 150ft, concrete and wood chippings. *Hangars:* two T2, nine EO-Blister. *Hardstandings:* nine 150ft diameter, forty-one 125ft diameter, one 75ft diameter. *Accommodation:* RAF Officers 155, SNCOs 504, ORs 1,434; WAAF Officers 10, SNCOs 19, ORs 420.

KEMBLE, Gloucestershire

ST960965, 4 miles SW of Cirencester on A429

Very few airfields have had roles that remained unchanged for more than fifty-five years, but Kemble is certainly one, performing the vital task of storage and maintenance since its inception, for both the RAF and the USAF.

Construction of this airfield astride the Fosse Way began in August 1936 as part of the Third Phase of the RAF Expansion Plan. It was to house an Aircraft Storage Unit and, in addition to three large hangars on the main technical site, a number of storage hangars and associated buildings were constructed on several dispersed sites. It opened as 6 ASU on 22 June 1938, its job being to receive and store aircraft, either as new airframes on delivery from the manufacturers, or on transfer from other units. It was then to equip, maintain, modify, store and issue them in response to demands from the ASU HQ at 41 Group Maintenance Command, RAF Andover. However, as a security measure the unit's title was changed to 5 MU, and it was to remain at Kemble for the rest of the station's life, the RAF's longest-serving MU.

The first aircraft to arrive were Hurricanes and Blenheims, delivered direct from the manufacturers for the installation of service equipment, such as radios and guns. With the declaration of war, operational aircraft arrived in the form of fourteen Wellingtons from 37 Squadron, based at Feltwell. They had deployed under Operation *Scatter*, but left again a few days later when the expected Luftwaffe attacks on their base did not materialise.

The need for more storage facilities at Kemble resulted in additional land being requisitioned and more hangars being erected. By the end of the year, 488 aircraft were in store, and many had to be stored in nearby fields. Servicing and guarding aircraft in the open became a problem, especially during the winter, and by April 1940 there were 629 aircraft on site, ranging from Lysanders and Battles to Beauforts and Wellingtons.

Due to problems in finding available aircrew to move the aircraft, it was decided to move 4 Ferry Pilots Pool from Cardiff. This unit took over C site, and flew a diverse set of aircraft, including

A 5 MU hangar in 1946, with Airspeed Courier, Auster Is and Miles Gull Sixes in store.

Hurricanes, Ansons, Beauforts and Hampdens, to train, deploy and collect aircrews. The throughput rate increased, and by 3 July 1940 the 1,000th aircraft to be despatched since the outbreak of war left 5 MU. Following the fall of France an Air Defence Flight of Hurricanes was formed to deter any attackers. One of its Hurricanes intercepted a Ju 88 on 25 July and shot it down, but celebrations were short-lived as the fighter went into a spin and crashed, killing its pilot. The Luftwaffe returned on 14 August, when two bombers dropped eighteen HE and four large oil incendiary bombs; nine Whitleys on B site were damaged, but no casualties were sustained. With the fear of invasion looming, Hinds were fitted with bomb racks, and bomber aircraft were prepared to attack enemy troops. The work of 4 FPP expanded during the summer to include the ferrying of aircraft to the Middle and Far East. On 9 September 1940 the Overseas Aircraft Deliveries Flight formed to take on this work, training with Wellingtons, Beauforts and Marylands, becoming the Overseas Air Deliveries Flight on 23 September. On 5 November No 7 (Service) Ferry Pilots Pool was formed to replace 4 FPP, which became HQ Service Ferry Pools.

By November 1940 the number of aircraft in store at any one time averaged 250, of about thirty-five types, and there were 657 civilian employees at the MU together with 300 RAF personnel. The Luftwaffe attacked again on 19 November, but although little damage was done, dispersal again became an issue, and aircraft were sent off to SLGs such as Stoke Orchard and Watchfield. These soon became full, and special camouflaged Satellite Landing Grounds were developed instead, at Barnsley Park, Berrow, Beechwood, Booker and Bush Barn.

Argosy C1s in open storage at 5 MU in the 1970s; XN847, ex-Near East Air Force, is nearest the camera.

Kemble-based Gnats of the Red Arrows at Greenham Common in July 1977.

No 7 (S)FPP was absorbed into HQ SFP on 20 February 1941. Shortly afterwards, on 1 April, the Service Ferry Training Squadron was formed within HQSFP to ensure that ferry pilots were adequately trained on type. During 1941 ferry pilots were being increasingly provided by the ATA, which took over the majority of shorter-range ferrying by November, so HQSFP was disbanded. SFTS was transferred to Honeybourne, becoming the Ferry Training Squadron, to train service pilots for long-range ferrying duties. The OAD Flight was re-titled the Overseas Aircraft Despatch Unit on 15 August 1941, and on 5 November moved to Portreath. In its place the Overseas Aircraft Preparation Flight was formed (subsequently re-designated the "OAP Unit, with Nos 1 and 2 Flights at Kemble, and Nos 3 and 4 at Filton. The Kemble flights became No.1 OAPU in December 1942

The construction of a runway had started in the autumn, and this was available for use in April 1942. New hangars were opened for the assembly of Hotspur, Horsa and Hamilcar gliders, while Hurricanes were being converted to fighter-bombers; one of the main outputs of the MU through the 1 OAPU was a stream of Wellingtons and Hudsons for the Middle East. The Luftwaffe visited Kemble again on 27 July 1942, when two Do 217s machine-gunned the parked aircraft but failed to hit anything.

Wellingtons, Beauforts and Hurricanes continued to be processed through into 1943, with Lancasters starting to arrive in February and Warwicks in August. In September the main runway was extended and work started on a secondary runway. Taxiways were also laid to connect the maze of dispersals to the west of the main airfield, some of which almost reached the village of Culkerton, $1\frac{1}{2}$ miles away. This was completed by January 1944, as work built up on Typhoons, Tempests, assault gliders (Horsa and Hamilcar) and Albemarle glider tugs, in preparation for the invasion of Europe. The imminence of D-Day was felt on 27 May when twenty-four C-47s arrived to collect Horsas for the USAAF. Work in support of the invasion air forces continued throughout the summer. Types such as the Buckingham then began to appear, and work started on upgrading Lancasters by installing Merlin 45 engines.

C-47s of the USAAF reappeared at Kemble on 5 September 1944 to use it as a forward base to take supplies, rations, ammunition and fuel to Douai in France to support the US offensive, stalled through lack of supplies. There were 225 aircraft involved, some making second trips, totalling 580 movements that day. Re-supply flights continued on virtually a daily basis until 12 December. In January 1945 Kemble was transferred to 47 Group, Transport Command, 5 MU then becoming virtually fully engaged in dealing with transport aircraft such as Dakotas, Warwicks, Yorks, Lancastrians and Stirlings.

The war over, units returned to the UK to disband, and their aircraft were brought to Kemble and other ASUs for storage. In December 1945 1,030 aircraft were in storage at 5 MU, the vast majority for disposal. The first auctions then started, and numbers gradually reduced as airframes were sold, scrapped, or put aside for future use. Kemble returned to Maintenance Command in 1946, and became one of the main MUs in the UK. Meteors and other jets started to appear, and in

Kemble is still home to Hunters – T7 WV372 is seen here outside the Delta Jets hangar in May 2005.

1952 the first of 580 Canadair Sabres arrived at Kemble, having been ferried over from Canada by Operation *Beechers Brook*. The aircraft were camouflaged in the paint shop, which later became the Surface Finish Section, justly renowned for the high standard of its paint schemes.

Hunters arrived in the mid-1950s and for the next thirty years 5 MU was to become the 'Hunter MU'. The aircraft were a familiar sight in the circuit through to the 1980s, but some were actually based there with a CFS detachment known as 4 Squadron. Gnats joined the CFS Hunters at Kemble and it was there in 1965 that the Red Arrows were formed, becoming the official full-time RAF Aerobatic Team in 1969. When the Hunters of 4 Squadron departed for Valley in April 1976, the Red Arrows remained and re-equipped at Kemble with the Hawk for the 1980 season.

The Red Arrows moved to Scampton in 1983 when 5 MU was closed and Kemble was transferred to the USAF. The station then became a maintenance base for A-10 Thunderbolts and other types used by the USAF in the UK. The Americans remained until 1992, and Kemble was officially closed in March 1993 in a ceremony that brought the Red Arrows back to their former base.

The extensive facilities at Kemble were subsequently leased by the MoD to several civilian companies. A flying club was established, Hunters reappeared operated by Delta Jets, and the Bristol Aero Collection has found a home in one of the hangars. The airfield was sold off by Defence Estates in 2000 to its users as the Kemble Heritage Group, and with regular air displays and other events held there, Kemble's continued future as an airfield looks good.

Main features:
Runways: 270° 6,000ft x 150ft, 320° 3,900ft x 150ft, concrete and asphalt. *Hangars:* one Type C, four Type D, two Type E, four Type L, four Lamella, eight Robin, four Super Robin, two Blister. *Hardstandings:* twenty spectacle. *Accommodation:* RAF Officers 36, SNCOs 89, ORs 897; WAAF Officers 4, SNCOs 6, ORs 166.

LAIRA, Devon

SX510554, 1¹/₂ miles E of Plymouth city centre, off A38

The RNAS had been considering the possibilities of extending the range of its airships in 1917 by establishing a network of secure moorings between its main bases that would double as safe havens in case of bad weather. Early in 1918 trials were carried out at Saltram Park, close to the old Plymouth Racecourse on Chelston Meadow. A site was selected that was conveniently sheltered by trees from all but an easterly wind. Despite airship SST2 being damaged during a visit on 15 March 1918, the trial was declared a success.

As the result, a mooring-out site was opened as a sub-station, taking its name from the Laira district of Plymouth. Commissioned with moorings for two SS or coastal airships, no buildings were erected, the ratings living in the nearby racecourse grandstand. Operations were flown under the control of C-in-C Devonport, concentrating on anti-submarine patrols over the Dockyard approaches and covering convoys passing along the South Devon coast. With the formation of the RAF, Mullion and its sub-stations such as Laira came under the command of 9 Group, but operational control was retained by Devonport.

Patrols from Laira were largely uneventful, the only major problem occurring just before the Armistice, when SS214 was wrecked there on 6 November. Operations continued for a few months after the war, but with the decision to withdraw non-rigid airships from sea patrol, Laira sub-station was closed.

The old Plymouth Racecourse had been used briefly in 1911 by the pioneering lady aviator Mrs Blondeau Hewlett, and flying was resumed after the Great War by the Berkshire Aviation Company, which took members of the public up in its Avro 504 biplanes for joyrides in return for a fee of 5 shillings. Attempts to start air services from Laira were made in 1923 with route-proving flights being made by Surrey Flying Services to Croydon and Manchester. However, the use of Chelston Meadow was not approved by the Civil Aviation Branch of the Air Ministry because of its many ditches, and further services were flown from a preferred site on the polo ground at Roborough.

Lake Down, home of 14 TDS, in 1917.

LAKE DOWN, Wiltshire

SU010393, 7 miles NNW of Salisbury, alongside A360

When it was decided to establish another flying training station on Salisbury Plain early in 1917 an area of pastureland to the north of Salisbury was requisitioned. Surrounded by tumuli and barrows, the 160-acre site covered a prehistoric field system to the west of the village of Lake, and was known as Lake Down.

Buildings soon went up alongside the landing ground, which was laid out in a roughly diamond shape. A technical site was established on its western edge, covering 30 acres and consisting of six paired GS sheds, an Aeroplane Repair Shed and two MT sheds. A number of Bessoneau canvas hangars were later added. The domestic and administration accommodation was built to the north on the opposite side of the road. Lake Down was connected to other military camps on Salisbury Plain by a railway network, a spur of which ended with an engine shed and water tower beside the airfield.

Lake Down seen in June 2006. The airfield covered the large light-coloured field, its sides then projecting further into a diamond shape. The woods in the centre of the photo cover the former main hangar area.

The water tower and railway engine shed at Lake Down in March 2009.

No 2 Training Depot Station formed at Lake Down on 15 August 1917 by moving in elements of 35, 19 and 9 Training Squadrons (from Filton, Hounslow and Mousehold Heath), becoming A, B and C Flights respectively. The unit flew Shorthorn, BE2C, BE2E, DH4, DH6, RE8 and HP0/100 aircraft, but did not remain at Lake Down for long, moving to Stonehenge in December to make room for day-bombing training.

No 2 TDS exchanged places with 107, 108 and 109 Squadrons, later joined by 136 Squadron, formed on 1 April 1918, the day that the RAF was born. All four squadrons flew DH9s, supplemented by a few other types. They had hardly settled when it was announced that 14 TDS would form at Lake Down, on 6 June. To make room, early in June 107 Squadron moved to Le Quesney in France, and 108 Squadron left for Kenley. The remaining squadrons disbanded, 136 on 4 July and 109 on 18 August.

Operating under the command of 33 Wing, which had its HQ nearby at Druid's Lodge, 14 TDS maintained the day-bombing training role at Lake Down. It had thirty-six Avro 504Ks, thirty-six DH4/DH9s and 858 personnel. With construction of the airfield's facilities completed in early August 1918, a full training programme was maintained. However, when the Armistice came in November, training started to run down. Activity eventually stopped at Lake Down, aircraft were grounded and 14 TDS moved to Boscombe Down towards the end of the year.

Lake Down remained open, and in mid-February 1919 the Sopwith Snipes and cadre personnel of 201 Squadron arrived from Bethencourt in France. They were joined by 14 TDS which returned from Boscombe Down during March, then flying BE2Es, BE12s, DH4s, DH9s and Avro 504Ks. It was re-designated 14 Training Squadron in June, but disbanded in September when 201 Squadron moved to Eastleigh. Lake Down was then closed.

Most of the technical and domestic buildings were removed following auction, and woodland now covers much of their former sites. The few buildings that remain of this well-appointed airfield are the workshops, engine shed and water tower of the military railway, which still stand alongside the main road.

LAND'S END (ST JUST), Cornwall

SW375292, 5 miles W of Penzance, on B3306

Captain Gordon Olley of Olley Air Services saw the potential of an air service between the Isles of Scilly and the mainland, and in 1935 purchased land between Sennen and St Just as a base. He made several proving flights using DH84 Dragons, and in May 1936 formed Channel Air Services to start a service between Land's End Aerodrome and St Mary's. Construction of the airfield (also known as St Just) was completed in 1937, giving a landing run of 2,100 feet, with facilities including a hangar (relocated from Squire's Gate Aerodrome, Blackpool), booking office and refuelling point. Regular daily services started on 15 September, using DH84 Dragon G-ADCR. The flight time of 20 minutes against the 4 hours taken by the *Scillonian* steamer meant that the service was soon a great success, more Dragons were obtained, and on 5 May the following year it was extended to Plymouth and on to Bristol. In December 1938 Channel Air Services and its routes were taken over by Great Western & Southern Air Lines. Three days later Western Airways also started operations from St Just with Dragons, to Swansea via Newquay and Barnstaple.

Although all civil air services were suspended with the outbreak of war on 3 September 1939, the need for speedy communications with the Isles of Scilly soon became apparent, and the service was reopened, the only internal air service in the south of the country. The three DH84s of Great Western & Southern, which now included G-ADDI, were camouflaged and re-started the schedule on 25 September. During the winter of 1939/40 the frequency was reduced to three flights per day, resulting in one Dragon being used for local searchlight cooperation. Military aircraft landed occasionally, such as the Lysanders of 16 Squadron flying anti-invasion coastal patrols from Roborough, an Army exercise in April 1941 resulting in the whole of the Squadron's A Flight moving in for a couple of weeks.

The air service was suspended on 3 June 1941 following the disappearance of DH84 G-ACPY just after having left St Mary's, presumed shot down by an enemy aircraft (it was later established that it had been attacked by an He 111). Flights were resumed on 27 October, but were stopped again by the Air Ministry a week later. The ban was lifted again on 12 January 1942, and limited services to Scilly resumed, with the result that it proved to be the only UK internal air route flown almost continuously throughout the war. For a period Land's End airfield was partially obstructed to deter enemy airborne landings, which restricted landings in certain wind conditions. A pasture near Sennen was therefore allocated as an alternative landing field should a diversion be required.

Visitors in 1943 included the largest aircraft ever to land at St Just, a Fortress, which made an emergency landing on 16 September. The pilot managed to bring the aircraft to a halt just before it hit the boundary wall at the end of the runway. The Observer Corps post atop nearby Carn Brea reported its arrival to the duty controller at the airport, who didn't believe them until he looked out of the window and saw the bomber suddenly appear over the slope at the far end of the airfield, taxying towards him! The aircraft, B-17F 42-30018 of 305th BG, had diverted following a raid on Nantes due to shortage of fuel. Once it had been checked over, everything portable was removed to enable it to lift off again on the 28th for St Eval with a minimal fuel load.

Full peacetime scheduled services resumed in May 1945 with DH89 Dragon Rapides. For a while from June the Proctors of St Mary's-based Island Air Services started calling in on freight and passenger charters. On 1 February 1947 Great Western & Southern, its routes and aircraft, were taken over by BEA, its Rapides becoming known as the 'Islander' Class. A number of other operators, including Murray Chown Aviation, Melba Airways and Olley Air Services, flew short-lived services from Land's End in the early 1950s. By 1953 BEA was well-established, Land's End to the Isles of Scilly being its busiest route, with 36,000 passengers, 50 tons of freight and 12 tons of mail being flown that season. Its three Rapides were kept very busy, making more than twenty round trips per day at peak times. In June 1961 Mayflower also started using Land's End to call in on its Rapide Service from Plymouth to St Mary's, until the end of 1963.

BEA Dragon Rapide G-AJCL RMA Sir Henry Lawrence is on its way to Scilly in 1963. The village of Pendeen can be seen beneath its wheels, and Land's End Airport under its starboard wing-tip, in the middle-distance.

A long-term Land's End resident in the 1960s, pristine Messenger 2A G-AJKK is seen in June 1966.

The veteran Rapides were worked hard by BEA, but in the mid-1960s it was decided to replace them. In an imaginative move, following trials with a Westland WS-55, it was decided to introduce helicopters to the route. Sikorsky S-61s were acquired, and the first scheduled rotary-wing services were started on 2 May 1964. The helicopters flew from Land's End until September, when they moved to a new purpose-built heliport built on Penzance's Eastern Green. The airport was then managed by Land's End Aero Club, established by aircraft restorer and businessman Viv Bellamy.

A new enterprise, Scillonia Airways, was formed at Land's End in 1965 by former BOAC pilot Captain Brian Neely. Services to St Mary's and Newquay were started in June 1966 with one Rapide, and that summer four more were added to the fleet, including some ex-BEA machines enabling pleasure flights to be made as well as more frequent services. By 1968 it was the last commercial operator in Europe to use the Rapide on scheduled services. Unfortunately, despite expansion plans, including the acquisition of Twin Pioneers, Scillonia's financial position deteriorated and it went into liquidation in May 1970.

Dragon Rapide G-AHKU Bishop *awaits its passengers at Land's End in July 1969.*

Viv Bellamy Camel replica 'C1701' seen in the hangar at Land's End in April 1977.

Island Air Charter was formed in June 1970 at Land's End with Islander G-AYCV for charter work, pleasure flights and cargo. More Islanders appeared in September when Brymon Aviation started regular charter flights to Land's End. Viv Bellamy formed Westward Airways (Land's End) in August 1971, using Rapide G-AIYR for pleasure flights and skydiving until 1978. The company also operated the Land's End Flying School as well as restoring vintage aeroplanes and making flying replicas; examples of the latter included the Hawker Fury, Fokker Triplane, Fairey Flycatcher, Sopwith Camel, DH2, Sopwith $1^1/_2$ Strutter and Supermarine S5 floatplane. Its many

BN2 Islander G-AXWR of Isles of Scilly Skybus in June 1994.

restorations included Fairey Albacore N4389, delivered to the FAA Museum Yeovilton in the spring of 1987 after four years' work. Much of this work took place in the original 4,080-square-foot hangar, but in early 1989 a new double hangar was erected alongside it, adding substantially to the airport's storage and maintenance facilities. The Isles of Scilly Steamship Company (ISSC) had by this time acquired Westward Airways and, as the main user of Land's End, also invested in the upgrade of the control tower and operations building.

The ISSC had formed Isles of Scilly Skybus in the spring of 1984 to complement its steamer services. In October 1984 it started freight services from Land's End to St Mary's using an Islander, and in March 1987 was allowed to carry passengers on the route. Its routes were later extended to cover Bristol, Exeter, Newquay and Plymouth, using a number of Islanders, supplemented by a DHC6 Twin Otter in 1993. In 2001 Land's End Airport was purchased by Ambercroft Properties Ltd, but its main user remained the ISSC. A second Twin Otter was added to the Skybus fleet in June 2002, and in August 2004 the company celebrated its 20th anniversary of operations, with a fleet of four Islanders and two Twin Otters flying from Land's End to Newquay, Exeter, Bristol and Southampton as well as St Mary's.

Westward Airways continued to operate Land's End Flying School, latterly with Cessna 152s and 172s and Piper Cherokees, but this operation became a casualty of the recession in 2009, closing down on 31 January. Skybus continues to fly services from Land's End, and the airport is a popular destination for visiting private aircraft, particularly during the summer.

The Bristol School, Larkhill, established in June 1910. Boxkite primary trainers and Bristol-Prier Monoplane advanced trainers are parked by the hangars.

LARKHILL, Wiltshire

SU135437 (Durrington Down), 2 miles NW of Amesbury
SU120455 (Knighton Down), 2 miles N of Stonehenge

Larkhill has a special place in aviation history as the home to many of Britain's pioneers of flight. Although the original airfield was abandoned years ago, it was established in the earliest days of flying and became the first military airfield in Britain. There is one main recognisable site, but aircraft have flown from several different locations in the area, all given the same name. The first flying at Larkhill was by the balloons of the Royal Engineers in the late 19th century, but powered aircraft were soon to appear.

During the summer of 1909 Horatio Barber, an early enthusiast, built an aircraft shed on Army land that he had rented near Larkhill Artillery Barracks, close to the junction of Tombs Road and the Packway in an area known as the Hill of the Larks, on Durrington Down. Barber flew an aeroplane of his own design, the Valkyrie, from the field nearby and was joined the following year by G. D. Cockburn and Captain J. D. B. Fulton of the Royal Artillery, when the War Office offered free use of the area for flying. In June 1910 the Bristol School of Aviation was established there to train military pilots. The first Army experiments in aerial reconnaissance were made shortly afterwards, and two Bristol Boxkites observed the September manoeuvres on Salisbury Plain.

On 1 April 1911 the Air Battalion, Royal Engineers, was formed, with its HQ and No 1 Company (with balloons, airships and kites) at Farnborough and No 2 Company (with aeroplanes) at Larkhill. The latter became 3 Squadron when the Royal Flying Corps was formed in May 1912.

Designer Pierre Prier with a Bristol-Prier P-1 monoplane at Larkhill in July 1911.

In August Larkhill was the venue for the first Military Aircraft Trials, mounted to find suitable aircraft designs for the Army. Interest was shown by a number of aircraft manufacturers, and although the Cody Biplane was selected as the winner, the two examples purchased as a result of the trials were soon replaced in service by BE2As.

Five of the original Bristol School hangars remain at Larkhill, seen here in April 2009 in use as Army accommodation stores. They are probably the oldest purpose-built aeronautical buildings in the UK.

Northrop SD-1 drone XT584 at Knighton Down in August 1976.

Hercules C1 XV186 uses the airstrip at Knighton Down in June 1995.

With the development of Upavon and Netheravon on more extensive sites nearby, aeronautical activity started to tail off at Larkhill. No 3 Squadron moved to Netheravon in June 1913 and the Bristol School departed for Brooklands a year later, having trained 129 pilots until that point. With the outbreak of war the local barracks expanded, and soon the airfield was covered in hundreds of corrugated iron huts.

Although flying at the original Larkhill airfield had ceased, a new site a mile to the north came into use in the 1920s. This was Knighton Down, used by aircraft taking part in exercises. Nos 2, 4, 13 and 16 Squadrons all used the area, the main location becoming known as RAF Larkhill from January 1936. Facilities were rudimentary, to say the least, with tents supplementing a sole wooden hut when the airfield was in use.

The first unit to be permanently based there was D Flight, which formed at Larkhill on 1 February 1940 as part of No 1 School of Army Cooperation. Equipped with a variety of types, including Piper Cubs, Stinson Voyagers, Taylorcraft Ds and at least one Gloster Gauntlet, the unit was formed to evolve and evaluate AOP tactics and methods. It went to France in mid-April to work in operational conditions, but a month later returned to the UK following the German offensive. The flight returned to Larkhill on 3 June, resuming its AOP work. It started training AOP pilots, sufficient to form the first AOP Squadron, 651, at Old Sarum on 1 August 1941. On 20 September D Flight was re-designated 1424 Flight, and took part with 651 Squadron in Exercise *Bumper*, a large firepower demonstration on Salisbury Plain commanded by General Montgomery. Both AOP units acquitted themselves well, and it was decided to form more.

By the end of 1941 a hangar had been built at Larkhill to provide cover for 1424 Flight's aircraft, which included a number of Tiger Moths. AOP pilot training continued into 1942 and on 1 October the importance of this activity was recognised when 1424 Flight was upgraded to become 43 OTU. It was increased in size and subsequently moved, with its thirty-two aircraft, to the much larger airfield at Old Sarum. For the remainder of the war Larkhill was little used, as AOP Austers tended to use unprepared fields for training.

Helicopters gradually took over from the Austers of the AOP squadrons in the 1950s, and their need for prepared airfields became even less than that of their predecessors. Knighton Down has, however, been a convenient operating area for helicopters visiting the School of Artillery over the years. An airstrip has been marked out there for exercises and displays taking place on the Larkhill

An aerial view of the former airfield in June 2006, now partly covered by roads and housing. The remaining Bristol hangars can be seen lower centre right.

ranges involving fixed-wing aircraft such as Middle Wallop Islanders and Lyneham Hercules. Needing little in the way of facilities, helicopters have also operated from other parts of Larkhill Garrison, at least one detachment of Sioux being attached to 49 Field Regiment, RA, between 1967 and 1969, hangared in storage sheds at Roberts Barracks.

Three hangars remain in place today on the site of the original airfield on Durrington Downs, and are used by the Army for storage. A plaque nearby confirms that it is the site of the first military airfield in the country.

Avro 504K F4241 of 8 TS, AFC, at Leighterton in 1918.

LEIGHTERTON, Gloucestershire

ST829924, 4¹/₂ miles SW of Nailsworth, alongside A46

Motorists calling at the Aerodrome Garage on the Bath-Stroud road high up on the Cotswolds may well speculate on the origins of its name as, although it is not far from Babdown Farm, the latter is not visible. The buildings were in fact constructed much earlier, as part of Leighterton airfield, a flying training station built for the Australians during 1917.

Opened in February 1918 as No 2 Station, it came under No 1 Wing of the Australian Flying Corps, which had its HQ at Tetbury. The field covered 172 acres, and had landing runs of 2,700 feet E/W and 3,450 feet N/S. The technical site ran alongside the main road and consisted of four aeroplane sheds and a repair hangar, together with stores, workshop and MT sheds. The domestic site was to the north of the airfield, and an air-to-ground firing range was set up and marked out at Long Newnton to the east, which became an airfield during the Second World War.

The first unit to arrive was 8 (Training) Squadron, AFC, which arrived on 18 February 1918 from Tern Hill. Flying Avro 504s, Pups and Camels proudly marked with an emu on their fuselages, its role was to train pilots to fly fighters. On the 23rd No 7 (Training) Squadron moved in from Yatesbury with Avro 504Ks, BE2Es, RE8s and DH6s, to train pilots and observers in reconnaissance; its aircraft were marked with a boomerang.

Flying from Leighterton was challenging, as its exposed position 630 feet above sea level and with deep valleys nearby resulted in turbulence and sudden downdraughts. Accidents were frequent, particularly to flimsy types such as the 504s and BE2s. More robust aircraft arrived in October 1918 when 7 Squadron received the Bristol F2B, and 8 Squadron the Snipe. By this time an Aircraft Repair Section had been established, and this dealt with most types in service at Leighterton and at

Aerodrome Garage, Leighterton, with the former Officers' Mess to the left, in March 2008.

the other Australian training station at Minchinhampton, except for the Snipe, which went to 3 (Western) Aircraft Repair Depot at Yate.

Intensive training carried on until the end of the war, then gradually tailed off, although the firing range was still in use in February 1919. The Australians moved out during the spring, but were replaced by 66 Squadron, which moved in from Yatesbury with Camels during March. It was joined in June 1919 by 28 Squadron, also with Camels, which had made a name for itself during combat in Italy. However, at the end of October the airfield closed, following the disbandment of 66 Squadron and the transfer of 28 Squadron to Eastleigh. The buildings were emptied and auctioned off, some of them reappearing in local villages in different guises. The Officers' Mess remained in place after the sale, and eventually became part of Aerodrome Garage.

The landing ground was used occasionally during the 1920s and '30s by private aircraft taking visitors such as the Prince of Wales to nearby country houses. The Bristol Gliding Club also flew from the airfield from November 1938, using bungees and cars to launch its Dagling and Grunau Baby gliders. The Dagling was written off in a fatal accident on 2 April 1939, and the club stopped flying on 23 July, with war inevitable.

During the Second World War Leighterton was used as an RLG by 9 SFTS Hullavington during the spring of 1940, before being laid out as a decoy site for Babdown Farm. Its usefulness was proven when it was bombed on two successive nights, 15 and 16 December 1940.

As well as the Aerodrome Garage, several other workshop and technical buildings still survive to the south just off the main road.

LONG NEWNTON, Gloucestershire

ST929920, 2 miles SE of Tetbury

Long Newnton was originally used during the First World War, when an air-to-ground firing range was laid out there for the AFC training squadrons based at Leighterton. It was reopened in late 1939 for the storage of ammunition, as a sub-site of 11 MU Chilmark. The stores were removed in July 1940 when it was selected as a decoy site for RAF Kemble, which occupied a similar topographical position 4 miles to the north-east. It was set out as a 'Q' site, a night decoy electrically lit to simulate an operational airfield.

It was not long before the suitability of Long Newnton as an airfield in its own right was realised, and 15 SFTS started using it as an RLG, bringing its Harvards across from Kidlington for night-flying training. Other units, such as 14 SFTS Lyneham, also used the airfield, but it was 3 SFTS South Cerney that decided to take it on as a SLG for its Oxfords in February 1941. Two runways of Sommerfield track were then laid, together with a concrete perimeter track. A control

Long Newnton control tower and operations building in June 2008.

tower and a number of buildings were erected, including four Blister hangars providing a technical site. In March 1942 No 3 SFTS became 3 (P)AFU, but continued to fly Oxfords, some based at Long Newnton. As more aircraft arrived more covered storage was needed, so a further half-dozen Blister hangars were erected around the airfield and a T1 hangar was added to the technical site.

In September 1943 the airfield was handed over to 15 (P)AFU, which also flew Oxfords, with its HQ at Ramsbury (later Castle Combe). The unit brought several flights in from Greenham Common to train, but heavy rain in October made ground conditions very difficult, and flying was curtailed until the spring of 1944. Bad weather again brought problems during the winter of 1944/45, and the airfield was hardly back to full operation when the war in Europe came to an end, and RAF flying training began to wind down.

No 15 (P)AFU left for Babdown Farm in June 1945, when flying ended at Long Newnton. The station then became a storage sub-unit of 11 MU once more, although by 1949 it was inactive. It was sold off in 1950 and returned to agriculture. Part of the perimeter track and a number of the airfield buildings remain, now in private use, including the T1 hangar, control tower, stores and accommodation.

Main features:
Runways: 214° 3,420ft, 272° 3,555ft, Sommerfield track. *Hangars:* one T1, six 69ft Blister, four 65ft Blister. *Accommodation:* RAF Officers 83, SNCOs 180, ORs 360; WAAF Officers 3, ORs 140.

LOPCOMBE CORNER, Wiltshire

SU 275356, 8½ miles NE of Salisbury on A30

In 1917 the RFC established a fighter training airfield alongside the Salisbury to Andover road (now the A343) a mile to the east of its junction with the present A30. The airfield was named after the road junction, 'Lopcombe Corner', and was roughly square-shaped, covering some 228 acres. On the eastern side of the airfield near Hollom Down Farm were technical and living sites, consisting of six aircraft and two storage hangars, an Aircraft Repair Shed and (later) a large number of wooden huts. (The RFC personnel initially lived in tents, but as winter approached they were billeted in local villages until barracks were provided at the airfield.)

Known to the locals as Hollom Down and also Jack's Bush, the camp opened on 5 September 1917 as No 3 Training Depot Station. It was formed by moving in elements of 54 and 62 Training Squadrons together with 28 Squadron (from Wyton, Gosport and Yatesbury), and merging them to

Avro 504K E1861 being re-assembled at Lopcombe Corner in 1917.

become A, B and C Flights respectively. The station operated a mix of aircraft, BE2Bs, BE2Es and DH6s being used for initial training, DH5s and Pups for more advanced work. Because the thin turf on the airfield's surface, typical of the local area, was soon cut to pieces by the tailskids of aircraft that kicked up the chalky soil, Lopcombe became notorious for its dust-storms, created by every take-off during dry weather.

Following the formation of the RAF on 1 April 1918, 3 TDS came under 34 Wing, 8 Group, with an establishment of thirty-six Avro 504Ks and thirty-six Camels, together with a strength of 839 Officers and other ranks. Training continued throughout the summer of 1918 in order to produce aircrews for the Western Front, and it was only after the Armistice in November that activity at Lopcombe slowed. There then came a severe cutback in flying, and 3 TDS gradually wound down during the early months of 1919.

Some of the accommodation vacated by TDS personnel was used to house the crews of squadrons returning from the continent. These included two SE5A units, 74 Squadron, which arrived from Halluin on 10 February, and 85 Squadron, flying in from Ascq on the 16th.

Mechanics are busy at Lopcombe, with a couple of Pups on the airfield.

A general view of Lopcombe in 1917.

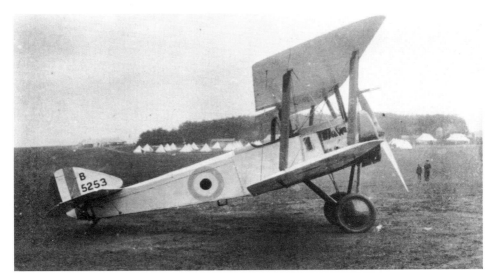

Pup B5253 Bluebird, *flown by Major Cogan, OC 3 TDS, early in 1918.*

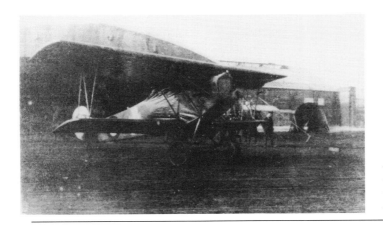

A captured Fokker DVII under evaluation at 3 TDS in early 1918.

A former Lopcombe airfield building, still in use in September 2006.

No 3 TDS disbanded on 15 May 1919 to become 3 Training Squadron, but it was not to last long in this guise, being finally disbanded on 20 June. Its place at Lopcombe was taken by a reconnaissance unit, 52 Squadron, which arrived just over a week later, on 28 June. It was in cadre form, having left its RE8 aircraft behind at its previous base, Netheravon. It was not long before the next disbandments took place; 74 and 85 Squadrons, which both stood down on the same day, 3 July. No 52 Squadron remained, but its personnel gradually dwindled until it too disbanded on 23 October 1919.

Lopcombe Corner was then declared surplus to requirements, and in November was closed to all aircraft except for emergency landings. Preparations for the disposal of the land and buildings then went ahead, and a series of auctions followed during 1920. Much of the airfield site remains as fields today, with a few of the former station buildings surviving as part of Hollom Down Farm or occupied as small industrial units.

LULSGATE BOTTOM (BROADFIELD DOWN), Somerset

ST504651, 6 miles SW of Bristol, alongside A38

The airfield with the delightful name of Lulsgate Bottom was opened as an RLG in September 1940 for the use of 10 EFTS, which flew Tiger Moths from Weston-super-Mare. Facilities were basic, and because of the airfield's small size and bad weather record it was initially little used. Flying expanded during 1941 and two Blister hangars were built to provide cover for the visiting aircraft.

Attention from the Luftwaffe came in November, and again in March and April 1941, not because of the airfield's importance, but because of its proximity to a Starfish site built at Downside as a decoy for Bristol. Nonetheless, it was decided to develop the site as 10 Group, Fighter Command, was short of operating bases in the region. Flying training stopped on 10 June 1941 when construction started on three runways for a new airfield to be known as Broadfield Down. Work was advanced but not complete when the first arrival appeared at the new airfield on 24 July. This was a Ju 88A-4 of 3/KG40 whose crew had been misled by a fake navigational beam transmitted from an RAF Meacon station near Weston-super-Mare. The Germans thought they had landed in France, and had dismounted to await transport – they were rather shocked when this turned out to be a British Army lorry full of armed troops! Their aircraft later joined 1426 (Enemy Aircraft) Flight at Collyweston.

The new airfield was officially opened by 10 Group on 15 January 1942 with its initial title of Lulsgate Bottom reinstated. The runways, hangars and technical facilities were complete, but it was to be several months before the domestic accommodation was ready for occupation. The first unit to arrive, on 24 January, came from Filton and was 286 Squadron, flying Lysanders, Hurricanes, Blenheims, Masters and Oxfords in the target facilities role. The author's father was among the ground staff that arrived that day, as an Airframe Fitter with M Flight. The Squadron was joined two days later by a detachment of 116 Squadron, an AA calibration unit with Hurricanes and Blenheims. The detachment didn't stay for long, leaving for Hendon on 1 March, but 286 Squadron flew hundreds of sorties from Lulsgate in support of RAF and Army units across the South West until 26 May when it moved to Zeals.

A few days after 286 Squadron's departure, on 1 June 1942, Lulsgate was transferred to 23 Group, Flying Training Command, as a satellite of 3 (P)AFU, South Cerney. Two flights of the unit arrived to take up residence with Oxfords, and both staff and pupils found their new base to be ideal for training. Accommodation was gradually expanded to cater for the extra training and support staff required, but the increased level of flying and the intensive nature of flying training inevitably resulted in an increase in flying accidents. Most were minor, such as heavy landings, and resulted in few injuries. Others were more serious and some proved fatal, as for example on the night of 22 September 1942, when Oxford I W6610 dived into the ground, killing both occupants. Visiting aircraft were also sometimes involved in mishaps, as on 15 October when two FAA Fulmars from 761 Squadron, Yeovilton, collided and crashed over the airfield, one pilot being killed.

A Standard Beam Approach system was installed during the spring of 1943 to enable a new unit, 1540 (BAT) Flight, to be formed at Lulsgate on 15 April with Oxfords to train 3 (P)AFU students. The BAT Flight remained at the station when the aircraft and personnel of the AFU departed for Southrop on 27 September. In its place came 3 FIS(A), which moved in from Hullavington and Castle Combe. The school was organised into five flights, A to E, and trained its pupils on Masters, Oxfords and Harvards. The SBA system enabled an increasing number of aircraft to use Lulsgate, including those of BOAC, which saw it as a useful diversion airfield in case of bad weather, fuel shortage or congestion at Whitchurch. Masters replaced Magisters at 3 FIS(A) during 1944, and in May the unit had ten on strength, together with fifty Oxfords. No 1540 BAT Flight had a complement of eight Oxfords in early 1945, and took these to Weston Zoyland when it transferred there on 6 February. In its place came the OTU Flight of 7 FIS(A) from Upavon with thirteen Oxfords.

Flying training continued uninterrupted at Lulsgate after the German surrender in May 1945, as war still raged in the Far East. However, it was eventually decided to reduce activity, and 3 FIS(A) was disbanded on 18 July. The unit's aircraft (by then mainly Oxfords and Harvards) and remaining staff were taken on by 7 FIS(A), and Lulsgate became a satellite of Upavon. Flying

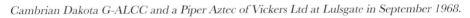

Cambrian Dakota G-ALCC and a Piper Aztec of Vickers Ltd at Lulsgate in September 1968.

training continued into 1946, but when 7 FIS(A)'s final course finished on 15 April it was closed and moved to Little Rissington, where it was to form the basis of a re-born CFS.

On 8 May Lulsgate was reduced to C&M, but was soon in use by the Bristol Gliding Club. In 1948 and 1949 its taxiways became the venue for motor racing, which then moved to Castle Combe. The gliding club moved to Nympsfield in 1955 following the decision by Bristol Corporation to purchase a 300-acre site at Lulsgate Bottom for the city's new airport. Work started immediately to improve the runways and erect a terminal building in the north-east corner of the airfield next to the A38. Bristol Airport was opened on 1 May 1957 by the Duchess of Kent with inaugural services by Aer Lingus and Cambrian Airways. The first year proved very successful, with 33,000 passengers and 608,000kg of freight passing through. The 3,930-foot runway was extended to 6,598 feet in 1963, allowing operation of larger four-engined aircraft and resulting in a steady growth of passenger numbers. The passenger terminal was extended in 1965 and a new freight transit shed was built three years later.

By 1972 annual passenger numbers had grown to 328,408, and although the collapse of Court Line the following year caused a fall in passengers, the inclusive tour charter market expanded during the 1980s with a number of carriers using Bristol. Radar systems were updated with an ILS in 1984 and the terminal was extended once more. The following year a new scheduled service to the Isles of Scilly was started by Brymon Airways. Paramount Airways, Bristol's first locally based charter airline, then started flights to Tenerife and Malaga. Aer Lingus increased the frequency of its services in 1989, followed by the arrival of Lufthansa and NLM, but Jersey European was then the largest operator from Bristol. Two years later Sabena and Crossair also commenced services, and by 1992 annual passenger figures were 843,000. In 1993 Aer Lingus started daily services to New York via Dublin using Airbus A330s.

By 1996 passenger numbers had reached 1.4 million per annum, and when, the following year, Bristol City Council sold its controlling interest to First Group the airport was re-launched as Bristol International. Although the passenger terminal was refurbished in 1998, this was only an interim measure, as on 3 March 2000 an entirely new building was opened as part of a major development that included diverting the A38 and installing a new ILS. The airport's first direct transatlantic services, to Toronto by Royal Airlines, then started in a year that saw passenger figures reach 2 million.

More investment followed the acquisition of the airport by Macquarie Bank and Ferrovial Aeroportas for £198 million in January 2001, South West Airports Ltd being formed as an

An Easyjet Boeing 737 waits for Air Southwest Dash 8 G-WOWC to clear the runway at Lulsgate in August 2005.

Bristol Airport in July 2006.

operating company. A new control tower was opened later in the year and, with the introduction of services by the low-fare airline Go (later absorbed by Easyjet) and new routes to Paris by Air France and Aer Arran to Dublin, annual passenger numbers leapt; by 2004 they stood at just under 4.6 million. Air Southwest started services to Manchester and Plymouth later that year, together with Isles of Scilly Skybus services to Newquay.

In 2005 the airport's 50th anniversary was celebrated with the doubling of passenger numbers and tripling of scheduled flights in less than five years. In May Continental Airlines started services to New York, followed by First Choice with charter flights to Florida, Dominica and Cuba in 2006. A £17 million runway resurfacing project was completed in May 2007. In 2008 new routes were introduced by Ryanair, Lufthansa and Flyglobespan, taking the number of scheduled routes from Bristol to seventy-seven and charter destinations to fifty-nine, encompassing 122 destinations in twenty-nine countries.

Bristol International's success as one of the prime South West airports continues, with ever-increasing passenger figures and a new expansion scheme announced in 2008. With the constant development that has taken place at the airport over the years little remains today of its RAF past.

Main features:
Runways: 030° 3,300ft x 150ft, 100° 3,900ft x 150ft, 160° 3,300ft x 150ft, concrete and tarmac. *Hangars:* one Bellman, three Double Blisters, one Single Blister. *Hardstandings:* six double fighter pens, three 20ft diameter circular. *Accommodation:* RAF Officers 128, SNCOs 125, ORs 572; WAAF Officers 4, SNCOs 10, ORs 204.

LYMINGTON, Hampshire

SZ342960, 1 mile E of Lymington

Lymington was one of twenty-three airstrips built along the South Coast to act as forward operating bases to support the proposed landings in France. Known as Advanced Landing Grounds, they were given limited facilities as they were only to be used for a short period. It was situated at Snooks' Farm, and was also known as Pylewell. Surveyed in 1942, it was laid out in the form of two temporary runways consisting of steel-mesh Sommerfield track. Also provided were seventy-five steel-mesh dispersals, several Blister hangars and a 74,000-gallon fuel storage area. Personnel were to live in tents.

During March 1944 the personnel of the USAAF's 50th Fighter Group (consisting of the 10th, 81st and 313th Fighter Squadrons) moved in, having recently arrived in the UK. When their P-47D Thunderbolts arrived the units started intensive training and were ready to fly their first mission on 1 May, a sweep along the French coast. Dive-bombing and machine-gun attacks on German installations, and transport and communications soon followed. Intensive daily missions continued from Lymington until 25 June, when the 50th FG moved to Carentan in France. The unit shot down six enemy aircraft during operations from the ALG, losing six P-47s. There was no further activity at Lymington, and the ALG was soon de-requisitioned and returned to agriculture. Although the steel-mesh runways and dispersals were lifted, the Blister hangars were left, one remaining in place today as a farm store.

Main features:
Runways: E-W 4,800ft, S-N 4,200ft, Sommerfield track. *Hangars:* four Blister. *Hardstandings:* seventy-five Sommerfield track.

Liberator I AM922 of 511 Squadron at Lyneham in October 1943.

LYNEHAM, Wiltshire

SU005785, 8 miles SW of Swindon, off A420

Situated on the edge of a plateau overlooking the valley of the Wiltshire Avon, Lyneham is unusual among today's front-line stations in that it was not opened or modernised during the 1930s RAF Expansion Scheme.

Selected as the site for an Aircraft Storage Unit, building started in 1939. RAF Lyneham was opened by 41 Group, Maintenance Command, on 18 May 1940 to house 33 MU. It consisted of a central group of four Lamella hangars with support buildings placed around them and four further groups of hangars around the perimeter of the grass airfield. Domestic accommodation was in huts, some on the main site, others on five dispersed living sites. The WAAF quarters and mess hall were in Lyneham village.

As an ASU, the MU was responsible for the receipt, storage, servicing, modification and issue of aircraft. The first types to arrive were Blenheims, Wellingtons, Proctors, Tiger Moths and Lysanders, and by September 1940 more than 150 aircraft were in store. Lyneham drew the attention of the Luftwaffe on 10 September when a single German aircraft machine-gunned the airfield, but without causing any serious damage or casualties. Nine days later an He 111 dropped an incendiary and two HE bombs onto one of the unfinished central hangars, causing severe damage and killing five workmen. The hangar was never completed to its full length, and today, as the Air Cargo Hangar (J4), it is shorter than the others. The last attack on Lyneham was on 15 March 1941, once again by a single aircraft that dropped four bombs and fired its machine-guns, damaging a couple of aircraft but with no casualties.

On 16 August 1941 No 14 SFTS moved from Cranfield to take over the airfield for flying training with Oxfords, and three days later control of Lyneham passed to 23 Group, Flying Training Command. This was not to last as, on 20 January, 14 SFTS moved to Ossington to make way for transport operations.

A Spitfire IXC outside D1 Hangar, 33 MU, in 1944.

No 44 Group, Ferry Command, took over Lyneham on 14 February 1942 and the Ferry Training Unit arrived from Honeybourne. Equipped with a variety of types such as the Wellington, Bombay, Beaufort, Mosquito and Hudson, the unit's role was to train crews to fly such aircraft over long distances on delivery to the Middle East, and was re-designated the Ferry Training & Despatch Unit on 28 March. It was joined in the ferry training role by 1445 Ferry Training Flight, formed at Lyneham on 27 February with Liberators, Halifaxes and Fortresses, and in June by 1444FTF, which flew Hudsons and moved from Horsham St Faith.

No 1425 Communications Flight had arrived from Honeybourne in April, and was soon flying Liberators on courier and passenger services to Africa and the Middle East. Renowned Liberator AL504 ('Commando') joined the flight in May and on 1 August left Lyneham carrying Sir Winston Churchill to the Middle East. Other VIPs carried by the unit later that month included General Alexander, Lord Alanbrooke, General Wavell and Air Chief Marshal Sir Arthur Tedder. The flight was brought up to squadron strength during the autumn, with twenty-five aircraft including Albemarles, and on 1 October was re-designated 511 Squadron. Another reorganisation on 3 November resulted in the FTDU being merged with 1444 and 1445 RTFs to form 301 Ferry Training Unit. Its A Flight trained crews on Blenheims, Beauforts, Beaufighters and Wellingtons, B Flight on Hudsons, and C Flight on Halifaxes and Liberators.

Hamilcar I LA643 at 33 MU in 1944.

Lyneham-based Comet C2 XK297 of 216 Squadron in 1957.

In January 1943 No 33 MU, which had previously dealt with a variety of types, became a mainly Spitfire holding unit. By the end of June 1943 it had 240 in stock, ranging from Mk Is to Mk IXs, plus some Seafires. At the end of the year it also took on the role of assembling and holding Hamilcar gliders, and was eventually to produce 250 of the type. SLGs, such as Townsend and Everleigh, were used for storage.

In early 1943 BOAC started to use Lyneham as one of its main terminals for passengers and freight, using Liberators and Dakotas, and was to continue to do so for two years. By the time of BOAC's arrival three hard runways had been built to cope with heavy transport aircraft, the first two in 1940 and 1941, later both extended, and a third, of 6,000 feet, two years later. With the formation of Transport Command in March 1943, Ferry Command was reduced to group status and, as 45 Group, assumed responsibility for RAF Lyneham. The aircraft of 511 Squadron continued to operate their scheduled routes, one of their Liberators, AL523, being lost on 5 July when, carrying the Polish leader General Sikorski, it went into the sea just after take-off from Gibraltar. Dakotas joined the unit in October, replacing Albemarles by the end of the year, and in November the York appeared.

In February 1944 No 525 Squadron transferred from Weston Zoyland, flying the Warwick transport on services to Gibraltar, extended to North Africa in March. The loss of two Warwicks during April led to them being replaced by Dakotas the following month. With the increased use of Lyneham by transport aircraft, it was decided to reorganise and relocate the remaining ferry units. On 16 March No 1 Ferry Crew Pool (which had been formed the previous August) and 301FTU were disbanded at Lyneham and merged to form 1 Ferry Unit at Pershore. Lyneham was transferred to 116 Wing on 24 July 1944.

By the autumn of 1944 Lyneham had become the main Transport Command base for southern England and was extremely busy, with more than 300 movements per day by the Dakotas, Liberators and Yorks of 511 and 525 Squadrons, B Flight of 511 Squadron was detached to form 246 Squadron on 11th October. Its Liberator VIIs were supplemented by Halifax IIIs a month later, with which the unit started flying routes to Cairo. It continued these from Holmsley South when the squadron was transferred there towards the end of December 1944.

The remaining squadrons, together with BOAC, maintained their busy schedules into 1945. There were many visiting aircraft, as foreign aircraft transited through and other RAF squadrons began using Lyneham as the UK terminal for overseas flights. These included 46 and 242 Squadrons, flying Stirlings to India. In July 1948 No 525 Squadron moved to Membury.

The end of the war resulted in increased activity not only to support occupying forces in Europe and the Far East, but also to repatriate Allied personnel. In October 1945 No 1409 Long Range Meteorological Reconnaissance Flight moved in with Mosquito IXs and PRXVIs, and

Britannia C1 XL660 of 99 Squadron flying from Lyneham in May 1970.

Liberator VIs, to reconnoitre the routes. On 1 December No 1389 VIP Flight formed, operating passenger and courier services with Lancastrians, leaving on 25 February 1946 for Bassingbourn. No 1409 LRMRF was disbanded on 13 May 1946, and although 511 Squadron followed on 7 October it was reformed again on 16 October with Yorks. Two more York squadrons appeared at Lyneham the following year, when 99 and 206 Squadrons reformed on 17 November 1947. It was not long before all three Lyneham York squadrons were to be heavily involved in operations, with the onset of the Berlin Airlift in June 1948. They spent the following year hauling supplies into the German capital from a forward base at Wunsdorf. This was not to be without cost, as four of Lyneham's Yorks were lost during the operation, two from 99 and two from 206 Squadron.

The arrival of 242 Squadron from Abingdon on 25 June 1949 heralded reorganisation at Lyneham. Together with 99 and 511 Squadrons, its Yorks were replaced with Hastings. No 206 Squadron retained its Yorks until disbandment on 20 February 1950, but was followed by 242 Squadron on 1 May. No 24 Squadron transferred briefly from Oakington in November 1950 to re-equip with the Hastings before moving on to Topcliffe in February 1951. It exchanged places with 53 Squadron, which flew its Hastings from Lyneham until January 1957, when it moved to Abingdon to re-equip with the Beverley. In May 1957 No 511 Squadron also moved out, to Colerne, where it later disbanded.

A formation of Hercules of the Lyneham Wing overflies the station in June 1994.

Hercules C2 XV301 makes a low run over Lyneham in August 2007.

Lyneham became the world's first military jet transport base in June 1956 when 216 Squadron formed with the Comet C2, but its operation required the demolition of two hangars to enable the main runway to be extended, to its present 7,830 feet. Another type new to Lyneham was the Britannia, which arrived to replace 99 Squadron's Hastings in June 1959. On 15 December No 511 Squadron reformed at Lyneham, also with the Britannia. The first Comet C4 arrived with 216 in February 1960, increasing the type's passenger capacity to ninety-four (from the C2's forty-four). Also operating in a VIP and medevac role, both variants operated until March 1967, when the last C2 left service. During the 1960s more than twenty Britannias and nine Comets operated from Lyneham, route-flying to Hong Kong via Singapore, to Australia and Africa as well as to Malta and Cyprus. The Britannia squadrons moved to Brize Norton in June 1970 but the Comets remained at Lyneham until 30 June 1975, when 216 Squadron disbanded.

A new terminal had opened in April 1967, replacing facilities dating back to the war years. Other new construction included Officers', Sergeants' and Airmen's Messes and living accommodation. This period also saw the demise of 33 MU. The unit had continued to support the Spitfire after the war, and in 1953 still had seventy-seven in long-term storage. Jets joining the Spitfires and eventually replacing

Hercules C5 ZH874 runs up beside Lyneham's terminal in July 2008.

them at the MU included the Meteor, Vampire, Canberra and Lightning. It was one of the latter that jumped the chocks during an engine run at Lyneham, and took to the air. The terrified Engineering Officer who was sitting in the cockpit managed to keep the aircraft under control and land it, albeit after several attempts! Eventually, with an ever-shrinking RAF, 33 MU closed on 31 December 1967.

On 1 August 1967 the first Hercules had arrived at Lyneham in the service of 36 Squadron, transferred from Colerne. A further six units appeared with the type (24 Squadron from Colerne in January 1968, 30 and 47 Squadrons in February 1971 from Fairford, 48 from Singapore in September 1971, and 70 Squadron from Cyprus in January 1975, followed by 242 OCU from Thorney Island that October). However, two (36 and 48 Squadrons) fell victim to defence cuts in November 1975 and January 1976 respectively. The Hercules has been the single type particularly associated with RAF Lyneham in the forty years since its arrival. With the Lyneham Wing the Hercules has been involved in a never-ending series of tactical and strategic operations and exercises, peace-keeping and humanitarian relief, ranging from the Falklands Conflict to the Gulf Wars and Afghanistan, and from Ethiopia and Nepal to the former Yugoslavia. Today Lyneham covers some 2,500 acres, has $3\frac{1}{2}$ miles of runways and 700 buildings accommodating 3,500 personnel and sixty Hercules. However, despite being such a hive of activity, the station's closure was announced as a cost-saving measure in 2003, to take effect in 2012. Although the units currently based at Lyneham are due to transfer to Brize Norton, it is hoped that a useful alternative role will be found for this important base.

Main features:
Runways: 252° 6,000ft x 150ft, 135° 4,800ft x 150ft, 006° 6,000ft x 150ft, concrete and tarmac. *Hangars:* four Type J, two Type K, eight Type L, thirty Blister. *Hardstandings:* thirty-two frying pan, one diamond, concrete apron for eighty aircraft. *Accommodation:* RAF Officers 290, SNCOs 263, ORs 2196; WAAF Officers 11, SNCOs 6, ORs 286.

MANNINGFORD, Wiltshire

SU130590, 2 miles WSW of Pewsey

CFS Upavon was looking for more RLGs following the outbreak of the war, due to an increase in the demand for flying instructors. One area selected was a pasture on Manningford Bohune Common, 2½ miles to the north of Upavon. Little preparation was required, and by the end of September 1939 the school's Tutors and Hart Trainers were busy as student pilots practised take-offs, circuit planning and landings. The site had its limitations, which is why it was chosen as a training airfield, but this meant that flying accidents did occur.

The CFS used Manningford until the spring of 1942, when it became 7 FIS and had no further use for the RLG, which passed to 29 EFTS Clyffe Pypard. This unit does not appear to have made much use of Manningford, but it was still in operation in 1946 when taken over by 2 EFTS Yatesbury. The school's Tiger Moths made good use of it for training until April 1947, when it was closed down.

The only equipment installed at Manningford was a windsock, and when this was taken down there was nothing to mark the field's former use.

MARLBOROUGH (HIGH TREES), Wiltshire

SU193678, 1 mile S of Marlborough off A346

Marlborough (also known as High Trees) was an unusual airfield, as not only did it slope away sharply to the north and south, but it was positioned on top of a railway tunnel! Opened by the Earl of Cardigan in 1935 as an unlicensed airfield, it had a couple of decent landing runs of up to 1,800 feet. The Earl flew his Avro 504N, which he kept in a barn alongside the main road, and other local fliers also brought their machines to Marlborough, which was listed by the AA as a recognised airfield.

In January 1936 the CFS started using High Trees for forced-landing training, mainly by Tutors and, later, Ansons. Other types that dropped in included Hawker Furies, one of which crashed there in May 1939. The Chilton Aircraft Company also used the airfield from 1937, to flight-test the DW1 Monoplanes that it manufactured nearby at Chilton Foliat. They were moved from the works by road, towed on their own wheels with outer wing panels removed. One of them, G-AFGI, was fitted with extra tankage for a long-range record attempt from High Trees, but the war intervened.

Chilton DW1 G-AFSV at High Trees in 1938; the hangar can be seen in the background.

Private flying stopped in September 1939 with the outbreak of war, and all four Chilton Monoplanes built were stored in the High Trees hangar, where they remained for the duration. The airfield, however, remained open as an SLG of Upavon. The intensity and nature of flying training invariably resulted in mishaps and accidents, and at least seven aircraft came to grief at Marlborough, including a Battle and a Blenheim; the latter overshot and fell over the embankment onto the railway.

Marlborough SLG remained in use until the spring of 1942 when Overton Heath was reopened, which 7 FIS, then in residence at Upavon, started to use in preference. Marlborough was eventually abandoned and returned to agricultural use. It was not reopened as an airfield after the war, although the Earl of Cardigan did use it for private flying into the late 1940s, and the barn that he used is still in place.

Fury K2094 of CFS came to grief at Marlborough in May 1939. A Tutor sits behind it.

MERRIFIELD, Cornwall

SX433566, 2¹/₂ miles WNW of Devonport on minor road off A374

Located on the western shore of the Hamoaze in the Tamar estuary close to Devonport Dockyard, Merrifield was established in early 1918 as No 16 Balloon Base for the operation of kite balloons. A sub-station was maintained at Torquay. Occupying 13 acres, the base consisted of six 100ft x 36ft balloon sheds, with support buildings nearby on Looking Glass Point. Domestic accommodation for the 185 crew of the base was aboard HMS *Valiant*, a hulk moored in the river nearby.

Six kite balloons were maintained for operations from Merrifield, one of which was permanently detached to Berry Head. The others were taken to sea aboard specially equipped naval escorts for convoy protection. Construction work at Merrifield was hardly complete when the Armistice was declared and, as kite balloons were then withdrawn from service, Merrifield was soon closed and its buildings removed.

Vampire T11s WZ456, WZ453 and WZ457 of 208 AFS, Merryfield, in 1953.

MERRYFIELD (ISLE ABBOTS), Somerset

ST342186, 4 miles NW of Ilminster

Work began during 1942 on the construction of a bomber station in the flat countryside near Ilminster, to be known as Isle Abbots. Three runways were laid, together with dispersals, hangars, airfield operations buildings and extensive domestic accommodation to house 3,200 personnel. Construction problems, such as filling in a canal crossing the site, meant that it was not until 12 February 1944 that the airfield was opened. By then its name had been changed to Merryfield, and it had been allocated to the IXth Troop Carrier Command of the US 9th AF. The first units to arrive, however, were 2815 and 2892 Field Squadrons, RAF Regiment, who were to defend the new station. They were followed, on 21 April, by US Army engineers, laying PSP alongside the main runway to enlarge the dispersal and marshalling areas for glider operations.

From 24 to 27 April a steady stream of aeroplanes and vehicles arrived at Merryfield to bring the four squadrons (99th, 100th, 300th and 301st Troop Carrier Squadrons) of the 441st Troop Carrier Wing. From its previous base at Langar, the Group brought more than seventy C-47s, together with a similar number of CG-4A Hadrian gliders. Training for D-Day started immediately, and by the end of May the Americans had become proficient at marshalling their gliders and tugs so that rapid hook-ups and concentrated take-offs could be made to achieve the rapid build-up of large formations of aircraft. On D-Day itself the C-47s of the 441st TCW dropped paratroops of the US 101st Airborne Division near St Mere Eglise to seize bridges and other key points, taking in reinforcements from 82nd Airborne Division by glider on D+1. Over the next few days they flew re-supply missions.

At the end of June the 61st Field Hospital was set up in Merryfield's south-east corner, staffed by the 813th Air Evacuations Squadron; casualties from Normandy started to arrive by air on 13 July. Following the detachment of three squadrons on Operation *Dragoon*, the landings in southern France, it was decided to move the whole Group to France, starting on 8 September. The airfield remained under the IXth TCC's control for another two months for the movement of freight and casualties.

Merryfield, disused in 1963.

At the end of November 1944 Merryfield was transferred to 47 Group, RAF Transport Command. No 238 Squadron was reformed there on 1 December, followed by 1315 (Transport) Flight a month later. Both were to fly the Dakota, joined by crews of 243 Squadron, detached for training on the type. These units were earmarked for overseas, and in mid-February 238 Squadron left for India. The crews of 243 Squadron and 1315 Flight continued to train until the end of the month, when they also left, for Morecambe for embarkation aboard ship for Australia.

The Halifax Development Flight was formed within 246 Squadron at Holmsley South on 15 November 1944, and this later moved to Merryfield. On 1 February 1945 it formed the basis of 187 Squadron, reformed at Merryfield to fly Halifaxes on trooping flights to India. However, the supply of suitable aircraft dried up, and it was decided to partially re-equip the unit with Dakotas. Freight runs were started to India in March, with passengers being carried a few weeks later – some of those returning in early May were liberated PoWs from Rangoon.

VE Day was celebrated at Merryfield, but the work of its units continued in support of the war against the Japanese. Services continued even after VJ Day, when a detachment of Dakotas from 525 Squadron at Membury started operating from Merryfield. When the detachment returned to its base on 17 September, 187 Squadron joined it, moving its trooping to Membury.

In its place came 53 Squadron, a former Coastal Command Liberator squadron that had joined Transport Command in June 1945 when its aircraft were converted for trooping. Following its arrival from St David's the unit started on the India run. After some 2¹/₂ months of successful operations from Merryfield it moved to Gransden Lodge on 3 December 1945, and was in turn replaced six days later by 242 Squadron, a Stirling transport unit from Stoney Cross. This unit also operated to the Far East, and had started to convert to the York. By January 1946 it was fully equipped with the new type and flew services to India, the Far East and the Azores from Merryfield until 2 May, then moving to Oakington.

Its residents gone, Merryfield started running down. The last aircraft to operate from the airfield during 1946 were four Oxfords of 1552 (RAT) Flight on detachment from Melbourne, departing just before the station closed on 15 October 1946

Retained on C&M, Merryfield was utilised from 1949 by Westland Aircraft for flight-testing the Wyvern, and that company continued to use it throughout the 1950s for air tests on Sabres and Meteors rebuilt by its repair unit at Yeovilton. The airfield was reactivated in November 1951 by

A Sea King HC4 of 848 Squadron training with underslung loads at Merryfield in July 2005.

Flying Training Command, forming 208 AFS with Meteor T7s and Vampire FB5s to train reserve fighter pilots for the Korean War. The threat passed, but the school continued, being re-titled as 1(FTS in June 1954 (and 9 FTS a month later!), eventually disbanding on 16 February 1955.

Two months later the station transferred to 1 Group, Bomber Command, and was used for training by Meteors and Canberras of 231 OCU on detachment from Bassingbourn. The unit moved on again to Wyton in November 1956, probably to accommodate the FAA, which needed Merryfield as a temporary base for the Sea Venoms of 766 Squadron while Yeovilton was closed for rebuilding. The unit trained all-weather fighter pilots and flew from Merryfield until work was completed in January 1958.

Other Yeovilton-based units, such as 700 Squadron, used Merryfield for training over the following couple of years, but in the early 1960s the hangars were sold and the airfield was virtually abandoned, becoming vandalised and derelict. However, Merryfield remained Government property and after about ten years the Navy showed an interest in using it once again as a satellite of Yeovilton. The wartime control tower was refurbished, runways repaired and the airfield reopened as RNAS Merryfield, HMS *Heron II*, on 22 February 1972. It was then used for training by Yeovilton's helicopter squadrons, and has been the venue for some large-scale tactical exercises. The airfield continues in this role today, with Lynx and Sea Kings often to be seen overhead.

Main features:
Runways: 280° 6,000ft x 150ft, 350° 4,200ft x 150ft, 040° 3,660ft x 150ft, concrete and bitumen. *Hangars:* two T2. *Hardstandings:* fifty spectacle. *Accommodation:* RAF Officers 124, SNCOs 825, ORs 2130.

Spitfire Is of 609 Squadron at Middle Wallop during the Battle of Britain, July 1940.

MIDDLE WALLOP, Hampshire

SU305393, 6 miles SW of Andover on A343

Planned as a standard bomber station under the pre-war RAF Expansion Scheme, work commenced on building Middle Wallop in 1938. Situated on a natural plateau to the south of the Salisbury-Andover road, it was laid out as a large grass airfield with maximum runs of 4,200 and 3,750 feet. A concrete perimeter track and hardstandings were added, together with five large hangars, seven barrack blocks and a host of support buildings to provide accommodation for two bomber squadrons. While still under construction, Middle Wallop's role changed to that of a fighter station within 11 Group, Fighter Command.

The first residents were in fact from Flying Training Command. These were the Oxfords and Masters of 15 SFTS, which arrived on 18 April 1940, their base at Lossiemouth being hastily required to house bomber units. When they arrived the SFTS staff found that the station had still not been finished, only one hangar and few of the buildings being usable. Although construction was to continue until January 1941, the airfield was serviceable, and the SFTS was able to recommence flying training. With the fall of France, however, Middle Wallop's role as a fighter station became of paramount importance, and its first operational squadron, 601, flew in its Hurricanes from Tangmere on 1 June. The unit immediately started flying patrols and bomber escorts, and on 7 June attacked Merville, a newly occupied Luftwaffe airfield from which it had itself flown only two weeks before.

On 11 June No 15 SFTS moved to South Cerney, and at 0900 the following morning RAF Middle Wallop was officially declared operational. This was initially under 11 Group, although it was planned that Middle Wallop would become a sector station under 10 Group, forming at Rudloe Manor to satisfy the need for more fighter defences to the west.

Blenheim Mk I fighters appeared in the circuit on 14 June when 236 Squadron arrived on transfer from Filton. The next day the advance party of 238 Squadron arrived with ten Hurricanes, to exchange with 601 Squadron, which returned to Tangmere on the 17th. The remainder of 238 Squadron, with another eighteen Hurricanes, arrived on the 20th. On the following day the personnel of 1 Squadron, RCAF, gathered at Middle Wallop, having arrived in the UK by ship two days earlier. There they received sixteen Hurricanes and began operational training. More unexpected and unwelcome visitors then started to arrive – from the Luftwaffe. The first of these was in the early hours of 27 June, when a lone German raider dropped four bombs, two of which fell on the airfield, but without damage.

Hurricane IIDs of 164 Squadron, KX413 nearest, at Middle Wallop in May 1943.

The Blenheims of 236 Squadron departed for Thorney Island on 4 July, the day that the Hurricanes of 501 Squadron flew in from Croydon for a three-week stay. No 501 exchanged places with 1 Squadron RCAF, which departed the following day just as 609 Squadron arrived, flying the Spitfire I, on transfer from Northolt.

The first victory by 238 was recorded on 11 July, when a Bf 110 was shot down off Portland Bill. The unit's Hurricanes, and the Spitfires of 609 Squadron, were joined by the Blenheim Mk IFs of 604 Squadron on 26 July. The latter had moved from Gravesend, and were engaged in developing night-fighter techniques with the ultra-secret Airborne Interception radar. With these squadrons Middle

Middle Wallop control tower, seen here in about 1952, is flanked by Tiger Moths and Austers of the AOP School. Oxfords and Spitfire LF16s of the Fighter Command Control & Reporting School can also be seen.

Tiger Moth N6791 of the Light Aircraft School, Middle Wallop, in 1955, with bomb-damaged No 5 Hangar behind.

Wallop could truly be termed operational by day and night. No 10 Group became active at Rudloe Manor on 4 August, with Middle Wallop as its Y-Sector HQ. The station's operations room then controlled squadrons at Boscombe Down, Warmwell, and later Chilbolton and Ibsley, as well as its own.

German activity over southern England increased during August, so that by the 11th Middle Wallop's squadrons were involved in daily contact with enemy fighters. Immediately after having flown operations on 14 August, 238 Squadron was transferred to St Eval, exchanging with 234 Squadron, whose Spitfires were active over the airfield that afternoon, shooting down a Ju 88. Between June 1940 and July 1941, Middle Wallop was on the receiving end of fourteen raids, the most intense being during August 1941. On the 13th a strong force of Ju 87s and Bf 109s made for the station; short of fuel, the Bf 109s turned back over the coast, and Middle Wallop was saved when the Spitfires of 609 Squadron, operating from Warmwell as a forward airfield, fell upon the Stukas and shot six of them down. The others scattered, but a lone Ju 88 of LG1 did manage to find Middle Wallop and drop five bombs, but without causing damage.

The station was not to be so lucky the following day. On 14 August the Luftwaffe sent over a larger number of smaller formations in order to dilute the fighter defence, which again resulted in a single Ju 88 getting through to Middle Wallop. It emerged from cloud in a shallow dive and dropped five bombs, three of which hit Hangars 4 and 5, one then hitting an air raid shelter behind Hangar 3 and the fifth landing next to the station HQ and Operations building. Six people were killed and fifteen injured, and six aircraft (three Blenheims and three Spitfires) were wrecked in the hangars. The raiders' euphoria was short-lived – the Ju 88 was intercepted by a 609 Squadron Spitfire and shot down near Redlynch to the south of the airfield.

As the Spitfires were being refuelled and rearmed later that afternoon, more Ju 88s appeared overhead, together with He 111s. Although more bombs were dropped, little further damage was done, but several UXBs hampered rescue and repair work. Airborne again, the Spitfires pursued the enemy bombers, Plt Off David Crook of 609 catching a Ju 88 west of the airfield and bringing it down just inside a new ammunition depot being constructed at East Dean; three of the five-man crew were killed, the rest taken prisoner. During another raid on the afternoon of the following day, a dozen Ju 88s escorted by Bf 110s made a low pass over the airfield, each Junkers dropping a 1,000kg bomb. These missed the main camp, though one aircraft was destroyed and another five damaged, together with two hangars. The Spitfires of 609 Squadron, held in reserve, took off as the bombs fell, and soon caught up with the raiders. In the ensuing battle they claimed one Ju 88 destroyed and three probables, plus four Bf 110s destroyed. A Blenheim of 604 Squadron, airborne at the time, was also caught up in the melee and was shot down by a 609 Squadron Spitfire, fortunately without injury to the crew.

Middle Wallop in the mid-1960s, with dispersals still alongside the main road, and No 5 Hangar having been rebuilt.

Middle Wallop was not raided en masse again, although there were further isolated attacks. Th Spitfires of 234 and 609 Squadrons continued to patrol the South Coast, intercepting raids during th following months until 234 transferred to St Eval on 11 September, and 609 to Warmwell on 2⒐ November. The latter was replaced by 56 Squadron bringing its Hurricane Is from Boscombe Down which continued operations from Middle Wallop until returning to North Weald on 17 December.

The first Beaufighters were received by 604 Squadron on 2 September, and began training on th new type. The unit's first success came on the night of 19/20 November when Flt Lt John ('Cat's-eyes' Cunningham intercepted and shot down a Ju 88, guided to the vicinity of its quarry by the Groun⒟ Controlled Interception radar station at Sopley. Further deliveries of Beaufighters to 604 wer⒠ painfully slow; by the end of 1940 the unit had only seven, but their limited numbers made themselv⒠ felt. During the winter 1940/41 offensive by the Luftwaffe the unit's interceptions steadily increase⒟ and it became the top-scoring night-fighter unit by downing thirty aircraft in a two-month period.

New arrivals that winter were the aircraft of 420 (Pandora) Flight from Christchurch. This unit ha⒟ been formed to drop mines by parachute into the paths of enemy bombers, initially using Harrows, the⒩ Wellingtons. Successful trials in November 1940 resulted in a number of Havocs being converted t⒪ carry the munitions, code-named 'Mutton'. The Havocs were delivered to the unit (which, on ⒑ December 1940, became 93 Squadron) between March and April 1941, but despite the odd success (a⒯ least one German bomber being brought down) the aerial mines were to prove of little value. With th⒠ increasing number of AI-equipped night-fighters in service, the experiment was abandoned and th⒠ Squadron disbanded on 6 December 1941. The remnants were immediately formed into 1458 Fligh⒯ to fly the Turbinlite Havoc. A Hurricane unit, 245 Squadron, was transferred from Chilbolton on 1⒌ December 1941 to resume its air defence role at Middle Wallop while allocating one of its flights t⒪ work with 1458 Flight as interceptors of any targets that the Havocs might locate. Despite the lack ⒪ success in intercepting any raiders, the Turbinlite units were given squadron status, 1458 Fligh⒯ becoming 537 Squadron on 8 September 1942, then consisting of one Havoc Flight and a Hurrican⒠ Flight. Relieved of its Turbinlite duties, 245 Squadron moved to Charmy Down on 26 October.

A succession of single-engined fighter units passed through Middle Wallop during 1942, mainly involved in bomber escort work, but also undertaking sweeps along the coast, protecting convoys and deterring raiders. In contrast to 537 Squadron, the Beaufighters of 604 had continued to operate with increasing success during this period. They eventually left on 7 December 1942 for Predannack, after 2¾ years at Middle Wallop, a very long time for a wartime fighter squadron on one station. Neither was 537 Squadron to stay much longer at the station, but for a different reason, as on 25 January 1943 it was disbanded, the Turbinlite project finally being terminated.

Middle Wallop was gradually improved and expanded. Two Sommerfield track runways were laid in 1942, and a number of fighter pens built around the perimeter track, together with sixteen Blister hangars. The first Mustangs appeared at Middle Wallop in the autumn of 1942, when 400 (RCAF) Squadron arrived from Odiham on 27 October to fly *Rhubarbs* along the French coast for just over a month; they returned again for a couple of weeks in January. Hurricane IIDs arrived on 5 February 1943, with 164 Squadron, having trained in ground-attack tactics at Fairwood Common. They continued at Middle Wallop before mounting operations on shipping and coastal targets, moving to Warmwell on 19 June.

The Mustangs of 414 Squadron also did a couple of stints in February, and again in April 1943, flying patrols from Middle Wallop to intercept low-level raids by German fighter-bombers along the coast. More Mustangs appeared on 1 June, when 16 Squadron flew in from Andover; the unit also mounted anti-fighter bomber patrols from Middle Wallop until moving to Hartford Bridge at the end of the month.

In the meantime, 406 (Lynx) Squadron had brought its Beaufighter VIFs from Predannack to replace 604 at Middle Wallop, but, with little Luftwaffe activity, it flew night intrusion missions over France, looking for transport targets. This work was carried on by 456 Squadron from 29 March when it arrived from Valley with Mosquito IIs, swapping places with 406. The last RAF night-fighter unit to be based at Middle Wallop was 161 Squadron; arriving on 16 August, it flew Mosquito XIIs on night patrols until November 1943, when it returned to Colerne.

Middle Wallop then underwent a change of ownership, being allocated to the USAAF as part of the build-up for the invasion of Europe. It became Station 449 of the 9th AF, and HQ of 9th Fighter Command, controlling all operations and training elements of the US Air Support Commands. The official handover took place on 10 January 1944, but flying units were already in residence by this time. On 11 and 12 November two squadrons of the 67th Tactical Reconnaissance Group (the 107th and 109th TRSs) transferred from Membury. Both were in the process of converting from the Spitfire to the Mustang, becoming operational on the latter in December, and both then started to carry out oblique photography of 160 miles of the French coastline in preparation for D-Day. They were joined in mid-March by the 12th and 15th TRS, both with Spitfires and a few Mustangs. The 15th TRS moved out on 17 May in an exchange with 10 Group, and was replaced by the F-5 Lightnings of 30th Photo Squadron from Chalgrove, which then undertook high-altitude photographic reconnaissance. The 67th TRG moved to the Continent on 2 July and Middle Wallop reverted to 10 Group control, starting operations to combat a new menace.

On 29 July the Mosquito IIs of 418 Squadron flew in to mount night *Anti-Diver* patrols to intercept V-1 flying bombs being launched against southern England. They were joined by the Mosquito XVIIs of 25 Squadron, also from Hurn. These patrols were particularly successful, 418 Squadron shooting down an average of one V-1 each night during the first three weeks of August. It flew 402 sorties from Middle Wallop before being withdrawn on the 21st, representing 14 per cent of the total night kills of V-1s.

During September No 3501 Servicing Unit & Pilot Replacement Pool arrived from Cranfield with some sixty aircraft on strength. It carried out the servicing of Spitfires, Typhoons, Tempests, Mustangs and Mosquitoes flown back from 2nd TAF squadrons for Base Inspections. This activity continued until 16 February 1945, when Middle Wallop was transferred to the Royal Navy as HMS *Flycatcher*. Its role was the formation and administration of Mobile Naval Air Operations Bases, mobile units that could move onto existing airfields to provide a maintenance and support base for carrier-based squadrons operating ashore. Five MONABs were assembled at *Flycatcher* (Nos.VI, VII, VIII, IX and X), four of which were later deployed to Australia, Hong Kong and Singapore. The only flying that took place during this period was by the Station Flight, and maintenance test pilot training by 700 Squadron from May 1945 until *Flycatcher* was paid off on 10 April 1946. Later that day Middle Wallop returned to Fighter Command, becoming Southern Sector HQ under 11 Group. On 28 April No 164 Squadron arrived from Tangmere, exchanging its Spitfire IXs for the LF16E in July. Renumbered as 63 Squadron on 31 August, the unit formed part of the fighter defence of the UK, moving to Thorney Island on 5 January 1948.

Some of the last Scouts in service, including XW738, at Middle Wallop in April 1994.

Middle Wallop as seen from a Hercules formation in June 1994.

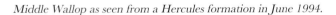

An Agusta A109 of 8 Flight takes off from Middle Wallop in October 2006.

Lynx AH1 XZ645 lifts off from Middle Wallop in April 2009.

On 1 February 1948 No 227 OCU arrived from Andover bringing a large number of Tiger Moths and Austers, which it used to train AOP pilots. The unit was renamed the AOP School on 1 May 1950 and became the Light Aircraft School on 3 April 1953.

The Fighter Command Control and Reporting School moved in from Rudloe Manor on 12 January 1946. Re-designated the School of Control & Reporting on 16 March 1953, its Balliols were formed into 288 Squadron, which also worked with Brigand night-fighter trainers of 238 OCU at Colerne. Re-designated the School of Fighter Plotting on 30 September 1957, it was disbanded on 1 March 1958.

Helicopters appeared at Middle Wallop for the first time on 1 April 1955 with the Joint Experimental Helicopter Unit. Formed to gain experience of helicopter operation, the unit found itself involved in the Suez Campaign, having been detached to Cyprus.

The Army Air Corps was formed on 1 September 1957 and formally took over Middle Wallop and the Light Aircraft School as the Army Air Corps Centre on 1 October 1958. The Chipmunks and Austers then came under the Elementary Training Flight, becoming the Basic Fixed Wing Flight when helicopter training was introduced. The basic Chipmunk and Westland Sioux phases of the course were later contracted out to Bristow, while military conversion and operational flying remained in Army hands.

A School of Army Aviation was created in August 1965, aircraft servicing coming under the control of REME. A rebuild programme provided new instructional blocks, extensions to messes and additional married quarters, the blitzed No 5 Hangar having been rebuilt only shortly before. In November 1966 the station's air strength consisted of eight Auster AOP9s, five Beavers, twenty-two Chipmunks, twenty-five Sioux and fifteen Scouts, together with twenty Hillers of Bristow Helicopters. The AAC's organisation at Middle Wallop has changed regularly over the years, but the title 'School of Army Aviation' remains in use today, its role currently being to conduct basic and advanced training of Army aircrew and groundcrew. It is an operating branch of the Army Training and Recruiting Division and consists of five squadrons numbered 668, 670, 671, 673 and 676. These undertake flying grading on the Slingsby Firefly 160, operational flying training on the AS350 Squirrel and conversion training on the Gazelle, Lynx, Bell 212 and Apache, as well as the training of groundcrews.

Despite recent redevelopment Middle Wallop remains essentially much the same as it did during the Second World War, with its five B Type hangars dominating what is today Europe's largest grass airfield. Every theatre of operations since the war has seen the presence of aircrew trained at Middle Wallop, not least the Falklands, Bosnia, the Gulf and Afghanistan. In 2007 the Army Air Corps celebrated its golden jubilee at Middle Wallop – fifty years of proud history recorded at the Museum of Army Flying situated alongside the airfield.

Main features:
Runways: 242° 5,340ft x 150ft, 185° 4,800ft x 150ft, Sommerfield track. *Hangars:* five Type C, sixteen Blister. *Hardstandings:* sixteen double fighter pens, nine single. *Accommodation:* RAF Officers 93, SNCOs 262, ORs 1,598; WAAF Officers 17, SNCOs 18, ORs 264.

MORETON, Dorset

SY762898, 4¹/₂ miles E of Dorchester, off minor road

Moreton was an RNAS Airship Station, built near Dorchester to plug a gap in convoy coverage off the South Coast. Work started on the station in 1918, some 355 acres of low-lying pastureland being acquired for it between the Dorchester-Wareham railway line to the south and the grounds of Woodsford Castle to the north. Construction of airship sheds, workshops and a gas plant was in progress when the Armistice was signed and work ceased immediately. The site was largely cleared after the war, although a number of buildings survived, and the track running westward out of High Woodsford village was originally part of the airship shed foundation.

Meteor I test-flown from Moreton Valence in 1944.

MORTON VALENCE (HARESFIELD), Gloucestershire

SO796104, 1 mile W of Haresfield village

Originally named Haresfield after the village nearby, this airfield was opened as an RLG for 6 AONS Staverton in November 1939. Pilots of the school's Ansons confirmed that it had potential, and during 1941 the airfield was upgraded. Three tarmac-covered concrete runways were laid, together with a perimeter track, and buildings erected, including three Blister hangars.

The airfield was reopened as Moreton Valence, and in August 1941 a permanent detachment was set up there by 6 AONS, training observers and navigators. On 17 January 1942 the unit was renamed 7 AOS, but the task remained the same. Shortly afterwards the Pilot Refresher Training Unit was formed at Moreton Valence with Masters, and later Tutors and Oxfords. Re-designated as the Refresher Flying Training School on 1 May, three weeks later it moved to Kirknewtown. No 6 AOS continued its work during 1942 and into the following year, receiving other types such as Dominies, Tutors, Tiger Moths, Magisters and Bothas; it was re-titled 6(O)AFU in June 1943.

During the summer of 1943 the MAP built construction hangars at Moreton Valence for the Gloster Aircraft Co, and extended the main runway. This was to cater for the Gloster F9/40, later known as the Meteor. All Meteor test-flying was then concentrated at Moreton Valence, joining a Bell YP-59A, which had been shipped to the UK for evaluation in exchange for a Meteor. The YP-59A was assembled by Gloster and test-flown alongside the Meteors.

Meteor PR10 prototype VS968 at Moreton Valence in March 1950.

Gloster GA5 (Javelin) prototype WD804 on the compass base at Moreton Valence in November 1951.

With the need for bomber crews much reduced, 6 (O)AFU closed in December 1944, but Moreton Valence was immediately taken over by 3 (P)AFU South Cerney as a satellite in place of Southrop. The unit's Oxfords used the airfield into the following summer, but after VE Day flying training started to contract, and the AFU closed. In July RAF Moreton Valence was transferred to 6 (P)AFU Little Rissington, which used it until December 1945. No 83 Gliding School had formed at the airfield in May 1944 to train ATC cadets on Dagling Primary and Kirby Cadet gliders.; this unit eventually departed for Aston Down in 13 October 1946, leaving Moreton Valence to the Gloster company.

Meteor flight testing and trials carried on at the airfield during the immediate post-war years. The Meteors that claimed World Air Speed Records in November 1945 and November 1946 were prepared there, and several record-breaking flights were made from the airfield, including time-to-height and altitude records. With the decision to concentrate much of the final assembly and all test work at Moreton Valence, the factory area was increased and the main runway extended. This was to accommodate the Javelin all-weather fighter, which first flew from the airfield as the GA5 on 26 November 1951. The first deliveries to the RAF came in December 1955, and although the last production Javelin flew out in April 1960, work continued, including the conversion of Javelin FAW7s to FAW9s and Meteor NF11s to TT20 standard.

Javelin FAW4 XA631 in 1956, used for operational reliability trials by Gloster.

Following cancellation of the P376, a supersonic Javelin, and reorganisation of the Hawker Siddeley Group, Gloster's aviation activities were run down. The last aircraft to leave Moreton Valence by air was a Javelin on 25 July 1962 and the airfield was deactivated. Subsequently sold off for industrial development, the M5 motorway now crosses the centre of the airfield, and few buildings remain to show that it was once a busy airfield and important aircraft factory.

Main features:
Runways: 223°, 6,300ft x 150ft, 162° 3,000ft x 150ft, 101° 3,000ft x 150ft, concrete and tarmac. *Hangars:* RAF: one Type A1, eight EO-Blister; MAP: one Type B1, four Type B2. *Accommodation:* RAF Officers 91, SNCOs 308; WAAF Officers 4, ORs 43.

Short 184 N1754 on Cattewater Pier in 1917.

MOUNT BATTEN (CATTEWATER), Devon

SX483533, 1 mile S of Plymouth, across the Sound

The importance of Devonport Dockyard meant that a seaplane base was needed in the Plymouth area during the First World War. The Cattewater was soon recognised as the most suitable location, with long stretches of open water sheltered by the mainland to the north, and the breakwater of Mount Batten peninsula to the south. Mount Batten was requisitioned as RNAS Cattewater in February 1917, and canvas hangars were erected together with workshops, support buildings and accommodation. Slipways were added and the breakwater used as a seaplane-launching pier.

Following the formation of the RAF in April 1918 two large hangars were built and the shipways into the Cattewater improved. Nos 420 and 421 Seaplane Flights were formed during May to operate the Short 184, followed by 347 Flying Boat Flight on 15 June and 348 a month later, to fly the Curtiss H16 and Felixstowe F3. The seaplane flights were absorbed by 237 Squadron, which formed at Cattewater on 20 August, and the two flying boat flights by 238 Squadron, which formed on the same day. On 15 October No 349 Flying Boat Flight was formed within 238 Squadron. With the end of the war, activity reduced, and on 15 May 1919 No 237 Squadron disbanded. No 238 remained as a holding and storage unit for spare flying boats and seaplanes until it, too, was disbanded on 20 March 1922, when RAF Cattewater was put into reserve.

Activity resumed at the station in 1928 with the formation of 482 (Coastal Reconnaissance) Flight on 15 December, to fly Southampton flying boats. On 1 January 1929 the unit was re-designated 203 Squadron and at the end of February left for Basrah. It was replaced by 204 Squadron, formed on 1 February, also with Southamptons.

Sunderland I P9600 of 10 (RAAF) Squadron outside Mount Batten's hangars in 1939.

RAF Cattewater was renamed RAF Mount Batten on 1 October 1929 as its importance as a maritime aviation base steadily grew. With seaplane catapults being fitted to RN capital ships, the RAF formed a number of catapult flights, with Mount Batten as their shore base. No 209 Squadron formed on 15 March 1930 with Iris flying boats, later converting to Singapores and moving to Felixstowe on 1 May 1935. No 204 Squadron remained at Mount Batten, and was progressively re-equipped, with Scapas in 1935, Londons in 1936, and its first Sunderlands in June 1939. When war broke out in September it shared the station with the Shark floatplanes of the Cooperation Flight of 2 AACU, which provided target-training for the RN Gunnery School, Devonport.

With six operational flying boats, 204 Squadron made its first anti-submarine patrol over the Western Approaches at dawn on 4 September. It was in the news two weeks later when one of its

A Luftwaffe target photo of RAF Mount Batten and its pier taken on 20 September 1940. Four Sunderlands and a Catalina are moored in the Cattewater.

Sunderlands, together with another from Pembroke Dock, alighted on the open sea seventy miles west of Scilly to rescue thirty-three survivors from the torpedoed SS *Kensington Court*. The unit left for Sullom Voe on 2 April and was replaced by 10 (RAAF) Squadron, also with Sunderlands, on transfer from Pembroke Dock. The Australians had been sent to Britain to collect their new Sunderlands, and were undergoing conversion training when the war broke out. Ordered by their Government to stay in Britain to assist the war effort, they were soon busy flying patrols from Mount Batten, and found themselves also acting as long-range transports, flying VIPs to North Africa and Malta. Their operational scoreboard opened on 1 July 1940 when P9603 captained by Flt Lt W. N. Gibson sank the U-26. However, with the Luftwaffe then in France, Plymouth was well within range, and the first raids came. On 15 July Mount Batten was attacked by two Ju 88s, which dropped bombs but with little damage. A much heavier raid came on 27 November, when one of the hangars was hit by an incendiary, destroying a Sunderland inside; another was sunk at its moorings, and two more damaged. More destruction was caused during raids in January and April 1941. Because of the station's vulnerability, and increasing congestion in Plymouth Sound, it was decided to return 10 (RAAF) Squadron to Pembroke Dock in May.

Three Short C Class flying boats that had recently joined 10 (RAAF) Squadron for courier and transport flights to Gibraltar and the Middle East remained at Mount Batten, but after the loss of one on 20 May the others were withdrawn. During 1941 No 10 (RAAF) Squadron used Mount Batten as a forward base for operations over the Bay of Biscay, together with other Sunderland squadrons, such as 95 at Pembroke Dock and 210 at Sullum Voe.

The Australians returned to Mount Batten on 31 December 1941, and remained there for the rest of the war. Another RAAF Sunderland squadron, 461, was formed at the station on 25 April 1942 from a nucleus provided by 10 Squadron. The OC, Wg Cdr Halliday, flew the unit's first operational patrol on 1 July, and it soon made a name for itself, one of its Sunderlands rescuing the survivors of the sunk destroyer HMS *Wild Swan*. Unfortunately, while attempting a similar rescue on 13 August, alighting on the open sea, the CO and his crew were lost. The unit moved to Hamworthy on 31 August 1942.

From May to August 1943 the U-boat offensive was reaching its climax, and Coastal Command achieved considerable success, Mount Batten's crews managing to destroy three of the fifty-seven U-boats sunk by the Command during the period. German long-range fighter presence over the Bay of Biscay was a major problem, however, and U-boats armed with flak guns also took their toll. This stimulated efforts to up-gun the Sunderlands, and it was such an aircraft fitted with additional fixed nose guns flown by Flt Lt Fry that attacked U-454 on 1 August 1943. Through heavy fire the Sunderland dropped its depth charges, sinking the U-boat; however, badly damaged, the flying boat crashed into the sea shortly afterwards, and seven of the thirteen-man crew perished.

Two days later Fg Off Williams's aircraft was intercepted by seven Ju 88s over the Bay of Biscay. One of the fighters attacked the boat head-on, causing much damage and killing the nose-turret gunner. A series of sustained attacks by the other Ju 88s were beaten off by the Sunderland's gunners, aided by Williams's skilful flying, but more damage was sustained, and four of the crew were wounded. They managed to fend off the fighters, damaging at least two in the process, as the pilot edged towards cloud, but once within it the Sunderland was able to circle until the Ju 88s eventually gave up.

On 8 January 1944 Sunderland EK586 of 10 Squadron captained by Fg Off J. P. Roberts attacked and sank U-426, the aircraft's nose guns effectively suppressing return fire from the submarine as its six depth charges were dropped. The Squadron flew one of the few Sunderland sorties on D-Day, and added to its score just over a month later when, on 8 July, W4030 captained by Fg Off Tilley caught U-243 on the surface about 130 miles south-west of Brest. The Sunderland went straight into the attack with depth charges, the rear gunner raking the U-boat's decks with machine-gun fire, killing its Commander and Coxswain. Crew members launched dinghies as the U-boat sank, and the Australians dropped a spare dinghy to survivors swimming in the water, as well as food-packs. They then radioed the crew's position to a nearby convoy and thirty-eight German seamen were later picked up. This was the sixth and final U-boat to be sunk by 10 Squadron's Sunderlands.

By September 1944 the U-boats had virtually all left the Bay of Biscay and the Western Approaches, but 10 Squadron maintained patrols into 1945. By the end of the war they had lost twenty-five Sunderlands, nineteen to enemy action and six in flying accidents, but had despatched five U-boats and damaged eight more, as well as sinking one warship and damaging eight others. The Australians finally left Mount Batten on 31 October 1945 after an incomparable period of operations, having spent most of that time at the one base, almost unheard of during wartime service.

Mount Batten's hangars in March 2005, in use as a marine centre.

RAF Mount Batten was placed on C&M on 5 October 1945, but on 1 January 1946 was transferred to Maintenance Command and reopened as 238 MU, a maritime storage unit. The flying boat moorings were maintained and used by visiting Sunderlands until the last UK squadron was disbanded in 1957, when Mount Batten became a centre for RAF Marine Craft activity. No 84 (Marine Craft Repair) Unit moved here in May 1946 and became part of 238 MU in January 1948. On 17 October 1953 the MU moved to Calshot, exchanging places with the Marine Craft Training School. When Calshot closed in 1961, 238 MU returned to Mount Batten and was amalgamated with the training school to become the Marine Craft Training & Support Unit.

It was joined by the School of Combat Survival & Rescue in 1959, which found Plymouth Sound and Dartmoor to be useful venues for its training courses. The following year No 3 (County of Devon) Maritime HQ Unit, Royal Auxiliary Air Force, joined it. Mount Batten remained one of the main centres for RAF Marine activity for the next twenty-five years, which only came to an end on 1 April 1986 when the RAF Marine Branch was disbanded, its role taken over by civilian contractors. The SCSR and 3 MHU remained in residence at Mount Batten until 1992, when the base became a victim of defence cuts. Both units moved to St Mawgan, and Mount Batten was put up for disposal. The site was sold off and in the late 1990s redeveloped into a water-sports centre using the slipways, hangars and some of the other RAF buildings, together with a number of new ones.

MULLION, Cornwall

SW705210, 2 miles NE of Mullion village, off A3083

Leaving Mullion at 0505 hours on 22 June 1917, HM Airship C9, a Coastal type craft, headed for its patrol area off Start Point. At 0730 a long, light green-coloured shape was observed just under the surface of the sea, 15 miles south of the Point. Although stationary, bubbles and an oily emulsion were rising from it. As a destroyer came to investigate, the object moved off at about 5 knots leaving an oily trail – obviously a submarine. The airship's pilot, Flight Commander J. G. Struthers RN, aimed a 65lb bomb at the shape and the destroyer moved in to drop two depth charges. Some wreckage and oil came to the surface, but with no further sighting and worsening weather, C9 was recalled at 1125. She struggled back to Mullion in heavy rain and strong winds, finally landing at 1555. Lizard Radio reported a U-boat being called by her base for several hours without response, but no positive claim on her sinking could be made – a common feature of submarine warfare.

Coastal Airship C9 being returned to its hangar in 1917, while two 1½-Strutters sit on the edge of the airfield.

The German submarine threat to blockade Britain had become reality in early 1915, with serious losses to shipping. It was therefore decided to establish bases in the West Country from which airships could patrol western waters. The Lizard was the natural choice for such a base, and a suitable location was found on downland between Mullion and Garras, adjacent to the village of Cury. The 320-acre site was cleared and work started during March 1916 on the construction of a large airship shed (300 feet long, 100 feet wide and 70 feet high), workshops and a hutted camp. Although still incomplete, the station was commissioned as RNAS Mullion during June 1916.

The first airship for Mullion, Coastal type C8, left its base at Kingsnorth on the Medway but unfortunately never made it, crashing into the sea off Start Point with the loss of three crewmen (only the W/T Operator survived). This tragedy resulted in the next two Coastals being delivered by rail and road. After assembly, the first of them, C9, made her initial test-flight on 18 June, and the first of many operational patrols on 1 July. The C Class was to see more action than any other British airship type, those stationed at the Cornish bases being amongst the busiest. Regular patrols along the coastline were uneventful until 10 September 1916 when the crew of C10 sighted a couple of vessels on fire off the Lizard. A U-boat was spotted as they moved in to investigate, but it had submerged before the airship could mount an attack. The destroyer HMS *Foyle* reached the scene as the U-boat resurfaced, but it dived when the *Foyle* opened fire. This was the first interception of a U-boat by an RNAS airship, and the crew had the satisfaction of knowing that they had driven it off.

The station's patrol areas stretched along the Channel eastwards to Plymouth Sound, and westwards past the Isles of Scilly. As well as anti-submarine patrols, its aircraft escorted convoys from the Channel into the Western Approaches. The construction of a second, smaller airship shed had been started in February 1917 to house a third airship, and was completed in June. A number of sub-stations were later established to extend the range of Mullion's airships.

To combat an increase in German submarine activity the Admiralty decided in the spring of 1917 to employ landplanes to supplement the airships. In mid-April four Sopwith 1½ Strutters arrived at Mullion, two of which were the two-seat bomber version and two the one-seat fighter version; a fifth arrived at the end of the month. To accommodate the Sopwiths a Bessoneau hangar was erected alongside the airship sheds. The aeroplanes were flown on coastal patrols and photographic reconnaissance until August 1917, when the pilots were transferred to the Western Front to make up combat losses in front-line squadrons.

Of the many patrols made, most were uneventful as sightings of U-boats were few and far between – this may well have been because sharp-eyed look-outs aboard the subs spotted the aircraft first! A surfaced U-boat was, however, spotted by C22 on 9 March 1917, moving towards a convoy off the Lizard. As the airship dropped it bombs the U-boat dived, and anti-submarine trawlers dropped depth charges. The sub was assumed sunk as a great oil slick appeared on the surface. C22 did not fare much better; a few weeks later she came down in the sea midway between Land's End and Ushant, but her crew of four were picked up.

A Sopwith 1¹/₂ Strutter at Mullion in June 1917.

C9 was in the forefront of the action after its first attack on a U-boat trail in February 1917. On 21 September, while standing by the torpedoed French steamer SS *Rouang* off the Lizard, its crew spotted a conning tower moving towards a Falmouth-bound convoy. They dropped two 100lb bombs and were rewarded with a violent explosion, air bubbles and oil, and were awarded a 'probable'. Just one week later, on 29 September, C9 attacked another U-boat off the Eddystone lighthouse, and once again was rewarded with the appearance of large quantities of oil.

South-westerly gales, common in the western Channel, were particularly hazardous for airships both on patrol and on the ground, but the effects were diminished at Mullion with the construction of wind-break screens at the end of both hangars. Such a gale almost meant the end for C9 on 3 October 1917. She was returning from patrol east of Bolt Head, having been recalled due to a bad

The ground handling party gets Sea Scout Zero into position at Mullion in 1918.

An aerial view of Mullion in 1918, showing the two airship sheds, and the airfield lower right.

weather warning, when her crew spotted an explosion among a group of six ships to the south. They swung the airship round and were overhead within a few minutes to see a torpedo track, with a sub at its source. Bombs were dropped and patrol vessels depth-charged the site as C9 headed for home. It arrived perilously short of fuel, having taken 6 hours to cover the 40 miles through gale-force winds.

Mullion was the most active of the airship stations during 1917, having flown 2,845 operational flying hours. More aeroplanes appeared at the base in early 1918 in the form of DH6s. Later, in May, DH9s arrived, and on 20 May No 493 (Light Bomber) Flight was formed with them. The DH6s were taken on by 515 (Special Duties) Flight, which formed on 6 June as part of 254 Squadron based at Prawle Point. On 20 August 1918 No 236 Squadron formed at Mullion and took command of all three flights there. Six Bessoneau hangars were erected to accommodate the aeroplanes.

The airships continued their patrols, working with the landplanes. As well as the twin-engined C (Coastal) Class, Mullion also operated the SSZ (Sea Scout Zero) Class, which was smaller and powered by a single engine. Many long patrols were flown by both types during 1918, but few U-boat sightings were made, mainly because the airships deterred them. The crew of C23a did, however, spot one on 10 May 1918 during a patrol along the north coast near Newquay. As it flew over Cranlock Bay at some 400 feet a U-boat surfaced. Its gun crew took up position and started firing, scoring several hits on the airship, which broke into two and fell into the bay. Of the crew of three aboard, two were saved, but the W/T Operator drowned.

Coastal C9 was deflated for the last time on 14 September 1918, after two years and seventy-five days' service at Mullion, during which time she flew an amazing 3,720 hours. The remaining Coastals were in poor condition by this time, and were gradually withdrawn from service. By the Armistice only one C Class remained at Mullion, together with seven SSZs and a single SS Twin (a locally produced twin-engined version of the SSZ nicknamed 'The Silver Queen'); it was the latter that made the last airship ascent from Mullion on 25 January 1919. The landplanes remained in operation until 15 May 1919, when 236 Squadron disbanded, the RAF then preferring flying boats for maritime duties.

RAF Mullion soon closed, its portable Bessoneau hangars being packed onto lorries as the airship sheds and most of the buildings were demolished. Today the airship shed floors survive, together with some of the roadways and a number of the heavy concrete bases of the wind-break screens.

NEEDS OAR POINT, Hampshire

SZ402978, 1 1/2 miles S of Bucklers Hard

Surveyed in 1942, work on Needs Oar Point started in the spring of 1943 as an ALG for occupation during the build-up to the invasion of Europe. Sited on low-lying ground near the mouth of the Beaulieu River in the New Forest, it was screened by trees to the north with clear approaches from the sea. Of the four ALGs to be built in the area, Needs Oar Point was the only one used by the RAF, the others going to the USAAF.

Construction was by 5004 Squadron, RAF Airfield Construction Service, which put down two runways, taxiways and dispersals of Sommerfield tracking. Four Blister hangars were erected for servicing and maintenance, but other facilities were minimal, as the ALG was to be used by highly mobile units living in field conditions. Nonetheless, farm buildings around the airfield were utilised; Park Farmhouse was the HQ, its outbuildings and barns becoming briefing rooms and equipment stores. From the completion of work in late 1943 the airfield remained unoccupied to avoid its existence being revealed, and to allow grass to grow through the mesh, aiding its concealment.

On 10 April 1944 units started to arrive in the form of the HQ and squadrons of 146 Airfield (later re-titled 146 Wing). Convoys of lorries arrived that morning from Tangmere, followed by the squadrons with their Typhoon IBs. These were 197, 257 and 266 Squadrons, with 193 Squadron arriving the following day. Being fully mobile, 146 Airfield had more than 200 vehicles and, with each squadron having thirty Typhoons, the ALG must have been crammed with equipment and personnel. To add to this congestion, Needs Oar Point was later nominated as the Emergency Landing Ground for the four FAA Seafire squadrons at Lee-on-Solent spotting for the battleships bombarding the French coast on D-Day.

The Typhoons immediately began operations, attacking coastal defences, radar stations, road and rail communications. Most of the Wing's aircraft were 'Bomb-phoons,' with bomb-pylons, but capable of being fitted with rocket racks if required. Nos 193 and 257 Squadrons bombed a rail tunnel on 19 May, successfully blocking it, and for a period were switched to *Noball* targets (suspected V-1 launching sites). On one day alone, 257 Squadron's aircraft fired 9,615 20mm cannon shells and dropped sixty-five 500lb bombs. The pace of these attacks steadily increased as D-Day approached, each squadron flying two or three missions per day.

On D-Day itself, the Wing's Typhoons were on cab-rank duty, on call to attack any strong point or other Army-designated target. At dawn, 197 Squadron had attacked a German HQ, leaving it in ruins. Attacks on communications continued over the following days, and a major coup was scored on 27 June when the Wing Leader, Wg Cdr Johnny Baldwin, led an attack on the HQ of the German 7th Army near St Lo, flying in at tree-top height to attack with bombs, rockets and cannon, while Mitchells flew over at height to distract the defences. The HQ was destroyed, the Army Commander, General-Lieutenant Dohlmann and most of his staff being killed.

This was to be one of the last of the Wing's operations from Needs Oar Point. On 29 June No 266 Squadron left for Eastchurch for a rocket-firing APC, and on 2 July 257 Squadron relocated to Hurn, followed by 193 and 197 Squadrons the following day. They moved to the continent within a few days and by 20 July were co-located at B3/Ste Croix sur Mer. On 17 July eight Typhoons of 193 Squadron led by Wg Cdr Baldwin had attacked an HQ area and strafed General Irwin Rommel's staff car, seriously wounding him and taking him out of the Battle for Normandy.

Needs Oar Point was abandoned as an airfield after the Typhoons left, but was later used by the RN for storage until de-requisitioned in 1946. Nothing remains of the SLG today.

Main features:
Runways: E-W 4,500ft x 150ft, N-S 4,800ft x 150ft, Sommerfield track. *Hangars:* four Blister. *Hardstandings:* thirty-six, Sommerfield track. *Accommodation:* Tented camp.

Maurice Farman Shorthorn No 343 being scrutinised at Netheravon during the RFC Concentration Camp in June 1914.

NETHERAVON, Wiltshire

SU165493, 6 miles N of Amesbury on A345

Netheravon can claim to be one of the oldest operational airfields in the UK, possibly in the world, having been in continuous operation since 1913. Constructed for the RFC on the edge of Salisbury Pain, it was laid out as two landing areas to the north and south of several aircraft sheds built on an east-west axis.

On 16 June 1913 No 3 Squadron moved in from Larkhill, followed two days later by 4 Squadron from Farnborough; both had a mixture of aircraft types on strength. During the summer of 1914 the whole of the Military Wing of the RFC, which then consisted of 700 personnel and seventy aeroplanes, assembled at Netheravon for an exercise. A few weeks later war broke out. Nos 3 and 4 Squadrons left for France to join the British Expeditionary Force, reaching Amiens on 13 August. They were replaced by 1 Squadron, which moved from Brooklands on 13 November for training until it, too, moved to France in March 1915. Netheravon continued in a training role, concentrating on the build-up of new squadrons for the Western Front. As training methods developed, it became one of a series of major school airfields, operating Reserve (later known as Training) Depot Squadrons (Nos 8 and 12) flying types as diverse as the Avro 504K and the HP0/400.

Following the end of the Great War Netheravon became a disbandment centre for returning RAF squadrons, but in 1919 No 1 Flying Training School was formed there to train new military and naval pilots. The school remained until it was disbanded on 1 February 1931 and a number of front-line fighter and bomber squadrons then passed through the station, some staying longer than others. On 1 April 1935 Netheravon was taken over by 23 Group and 6 FTS was reformed there, with Tutors, Audaxes and other members of the Hart family. It also received Ansons before moving to Little Rissington in August 1936. It was replaced by 1 FTS, which had been reformed at Leuchars as an advanced flying school with Tutors, Avros 504Ns and Hart Trainers. Training mainly FAA students, the school received Harvards during the spring of 1939, which it flew alongside the biplanes.

When war came again in September 1939 security measures were tightened, defences were dug and 1 FTS re-designated as 1 SFTS. It had a large fleet of aircraft, and Netheravon's circuit was soon saturated as training was stepped up. To relieve the pressure it opened a number of RLGs, including Castle Combe, Shrewton and High Post. Netheravon saw little enemy activity, but on 21 July a Hart of 1 SFTS was shot down by a Bf 110 and its pilot killed. The German fighter headed for the coast, but was caught by three Hurricanes of 238 Squadron Middle Wallop and forced down near Goodwood, its crew being captured.

The end of 1941 saw a radical change for Netheravon when the airfield became a centre for the newly created airborne forces. This was mainly because of its proximity to Salisbury Plain, which had vast tracts of training land available for the use of gliders and paratroops. A new formation, 38 Wing (later to become 38 Group), was established at Netheravon to control RAF airborne support activities and to coordinate them with those of 1st Parachute Brigade, whose HQ was at nearby Bulford Camp. The HQ of 6th Airborne Division was subsequently set up at Syrencote House to the south of the airfield.

The Parachute Exercise Squadron (later numbered as 297 Squadron) arrived in January 1942 with Tiger Moths; these were soon supplemented with Whitleys, then were withdrawn from front-line bombing operations. The unit was joined the following month by 296 Squadron, which used Hart and Hector biplanes to tow Hotspurs. Military glider pilots were seen as specialists, distinct from other aircrew as they had a secondary role; this was because, having landed their glider, they were expected to pick up their weapons and join the battle. They were recruited into the Glider Pilot Regiment (GPR) and received full elementary flying training on the Tiger Moth or Magister before moving on to the Hotspur glider trainer and Horsa operational glider.

When 1 SFTS was disbanded in March 1942, Netheravon became a purely airborne-orientated base. A demonstration of paratroop-dropping and glider insertion was laid on for the Prime Minister, Sir Winston Churchill, in April 1942, and a series of exercises followed. These culminated in Exercise *Brimerston* on 11 July, when ground-attack Hurricanes softened up the landing area and smoke was laid by Blenheims before twenty-five Whitleys dropped paratroops and four more released gliders, followed by a wave of Hectors releasing more gliders.

By the end of June both squadrons had moved to Hurn, but on 3 August No 295 Squadron formed at Netheravon to train pilots in paratroop and glider operations using Whitleys, later Halifaxes. A few days later the Glider Pilot Exercise Unit formed from a detachment of 296 Squadron, providing refresher flying for qualified GPR pilots, using Tiger Moths, Hectors and Hotspurs. Training towards the end of the year focused on the first British glider operation, a commando raid on the Norsk Hydro Plant at Vermok in Norway. Although unsuccessful, it proved the viability of gliders for assault.

In January 1943 No 235 MU formed at Netheravon to support airborne equipment and to recover and repair gliders, with 3 Mobile Parachute Servicing Unit to repair parachute drop equipment. The latter unit moved to the Mediterranean a few months later, replaced by 4 MPSU. On 1 May No 295 Squadron moved to Holmsley South, and the Heavy Glider MU, from Hurn, replaced it. Training and exercises continued throughout 1943, becoming more focused with the general feeling that a big operation was impending.

HM the King views a Tetrarch tank deplaning from a Hamilcar during a visit to Netheravon in May 1944.

Horsas out to grass at Netheravon in October 1945.

On 15 January 1944 the Air Transport Tactical Development Unit was formed at Netheravon to conduct trials on airborne equipment, flying a variety of types including the Halifax, Oxford and Mosquito. It was joined in March by 1677 (Target Training) Flight, which flew Martinet target tugs to train the tail-gunners of 38 Group's squadrons.

Training for the invasion of France began in earnest in the spring of 1944, the emphasis being on precision nocturnal glider and parachute landings. Nineteen major airborne exercises were held during the build-up to D-Day, in order to hone the participants' skills and build their confidence. Fields were found replicating those near targets, such as one near Netheravon that resembled a field near the Caen Canal Bridge. It was into this that the glider pilots flew, again and again, by day and night. Although no D-Day missions were flown from Netheravon itself, the training undertaken there paid off; for example, the three gliders that were to land beside the Caen Canal Bridge did so with so much precision that the nose of the first Horsa went through the boundary wire of the enemy defences. The Germans were so taken by surprise that the bridge was captured within a matter of minutes.

The war moved on, and by mid-June a lot of used gliders were sitting around on the Normandy LZs. As glider reserves in the UK were sorely depleted, work started on reclaiming these veterans for reuse in future operations. A Dakota Flight was formed within 1 HGSU (the HGMU re-titled in March 1944), which was to recover airworthy gliders by snatching them off the ground. Thirty-nine Horsas were safely retrieved in this way by the end of August, while many more were taken apart on the LZs and returned by LCT.

Gazelle AH1 ZA773/F of 7 Regiment rests alongside an A Type hangar at Netheravon in June 2002.

The value of the stocks of gliders retrieved and repaired by 1 HGSU was to be realised in September 1944, with the mounting of Operation *Market Garden*, the airborne carpet for the planned armoured thrust to the bridge over the Rhine at Arnhem. Netheravon's involvement was similar to that of D-Day, providing a centre for training and the build-up to the operation, but on the day itself units jumped off from bases further east, closer to their objectives. As the operation started, on 17 September, it was hoped that follow-up glider recovery could start as the troops moved forward, but this proved impossible as the Germans, overrunning the LZs, systematically destroyed the gliders to prevent their reuse.

Operation *Varsity* (the glider and paratroop landings in support of the Rhine Crossing by the 21st Army Group) was the last major Allied airborne operation of the war. Netheravon's units were once again involved, providing Horsas and Hamilcars, new and repaired, which were wheeled out of the hangars, connected to tugs and delivered to the assault airfields; 150 gliders were supplied by 1 HGSU, without which the operation could not have taken place.

In mid-1945 Transport Command took over 38 Group and on 31 August the ATTDU was re-titled the Transport Command Development Unit, before moving to Harwell in mid-September. Following the war's end, gliders were stored in reserve at Netheravon, airborne training continued , nos 27, 53 and 187 Squadrons flying Dakotas from the station flew from the station. However, the last RAF flying unit, 27 Squadron, departed in 1950, and Netheravon became the RAF Police Training Depot.

With the transfer of Netheravon to the Army in 1963, flying started once again, and its airborne connection was resumed with the arrival of the Army Parachute Association. Helicopter operations were started by 6 Flight, AAC, with Scouts, succeeded by 7 Regiment, flying Gazelles. Although sport parachuting continues from the airfield today, the withdrawal of the Gazelle from AAC service resulted in the disbandment of 7 Regiment in March 2009. A good number of the original buildings still stand at Netheravon, including the hangars and the Officers' Mess, which still carries the badge of the RFC above the front door.

Main features:
Runways: E-W 6,000ft, NE-SW 4,200ft, SE-NW 4,500ft, grass. *Hangars:* two Type A, two Cathedral, three Flight Sheds, one Bessoneau. *Accommodation:* RAF Officers 142, SNCOs 152, ORs 1,050; WAAF Officers 10, SNCOs 13, ORs 362.

NEWLYN Cornwall

SW468281, 2 miles S of Penzance on minor road

Commissioned in January 1917, the seaplane base at Newlyn on Mount's Bay in west Cornwall resulted from the Admiralty's urgent requirement to extend coastal anti-submarine defences. Known as RNAS Newlyn/Land's End, the station was built between Newlyn Harbour and Carn Gwavas on a narrow strip of land that had earlier been reclaimed using spoil from nearby Penlee Quarry. Three Bessoneau hangars were erected on a hardstanding reached from the sea by a slipway that consisted of two rails laid on sleepers upon which a trolley was mounted to carry the floatplanes. A second slipway was later added. York House nearby was requisitioned for the use of the officers, the ratings living in two houses in Newlyn.

The first aircraft, Short 184 floatplanes Nos 8049 and 8350, were delivered on 20 January 1917. When others arrived the hangars became so cramped that storage had to be found at the Trinity House depot in Penzance Harbour. A large aircraft shed, 180 feet by 60 feet, was therefore erected at Newlyn to house the six floatplanes on strength at the end of 1917.

The Newlyn-based Short 184s saw a fair amount of action, their first attack being on 16 March when 8350 bombed a U-boat 10 miles off Dodman Point, albeit non-conclusive. Further attacks, on 16 August and 8 September, were made on U-boats seen off Wolf Rock, but again with no definite result. On 19 December a much more successful result was achieved when N1606 located a U-boat 10 mile south-west of the Lizard. The sub was following a convoy and fired torpedoes that were spotted by N1606's crew. They dropped two 100lb bombs, and oil and air bubbles were seen rising to the surface.

Newlyn was also used as a staging post by aircraft from other bases. Tresco-based Curtiss H12 Large America 8652 was the first of these, landing with engine trouble on 11 March 1917; 8654 arrived early in May, lost in fog, while another landed short of fuel in June 1918.

The Newlyn floatplanes cooperated with flying boats from Tresco and airships from Mullion and its outstations in continuous patrols to protect convoys moving in and out of the English

An aerial view of Newlyn seaplane base in 1917, before the large aircraft shed was built to the left of the three Bessoneaus.

Channel. Like all maritime patrols, this work was monotonous, uneventful, and only rarely interrupted by sudden action. On 24 March 1918, during renewed U-boat activity, Short 184 N1618 dropped two bombs on a submarine; N1609 also attacked one on 29 April and N1767 another on 6 May, but all without perceived result. However, when N1616 bombed a U-boat off north Cornwall on 16 May, oil was seen and a probable sinking was claimed.

Following the formation of the RAF on 1 April 1918, the seaplane bases were reorganised. On 20 May two units were formed at Newlyn, 424 and 425 (Seaplane) Flights, the resident aircraft being divided between the two (each with a nominal strength of six floatplanes). On 20 August No

Ready for launch at Newlyn, this Short 184 is armed with a depth charge and a 112lb HE Mk 3 bomb. Three more bombs can be seen in the foreground.

Seen at Newlyn early in 1918, Short 184 N2631 is armed with bomb and depth charge.

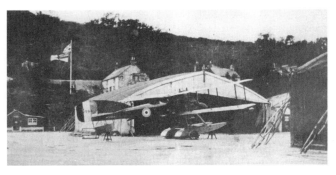

Short 184 N2928 on its beaching trolley between two of Newlyn's Bessoneau hangars in 1918.

235 Squadron was formed to control and coordinate the activities of both flights under 71 Wing, based in Penzance, and a number of Short 320 floatplanes arrived to boost the squadron's strength.

Sporadic contacts were made during the summer of 1918, such as that by N1770, which attacked an oil slick on 13 July. With the Armistice came a reduction in flying, although patrols were still mounted to spot and explode mines left over from hostilities. Newlyn was eventually decommissioned during February 1919, No 235 Squadron disbanding on 22 February. Although the Bessoneau hangars were removed, the station was retained by the Air Ministry as an emergency base until 1922 when it was declared no longer suitable for operations. Although the site of the base still exists as part of Penlee Quarry works, the area is due for redevelopment.

NEW ZEALAND FARM (LAVINGTON), Wiltshire

ST967505, 5¹/₂ miles SW of West Lavington

In 1940 CFS Upavon established an RLG at Market Lavington Hill on the northern edge of Salisbury Plain, but soon found that air currents made it unsafe to use. A more suitable site was found not far away to the south-west on Chickerell Down, and this was opened on 9 October 1940 as Lavington RLG. It was renamed shortly afterwards as New Zealand Farm, upon which the airfield was located. The farmhouse, set in a large copse, was demolished to make way for a small camp of wooden huts for storage and accommodation. Two runways were laid out on the grass, one orientated N-S and the other E-W, and three Blister hangars were later provided to give cover and maintenance facilities, together with a small wooden watch office.

The RLG was initially used for night-flying training by Oxfords and Masters, with goose-neck flares giving approach and runway lighting. The flares attracted an unwelcome visitor on the evening of 14 April 1941 during night-flying training, when a German bomber dropped ten bombs, only one of which hit the airfield, causing no damage. Accidents were surprisingly few in the circumstances, but a couple of fatal ones did occur during 1941: Master T8678 crashed on 30 April, and Oxford V3502 on 16 September. Beam Approach landing equipment was installed in the spring of 1942, and more buildings were added to increase accommodation. The parent unit changed on 1 April when the CFS was disbanded and replaced at Upavon by 7 FIS (later 7 FIS(A)), but for New Zealand Farm this meant only that Magisters replaced Masters in the circuit.

On 15 January 1942 a Wellington force-landed, returning from a raid. Another landed eleven days later, followed by a Halifax on 17 April and a Whitley on 17 June. On 4 May No 1537 (BAT) Flight formed at Upavon and its Oxfords were soon making use of New Zealand Farm, illumination having been upgraded with sodium lighting a couple of months before. A revision in 7 FIS(A)'s training syllabus required each course to spend two weeks at the Farm for intensive night-flying training. This scheme was successful and training was proceeding well until 1 November 1943, when all flying was stopped as a result of the Army's need to expand its Salisbury Plain training range. The RAF was given eviction notices, as were the civilian inhabitants of Imber village a mile to the south. New Zealand Farm transferred to the War Office on 17 December 1942.

Aircraft reappeared just over a year later when, from March 1944, the Piper L-4 Cubs and Stinson L-5s of the 153rd Liaison Squadron, US Army, started using the former RLG for training. In June they moved to the continent with the invasion forces, but were replaced by the 125th LS, which flew its L-5s from the airfield for a few weeks before leaving for France in August 1944. After the war New Zealand Farm became an outstation of the A&AEE Boscombe Down, and was used for weapon trials, and observation bunkers were built for photographic and visual assessment. The airfield has since been returned to Army control, and the runways are maintained for the use of tactical transport aircraft (mainly Hercules) on military exercises.

NORTH STOKE, Gloucestershire

ST717687, 3¹/₂ miles NW of Bath

Due to the shortage of suitable landing grounds for flying training in 1943, Landsdown Racecourse was surveyed as a potential site. Following its inspection in May by Wg Cdr Gosnell, OC/2 FIS(A), Hullavington, the site was prepared for flying.

The grandstands accommodated the personnel who removed the racecourse railings, and after minimal preparation an E-W runway was laid out on the turf to enable flying to start. Oxfords were soon in the circuit, as well as the occasional Harvard, Magister and Master. Although 3 FIS(A) moved to Lulsgate Bottom in early October 1943, it continued to use North Stoke as an RLG. The airfield could be a tricky place from which to fly, but despite this there were few accidents – the only one of note being an Oxford, which was badly damaged during a heavy landing on 7 March 1945.

No 3 FIS(A) was disbanded on 5 July 1945, its aircraft and staff absorbed by 7 FIS(A), also at Lulsgate. This unit also used North Stoke, but only for another month or so. Having no further need for it, the RAF handed the site back to its owners on 22 August 1945. Bath (Landsdown) Racecourse was re-established after the war and resumed its place in the racing calendar, which it maintains today. It has retained its association with aviation, as light aircraft and helicopters often fly in for race meetings.

OATLANDS HILL, Wiltshire

SU095405, 3¹/₂ miles W of Amesbury on A303

Opened as a satellite of Old Sarum in June 1941, Oatlands Hill was not an ideal airfield, occupying a low hill to the west of Stonehenge. It was pretty basic, consisting of three grass runways and four Blister hangars, together with a few buildings dispersed along the perimeter and in trees nearby.

The first unit to use the airfield was 239 Squadron, flying Tomahawks from Old Sarum on detachment from its base at Gatwick. In September 41 OTU, also at Old Sarum, began to make use of the airfield; flying Tomahawks, Harvards and Magisters, it trained fighter-reconnaissance pilots. The unit received Mustang Is in April 1942, but found Oatlands Hill to be challenging to fly from, and there were a number of accidents, both in the air and on the ground.

Despite the camouflage and dispersal of the buildings, the airfield was raided on 29 September, two bombs being dropped, but with no damage. No 41 OTU left the area in November 1942 and

Tomahawk AH784 of 41 OTU stands at Oatlands Hill in 1942.

was replaced by 43 OTU, an AOP training unit, which also used Oatlands Hill for flying training and for practising operations in the field, coming out from Old Sarum for the day or for week-long field exercises. This changed on 17 February 1944, when the whole of 43 OTU moved out of Old Sarum, which was required for D-Day preparations, to take up residence at Oatlands Hill. Its new home was still pretty basic, its hangars and buildings scarcely able to accommodate the unit's thirty Austers and more than a hundred personnel. When facilities became available at Andover they gratefully moved there on 10 August 1944.

The last surviving Blister hangar at Oatlands, seen in 2001.

Although then put on C&M, Oatlands Hill was still occasionally used by nearby units; for example, in early 1945 No 655 Squadron spent a month there on detachment. Old Sarum continued parenting the airfield until 13 May 1946 when it was finally closed. Most of the buildings were gradually cleared, the last Blister hangar being demolished in 2005. A couple of buildings remain, the former sick bay being used as a dwelling house.

Main features:
Runways: NE-SW 4,800ft, E-W 3,600ft, N-S 4,200ft., grass. *Hangars:* four Blister.
Accommodation: RAF Officers 5, SNCOs 7, ORs 183.

OKEHAMPTON (FOLLY GATE), Devon

SX575970, 1½ miles NW of Okehampton on A386

This little airfield dates back to 1928, when it was first used by army cooperation squadrons taking part in exercises on Dartmoor. Although situated on a hill, it was the flattest area that could be found in the vicinity, not far from the Army camps of Okehampton, a few miles to the south. It was mainly used during the summer by 13 and 16 Squadrons flying Bristol F2B, Atlas and later Audax aircraft, unit personnel being accommodated in tents on the airfield. These detachments continued until the summer of 1939, both squadrons then flying the Lysander.

The airfield remained unused after the outbreak of war, but in August 1940 the Lysanders of 16 Squadron returned to fly coastal patrols to counter the threat of invasion. The HQ and A Flight moved on to Weston Zoyland on 15 August, but other flights continued to use Folly Gate until the autumn, when the Squadron moved its forward operating base to Roborough. Apart from brief use by 225 Squadron's Lysanders during November for artillery observation training, the airfield was deserted for the winter.

Folly Gate became a satellite of Weston Zoyland in May 1941 and was again regularly used by 16 and 225 Squadrons working with Army units during Corps exercises. Detachments continued until April 1942 when the airfield was taken over by 43 Group, Maintenance Command, as a Forward Holding Unit for aircraft spares. No 73 MU had been formed during March for this purpose, and a number of large sheds and wooden huts were erected to accommodate the unit, which became operational in December.

Aircraft movements were then few and mostly unexpected. The first of these came shortly after the MU's formation when in April a Whitley of 58 Squadron, Chivenor, made a forced-landing on one engine, unfortunately becoming badly damaged after hitting an obstruction. A USAAF Tiger Moth crash-landed in April 1943, its pilot uninjured. US Army Piper L-4 Cubs flew from Okehampton late in 1944; these were from the 227th Field Artillery Battery of 29th Infantry Division, detached for a short period during an artillery practice camp in 1944.

With the end of the war in Europe, 73 MU closed on 24 July 1945, responsibility for its tasks having been transferred to 7 and 225 MUs. Sporadic use was made of the airfield after the war, AOP Austers using it until the early 1950s, when the site was finally closed and the buildings sold off. Little now exists of the airfield, apart from several buildings, one utilised as a village hall.

Main features:
Runways: N-S 2,520ft, NE-SW 2,520ft, E-W 2,490ft, SE-NW 2,520ft, grass.
Accommodation: RAF SNCOs 7, ORs 81; WAAF Officers 2, SNCOs 2, ORs 64.

OLD SARUM (FORD FARM), Wiltshire

SU153335, 2 miles N of Salisbury

Situated in an idyllic setting overlooked by an ancient castle, not far from the cathedral city of Salisbury, Old Sarum airfield buzzes with activity, particularly at the weekends. It is one of the oldest airfields still in use, having started life in 1917 on land requisitioned from Ford Farm, which gave its name to the original airfield. A double line of Belfast-truss hangars was erected, together with many wooden huts, and in August 1917 Nos 98 and 99 Squadrons moved in, from Harlaxton and Yatesbury respectively, followed by 103 from Beaulieu the following month. Day-bomber squadrons equipped with various aircraft types, they trained at Ford Farm before leaving for the Western Front in the spring

Old Sarum in the 1930s, with Brisfits and Grebes in residence.

of 1918. By that time the airfield had been renamed Old Sarum and the resident unit was No 11 TDS, which remained until the end of the war, training student pilots on Avro 504K, DH4 and DH6 aircraft.

Old Sarum was one of the few airfields to be retained by a much-reduced RAF after the war, and the School of Army Cooperation moved there from Stonehenge in March 1920. Having been set up to improve the operational relationship between the Army and the RAF, the school ran courses for Army liaison officers and the crews of Army cooperation squadrons (concentrating on artillery-spotting and tactical reconnaissance). Its Cooperation Squadron, flying Bristol F2Bs, was re-designated 16 Squadron on 1 April 1924, and continued to work with the SofAC. Later re-equipped with Audaxes and Hinds, in 1938 it became the first to receive the Lysander. No 13 Squadron was reformed at Old Sarum with Audaxes on 3 May 1935, and also worked with the school until moving to Odiham in February 1937. Four months later 59 Squadron also reformed there with Hectors, receiving Blenheim IVs in May 1939, just before moving to Andover.

Audax K3698 of 16 Squadron flying near its base at Old Sarum in June 1936.

Squadron Leader Charles, OC 16 Squadron, chatting with his pilots at Old Sarum in 1939.

The School of Army Cooperation was operating Lysanders, Ansons and Blenheims in the late 1930s. When the war started an element was moved to Andover and reformed there on 21 October 1939 as 2 SofAC, that at Old Sarum becoming 1 SofAC on 20 December. The crews of 16 Squadron undertook test and evaluation work, including gas-spraying techniques, but on 17 February 1940 they were moved to Hawkinge prior to joining the AASF in France.

A concept that the SofAC had developed was the use of light aircraft to aid communications and reconnaissance in the field, as Air Observation Posts. After evaluating a number of different types, the Taylorcraft Plus D was chosen to equip a trials unit, D Flight, which was formed by the school on 1 February 1940 at Larkhill for field trials. The unit left for France in mid-April, but was back again in June following the German breakthrough, having gained some useful operational experience, albeit some of it a bit close for comfort!

More Lysanders had appeared at Old Sarum just after 16 Squadron had left. These were with one of the first RCAF units to reach Britain, 110 (Army Cooperation) Squadron, which brought with it a dozen Canadian-built Lysanders. They did not stay long, exchanging places with another Lysander unit, 225 Squadron, at Odiham on 9 June. From Old Sarum 225 Squadron carried out daylight anti-invasion patrols along the South Coast between Selsey Bill and St Albans Head, then at the end of the month it moved to Tilshead.

Old Sarum was largely ignored by the Luftwaffe, but on 21 October 1940 a lone Ju 88A-1 of KG51 strafed the airfield at low level. It was chased by two Spitfires of 609 Squadron Middle Wallop, which shot it down near Lymington – the Squadron's 100th victory. During another attack on the night of 11-12 May 1941 a German bomber dropped incendiary and HE bombs, burning out one hangar, the Sergeants' Mess and the Signals Section.

Concerns over the vulnerability of the Lysander led to the introduction of fighter-reconnaissance aircraft, initially Tomahawks, to conduct tactical reconnaissance missions. On 20 September 1941 No 1 SofAC formed 41 OTU to train pilots in this work with twenty Tomahawks and a number of Harvards, Magisters and target tugs. One of the first units to adopt this role, 239 Squadron flew in its Tomahawks on regular detachments to the school from its base at Gatwick to take part in demonstrations and exercises. The OTU later received Mustang Mk Is to supplement

Three Lysanders of 16 Squadron take to the air from Old Sarum in 1939.

Old Sarum resident Auster I LB312, restored and owned by John Pothecary and seen here in June 2005, has spent much of its career at the station, having served there with 43 OTU.

Tiger Moth G-EMSY seen beside its residence, one of the First World War GS Sheds at Old Sarum, in August 2006.

and later replace the Tomahawks. Conventional Army cooperation training was still maintained by No 1 SofAC using Lysanders, and AOP development continued. In August 1941 it formed 651 Squadron with the Auster AOP1, from a nucleus of D Flight at Old Sarum. This was the first of twelve AOP squadrons, nine of which – Nos 651, 652, 653, 654, 655, 658, 660, 661 and 662 – were formed with Austers at Old Sarum between 1941 and 1943.

No 41 OTU moved to Hawarden in November 1941 and was replaced by 43 OTU, which had been formed with Auster AOP1s at Larkhill. Flying thirty-two Austers, it continued training AOP pilots at Old Sarum and also assisted with the formation of new AOP squadrons. In February 1944 the unit was moved to Oatlands Hill to make room for higher-priority work, preparations for the invasion of Europe, Old Sarum having been selected as a concentration area for RAF ground units going with the seaborne invasion force. All RAF vehicles involved in the landings went through Old Sarum for waterproofing so that they could wade ashore from LCTs. The vehicles then went into open storage on the airfield until needed. Six RAF Servicing Commandos also came to the station during May ready for the big day. On the morning of 1 June, road convoys started moving out from Old Sarum, heading for assembly areas near the coastal ports. Within a week or so the airfield was clear again. The Servicing Commandos returned to regroup in July and August, several going on to the Far East.

In December 1944 No 1 SofAC became the tri-service School of Air Support, its flying role being limited to battlefield demonstrations. In May 1947 the name was changed again to the School of Land/Air Warfare, but training continued for officers of all three services. Flying after the war was mainly by the Ansons, Dominies and Chipmunks of the Station Flight, and the Cadet and Sedburgh gliders of 622 Gliding School ATC. The Helicopter Development Unit formed on 1 June 1961 with Sycamores and Whirlwinds to work with SLAW, and was absorbed by the school when it became the Joint Warfare Establishment in March 1963. Old Sarum was transferred to the Army Department in December 1971 and the JWE disbanded in July 1976. Flying continued at Old Sarum until November 1978 when 622 GS moved to Upavon. The station was finally closed as a military base in 1979, and two years later the airfield and hangars were sold to the Edgeley Aircraft Company for the manufacture of the Optica spotter aircraft. After a disastrous fire that destroyed two hangars and several aircraft, the company moved to Hurn.

Flying still continues at Old Sarum today, the main residents currently being the Wiltshire Aero Club and the Old Sarum Flying Club. Although development is taking place around the airfield, many of the original First World War buildings still remain in place, including several hangars, a workshop and station HQ. Other buildings survive from the Second World War, including the messes and domestic site. Today Old Sarum remains in good health as one of the oldest active airfields in the UK.

Main features:
Runways: NE-SW 3,600ft, grass. *Hangars:* four GS Type, two Blister. *Hardstandings:* eighteen Sommerfield track. *Accommodation:* RAF Officers 172, SNCOs 84, ORs 1,131; WAAF Officers 7, SNCOs 3, ORs 258.

Old Sarum Castle and airfield in June 2006.

OVERLEY, Gloucestershire

SO965046, 4 1/2 miles NW of Cirencester

The site for a new SLG for 20 MU Aston Down was selected near Overley Wood in late 1940. Such SLGs were used for the storage of reserve aircraft by the ASUs, on sites that could be easily concealed, often near woodland so that aircraft could be hidden under the trees or in small clearings.

Work on laying the runways and preparing dispersals of Sommerfield track took place the following year, and the SLG was ready for its first aircraft in March 1942, which soon started to arrive from Aston Down. It was not long before the airfield drew the attention of a nearby flying school, 3 SFTS South Cerney, which started to use it as a useful RLG for practising landing and take-off techniques in its Oxfords.

The runways were extended in October 1942 to take four-engined aircraft, and a number of buildings were erected, including a Super Robin hangar and HQ. Other MUs used Overley during 1944 and the airfield was regularly used for training until at least 23 March 1945, when Oxford AS894 of 3(P)AFU overshot and crashed. With the end of the war the dispersals were gradually cleared of aircraft, which were flown to Aston Down. The site was abandoned in October 1945 after it had been cleared of some 16,000 square yards of track. Little can be seen today apart from the remains of the HQ building.

In this shot of RNAS Padstow taken during the summer of 1918, eleven DH6s can be seen beside the three Bessoneau hangars. A fourth was later added.

PADSTOW (CRUGMEER), Cornwall

SW898765, 1 1/2 miles NW of Padstow

Towards the end of 1917 German U-boat Command, frustrated by the convoy system, moved its operations closer to the British coastline. The result was that, of the shipping lost to U-boats in January 1918, some 60 per cent was sunk within 10 miles of the shore. To counter this activity the RNAS urgently needed to increase inshore patrols and provide support bases. A site was selected for such a base at Crugmeer near Padstow and a 50-acre airfield was established with three Bessoneau hangars (a fourth was later added) and a number of wooden buildings supplemented by tents. A landing run of 1,500 feet was laid out on sloping ground along the cliff-top, and a mooring mast erected on the edge of the airfield to cater for visiting airships. The base was commissioned as RNAS Padstow/Crugmeer in March 1918.

Padstow-based DH6 C5194 force-landed at sea, but was taken in tow by a collier and landed at Newlyn, where it is seen here being inspected on 4 July 1918.

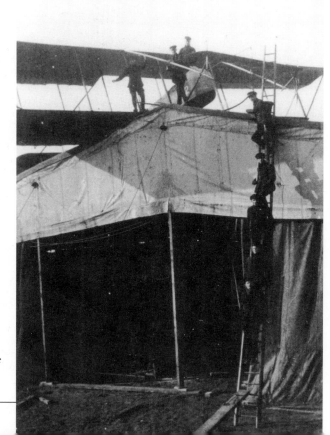

Another mishap, this time to a Maurice Farman, which appears to have landed on the roof of one of Padstow's hangars!

A dozen DH6 biplanes operating from the airfield were split into two sections, which became 500 and 501 Flights on 31 May. DH9s also arrived and these were formed into 494 (Light Bomber) Flight on 30 May. All three flights were parented by 250 Squadron, which formed at Padstow on 18 May as part of 71 Wing RAF with its HQ at Penzance.

Padstow was found to be one of the more difficult landing grounds from which to fly, particularly for the DH6 with its unreliable powerplant. With bombs aboard they were often unable to climb above the cliffs on return, and were forced to fly up a nearby valley, conveniently positioned just south of Gunver Head. Detachments were therefore often made to Westward Ho! During their lonely 2-hour patrols Padstow's pilots rarely saw any sign of the enemy, but were obviously a deterrent as the U-boats only seemed to attack when the aircraft were grounded due to bad weather. A number of DH6s were lost or damaged, but often by accident rather than enemy action; several force-landed at sea, the crews being rescued and the aircraft usually being towed back to shore, sometimes to fly again! Of the few attacks made by Padstow's aircraft, a DH6 flown by Captain H. Goodfellow dropped a bomb on a U-boat seen 3 miles off Trevose Head on 23 July 1918, and Lieutenant A. C. Tremellon released another four days later in similar circumstances, but neither attack proved conclusive. On 13 August Lieutenant H. H. Shorter spotted a U-boat off Newquay and dropped two bombs, but his elation was short-lived as both failed to explode.

After the Armistice flying finished at Padstow but the LG remained open until mid-May 1919 when 250 Squadron was disbanded. The site soon returned to agriculture and RNAS/RAF Padstow became just a memory. During the Second World War a radio station was built on the former airfield and a number of Maycrete buildings erected, some of which are still in use by local farmers.

S-61N G-ASNM of BEAH at Penzance Heliport in June 1966.

PENZANCE HELIPORT, Cornwall

SW487313, on Eastern Green, Penzance, alongside A30

The first flight to be made in Cornwall was from Poniou Meadow, east of Penzance, on 23 July 1910 by Claude Graham White in his Farman Biplane. He had chosen the location because 200 warships of the combined British fleets were at anchor in Mount's Bay, and he wished to demonstrate their vulnerability to air attack by flying over them. He flew for 15 minutes and circled the flagship, HMS *Dreadnought*, making a lasting impression on the thousands of people watching, and proving that aviation had arrived in the county, less than two years after Sam Cody had made the first flight in the UK at Farnborough.

BEAH WS-55 Whirlwind King Arthur *operating from Penzance in July 1966.*

It was fitting therefore that a spot nearby, since known as Eastern Green, was selected as the site for a purpose-built heliport, the first of its kind in Europe, as the centre for the first scheduled passenger helicopter service in the UK. Although Sikorsky S-61Ns had taken over from the DH Dragon Rapides on BEA's service to the Isles of Scilly from Land's End in May 1964, the airport did not have a good weather record so another operational base had been sought. Not only did the Penzance site have better weather, but it also had convenient road and rail links. The proposed heliport's site was on 14 acres of reclaimed marshland, and construction started in 1964 on a self-contained passenger terminal and maintenance base. The helicopters started operating from the new heliport in September and the service soon became firmly established. By the end of 1964 more than 36,300 passengers had been carried, the total for the first full year (1965) being 54,500. Passenger numbers steadily increased, year by year, as did regularity, which went from 88 per cent (the highest figure for Rapide operations) to virtually 100 per cent. The company also established one of the highest levels of technical reliability on the route of any scheduled service in Europe. Two Sikorsky S-61N helicopters were initially used on the route, G-ASNL and G-ASNM, which also carried cargo and freight, including flowers from 1966. Specialist airlift work was also undertaken, the S-61N having a useful underslung lifting capacity of $2^{1}/_{2}$ tons.

During March and April 1967 Penzance Heliport became the centre for helicopter operations following the wrecking of the *Torrey Canyon* off Land's End. In support of salvage attempts to save the stricken ship, a BEA S-61N was leased by Dutch salvors Wijsmuller to take compressors, equipment and personnel out to her. Other early arrivals were a Brantly B2 bringing newspaper reporters and an Alouette II camera-ship. Naval helicopters on oil-slick surveillance called in, but once the oil started to appear on Cornish beaches Army and RAF helicopters came in to assist the cleansing parties. Middle Wallop-based Sioux and Scouts were the first of these to arrive, followed by Wessex HC2s of 72 Squadron and Whirlwind HAR10s of 230 Squadron from RAF Odiham. The choppers carried personnel and equipment into coves inaccessible by road, and were invaluable in carrying thousand of drums of chemical detergent for the beach parties to spray onto the oil in order to disperse it. This work continued well into April.

During October 1968 the 250,000th passenger was carried on the Penzance-Isles of Scilly service, and traffic steadily grew. However, the increasing demand for helicopters on North Sea oil operations in the 1970s and the need for increased crew training resulted in S-61s being withdrawn from the route during several winters. As replacements, Sikorsky S-58Ts were leased to operate from Penzance or BN2 Islanders from Land's End, but these arrangements were not popular with passengers. The purchase of more S-61s, together with the installation of a flight simulator at the main BEAH base at Aberdeen later obviated the need to take an S-61 off-station.

Sioux AH1 XT163 at Penzance Heliport in March 1967, during the Torrey Canyon *operations.*

BEA Helicopters became British Airways Helicopters in 1972 following the merger of BEA and BOAC, and its success continued, the millionth passenger being flown on the Penzance-IoS route in July 1979. The flight safety record of the BEAH/BAH operation has been extremely high over the years, and has only been marred on two occasions. The first was when S-61N G-AWFX crash-landed on a training flight near the heliport on 31 October 1968, damaging its port sponson, but without injury to the crew. The second was far more serious, when on 16 July 1983 a combination of factors caused S-61N G-BEON to crash into the sea 2 miles short of St Mary's. Of the twenty-six passengers and crew aboard, there were only six survivors. In 1986 came a change of ownership when BAH was sold to the Maxwell Group, becoming British International Helicopters. The fiftieth anniversary of scheduled air services to the Isles of Scilly was celebrated in 1987.

A single S-61N is based at Penzance all year round, supplemented by a second during the summer. Other helicopters use the heliport, including S-61Ns and S-76s on oil exploration work, and

Wessex HC2 XT671/W of 72 Squadron, Odiham, was also flying Torrey Canyon *operations from Penzance during March 1967.*

S-61N G-BFFJ of British International at the heliport on a maintenance day in May 1999.

n additional S-61N on the route to Tresco. Between 1989 and 1993 Westland WG30 G-BKGD was ased at the heliport, operating a new Penzance-St Mawgan service, as well as supporting the route o Scilly. The fourteen-seater helicopter flew more than 30,000 passengers during this time.

The S-61N that has predominantly operated the service since 1975 is G-BCEB, originally built s a land-based S-61L, later modified to amphibious S-61N standard. With integral baggage lockers n the lower hull, 5-minute turnarounds are possible, with engines running and rotors turning, a echnique pioneered on the route. The standard twenty-eight-passenger layout has been increased o thirty on G-BCEB, which at peak times can be raised to thirty-two.

British International S-61N G-BCEB lands at Penzance Heliport during a busy day in September 2007.

Passenger numbers on the service have grown steadily since 1964, the figure for 1992 representing an increase of almost 50 per cent on the first full year of service. The highest number of passengers flown in one day was 1,125 on 5 June 1999, and the highest flown in one day by one helicopter was 730 by G-BCEB on 4 June 1988. By the thirtieth anniversary of the service in May 1994 some 2,233,000 passengers had been carried, and on the fortieth anniversary the figure was 3,250,000, running at a rate of around 100,000 per annum.

During the summer on peak Saturdays twenty-six daily return flights are made, and extra flights are operated when required. In high summer the first scheduled departure often leaves Penzance at 06.45, the last from St Mary's at 20.40. Transit time is 20 minutes, flown at 120 knots between 500 to 3,000 feet. The S-61N is fully equipped with weather radar, full instrumentation and ground proximity warning systems, and is flown by a crew of two pilots and one cabin attendant. It is fully amphibious and can be safely landed at sea – this procedure is regularly practised by pilots, and an S-61N can sometimes be seen water-borne in Mount's Bay. Routine servicing is carried out at night and on Sundays, heavy maintenance being undertaken at Penzance for other company helicopters as well as those home-based. The heliport itself was upgraded in 1992 to extend passenger facilities, but otherwise its original design has stood the test of time well.

As well as being BIH's base, Penzance Heliport is also open to other users. The Trinity House MBB105, Devon & Cornwall Police MBB105 and Cornwall Air Ambulance EC135 often call in, as do private users. British International's parent company, Brintel Helicopters, is part of the Canadian-based CHC Helicopter Group, and in late 1999 Brintel was merged with Bond Helicopters to form Scotia Helicopter Services. British International operates one of the largest fleets of S-61s, with eight in service. As well as two on the Penzance-Scilly route, four spend most of their time on oil work in Scotland, while two more operate in support of British forces in the Falkland Islands, based at RAF Mount Pleasant. Although several replacements have been suggested for them, including the Westland EH101 Heliliner (the civil version of the Merlin), the S-61Ns of BI continue to ply their way between Penzance and the Isles of Scilly, and will probably continue to do so for some time to come, on the world's longest-established scheduled passenger helicopter service.

PERRANPORTH, Cornwall

SW740528, 1½ miles SW of Perranporth on B3285

Land was requisitioned at Perranporth in July 1940 to build a satellite airfield for Portreath, 4 miles to the north. Located in a dramatic spot overlooking the Cornish cliffs, the new station was intended for one fighter squadron, with basic facilities (one T2 and a few Blister hangars, a watch office and some flight huts). The MT section on the northern edge of the airfield utilised an old explosives factory, but the domestic sites were all away from the airfield. The three runways were connected by a perimeter track, off which there were a number of blast pens.

The airfield opened in April 1941, with 66 Squadron bringing its Spitfires in from Exeter on the 27th. The unit stayed until 14 December, flying coastal patrols and escorts for St Eval-based PR Spitfires and bombers targeting northern France. This set the pattern for the succession of Spitfire squadrons passing through Perranporth. An ASR Flight formed in May 1941 with Lysanders becoming part of 276 Squadron and moving to Portreath in November.

No 310 (Czech) Squadron arrived in December, continuing the patrol work, but after its replacement by 19, 130 and later 234 and 610 Squadrons, fighter sweeps were initiated across the Channel. Sergeant G. Eames of 610 Squadron ditched during a shipping patrol on 11 April 1943 and established a somewhat unenviable record, floating for nearly two weeks in his dinghy until rescued!

With two and sometimes three Spitfire squadrons in residence, Perranporth's facilities were upgraded, with runway extensions, more dispersals and a briefing room being added during the spring of 1943. Nos 412 (RCAF) and 610 Squadrons arrived in April to fly *Ramrods* and sweeps along the Channel and over northern France. Escorts were also flown, 610 covering Whirlwind fighter-bombers attacking targets on the Cherbourg peninsula. Joined by 132 Squadron in May the three units stayed until June, when they were replaced by a Polish Wing of 302 and 317 Squadrons.

The first non-Spitfire unit to be based at Perranporth came on 18 September when the Typhoons of 183 Squadron arrived from Tangmere for fighter-bomber operations over the Brest peninsula; however, needing longer runways when fully bombed-up, they soon left for Predannack. The Australians of 453 Squadron had arrived on 20 August and flew offensive patrols to protect

Spitfire VBs of 130 Squadron line up for another mission at Perranporth in early 1942.

The proximity of Perranporth's dispersals to the cliffs can be seen in this photo of groundcrews preparing one of 453 Squadron's Spitfire VBs in 1943.

Perranporth's underground Battle HQ nestles amongst the vegetation in August 2005.

Allied aircraft bound for the Middle East from Cornwall, as well as Sunderlands operating from Mount Batten and Pembroke Dock. The flying boats had been attracting the attention of marauding packs of Ju 88 and Bf 110 fighters, and on 8 October two Bf 110 finger-fours were spotted by the Aussies 100 miles south-west of the Isles of Scilly. The Spitfires went into the attack and after a furious dogfight five of the Bf 110s, which were from II/ZG1, were shot down for the loss of two Spitfires, one RAF pilot later being rescued by RN destroyer. No 66 Squadron had arrived on 17 September 1943 with Spitfire VIs from Kenley and, later in the month, during an SAR operation near the Isle of Butz for survivors from a British ship, intercepted four FW 190s. Two were shot down without loss, but success was marred when two Spitfires collided in the circuit on their return to base.

Two Free French Spitfire V squadrons, 340 and 341 (arriving from Drem on 9 November and Biggin Hill on 11 October) formed 145 Wing at Perranporth as part of the reorganisation of the RAF in preparation for the invasion of France. They re-equipped with the Spitfire IX and, joined by 329 Squadron on 12 March 1944, flew convoy patrols and *Insteps* before leaving for Merston at 145 Airfield in mid-April.

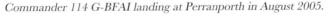

Commander 114 G-BFAI landing at Perranporth in August 2005.

Perranporth played an important part during the build-up to D-Day, being taken over by 19 Group Coastal Command as the base for anti-submarine and anti-shipping operations. These were to be carried out by three FAA squadrons, 816 flying Swordfish, arriving from Crail on 20 April, and two Avenger squadrons, 849 from Macrihanish on the same day and 850, flying in from Lee-on-Solent three days later. Operations commenced on 30 April when six Avengers of 849 Squadron and five of 850 went on an offensive sweep off the French coast while 816's Swordfish flew a line patrol. Activities increased as D-Day approached, with operations also being flown from St.Eval and St.Merryn. By 4 June eighteen Avengers and six Swordfish were regularly flying patrols round the clock. These continued until the end of July, with little action taking place, although on 20 July Avengers of 850 Squadron spotted two He 177s attacking a destroyer off Ushant and went into the attack, claiming one damaged.

Following the naval squadrons' departure in August 1944 Perranporth was reduced to C&M. Transferred to 46 Group, it was reopened on 23 November, and used until February 1945 to accommodate Transport Command Staging Post personnel awaiting transport to the continent. Returned to C&M, parented by St Mawgan, the airfield briefly became the base for 95 Gliding School, but was finally closed on 6 April 1946. The Air Ministry de-requisitioned the airfield in 1951 for licensing by Newquay Council as a commercial airfield; limited operations started for scheduled services and pleasure flights, but closed at the end of the 1952 season.

The Cornish Gliding Club started flying from Perranporth in 1957 using the old MT site, later building extra hangars. Gliding expanded rapidly at the airfield and within a year it was one of the most active in the county. The club has continued to operate at Perranporth ever since and this in turn has encouraged an expansion of general aviation at the airfield. The control tower was refurbished in the 1980s and is now fully operational. Today Perranporth is a very active airfield with substantial parts of the original runways still in use, and new hangars have been built to cater for this expansion. As well as the tower, wartime buildings still extant include many of the fighter pens and the battle HQ.

Main features:
Runways: 058° 4,200ft x 150ft, 100° 3,300ft x 150ft, 198° 3,300ft x 150ft, tarmac. *Hangars:* one Teeside, four O-Blister, two EO-Blister. *Hardstandings:* twenty fighter pens. *Accommodation:* RAF Officers 48, SNCOs 69, ORs 917; WAAF Officers 1, SNCOs 1, ORs 40.

PORTLAND, Dorset

SY682746, 3 miles S of Weymouth

When Squadron Commander Charles Simpson flew his Short Amphibian from HMS *Hibernia* in Portland Harbour on 27 May 1912, it was the first flight in the UK from the deck of a ship while under way. Aviation returned to Portland in September 1916 with the opening of an RNAS seaplane unit to help combat the U-boat offensive. Four Short 184 floatplanes were flown, from basic facilities including a hangar and slipway. Few U-boat sightings were made during patrols, although one, made by exchange USN officer Ensign J. F. McNamara, resulted in the first attack on a submarine by a US aviator when he bombed a U-boat.

The RAF took over the base in April 1918 and in May formed its aircraft, then Short 184s, (and later 320s) Wight Seaplanes and Fairey Campanias, into 416 and 417 (Seaplane) Flights. On 20 August No 241 Squadron was formed to administer the flights, also taking on 513 (Special Duty) Flight at Chickerell with DH6 landplanes. RAF Portland carried on as part of 10 Group until 241 Squadron and its flights were disbanded in June 1919.

Although Portland naval base stayed open, little flying took place there and it was not until 24 May 1939 that naval aircraft were based again in the area, when 771 Squadron was formed at Portland as a Fleet Requirements Unit to tow targets for ships' AA gunners. It consisted of two flights, X Flight flying landplanes from Lee-on-Solent and Y Flight with four Swordfish floatplanes at Portland. When the Squadron split on 28 September, Y Flight became 772 Squadron, continuing to fly targets for warships at Portland until 14 July 1940, then moving to Campbeltown when the base was evacuated following the fall of France.

Reinstated, Portland naval base became home for the Anti-Submarine School in 1946, which then started evaluating helicopters in the ASW role. Sikorsky R-4 Hoverflies were flown initially, as were more modern types as they came into service. FAA helicopter squadrons visited Portland to

Three Short 320s on the slipway at RAF Portland in 1918.

work with the school and eventually it was decided to build a new flying station there. A landing ground and two hangars were built on the playing fields alongside the old Fleet Canteen, which was converted into the SHQ, operations centre, workshops and control tower. Shortly after RNAS Portland was commissioned as HMS *Osprey* on 24 April 1959, the Air ASW School, together with 815 Squadron with Whirlwind HAS7s, moved in from Eglington. The Squadron disbanded on 28 August and immediately reformed as 737 Squadron, the Anti-Submarine Operational Flying School.

Portland Naval Base became the venue for the operational sea training and working-up of warships' crews in 1958, with the transfer of HQ Flag Officer Sea Training, which started to use helicopters (initially Dragonflies) for communications, based at *Osprey*. No 771 Squadron reformed there on 11 July 1961 as the Helicopter Trials & Training Squadron with Dragonflies, Whirlwinds and a couple of Wasps; it subsequently took over the Portland SAR task. In July 1962 No 737 Squadron converted to the Wessex and in 1970 took over the parenting of Wessex Flights in 'County' Class destroyers. No 829 Squadron transferred from Culdrose in December 1964 as the parent unit for Wasp ships' flights, absorbing the SAR and training role of 771 Squadron, which then disbanded.

In the late 1960s the first of several redevelopment programmes was started. Part of the harbour was filled in to increase the size of the helicopter operating area by 12 acres. New hangars and workshops were built near the fuel storage area, and the approaches to the runway were tidied up. As more ships'

Portland-based Wessex HU5 XS496 of 772 Squadron in July 1983.

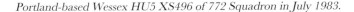

The former RNAS Portland HQ building with flying control and hangar, seen in August 2006.

flights were commissioned, 829 Squadron increased in size and 771 reformed on 23 June 1967 with Whirlwind HAS7s to take over part of its training task. The remainder of 829's training commitment was transferred to 703 Squadron, which reformed at the station on 22 January 1972 with Wasps.

On 6 September 1974 No 772 Squadron reformed from part of 771, which then moved to Culdrose, leaving 772 with the Portland SAR commitment using six Wessex HAS1s – these were replaced by HU5s in 1976. In 1977 the unit took on the parenting of Wessex HU5 Flights aboard the RFAs. No 701 Squadron was reabsorbed by 829 in January 1981, and in August 1982 the latter took over the Wessex 3 ship-borne flights from 737 Squadron, which disbanded on 27 February 1983. Nos 702 and 815 Squadrons moved in from Yeovilton on 19 July 1982, the former providing conversion and operational training on the Lynx, the latter parenting ships' flights operating the type. No 829 Squadron then started converting to the Lynx while continuing to support the Wasp ships' flights. The units supported by both squadrons were involved in the Falklands Campaign, and later the Armilla Patrol and relief operations in Lebanon, Aden and the Caribbean. In September 1986 No 829 started to parent a number of the Lynx ships' flights transferred from 815 Squadron. More flights moved across in 1987 and 1988, the Squadron eventually having thirty aircraft on strength. In March 1988 No 772 Squadron re-equipped with the Sea King HC4 (Commando).

Many of Portland's units were deployed to the Persian Gulf between August 1990 and February 1991, and were at the centre of the action there. More reorganisation came on 26 March 1993, when 829 Squadron was disbanded into 815, making it the largest helicopter squadron in the world. More improvements were made to facilities during the mid-1990s, but, despite this, plans to

S-61N G-BPWB Portland Castle *of HM Coastguard at Portland in August 2006.*

close the naval base and its air station due to economy measures were announced in 1995. On 30 September No 772 Squadron was disbanded and its place taken, not by another naval air squadron, but an SAR unit of HM Coastguard flying Sikorsky S61s operated by Bristow Helicopters.

Nos 702 and 815 Naval Air Squadrons continued to operate from the station until March 1999 when RNAS Portland closed and the squadrons transferred to Yeovilton. Having been taken over by the South-West Regional Development Agency, the buildings of the former air station have since been adapted for use by a number of industrial and marine companies. The airfield itself remains one of the main operating bases of the HM Coastguard SAR organisation, which flew the S-61 until August 2008, when it was replaced by the Agusta-Westland AW139.

Horsley J8606 of Porton Down Special Duty Flight fitted with a spray device at Boscombe Down in about 1932, with Hinaidis of 10 Squadron behind.

PORTON DOWN, Wiltshire

SU205365, 5 miles NE of Salisbury

Porton Down has been the centre for research on protective measures and offensive means involving chemical warfare since 1916, when the Royal Engineers Experimental Station was established there. The establishment had a landing ground from which aircraft operated in support of trials from the 1920s to the 1940s, and helicopters still use the site today.

Aircraft bombing trials on Porton ranges were planned in 1918 but the Armistice obviated the need for them. In fact, there is no evidence that aerial bombs were actually charged with chemical agents at REES during the First World War. Trials for the delivery of chemical warfare agents by aircraft were undertaken on the ranges and, following the successful use of an Avro 504 in 1926, it was decided to form a special flight to develop these activities. A landing ground was laid out, but rather than build hangars at Porton Down, the Bristol F2Bs of the new Porton Experimental Flight were based at Old Sarum. The flight moved to Netheravon on 12 September 1928, then having a Fairey Fox, two Hawker Horsleys and a Blackburn Dart on strength. Smoke and chemicals were normally released from bombs, but in the 1930s spray tanks were devised to be fitted to aircraft with nozzles to emit smoke indicating dispersion patterns. Later developed to spray chemicals and smoke operationally, this equipment was given the title Smoke Curtain Installation (SCI) to disguise its real role.

The Porton Experimental Flight of the Chemical Defence Experimental Station (as it became in 1930) moved to Boscombe Down in February 1930 when accommodation became available at the newly reopened airfield. Shortly after moving, the flight was re-equipped with a Wapiti and a Hart and renamed the Special Duty Flight. Its work, which included aiding the RAF Anti-Gas School at Rollestone as well as trials, was obviously taken seriously as the SDF's fleet was updated as the aircraft types in front-line service changed. At the outbreak of the Second World War it had a Lysander, a Battle, a Whitley and a Wellington on strength.

Nimrod K3657, fitted with SCIs, at Porton Down in July 1937.

Hunter F6 XE601 sprays training agent during an NBC 'Battle Run' exercise at Porton Down in 1995.

In the late 1930s the British offensive chemical weapons stockpile was small compared to that of other countries. With war on the horizon a priority programme was started to increase stocks of air-launched chemical weapons such as chemical bombs and SCIs. The RAF took a major role in the distribution and storage of these weapons, and sixty RAF stations and twenty-nine MUs were to eventually hold large amounts of them. The RAF also had a decontamination organisation, each station having squads to treat areas of contamination under the control of a Gas Defence Centre. These weapons and their countermeasures, as well as the protective clothing and decontamination equipment, were all developed at the CDES.

A larger higher-capacity version of the SCI was developed by the CDES in 1939 for installation in aircraft bomb bays; one could be fitted into a Whitley and two into a Wellington. The standard SCI continued to be used for smoke delivery as, being externally mounted, it could easily be replaced during an operational turnaround. Originally fitted to light bombers, clearance trials broadened the aircraft that could be fitted and later included such types as the Typhoon and Tempest. SCIs were used in action in August 1942 during Operation *Jubilee*, the Dieppe landings; two Boston squadrons laid smoke using SCIs and phosphorous bombs, aided by four Blenheim squadrons that dropped smoke bombs. The resulting smoke screens blinded enemy gun batteries during the landings, and further smoke covered the withdrawal. Such operations were repeated and were particularly successful during the D-Day landings.

Porton Down's Hard Target, in June 2002.

At some stage during the war the 'hard target' was constructed on Porton Down ranges. This massive reinforced concrete wall, some 50 feet square, was built as an artillery and aircraft target, and it still bears the scars of many ordnance strikes. The airstrip at Porton Down was mainly used for communications during the war, trials aircraft usually flying from Boscombe Down. In 1942 the CDES Special Duty Flight was absorbed into the A&AEE's C Squadron, as C Squadron Test Flight. Its title changed again in 1944 to Communications & Special Duties Flight, then operating a Cub, Auster, Swordfish, Thunderbolt, Mosquito, Stirling and Lancaster, and flying until the end of the war.

After 1945 aviation continued to figure in the work of the CDES (which became the Chemical Defence Experimental Establishment in 1948). A helipad was marked out on the landing ground, which was still used for communications and the occasional trial such as in 1956 when the Colonial Office Insecticide Research Unit tested a chemical spray attachment on its Auster Autocar. Post-war, aircraft have been provided by the A&AEE for chemical, biological, pesticide and meteorological trials by Porton Down, from the late 1940s, when an Anson fitted with tanks and a rotary atomiser was provided for an anti-locust trial, to the 1990s, when a Hunter was flown with spray tanks to simulate chemical attacks on troops taking part in tactical training during the Porton Down 'Battle Run'. Helicopters have regularly used the range facilities, from Whirlwinds in the 1950s to Gazelles and Chinooks today. The establishment itself has been enlarged, and continues as the HQ site for the MoD's Defence Science Technology Laboratory (Dstl).

PORTREATH, Cornwall

SW670460, 1 mile NE of village

Another Cornish cliff-top airfield, Portreath was very busy during the Second World War, with resident units vying for circuit space and dispersals full of aircraft passing through on ferry flights to and from the Mediterranean. The latter were hazardous at the best of times due to the vagaries of the weather over the Bay of Biscay, but doubly so given the presence of enemy fighter patrols looking for easy prey. Operation *Beggar* was just such a mission, involving the ferrying of Horsa gliders towed by Halifaxes to North Africa in preparation for the invasion of Sicily. The first four combinations, flown by 295 Squadron crews, left Portreath for Morocco on 3 June 1943. Only two got there, the other two Halifaxes returning to Portreath, one with an unserviceable glider, the other having lost its Horsa due to a broken tow rope; the glider floated for 10 hours in the Bay of Biscay before its crew were rescued. Deliveries went smoothly for the next fortnight, fourteen gliders being successfully delivered to Sale. On the 14th a combination met up with two FW200 Condors and, despite casting off its glider and taking evasive action, was shot down. Altogether two Halifaxes and four Horsas were lost, with another of the Horsas crashing on arrival at Sale. The operation was nonetheless a tremendous feat by any standards.

Land for an airfield on Nancekuke Common, Portreath, was requisitioned in July 1940 and, after several minor roads were closed, construction started. Initially three tarmac runways were laid, a fourth being added latter. Double fighter blast pens were dispersed along the perimeter track together with four Blister hangars (later supplemented by a further four), and four T2 hangars on

Portreath's first resident was 263 Squadron, which flew its Whirlwinds on operations from the station during March and April 1941. P6984 was one of these, pictured at Exeter in January.

the technical site. Extensive domestic sites were built to the south of the airfield. RAF Portreath was opened on 7 March 1941, the first resident being 263 Squadron, which flew in its Whirlwinds from St Eval on 18 March. Engaged on convoy patrols in the Western Approaches, the unit stayed for three weeks before moving to Filton on 10 April. It was replaced by the Spitfire IIAs of 152 Squadron, which had arrived from Warmwell on the 9th and immediately started night patrols; they reverted to day combat patrols after losing two aircraft in accidents.

Discovering that Portreath was operational, the Luftwaffe made two attacks during April without causing any damage, but a more determined raid on 9 May resulted in the death of one airman and the wounding of three others, together with the destruction of three aircraft and damage to two others. Portreath became a sector station when a new sector operations room was opened at nearby Tehidy Farm, replacing the previous one at St Eval, and also becoming

Spitfire Vs of 130 Squadron at Portreath in October 1941.

responsible for Perranporth and Predannack. The first of many Blenheims arrived in early May 1941 when 2 Group squadrons started using Portreath as a forward airfield for raids into France, No 152 Squadron providing escorts for some of these operations.

Portreath's potential as a forward airfield was also realised by the ferry organisation, and in June 1941 the Overseas Air Deliveries Flight, Kemble (becoming the OADU in August), set up a detachment at Portreath. This unit prepared aircraft for long-distance ferry flights, initially across the Bay of Biscay to Gibraltar, subsequently to North Africa, then across the Mediterranean to the Far East. The remainder of the unit moved to Portreath in early November, having by then become the OADU. It was re-designated 1 OADU on 26 January 1942. No 130 Squadron was formed at Portreath on 20 June and worked up with Spitfire IIs, becoming operational in September. Later with 313 Squadron, which arrived with its Spitfire VBs from Warmwell on 29 November for a short stay, 130 flew convoy escorts and offensive sweeps as well as providing cover for Blenheims withdrawing from raids on the French ports.

The ferrying of whole units to the Mediterranean started during the summer of 1941 to counter the build-up of the Afrika Korps by taking action against Axis shipping. The Blenheims of 2 Group were the first to go, 82 Squadron leaving for a five-week detachment on 11 June. The main runway was only just long enough for a fully loaded Blenheim, and many heart-stopping take-offs were made, aircraft often disappearing over the cliffs to reappear agonisingly long seconds later, struggling for height over the sea. Fighter squadrons came and went on operational detachments during this time; among the major efforts by the Portreath sector were the two Operation *Veracity* daylight attacks on the *Scharnhorst* and *Gneisnau* at Brest during December 1941. During the second, made on the 30th by three Halifax squadrons, the escorting Spitfires shot down six German fighters and damaged eleven more.

A detachment of 276 Squadron Lysanders arrived at the station on 21 October 1941 to fly ASR patrols, and soon proved their effectiveness. On 7 January 1942 a Wellington of 15 OTU ditched 2 miles off Portreath and the Lysanders made four searches for survivors. Less than 2 hours later a PRU Anson ditched, and a Lysander, airborne within 8 minutes, successfully located the floating aircraft. In the autumn of 1942 Portreath was cleared for Operation *Cackle*, the supply of RAF and USAAF aircraft in the build-up for Operation *Torch*. More than a hundred aircraft were to be seen at Portreath in the period towards the end of the year, often because of delays due to the weather or diversions. Accommodation of crews put a strain on the station's facilities and a tent-town was erected to provide shelter. On 6 November, for example, sixty-six C-47s arrived, leaving the next day for North Africa. On the 9th, with the station already stretched to the limit, nineteen B-17s of the 306th BG arrived, having been diverted after a raid on St Nazaire, joining eighty-eight aircraft already occupying the dispersals.

Portreath from the air in about 1950, clearly showing its four-runway layout and proximity to the cliff-tops.

There were accidents – nine men were killed on 8 December 1942 when a Hudson and a Beaufort flew into cliffs after take-off. Considering the difficult conditions, with inexperienced crews flying overweight aircraft, such accidents were comparatively few. Some losses were also due to interception by German fighters. In an attempt to combat this, six long-range Mustangs were detached from 400 (RCAF) Squadron at Dunsfold during December to provide escorts. Many aircraft that did not make it to Gibraltar were later found to have in fact force-landed in Portugal and been interned. A steady stream of aircraft on ferry flights passed through Portreath during the first half of 1943, including 124 B-24s of the 44th, 93rd and 389th BGs en route to North Africa during June for raids on the Ploesti oil refinery. In May the airfield was used by forty-six P-47s of the 78th FG to provide escorts for the bombing of Brest and other western French ports. In early June two more Mustang squadrons, Nos 414 and 613, provided detachments to escort Coastal Command aircraft in the Bay, due to an increase in losses to German fighters.

A new sector operations room opened at Tregaea Hill in July, Portreath's operations by then being mainly concerned with coastal strike and anti-fighter operations over the Bay of Biscay. These involved the Beaufighters of 235 Squadron, which arrived from Leuchars on 29 August, and 143 Squadron from St Eval on 16 September. They left in February 1944 and were replaced by the Mosquito IVs of 248 Squadron, which also had a few Mk XVIIIs fitted with 6-pounder Molins guns designed to punch a hole through U-boat hulls. On 10 March four Mk IVs escorting two Mk XVIIIs spotted a German naval force off the north Spanish coast accompanied by ten Ju 88s. A number of individual combats ensued, the Mosquitoes shooting down three Junkers, as well as attacking the convoy.

The Beaufighters of 235 Squadron returned on 27 March 1944 and with 248 formed 153 Wing in preparation for the invasion of Europe. On 11 April they attacked four ships and eight Ju 88s escorting a U-boat, downing two Ju 88s for the loss of two Mosquitoes. Operations continued throughout May, increasing in frequency during the build-up to the invasion. On D-Day 248 Squadron flew five missions, on the last of which ten Mosquitoes escorted thirty-one Beaufighters on a *Rover* in the Bay of Biscay. Three destroyers were attacked by the Beaufighters and the Mosquitoes claimed an escorting Ju188. Late in June 235 Squadron also received Mosquitoes and joined 248 on strikes and Beaufighter escorts along the French coast, from Brest to the Gironde.

The Portreath Wing also provided air defence for RN operations in the area (a risky business as the Navy tended to regard any aircraft as hostile!). On 21 July, in appalling weather while covering a destroyer flotilla off Ushant, 235 Squadron crews sighted a number of Hs 293 glider bomb-carrying Do 217s. The two Mosquitoes intercepted one and set it on fire before going after another, which blew up after several bursts of cannon fire. Another four such Do 217s were intercepted by a formation of twelve Mk VIs of 235 Squadron and two Mk XVIIIs of 248 during a patrol on 9 August; two Dorniers were shot down and the others damaged. Activity over the Bay of Biscay tailed off after this, the final sorties being made in the area on 7 September. No 235 Squadron had already departed for Banff by this time, and 248 followed on 12 September.

Portreath was left to the ASR squadrons and 1 OADU. Although 276 Squadron departed on 18 September, a detachment remained that was joined by others from 275 and 277 Squadrons throughout the remainder of 1944 and into 1945. The airborne lifeboat-equipped Warwicks of 276 were transferred to 277 Squadron in November and remained at Portreath with a 275 Squadron Walrus detachment until February 1945, when both units left. Diversions continued to be handled, but, with the OADU then being the only resident unit, Portreath was transferred to 44 Group in early May 1945. During that month more than 200 replacement aircraft were delivered overseas and a Transport Command Briefing School was established. Such movements declined with the opening of overland routes to the Middle and Far East; therefore, following the departure of 76 Squadron Dakotas to the Far East in September 1945, the OADU was transferred to St Mawgan. The Briefing School left on 8 October and the following day the ATC closed.

In December 1945 Portreath was reduced to C&M and, after briefly being used by 7 (Polish) Resettlement Unit, was closed towards the end of 1946. The airfield lay abandoned until May 1950 when it was taken over by the Ministry of Supply, later becoming an outstation of CDEE Porton Down. Named Nancekuke, it was used for the production of chemical agents for research purposes. When the outstation closed in 1979 the airfield was transferred to the RAF as the site of a new air defence radar station. No 1 Air Control Centre arrived from Wattisham early in July 1979 with Type 93 mobile radar systems (later replaced by Type 101s), and the station was formally reopened as RAF Portreath on 1 October 1980.

Today the airfield looks much the same as it did during the Second World War, the main difference being the radar dome and buildings at its centre. Many of the wartime buildings were demolished when CDEE Nancekuke closed, but several survive, including the combined mess, several re-covered Maycrete huts and eighteen air raid shelters.

Main features:
Runways: 194° 4,050ft x 150ft, 283° 5,400ft x 150ft, 336° 3,450ft x 150ft, 242° 4,050ft x 150ft, asphalt. *Hangars:* four Teeside, eight EO-Blister. *Hardstandings:* twenty-two. *Accommodation:* RAF Officers 159, SNCOs 171, ORs 1,896; WAAF Officers 10, SNCOs 8, ORs 487.

PRAWLE POINT, Devon

SX778368, 3 miles SE of Salcombe

Another RNAS station built to combat the upsurge in U-boat attacks in early 1917, Prawle Point was opened in April of that year. Situated on a headland in the South Hams, the most southerly point in Devon, the rectangular landing ground covered some 50 acres. Facilities were the minimum to enable the operation of four Sopwith 1½ Strutters, men and machines being provided with tents of varying sizes. Regular patrols were flown from the base until August, when the aircrews were transferred to the Western Front where they were urgently needed to replace losses.

The landing ground was back in use during May 1918 under the control of the RAF, which had upgraded it with the provision of four Bessoneau hangars, offices, a mess and two cookhouses. Three flights were formed: 492 (Light Bomber) Flight with DH9s on 30 May, joined a week later by 517 and 518 (Special Duty) Flights with DH6s. All were part of 254 Squadron, 72 Wing, under the control of 9 Group Devonport, and spent many fruitless hours patrolling the South Devon coast looking for U-boats. That they saw none was probably due to their deterrent effect.

Prawle Point camp was in the process of being upgraded when the Armistice came in November 1918. Work stopped and flying diminished until 22 February 1919 when 254 Squadron disbanded. The base remained open, however, and by August 1919 was occupied by the Artillery Cooperation Squadron, which also used 1½ Strutters amongst other types. This unit did not stay long before moving to Stonehenge. Prawle Point closed in early 1920, the land soon reverting to agriculture.

PREDANNACK, Cornwall

SW685162, 2 miles S of Mullion on A3083

Intruding was always an exciting business, but never more so than for four crews of 264 Squadron on the night of 20/21 June 1943. Led by their CO, Wg Cdr Allington, they set off in their Mosquito NFIIs heading for Lake Bicarosse, south-west of Bordeaux, a base for German flying boats operating in the Bay of Biscay. Despite poor weather they found the base, shot down two three-engined BV138s in the circuit, then set about other flying boats on the lake. The Mosquitoes headed for home unscathed, and it was later confirmed that they had destroyed two BV138s and two BV222 six-engined flying boats, with hangars and other installations badly damaged. It was a tremendous success for the Predannack-based night-fighters.

In July 1940 780 acres of rough heathland on the Lizard peninsula were requisitioned for an airfield at Predannack. The main contractor, Trethowan of Constantine, immediately started work, later aided by No 1 Works Area (Field), RAF Works Service. Construction went well despite delays caused by damage to newly completed runways following a Luftwaffe raid on 10 April. Endowed with four runways to make the most of varying wind directions across the coast, the airfield was eventually provided with Bellman and Blister hangars, together with a good number of dispersals on the northern and southern perimeter tracks. Most of the domestic sites were to the east. The airfield was opened as a satellite of Portreath in May 1941 to accommodate night-fighters to work with a GCI station that had been opened at Treleaver. This was a bit premature, as the first residents, 247 Squadron with Hurricane IIs (arriving from Portreath on 18 June), found conditions very primitive, with accommodation incomplete and the airfield a sea of mud.

After a slow start the squadron started operations, its first victory coming on 7 July when Flt Lt Kenneth Mackenzie shot down a Ju 88. It then began night sweeps over France, and Flt Lt John

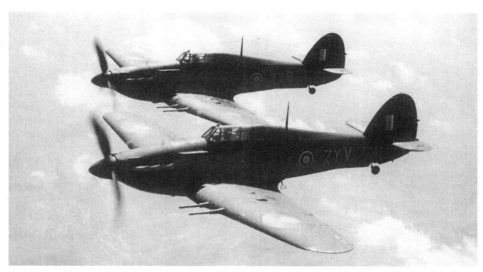

Hurricane IICs BE634 ZY-V and BD936 ZY-S of 247 Squadron on patrol from Predannack in April 1942.

Mosquito XVIII PZ468 of 248 Squadron is fitted with a 6-pounder Molins gun, which made its operational debut from Predannack in November 1943.

Carver brought down a Do 17 in August. He also claimed an He 111 in September, but was shot down by flak over Lannion airfield on the 29th, becoming a PoW. A detachment of 600 Squadron, with Beaufighter IF night-fighters, had been flying from Predannack since 18 June, and on 6 October was joined by the rest of the squadron.

The Luftwaffe also did its fair share of intruding, a Ju 88 following a Beaufighter into Predannack's approach on 12 October 1941, shooting up the airfield. Two aircraft were damaged by another raid on 14 December. To combat these intrusions more nocturnal RAF resources were brought to bear. In November the Turbinlite Havocs of 1457 Flight transferred from Colerne to operate with 247 Squadron. The first operational patrol was made on the night of 29 January 1942, but the first contact was not until 30 June, when a Ju 88 was illuminated but evaded the Havoc with a stall turn. Another contact on 4 August was lost before the Hurricane could get into position. Becoming 536 Squadron in September, the unit moved to Fairwood Common, and the last 247 Squadron detachment rejoined the main squadron at Exeter, where it had moved in May.

Predannack was seen as a useful forward airfield and a number of units deployed there for a variety of fighter and fighter-bomber operations, usually staying for only a few days. Bomber escort missions included daylight strikes against the *Scharnhorst*, *Gneisnau* and *Prinz Eugen* between 10 December 1941 and 20 January 1942. Units that regularly used Predannack included 118 Squadron Ibsley, flying Spitfire VBs on daylight sweeps, and 120 Squadron Ballykelly, with Liberator IIIs. The latter became part of a changing emphasis for Predannack, with activity becoming centred on anti-shipping and anti-U-boat work in the Western Approaches and Bay of Biscay, as well as countering Luftwaffe operations in the area. During their time on the Lizard during 1942, 120 Squadron's Liberators severely damaged at least four U-boats, including the U-89 and U-653, which had to return to port for repairs, but lost two aircraft in the process.

Meanwhile, the home-based squadrons were also busy. On 7 March a 600 Squadron crew intercepted an He 115 floatplane just off Lizard Point and despatched it into the sea. Things were not so easy for Plt Off Harvey and Fg Off Wicksteed on 7 June when they shot down an He 111, as they were themselves brought down by return fire. Having got into their dinghy, they paddled towards the northern Cornish coast, eventually reaching Portreath beach safely. The unit left for Church Fenton on 2 September 1942, replaced by 406 (RCAF) Squadron, which saw little action during its three-month stay, its Beaufighters being used mainly for SAR.

Predannack's position made it a natural location for emergency landings as well as forward operations, providing a safe haven for many 'heavies' during 1942. On 20 October, for example, a Liberator of 224 Squadron, Beaulieu, crash-landed after having been damaged by its own depth charges during an attack on a U-boat. The airfield was also used as a jumping-off point for North Africa during November and December 1942 as units moved up for Operation *Torch*. C-47s of the 60th TCG staged through on 7 November and P-39s of the 81st FG at the end of December on their way to Gibraltar. Other users included 138 and 161 Squadrons, which used Predannack as a forward base for the nocturnal delivery of agents and supplies to the French Resistance by Albemarle, Havoc, Hudson and Lysander.

In September 1942 a detachment of 263 Squadron Whirlwinds arrived from Warmwell to start anti-shipping strikes from Predannack using cannon and later bombs, maintaining these until June the following year. On 7 December No 604 Squadron moved in its Beaufighter IF night-fighters from Middle Wallop for patrols across the Bay of Biscay and along the French coast looking for German fighters. More Beaufighters arrived on 18 January, this time Mk VICs of 248 Squadron. The unit had transferred from Talbenny to become Predannack's first permanent Coastal Command squadron, and its longest serving. From its new base it began long-range patrols across the Western Approaches, acquiring a steady score of Ju 88s for the odd Beaufighter lost. During a notable sortie on 9 February 1943, three Beaufighters attacked four Ju 88s, shooting them all down. Shortly afterwards, when a Wellington of 304 Squadron from Dale made a hasty landing at Predannack after being damaged by four Ju 88s, three of 248 Squadron's Beaufighters took off and chased the enemy fighters, shooting them all down.

No 141 Squadron took over as the resident night-fighter unit, flying in its Beaufighters IFs from Ford to exchange places with 604 Squadron on 18 February. It also began flying daylight intruder operations, attacking shipping and trains along the French coast as well as *Instep* patrols, escorting shipping raids. The Beaufighters of 248 Squadron continued to maraud over the Bay, shooting down a Ju 88 on 10 March and an FW200 Condor two days later. French pilot Lt Maurice Guedj suffered an engine failure following the first attack, but managed to nurse his Beaufighter for more than 200 miles back to base. This was a tremendous feat, as engine failures then accounted for more losses than enemy action. There were other losses – over-confidence resulted in the loss of X7751 of 141 Squadron on 26 April when it hit a building during an airfield beat-up.

The increasing level of daylight raids by the USAAF over France during 1943 resulted in more unannounced visitors. These usually appeared in ones or twos, but on 1 May fifteen of the 360th BG put down at Predannack, having been badly mauled over St Nazaire. The first Mosquitoes appeared at Predannack on 30 April, when 264 Squadron Colerne began to use the airfield for shipping recces and night-rangers. It was joined by detachments from 456 Squadron Middle Wallop, also flying Mk IIs, in June, as more and more *Insteps* were being flown to clear the Bay of the Luftwaffe. A detachment of Beaufighter XICs of 236 Squadron arrived in May armed with rocket projectiles, making their first attack against a U-boat on 29 May, but with no result. Three days later U-418 was intercepted to the south-west of Brest, attacked and sunk, the first time that rocket projectiles had been used successfully in the Atlantic. No 307 Squadron had also began flying detachments with its Mosquito IIs from Fairwood Common in June, then, re-equipped with the Mk VI, moved to Predannack on 7 August. Initially flying night rangers, by June the unit had gone over to daylight *Instep* patrols. HMS *Sheffield* was used for a time as a radar picket ship to extend fighter control into the Bay, and this soon brought results; the Poles destroyed five out of twelve aircraft intercepted, and continued *Insteps* until moving to Drem in November.

No 248 Squadron had converted to the Beaufighter X in June and started detachments with them to Gibraltar. On 9 July, while escorting a Hudson, the aircraft came across four FW 200s, destroying one and damaging another. Three days later they attacked a U-boat, setting it on fire. In October a detachment of 618 Squadron Skitten brought a new Mosquito variant, the Mk XVIII, to Predannack. This was armed with a 6-pounder Molins gun, designed to pierce U-boat pressure hulls. The first operational use of the weapon came on 7 November, when U-123 was attacked near its home base of Lorient. Although several shells were seen to hit the boat's conning tower, it escaped back to base. This and other operations were made in conjunction with 248 Squadron, which received the Mosquito VI in December. In January 618's detachment was absorbed by 248 Squadron, which continued operating both versions of the Mosquito before moving to Portreath on 17 February.

Other changes during late 1943 included the arrival of the Typhoons of 183 Squadron from Perranporth on 14 October. They flew operations over the Brest peninsula, as well as providing escorts for anti-shipping strikes, often with 248 Squadron. The Mosquito IIs of 157 Squadron replaced those of 307 from 9 November 1943 on shipping patrols over the Western Approaches, and soon drew blood, claiming a Ju 290 on 20 November together with its Ju 88 escort. Eleven days later three Ju 88s were shot down for the loss of one Mosquito and crew.

The runways at Predannack were extended during 1943, enabling continuous operation by larger aircraft. The Wellington XIVs of 304 Squadron moved out of Davidstow Moor in December 1943 and spent almost three months flying anti-submarine operations from Predannack. Bad weather reduced sightings, but during January 1944 they destroyed one of the three attacked. On 1 February the Typhoons of 183 Squadron departed for Tangmere, and on the 17th 248 Squadron moved to Portreath after more than twelve months at Predannack. The Wellingtons of 304 Squadron left for Chivenor on the 19th and were replaced by the Liberator Vs of 311 Squadron from Beaulieu four days later. These too were fitted with rocket projectiles for operations against U-boats tempted to make their final run home on the surface. However, by this stage in the war U-boat skippers were extremely cautious and opportunities to use this specialised weapon were few.

The Mosquito VIs of 157 Squadron left for Valley on 26 March 1944, having been replaced the day before by the Mk XIIIs of 151 from Colerne. Flying night patrols, *Rangers* and anti-shipping escorts, 151's crews were fully extended during their time at their new base. On 11 April, while escorting 248's Mosquitoes to St Nazaire, they claimed seven enemy aircraft for the loss of two of their own – this brought 151 Squadron's wartime total to 100. The OC, Wg Cdr C. H. Goodman, together with his AI Operator Fg Off W. F. Thomas, had a field day on 4 May, shooting down four He 111s near Dijon airfield, bringing Goodman's personal score to twelve. At the end of April 1944 Nos 1 and 165 Squadrons formed a Spitfire IX Wing at Predannack for *Instep* operations to catch Ju 88s attacking shipping. Shipping recces were also flown, and on 19 May resulted in a strike being mounted on four merchantmen and their escorts off Ushant. The Spitfires escorted Coastal Beaufighters and drew flak as the attack went in; two merchantmen were damaged and one destroyer escort sunk for the loss of two Beaufighters.

On 28 April the Leigh Light Wellington XIVs of 179 Squadron transferred from Gibraltar to form 152 (GR) Wing with 311 Squadron, patrolling the Western Approaches in the build-up to D-Day. In early June seventeen Liberator Vs and VIs, together with fourteen Wellington XIVs, were engaged in Operation *Cork* from Predannack, preventing German naval forces interfering in the Normandy landings from the south. On 4 June the Predannack Spitfire Wing was ordered to give cover to a massive convoy assembling at Falmouth, and on the night of 5/6 June six Liberators and Wellingtons were airborne to give additional cover to the cross-Channel convoys. That evening fifteen U-boats left Brest, but U-415 was soon spotted and attacked by one of 179's Wellingtons and badly damaged; unable to dive she limped back to base with U-256. They were luckier than the U-955 and U-970, which were sunk by other 19 Group aircraft that night. During the following week air operations were hampered by low cloud, but the Spitfires managed a limited number of sorties, strafing German road convoys in Normandy and, armed with 500lb bombs, attacking radar installations. On 15 June they attacked shipping in St Peter Port, Guernsey, before leaving for Harrowbeer four days later.

'Wild Goose' elevated on the rail trolley at Predannack.

The U-boat war moved away from the Channel area later that summer, and with it went 311 and 179 Squadrons, the former to Tain on 7 August and the latter to Chivenor on 6 September. No 152 (GR) Wing was disbanded the following day. The Mosquitoes of 151 Squadron soon followed, leaving for Castle Camps on 8 October. Predannack then became a rest and re-equipment station for fighter units. The first customers were 264 and 604 Squadrons of 142 Wing, which flew in from B17/Carpiquet on 24 and 25 September. No 264 left again on 30 November for Colerne and 604 on 5 December for Odiham, to be replaced by 222 Squadron, which arrived on 2 November and 33 on 15 December. Both were Spitfire LFIX units withdrawn from B65/Maldeghem to re-equip with the Tempest V at Predannack, departing for B77/Gilze-Rijen on 21 February 1945. That same month Nos 349 and 485 Squadrons flew in from B77 to exchange their Spitfire IXEs for Tempests. However

The 'Swallow' 'swing-wing' UAV on its launch trolley.

Slingsby T31 WT875 of 626 GS about to be launched at Predannack in June 1970.

due to serviceability problems both had to return to the front at B106/Twenti with Spitfire IXBs!

VE Day was celebrated at Predannack with no flying units present, but on 17 May No 151 Squadron returned with its Mosquito XXXs. It was joined on 14 June by another returnee, 406 Squadron, also with Mk XXXs. The latter was disbanded on 1 September and was not around for the Battle of Britain display on 15 September 1945. The crowd of 4,000 visitors were treated to a flypast by nine Mosquito XXXs of 151 Squadron returning from a massed flypast over London. After a couple of detachments to Lubeck in January and March, the Squadron moved to Exeter on 19 April 1946.

On 1 June 1946 Predannack was reduced to C&M and lay abandoned for several years. Its isolation attracted Vickers Ltd to use it for experiments in the early 1950s using a number of model variable-geometry aircraft designed by Dr Barnes Wallis. A ramp and launching track were built alongside the main runway to enable his 'Wild Goose' and 'Swallow' designs to get into the air; although successful, the work was stopped in October 1954.

Four years later Predannack was reopened, as a satellite of RNAS Culdrose to provide a helicopter pilot training area. An FAA Fire-Fighting School was also established on the airfield. The gliders of 626 GS had operated from the airfield from August 1965 to June 1966 while the runway lighting at Culdrose was being relaid, and during the summer of 1968 the unit moved to Predannack. A Bessoneau hangar was erected to house the Sedburgh T21 and Cadet T31 gliders flown by the school. The author was one of the first students to train at the newly relocated school, and went solo in T31 WT875 on 21 July 1968. GRP Vikings replaced the veteran wood-and-canvas gliders in 1985 and, with updated facilities and a permanent hangar built in 1994, as 626 VGS the school still operates from Predannack as the airfield's longest-serving unit.

The main runway was resurfaced in 1971 to allow fixed-wing aircraft to land, and for most this was their last flight before succumbing to the FAA Fire School. A new control tower and office block were built in the 1990s to support ongoing helicopter training at Predannack. Evidence of the airfield's wartime past abounds, with shelters and dispersals still in evidence, and a number of derelict and refurbished buildings.

Supermarine 508 prototype VX133, burned at Predannack in June 1970, was one of several unusual aircraft that sadly have been sacrificed at the FAA Fire School over the years.

Predannack's unusual four-runway layout is apparent in this 1985 photo. The 'Swallow' launch track can be seen running parallel to the main runway.

Main features:
Runways: 012° 4,080ft x 150ft, 238° 5,103ft x 150ft, 282° 4,323ft x 150ft, 322° 3,015ft x 150ft, tarmac. *Hangars:* one Bellman, six O-Blister, six EO-Blister. *Hardstandings:* seven SE, eleven TE. *Accommodation:* RAF Officers 118, SNCOs 213, ORs 1,577; WAAF Officers 3, SNCOs 2, ORs 240.

This line-up in front of Rendcomb's hangars in 2005 includes a Dragonfly, Dragon, Chilton DW1 and Yak 18.

RENDCOMB, Gloucestershire

SP350850, 1¹/2 miles NE of North Cerney

Opened in early 1916, an aerodrome was built at Rendcomb as a training station. It lay to the east of White Way with the North Cerney to Calmsdon road forming its southern edge. The first unit to arrive was 48 Squadron, from Netheravon on 8 June 1916, with an assortment of aircraft including BE12s. Re-equipped with Bristol F2A Brisfits in March 1917, it shortly afterwards moved to France in time to take part in the Battle of Arras.

In August 1916 No 21 Wing established its HQ at Cirencester, and formed 38 Reserve Squadron at Rendcomb on 1 August from an element of 48 Squadron. Re-titled 38 Training Squadron on 31 May 1917, it flew RE7s, RE8s, BE2Es and Avro 504Js as well as Bristol F2s. Another Brisfit unit, 62 Squadron, arrived from Filton on 17 July, working up at Rendcomb before leaving for St Omer on 23 January 1918. No 110 Squadron formed at the airfield on 1 November 1917 from a nucleus of 38 TS and, flying a number of types including BE2Cs and Ds, left for Dover on 12 November.

No 45 Training Depot Station opened at Rendcomb on 15 August 1918 by re-designating 38 TS. Comprising elementary, advanced and operational squadrons, it trained its students using BE2Es, Brisfits and Avro 504Js and Ks. An element of the TDS was detached on 30 September 1918 and, joining elements from 1, 5 and 36 TDSs, became 138 Squadron at Chingford. No 59 TS arrived from Gosport during 1918 with RE8s, F2Bs and DH6s; on 15 August it was disbanded at Rendcomb and merged with 24 TS to become 24 TDS at Collingstown.

Flying training continued at Rendcomb after the Armistice, and into the following year, and although 45 TDS was disbanded and reformed as 45 TS in June 1919, peacetime rationalisation eventually caught up with Rendcomb. The TS closed on 8 July, and the airfield in 1920.

By 1921 Rendcomb had returned to agriculture, and as part of a dairy farm may well have supplied the inhabitants of nearby RAF Chedworth during the Second World War. Although the hangars had been removed, some of the other buildings remained in place, including the station workshops, stores, rifle range, engine shed, combined squash court/emergency hospital, machine-gun butts and a couple of living huts.

Boeing Stearmans of the Guinot aerobatic team during training at Rendcomb in May 2008.

The former airfield slumbered on until the late 1980s, when aerobatic pilot Vic Norman purchased the 65-acre site and, with business partner Torquil Norman, set about restoring it as a functioning airfield, aiming to recapture its Great War setting in the process. One of the original brick-built buildings was rebuilt as an Officers' Mess, and a double row of wooden period hangars erected alongside. The engine shed was converted into offices and briefing rooms. A First World War atmosphere has indeed been successfully recreated at Rendcomb, and at its official reopening on 15 September 1991, with one genuine SE5A, four SE5A replicas and further replicas of Sopwith Camel, DH5, Fokker DVII and Fokker Triplanes beside the hangars, the airfield certainly looked the part. Rendcomb remains open as a private airfield, and is the base of the Guinot aerobatic team and its Boeing Stearmans.

ROBOROUGH (PLYMOUTH), Devon

SW503605, 3¹/₂ miles NE of Plymouth off A386

The original Plymouth Airport at Chelston Meadow did not prove particularly suitable, and in the autumn of 1923 Roborough Polo Ground was rented for a trial air service to Birmingham, Manchester and Belfast. However, it did not prove commercially viable and soon closed. The Plymouth & District Aero Club started using the field some years later, and when Plymouth Corporation decided to open an airport, Roborough was the natural choice. The polo ground itself and several adjoining fields were purchased and the airport was officially opened by the Prince of Wales on 15 July 1931. The Great Western Railway started limited regular air services to Cardiff in April 1932 and was later joined by a number of others, including Railway Air Services and Jersey Airways.

Although the airport was regularly visited by service aircraft, the first unit to be based there was 15 Group Communications Flight, which formed at Roborough on 13 June 1939, with a Magister, Vega Gull and Envoy, plus two Walrus. The group HQ that it served had been transferred from Lee-on-Solent to Mount Wise Barracks, Plymouth, and it was joined by Swordfish of 814 Squadron, using the airport as a shore base having disembarked from HMS *Ark Royal* on 28 August.

More RAF aircraft appeared on 1 August 1939, when 46 E&RFTS was formed at Roborough. Using Audaxes, Hinds and Tiger Moths, the school was operated by a civilian company (Portsmouth, Southsea & Isle of Wight Aviation Ltd) on contract to the Air Ministry. The arrangement was not to have a long tenure, as on 2 September 1939, the eve of the declaration of war on Germany, the school was disbanded, and the Swordfish departed on 3 October to embark aboard HMS *Hermes*.

With the outbreak of war scheduled passenger services ceased and the airport was requisitioned by the Admiralty, becoming part of HMS *Drake*. Communications flying increased and in November 2 AACU started using Sharks to tow targets for the Gunnery School at Devonport. The AACU detachment left for St Eval in April 1940, but more biplanes arrived towards the end of May when the Swordfish of 819 Squadron transferred from Ford. More Swordfish, this time from 815 Squadron, arrived on 12 June, and both squadrons embarked aboard HMS *Illustrious* as it departed for Bermuda on 21 June.

Even more biplanes appeared at the end of July, when the Gladiators of the Sumburgh Fighter Flight landed at Roborough, having taken the best part of a week to fly from the Shetlands! The unit already had an enviable combat record, having flown more than 500 patrols with two probable kills – an He 111 and Do 17. Once at Plymouth the flight was disbanded and reformed as 247 Squadron, becoming operational on 13 August. Gladiators were kept at readiness by day at Roborough, with a detached flight by night at St Eval.

Facilities at Roborough were very basic. Although a few personnel were billeted in nearby houses, most were accommodated in bell tents until a number of huts could be provided. A Blister hangar was erected to supplement the three flying club hangars on the airfield, which had two grass runways. Four three-bay concrete and brick blast pens were later added.

Also in August 1940 a detachment of Lysanders from 225 Squadron, Tilshead, started daily dawn and dusk patrols, looking for signs of enemy activity along the South West coast. It was replaced by another from 16 Squadron, Weston Zoyland, whose Lysanders combined coastal patrol with ASR duties. One of the squadron's aircraft, piloted by the OC, Wg Cdr Hancock, crashed on take off from Roborough on 9 February, killing its crew. Sqn Ldr Walker assumed command, but he was killed the following day when his Lysander was shot down by four Bf 109s near Exmouth. The unit maintained an intermittent ASR detachment at Roborough until this was taken over by 276 Squadron, Harrowbeer, in October 1941, initially with Walruses. Lysanders were still seen at the airfield into 1942, from units taking part in live shoots on the Okehampton ranges.

Shuttleworth's Gladiator is marked up as N2308/HP-B of 247 Squadron, which reformed at Roborough in August 1940.

Anson C19 TX222 of 19 Group Communications Flight at Roborough in April 1955.

Meanwhile 247 Squadron, the only unit to fly Gladiators during the Battle of Britain, had its first combat on 28 October 1940, when Plt Off Winter intercepted an He 111, but without result; the same pilot claimed another He 111 damaged nine days later. Following replacement by Hurricanes in December, there was little action and the Squadron HQ moved to St Eval on 10 February 1941, leaving a detachment at Roborough until May, when the whole squadron moved to Portreath. Its departure brought the brief operational life of Roborough to an end. The airfield's relatively small landing area limited the operation of fighters such as the Hurricane, and the larger alternatives of St Eval and later Harrowbeer gave much better operational margins.

With the formation of 19 Group, Coastal Command, at Mount Batten in February 1941, its Communications Flight replaced that of 15 Group, which moved its HQ to Liverpool on 15 February. In June No 2 AACU returned, flying Hectors and Gladiators, but easily the largest aircraft seen at Roborough during the war was Fortress I AN523 of 90 Squadron, which crash-landed on 16 August. The bomber had been attacked by seven Bf 109s during a raid on Brest, but its pilot had managed to shake them off 30 miles from the South Coast. The Fortress unfortunately overran, hit an anti-tank ditch, broke up and caught fire, killing three of its seven crew.

In May 1942 Roborough transferred from Admiralty to Air Ministry control, parented by Mount Batten. Activity remained much the same, with C Flight of 2 AACU being the main resident, its main task remaining that of towing targets and gun-laying for Devonport Gunnery School. In February 1943 C Flight was re-titled 1623 Flight, and on 1 December became 691 Squadron. It had been flying Defiants, Battles and Gladiators, but then came Hurricanes, Oxfords and, unusual for an RAF unit, Barracudas. The Squadron moved to Harrowbeer on 21 February 1945.

An aerial view of Roborough in 2004.

Dash 8 G-WOWB of Air Southwest taxies in at Roborough in August 2008.

The Martinets of 3 APC arrived in early 1945 to provide target facilities for RAF units in the area, and they remained at Roborough until May. With the end of the war in Europe, activity declined at Roborough; only 19 Group Communications Flight remained, flying Ansons and Dominies. No 82 GS was formed at this time, providing flying training for Air Cadets until moving to Harrowbeer in February 1948.

The airport reopened in 1946, operated by the Straight Corporation on behalf of the City Council. The Plymouth & District Aero Club carried out flying training and some charter work using a Messenger and later a Gemini, and Jersey Airlines began services in April 1952 using Rapides. Various airlines and flying clubs have made use of Roborough ever since.

Its use by the military has also continued. Although 19 Group Communications Flight disbanded in April 1960, early the following year the Britannia Royal Naval College Air Experience Flight was formed to provide air experience and pilot screening for officer cadets from Dartmouth. Under a contract with the then airport owners, Airwork, seven Tiger Moths were flown initially, replaced by twelve Chipmunks in 1966, and the Flight was subsequently renamed the Royal Navy Training Flight. After twenty-five years' service these were in turn replaced in 1991 by Grob Tutors, and in December 2001 the flight was commissioned as 727 Squadron, moving to Yeovilton in December 2007. From the late 1960s until 1972 a number of helicopter detachments used a hangar at the airport to work with RM units in the Plymouth area. These started with the Sioux of Air Troop, 41 Commando, and were followed by 45 Commando, 95 Commando and 666 Squadron AAC.

Brymon Airways took over management of the airport in May 1975 and embarked on a series of improvements, including a new control tower, more hangarage, and a new SW/NE tarmac runway of 2,480 feet. As an airline it established a network of services from Roborough using Twin Otters and Dash 7s. Navigational aids and approach lightings were improved during 1984/85. Brymon was bought by British Airways in 1993, and continued to fly into Roborough until it withdrew from the region in 2003. The void was filled by Air Southwest, part of Sutton Harbour Holdings, which also now owns Plymouth City Airport. The airline flies DHC Dash 8s on routes to various destinations, including Gatwick, Manchester, Bristol, Leeds/Bradford, Jersey, Cork, Dublin, Glasgow, Newcastle and Grenoble. The airport has a busy General Aviation Centre, which provides flying training as well as facilities for business and leisure flights.

Main features:
Runways: NW-SE 2,400ft x 300ft, NE-SW 2,700ft x 300ft, E-W 1,800ft x 300ft, grass. *Hangars:* three Civilian, one Blister. *Hardstandings:* four three-bay concrete/brick pens. *Accommodation:* RAF SNCOs 16, ORs 320; WAAF SNCOs 16, ORs 50.

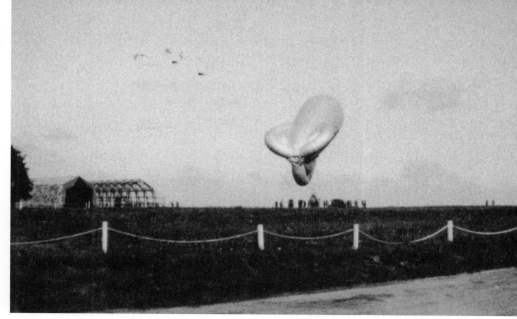

A barrage balloon at No 2 Balloon Training Unit, Rollestone, in 1939.

ROLLESTONE, Wiltshire

SU088439, 1 mile E of Shrewton

The grass airfield at Rollestone was first used to accommodate No 1 Balloon School, which had been set up there in July 1916 to train personnel in the use of observation balloons. The unit survived post-war reductions, operating throughout the 1920s and 1930s and, after several name changes during that time, became the RAF Balloon Centre on 3 November 1931. The following year a large balloon hangar was built to house two large Type R balloons, replacing two earlier canvas hangars. Beech trees were planted beside the hangar to provide sheltered anchorages for further balloons. A small Nissen hangar was built to the rear and to the north of the main sheds.

In December 1936 the Centre became No 2 Balloon Training Unit, was transferred from 22 to 24 Group, Training Command, and in February 1939 moved to Cardington. Rollestone was then closed for refurbishment and the construction of additional buildings before being reopened in June 1939 to accommodate the RAF Anti-Gas School, which moved from Uxbridge. The possibility of gas warfare was taken very seriously and, as airfields would have been prime targets for such attacks, the RAF ensured that its personnel were fully trained against noxious agents, particularly in the areas of protection, detection and decontamination. Instructors were trained at Rollestone to teach RAF personnel at other schools and stations.

In September 1939 a number of fields between the A360 and B386 were requisitioned and the area was used to give students some experience of aerial gas attacks and how to deal with them. Aircraft from 1 FTS, Netheravon, and the Special Duty Flight, CDES Porton Down, would fly over to spray troops with a training agent to simulate a gas attack. A Landing Ground was laid out to the south-west of Rollestone Camp to enable the aircraft to refuel and replenish their tanks. From March 1940 the SD Flight took over all gas-related aerial training, but 1 SFTS (as it had become) continued to use the LG for training.

In late 1939 a Manby Screen was built on the airfield; this was a sheet-metal-covered steel framework, 1,000 yards long and 50 feet high, designed to enable fully laden aircraft to take off in a crosswind of up to 30mph. Originally constructed at Manby, the war had started before it was fully tested, and with Manby required operationally, the screen was re-erected at Rollestone for further tests. A Tutor, Hurricane and Master were used in apparently successful trials, but the system was never adopted and the screen was demolished in November 1941. Whether or not it was attracted by the screen is difficult to say, but early on 12 May 1941 an enemy aircraft dropped eight bombs on the LG, then made a low run over the camp as it was engaged by a machine-gun post. No damage was done apart from a few broken windows.

Re-clad balloon sheds at Rollestone Camp in March 2007.

The Operational & Refresher Training Unit, Thruxton, used the LG during 1944 to maintain the currency of glider pilots using Hotspurs and Tiger Moths. The RAF Anti-Gas School reduced its training activity following the end of the war in Europe, and in October 1945 moved to Sutton-on-Hull. The LG was then in use by AOP Austers, and on 16 November 1945 No 657 Squadron arrived from Goslar in Germany, staying for six weeks before moving on to Andover.

On 25 July 1946 the LG was closed and Rollestone Camp transferred to the Army, which has used it ever since, apart from a spell between November 1980 and December 1981 when it was used as a temporary civilian prison. Although the LG has long since reverted to farmland, flying took place in the 1950s from a landing strip across the old coach road to Devizes which runs past the camp. The camp is still much the same as it was, with the two-bay balloon shed and hangar still standing, although both buildings are now offices, with floors added.

ST EVAL, Cornwall

SW873685, 6 miles NE of Newquay

On the night of 8 June 1944 the crew of St Eval-based Liberator G-George of 224 Squadron were on a 'Channel-Stop' sortie, patrolling between Scilly and Ushant looking for any U-boats threatening the mass of Allied shipping in the Channel on D-Day+2. Suddenly the radar operator reported a contact 12 miles ahead. In bright moonlight the Liberator slowly descended and at 3 miles a submarine was spotted on the surface. As the Liberator ran into the attack it came under fire, which it returned. At 50 feet the pilot, Fg Off K. O. Moore, released a stick of six depth charges as the aircraft tracked over the target. It was a perfect straddle, three charges to either side, and the U-boat broke up amongst the explosions. Jokingly, Moore said 'Now let's get another one,' and they did just that! Twenty minutes later another contact was picked up 6 miles away. Again they ran in sighting a U-boat at $2^{1}/_{2}$ miles. It was a duplicate of the first attack, with the same results.

St Eval remained an operational station for all of the twenty years it was open. During the war it was a microcosm of the RAF, with day- and night-fighters, bombers, anti-shipping, anti-submarine, photographic and meteorological patrols, as well as air-sea rescues being flown from the station. There were many successes during that time, but none more outstanding than G-George's double kill.

Beaufort I W6498 Killer of 42 Squadron in mid-1941. Based at Leuchars, the unit flew detachments from St Eval for fifteen months from March that year.

An airfield at St Eval was planned in 1937 as part of the RAF Expansion Scheme. It was eeded to support anti-submarine patrols around the Cornish peninsula, strategically important in ontrolling Britain's sea lanes. However, the plan was not without opposition, as it meant emolishing a small hamlet, although its church remained in place, and was to become a local andmark. Work started on the new airfield in 1938, and by the outbreak of war the site had been leared and four C Type hangars were being erected, but little else. Wooden huts soon sprouted up ll over the place, as accommodation was urgently needed for RAF personnel moving in. Despite its nready state – work on the runways hadn't even started at this point – St Eval officially opened on October 1939 when the Ansons of 217 Squadron arrived from Warmwell. They soon started onvoy protection and anti-submarine patrols, joined by 6 Coastal Patrol Flight, formed at the ation on 15 January 1940. With impressed Hornet and Tiger Moths, it flew 'Scarecrow' patrols ver coastal waters from Land's End to Start Point to deter U-boats, disbanding on 31 May.

Bomber Command Whitleys joined the maritime war early in 1940, starting a number of short etachments to fly anti-submarine patrols from St Eval. They were joined by 42 Squadron in April, sing the airfield as a forward base for its Beauforts from Thorney Island. The arrival of more eauforts, for 217 Squadron, heralded a change in role, and while some crews converted to these orpedo bombers, others continued convoy patrols with Ansons. Construction of three runways egan in the spring of 1940, with flying going on around the construction crews. With the fall of rance the Spitfire Is of 234 Squadron arrived from Church Fenton to give inshore convoy rotection. Their first victory came on 8 July when a Ju 88 was destroyed; two more were claimed ter in the month. Much stranger shapes appeared on 20 June when a Farman 222 and Potez 540 nded; followed in July by several Martin 167 bombers, they all carried escaping Frenchmen.

Hudson I P5143 flew with 206 Squadron from St Eval in June 1941.

Due to the Admiralty's concern over the use of the Biscay ports by the Kriegsmarine, tw
Spitfires of the PRU were detached from Heston on 1 July to carry out daily photo runs over th
ports. This became a dangerous occupation as the Germans were aware of their visits and tried t
stop them. To conceal the aircraft several trial colour schemes were used, including green, whi
and pink, before PRU blue was adopted.

In early June a detachment of Blenheim IVs from 236 Squadron, Thorney Island, a Coast
Command fighter reconnaissance unit, had started operations from St Eval. Its first victory came o
11 July, followed by another in August, by which time the whole squadron had moved in for a si
month stay. The Blenheim crews flew patrols along the French coast, later extending these furthe
out to look for FW 200 Condors, as well as escorting Sunderlands and later 217 Squadron
Beauforts on raids. Increased nocturnal activity by the Luftwaffe forced 234 Squadron to start nig
patrols, but the Spitfire was quite unsuitable, and after several accidents the unit transferred t
Middle Wallop, replaced by the Hurricanes of 238 Squadron on 14 August. These wer
supplemented by 'night flight' Gladiators detached from 247 Squadron at Roborough.

Shortly after a sector operations room was opened on the station, a series of air raids came in,
hangar being badly damaged and six Blenheims destroyed on 21 August. The next night
pyrotechnics store was hit and, with all manner of flares and rockets exploding, the German pilo
must have thought they had obliterated the station! A Harrow of 271 Squadron was destroyed on 2
August, but little damage was done on the night of 26th/27th, as a dummy flare-path had been lit o
a Q site 3 miles to the north-east, which was bombed for several hours.

The Spitfires of 234 Squadron returned from Middle Wallop on 11 September, exchanging plac
with 238 Squadron. The unit had been badly mauled during the Battle of Britain, one day losing nir
out of twelve aircraft. It remained at St Eval for five months, and was involved in occasional comba
one of which took place in November during a shipping escort, taking HMS *Javelin* into Devonpor
when three Do 17s were shot down. During the autumn St Eval was used as a forward base for attac
on invasion barges being assembled in the French ports – even the Ansons of 217 Squadron wer
involved. This was their swansong, as by December the Squadron had completed conversion t
Beauforts and was soon using its new mount in bombing, sea-mining and anti-submarine work.

Accurate weather forecasts were of paramount importance to flyers, particularly those c
Coastal Command embarking on long patrols into the Atlantic. On Christmas Eve 1940 No 40
(Meteorological) Flight was formed at St Eval with four Blenheim IVs, tasked with gatherin
weather data over the Western Approaches. The unit was re-designated 1404 Meteorological Fligl
on 1 March 1941, and more types were added to its fleet, including the Hudson, Hampde
Albemarle, Ventura and Mosquito. Disbanded on 11 August 1943 to become 517 Squadron, tl
unit moved to St David's that November.

In January 1941 No 247 Squadron, Roborough, converted to Hurricanes, and maintained
night detachment at St Eval until moving to Portreath in May. St Eval's runways had bee
completed by the New Year, and with the construction of the C Type hangars well advance
almost nightly attacks were started by the Luftwaffe. On 25 January 1941 one of seven 250kg bom
dropped hit an air raid shelter near the watch office, killing twenty-one people. As the attac
intensified many personnel were moved off-base into requisitioned hotels and guest houses; tl
Watergate Bay Hotel became an Officers' Mess and was used for many years afterwards. Insho
convoy patrols were forcing the Germans to use long-range Condors to attack shipping further o
to sea. No 263 Squadron's Whirlwinds arrived in February 1941 to attempt interceptions, but m
with little success and moved to Portreath a month later. The Spitfires of 234 Squadron left fc
Warmwell on 24 February, and 236 Squadron moved to Carew Cheriton on 21 March, to k
replaced by another Blenheim IV unit, 53 Squadron, from Thorney Island.

The *Scharnhorst* and *Gneisnau* were in Brest Harbour for repair in the spring of 1941, ar
when PRU photos showed that the *Gneisnau* had left dry dock on 5 April and appeared ready fc
sea, a low-level torpedo strike was ordered. The only unit readily available was 22 Squadron, whic
had maintained a detachment of Beauforts at St Eval since April 1940 from its base at Nort
Coates. Six crews were detailed for a strike at dawn on 6 April, to fly three Beauforts with bom
and three with torpedoes. Due to heavy rain during the night, two of the bombers became bogge
down; the third managed to take off, but lost its way in heavy cloud, as did one of the torpec
carriers. Flying independently, the Beauforts were to rendezvous near Brest, but poor weath
prevented this and Fg Off Kenneth Campbell, flying N1016, decided to make the attack alon
There was little chance of twenty-four-year-old Campbell and his crew surviving, but he ensur
that his torpedo ran straight and true as he crossed the mole into the inner harbour just before tl

Beaufort was shot down into the water. The *Gneisnau* was severely damaged and put out of action for nine crucial months. Fg Off Campbell was posthumously awarded the VC almost a year later, probably on the evidence of French Resistance members who witnessed the attack.

The Luftwaffe continued to show an interest in St Eval. Two particularly heavy raids in May caused the destruction of three Blenheims and damage to more than a dozen other aircraft. The Officers' and Sergeants' Messes were virtually demolished and two hangars so badly damaged that canvas portable Bessoneau units were set up inside the shells. Despite this, the effectiveness of St Eval's units continued to increase. The Hudsons of 206 Squadron, newly-arrived from Bircham Newton on 30 May, were soon out on patrol. They scoured the Bay of Biscay to find targets, such as blockade-runners, for the Beauforts of 217 Squadron, which were joined again by 22 Squadron transferred from Thorney Island on 28 October. No 206 Squadron had left for Aldergrove on 20 August, and was later replaced by 53 Squadron, which returned with Hudsons on 20 October. They stayed until leaving for Limavady on 17 December, exchanging places with 224 Squadron.

Movements in early 1942 included the arrival of 86 Squadron from North Coates with Beauforts on 10 January, replacing 22 Squadron, which left three weeks later for Thorney Island. No 224 Squadron left for Limavady on 19 February, and three days later the Whitleys of 502 Squadron transferred from Bircham Newton. This was not the first appearance of its Whitleys at St Eval, as the squadron had flown detachments from the station since early 1941. By 1942 the unit had started to receive the ASV-equipped Mk VII. Hampdens arrived with 415 (RCAF) Squadron from Thorney Island on 11 April. Flying in the torpedo bomber role, they mounted their first sortie from St Eval on the 27th. More of the type arrived later in the month, when a detachment of 489 (RNZAF) Squadron, also from Thorney Island, moved in as part of a Coastal Command effort to counter a new peak in the threat to transatlantic convoys from German submarines and surface ships.

To boost St Eval's anti-submarine capabilities, the Whitleys of 58 Squadron had been transferred from Linton-on-Ouse on 8 April 1942, and in June they too received the Mk VII before leaving for Stornoway in August. The Hudsons of 53 Squadron returned in mid-May to boost the recce capability. Nine examples of another type new to St Eval, the Lancaster, arrived on 14 July, detached from 61 Squadron, Syerston, on reluctant loan from Bomber Command. They soon proved their worth, for three days later Flt Lt P. R. Casement's crew sank U-751, damaged earlier in the day by a 502 Squadron Whitley. The Lancasters stayed for six weeks, searching for U-boats and blockade-runners.

In August the first of several detachments of Whitleys from 10 OTU, Abingdon, were made, to give student crews some operational experience. If not very experienced, they proved better than nothing and at least prevented U-boats from spending much time on the surface. Several squadrons were formed from the PRU on 19 October 1942, the detachment then at St Eval (B Flight) becoming A Flight of 543 Squadron; they continued to keep a wary eye on activities in western France. During the same month eight B-24 Liberators of the 409th BS, 93rd BG, USAAF, arrived on secondment to Coastal Command from the 8th AF. They were at St Eval to gain experience in the anti-submarine role, and started an influx of USAAF units (which referred to RAF St Eval as USAAF Station No 129), the 409th being replaced after a month by the 1st and 2nd Antisubmarine Squadrons of the 480th Antisubmarine Group. They mounted their first operation on 16 November and left for Morocco in March, having flown more than 210 missions and making twenty U-boat sightings and eight attacks. The only kill claimed was U-519, but this was amended after the war from Kriegsmarine records to U-52 damaged. Two aircraft were lost in action, while another flew into cliffs near Hartland Point.

From October 1942, 161 Squadron maintained a detachment at St.Eval to fly agents and supplies into Occupied France during nocturnal operations by Albemarle, Havoc, Hudson and Lysander. During the build-up to the invasion of North Africa in November 1942, most of the Allied air fleet staged through the Cornish airfields, including St Eval. This put a tremendous strain on the station, with up to seventy-two aircraft being present at any one time. Most of the anti-submarine aircraft were therefore detached to Beaulieu and Holmsley South, still using St Eval as a forward base. The squadrons returned during the spring of 1943, having received the Halifax GRII, at 502 Squadron on 25 March and 58 Squadron on the 31st.

The Whitleys of 10 OTU continued to fly patrols, making their first kill on 22 March when Flight Sergeant J. A. Marsden attacked and sank U-665 off the Irish coast. The following month, on the 29th, Flt Lt A. R. Laughland and his crew of 224 Squadron (the unit having returned from Beaulieu six days before) sank U-332 with their new Liberator V. May was very successful for 58 Squadron, which sank U-528, then U-266, U-463 and U-563, two of which were destroyed by the OC, Wg Cdr Oulton, and his crew. On 14 June No 10 OTU made its second kill, a U-boat off

Cape Ortegal; however, the boat's AA fire brought down the Whitley, Sgt S. J. Benson and his crew having to take to their dinghy and becoming PoWs. More USAAF units arrived in July, this time from the 479th Antisubmarine Group (4th and 29th Antisubmarine Squadrons). Although they only stayed a month, they shared in the destruction of U-558, U-404 and U-706, for the loss of one B-24 to flak. When they moved to Dunkeswell in August they were replaced by a series of USN patrol squadrons flying the PB4Y-1 version of the Liberator – first came VP-103, followed by VP-105 and VP-110 in September. By the end of October all US Liberator operations centred on Dunkeswell.

Extensions and improvements to the airfield at St Eval during 1943 by Canadian Engineers did nothing to reduce the hump in the main runway, which contributed to many heavy landings and several accidents. One of the worst occurred just before the last 10 OTU detachment left in August 1943 when, during take-off, a Whitley hit a USN Liberator taxying across the runway, hidden from view by the hump. The Whitley caught fire and both aircraft were destroyed when its depth charges exploded, with several fatalities.

On 30 June Nos 58 and 502 Squadrons left for Holmsley South. During July two U-boats were destroyed by the Liberators of 224 Squadron; on the 3rd U-628 was sunk by Sqn Ldr Cundy and crew and on the 8th U-514 was caught by Sqn Ldr Bullock. The latter's aircraft was fitted with a Leigh Light and armed with rocket projectiles as well as depth charges and mines. Beaufighters were to be seen at St Eval during that summer, when several Mk VIs of 235 Squadron were detached from their base at Leuchars during May and June to fly patrols over the Bay of Biscay. They were followed in August by 143 Squadron, which transferred its Mk XICs from North Coates at the end of August to provide air cover for anti-submarine aircraft suffering at the hands of German fighters. The unit shot down a number of Ju 88s and also sank two ships with RPs before moving on to Portreath in mid-September.

A detachment of four USAAF B-17s arrived on 8 September to undertake long-range weather patrols. They were attached to 517 Squadron, and moved with them to St David's in late November. More construction work during the winter included the installation of a FIDO system, the effectiveness of which was demonstrated by trials in April 1944. Its use over the following twelve months enabled St. Eval's aircraft to maintain operations despite the weather. Two Wellington GRXIV squadrons, 407 and 612, operated from St Eval for a time towards the end of 1943, arriving in early November and returning to Chivenor a month later.

For most of 1944 St Eval was a major Liberator base, and from April its four squadrons gave the Cornish airfield the most powerful anti-submarine force in the RAF. No 224 Squadron had been joined by 53 Squadron on 3 January, returning from Beaulieu re-equipped with Liberator Vs, and on the 14th came 547 Squadron from Thorney Island. The fourth Liberator unit, arriving from Davidstow Moor on 12 April, was 206 Squadron flying the latest version of the Liberator, the Mk VI (armed with a nose turret). St Eval's aircraft flew anti-submarine patrols by day and night, and as D-Day approached these increased, with 5,135 operational hours being flown during June. They were rewarded with a number of sightings and made several attacks. Flt Lt J. W. Carmichael and his crew of 53 Squadron made the first U-boat kill during this period when, on the night of 6/7 June, he attacked and sank U-629. On the following night Fg Off Moore of 224 Squadron made his famous patrol, sinking U-373 and U-441. Two more U-boats were destroyed later in the month, one shared with Mosquitoes, the other with four RN vessels. However, six Liberators were lost in action during the month.

On 11 July No 206 Squadron moved to Leuchars. During August 53 Squadron sank two more U-boats, U-608 north-west of La Rochelle on the 10th and U-618 near Lorient on the 15th, but lost three aircraft during the month. U-boat activity in the Bay of Biscay started to reduce after this, and during September (as the French ports were captured by the Allies) virtually ceased. However, U-boats continued to threaten shipping in other areas, so on 11 September 224 Squadron was moved to Milltown, two days before 53 Squadron left for Reykjavik. The last to leave was 547 Squadron for Leuchars on 1 October.

They were replaced by 282 Squadron from Davidstow Moor with its ten ASR Warwicks, fitted with airborne lifeboats. St Eval's runways had taken quite a beating, and were resurfaced during October, 282 moving to St Mawgan until 1 November, when 179 Squadron arrived from Chivenor shortly afterwards replacing its Wellington GRXIVs with Warwick GRVs. Anti-submarine patrol resumed, and on 24 February 1945 Flt Lt A. G. Brownsill and crew sank U-927 off the Lizard. On 6 March No 304 (Silesia) Squadron, from Benbecula, joined 179 on patrols with its Wellington XIVs and it was this unit that recorded the final U-boat kill from St Eval, when W/O O. R. Marczak's crew sank U-321 off south-west Ireland on 2 April. (This was in fact the unit's sole victim in more than

2,400 sorties and sixty attacks, during which it had lost eighteen aircraft.) Both squadrons continued patrols after the end of the war, in case any U-boats had not received the surrender message.

The Poles left for North Weald in early July, and were replaced on the 20th by 224 Squadron from Milltown, still operating Liberators. This unit had sunk twelve U-boats and damaged three more, the second highest squadron total in Coastal Command. In the meantime, on 9 July, 282 Squadron had disbanded, its SAR task taken over by 179 Squadron. The Liberators of 224 Squadron were stripped of their operational equipment and used to repatriate POWs from India at the end of the war with Japan. In February 1946 No 179 Squadron received its first Lancaster GR3s, and on 1 June was split into two, Y Flight becoming 210 Squadron; the remainder soldiered on until the end of September, when it was disbanded. The following month 224 Squadron reluctantly relinquished its much-loved lend-lease Liberators, in exchange for Lancaster GR3s.

With the arrival of 203 Squadron from Leuchars in January 1947, a St Eval three-squadron Lancaster Wing was formed, which got down to its peacetime role of SAR, with meteorological flights and exercises with the fleet thrown in for good measure. During the early spring of 1947 a joint RAE/Vickers team arrived with a Mosquito BXVI to start trials with air-launched transonic rocket models. The team stayed for eighteen months, using a range off the Isles of Scilly. Conducting research into the aerodynamics of supersonic flight, they managed, on the very last flight trial on 9 October 1948, to attain a speed of Mach 1.38.

No 224 Squadron had been disbanded in November 1947, and the other squadrons found it difficult to maintain their operational commitments due to lack of personnel and the limitations of the Lancasters, which were overdue for replacement. This came in November 1951, when the Shackleton MRIs of the newly reformed 220 Squadron arrived from Kinloss. No 42 Squadron reappeared at St Eval on 28 June 1952, when it reformed with Shackleton MR1As (the unit flew Beauforts on detachment from Thorney Island between April and June 1940). It was followed by 206 Squadron, which reformed on 26 September, also with MR1As, and when 203 and 210 squadrons left for Topcliffe, St Eval was completely Shackleton-equipped.

Due to the length of its runways, St Eval had been designated as one of twelve Master Diversion Airfields around the country, always open to receive aircraft diverted by weather or emergency. These varied from the forty-odd Canberras diverted one afternoon from Lincolnshire to large airliners when Heathrow was fogged in. All three St Eval squadrons took part in the Coronation Review flypast over Odiham in July 1953, putting up eighteen aircraft; by then they had all started to receive the improved Shackleton MR2. The Wing was completed by 228 Squadron, which reformed on 1 July 1954, also with the MR2. All available aircraft were sent to Blackbushe in January 1956 to help uplift 1,200 troops of 16 Parachute Brigade to combat EOKA terrorists in Cyprus, and an even bigger uplift was carried out during the Suez Crisis. Additional roles followed: 42 Squadron trained in medium-level bombing to undertake colonial policing, sending a detachment of two aircraft to Aden in January 1957, where it was maintained for two years, while 206 ferried stores to Christmas Island and flew meteorological sorties in support of the weapons tests that culminated in the dropping of Britain's first H-bomb by a Valiant on 15 May 1957.

Due to the close proximity of the larger and more modern Coastal station of St Mawgan, coupled with the introduction of the planned new MR3 version of the Shackleton (considered too heavy for operational flying from St Eval), the decision was made to run down the airfield for

St Eval-based Liberator GRVI EW309 of 224 Squadron in August 1944.

Wellington GRXIVs of 304(Silesia) Squadron in April 1945, with St Eval church in the background.

closure. The transition started in November 1956, when 228 Squadron moved to St Mawgan, followed by 220 in December. St Eval soldiered on for a few more years, 206 Squadron moving to St Mawgan on 7 January 1958, exchanging places with 228, which returned to St Eval a week later. However, once 42 Squadron moved to St Mawgan in mid-October 1958, it was only a matter of time before St Eval closed. It had also been decided to shut down 228 Squadron, and on 6 March 1959 a parade was held to disband the Squadron and close RAF St Eval. The station then went onto C&M, its quarters retained for St Mawgan personnel.

No 626 GS transferred from St Mawgan in 1961 and used the airfield for its winch-launched gliders until moving to Culdrose in May 1964. Portions of the taxiways were used for motor racing

Warwick GRV PN811 on patrol from St Eval in April 1945.

Lancaster ASR3s, PB641 nearest, of the St Eval Wing in 1948.

or a while, but much of the airfield was later fenced off for the aerials of a radio transmitter station. Although the runways and taxiways remain in place today under the radio masts, most of the buildings have long since gone, including the three massive hangars. The Parish Church of St Eval, a local landmark dating back to Norman times, still stands sentinel over the former RAF Station. It contains many items of aviation interest as the Church of Coastal Command, and a memorial nearby commemorates the 974 aircrew lost flying from St Eval during 1939-45, and the twenty-two personnel killed in bombing raids on the station.

Main features:

Runways: 261° 5,949ft x 150ft, 201° 5,910ft x 150ft, 320° 4,800ft x 150ft, concrete and tarmac. *Hangars:* three Type C, two T2, one Bellman, five 69ft Blister, two 45ft Blister. *Hardstandings:* forty-eight spectacle, eighteen circular. *Accommodation:* RAF Officers 18, SNCOs 168, ORs 1,116.

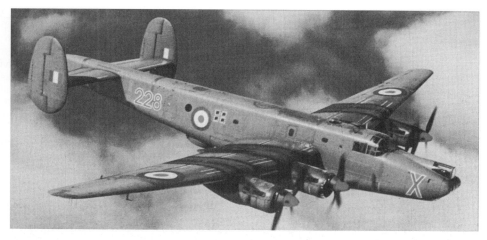

Shackleton MR2 WR960 of 228 Squadron, based at St Eval in 1956.

Hurricane IIC BE500 of 87 Squadron in November 1941, when operating from St Mary's.

ST MARY'S, Isles of Scilly

SV922104, 1mile E of Hugh Town

The first airfield established on the island of St Mary's was on the golf course, when Captain Gordon Olley persuaded the golf club to rearrange some of the bunkers so that the fifth and seventh fairways could be used as runways by his aeroplanes. This was for an air service to be established to the mainland, which was started on 15 September by his Channel Air Services initially using DH Dragon G-ADCR based at Land's End. More Dragons were employed as the route became popular, and in May 1938 the service was extended to Plymouth and Bristol. The airline and route were taken over by Great Western & Southern Air Lines in December 1938, but due to competition from the golfers the aircraft had to move, and a more permanent airfield was subsequently established at High Cross, first used on 25 July 1939.

After just two months of use, arrivals at the new airport suddenly stopped with the suspension of all civil flying due to the outbreak of war. However, due to the need for speedy communication with the islands it was decided to reinstate the air service, and the three DH84 Dragons were back on the route again on 25 September, having been hastily camouflaged. This was one of the few civil air services to continue during this time, the Dragons plodding back and forth with amazing regularity. The steeply sloping surface and maximum run of 1,350 feet added to the challenges of the often appalling weather in flying from St Mary's, especially during the winter.

Due to an increase in Luftwaffe activities off the South West coast it was decided to send a detachment of Hurricanes to the islands in the early summer of 1941. Having practiced on a strip marked out on their airfield at Charmy Down, six pilots of 87 Squadron, led by their OC, Sqn Ldr an 'Widge' Gleed, flew in on 19 May. The first fighter, 'LK-A', the OC's Hurricane, had hardly been refuelled when a flare went up from a nearby AA battery indicating the sighting of a hostile aircraft. Plt Off Ian Badger jumped in, started it up and, on lifting off, saw an He 115 just 5 miles away. The floatplane's pilot, no doubt greatly surprised, jettisoned his bomb load and took evasive action, but this was to no avail as the Hurricane shot the Heinkel down into the sea.

With field telephones laid from the airport to OPs around the islands, two Hurricanes were kept on constant readiness should the Luftwaffe return. They were scrambled again less than a week later when, on the 24th, despite low cloud and rain, a German raider was reported nearby. Sqn Ldr Gleed and Sergeant L. A. Thorogood were up, but due to the murk couldn't see much, so returned to base. As they approached to land, a Do 18 emerged from cloud right over the airfield, firing its nose gun. The Hurricanes pursued it, and after several bursts of MG fire the seaplane went into a left-hand turn into the water. On 28 May a Ju 88 was located and attacked 10 miles south of the islands by the OC and Fg Off Roy Watson, leaving it badly damaged. On 3 June another raider, an He 111, shot down Dragon G-ACPY soon after it had taken off from St Mary's; this resulted in air services being suspended, although they were resumed on 27 October, only to be suspended again on 4 November. They were eventually reinstated on 12 January 1942, and operated throughout the remainder of the war.

Little in the way of facilities existed on St Mary's airfield, the Dragons overnighting at Land's End. The RAF groundcrews lived in bell tents alongside their dispersals on the south side, while the pilots were accommodated in Hugh Town. Auxiliary tanks extended the Hurricanes' range and on 8 July an He 111 was intercepted and shot down 30 miles south of St Mary's. Another Ju 88 was downed on 18 August, followed by a further one ten days later. The first fighter to be encountered, a Bf 110, was sighted near the islands on 21 October; the Hurricanes gave chase and, after several bursts of fire, one killing its rear gunner, the Messerschmitt ditched. The German pilot had no dinghy, so one of the Hurricane pilots, Plt Off Musgrove, threw out his own. He then radioed his position and heard later that the German had been picked up.

This was to be the final claim made by 87 Squadron's Scilly detachment, although it continued through the winter months of 1941/42. Boredom was relieved by army cooperation exercises with local troops in January 1942, but the first RAF casualty on the islands occurred when one pilot flew too low and hit HT cables. The detachment became 1449 Flight in April 1942, retaining six Hurricanes, six pilots and thirty-three groundcrew. Enemy activity remained low, but the fighters were often tasked with providing escorts for returning British and US bombers. Airfield improvements during the year included a tarmac extension to the easterly end of the main grass strip and the erection of a Blister hangar, wooden watch tower and three Nissen huts. These were ready for use by October, when most operations were in support of the Walruses of 276 Squadron engaged in ASR work. Occasional interceptions of enemy aircraft still took place, but were inconclusive.

The odd accident occurred, such as on 12 August 1942 when Hurricane Z3658 hit the foremast of the RMS *Scillonian* while beating it up, and went into the sea. Just as spectacular were the odd emergency landings made by large aircraft at St Mary's inadequate airfield. These included

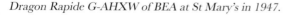

Dragon Rapide G-AHXW of BEA at St Mary's in 1947.

two St Eval-based aircraft, a Whitley of 10 OTU with engine failure, which overshot and crashed on 27 January 1943, and a battle-damaged Liberator of 547 Squadron, which skidded into a wall after landing, killing the pilot, Fg Off Dixon, although his crew of eight survived.

Although 1449 Flight had ten Hurricanes on charge in June 1944, it only had six pilots; on the evening of the 5th it put up six fighters to patrol the coast from Land's End to Dartmouth, maintaining patrols throughout the following day. Following the Normandy landings the war moved away from Scilly and, on 17 September 1944, No 1449 Flight was disbanded. A week later RAF St Mary's was reduced to C&M. Great Western & Southern Air Lines then had the airfield to itself, and resumed full peacetime services in May 1945, with DH89 Dragon Rapides. Island Air Services was formed at the airfield in June 1945 and, with two ex-RAF Proctors, flew a limited freight service to the mainland. The company acquired Rapides for a service to Heathrow, and relocated to London in 1948, winding up its Isles of Scilly services. In February 1947 the Great Western & Southern operation was taken over by BEA, including its Rapides.

A new control tower and terminal were built in 1949 and the route continued to grow, with 18,000 passengers being flown to St Mary's in 1953, and 29,100 in 1959. In 1961 a new operator Mayflower Air Services, started running from Exeter and Plymouth with Rapides, maintaining this until 1963. Other operators who put in brief appearances on services to St Mary's during the 1960s included Scillonian Air Services, British Westpoint and Westward Airways, the latter flying Islanders.

The next major change for St Mary's came in 1964 when, on 2 May, BEA started a helicopter service with twenty-four-seat Sikorsky S61s replacing the eight-seater Rapides. Two S61Ns, G-ASNI and G-ASNM, commenced services from Land's End on 2 May, until September, when BEA's new purpose-built heliport was opened in Penzance. Passenger numbers for the first full year of S61 operation (1965) were 54,500. Rapides reappeared at St Mary's during the summer of 1966, when Scillonia Airways started a service from Land's End. The last commercial operator to operate Rapides on scheduled services in Europe, it flew five aircraft until May 1970, when it went into liquidation. The wrecking of the Torrey Canyon off Scilly brought extra traffic to St Mary's in March and April 1967, with the arrival of press aircraft and military helicopters to support the beach cleaning parties.

The BEAH S61Ns were also flown on operations in support of the North Sea oilfields, and increased demands resulted in them being withdrawn from the Isles of Scilly route for brief periods. During the winter of 1975 they were replaced by Sikorsky S58Ts, and in 1976/77 by Islanders flying from Land's End, until more S61s were added to the fleet. Islanders had also reappeared in June 1972 in the hands of Brymon Aviation on a route from St Mawgan; these were later supplemented by Twin Otters, adding services to Exeter, Plymouth and Jersey. With passenger arrivals reaching 64,000, a new passenger terminal was opened at St Mary's in 1975. In August 1976 Bond Helicopters, on contract to Trinity House, started using St Mary's as a base for its Bolkow Bo105 helicopters to replenish Bishop Rock and other lighthouses in the Isles of Scilly.

The main operator to St Mary's remained BEA Helicopters, which became British Airways Helicopters in 1972; seven years later it flew its millionth passenger on the route. In 1986 British Airways sold BAH to the Maxwell Group to become British International Helicopters. The Penzance-Isles of Scilly helicopter service has a high serviceability rate (virtually 100%) and an excellent safety record. The latter has been marred by only one fatal accident, when S61N G-BEON was lost 2 miles out from St Mary's on 16 July 1983 in poor visibility, with only six survivors from the twenty-six passengers and crew aboard. By the late 1980s British International was flying 90,000 passengers per annum to the islands, and in 1991 carried its two millionth passenger.

The challenging approach to St Mary's, seen in October 2006.

Fixed-wing traffic remained important, however, and an 1,800-foot tarmac runway was laid at St Mary's in 1991. This was too late for Brymon, which had withdrawn from the route at the end of the 1990 season. However, Isles of Scilly Skybus, formed by the Isles of Scilly Steamship Company, took over the route. This company had started flying freight to St Mary's from Land's End in October 1984 and passengers from March 1987 using Islanders, and acquired a Twin Otter to cover its extended routes in 1993. Improvements were made to St Mary's terminal building in 1994, and in 1997 the apron was extended to take six helicopters. The terminal was improved again in 2004, when IoS Skybus celebrated the twentieth anniversary of its operations, having by then acquired a second Twin Otter. Aircraft movements in 2006 totalled 9,622, and 128,694 passengers passed through the airport.

Sikorsky S61 G-BCEB ('Echo Bravo') usually operates the service to St Mary's, backed up by a second S-61N during the summer; the helicopter notched up thirty-five years on the route in 2009. The airport is now owned and operated by the Council of the Isles of Scilly and is one of the archipelago's main gateways for passengers and freight, especially for the export of flowers. It is also used by SAR and ambulance helicopters of the emergency services, and is the main base for the islands' fire and rescue service. Today it is the tenth busiest regional airport in the UK, with some 150,000 passenger movements per year.

Main features:
Runways: NE-SW 1,998ft, grass and tarmac, N-S 1,800ft, NW-SE 1,779ft, grass.
Hangars: one Blister. *Hardstandings:* two tarmac. *Accommodation:* RAF SNCOs 5, ORs 73.

Lancaster GR3 RF325 of the SMR at St Mawgan in 1956, the last Lancaster in RAF service.

ST MAWGAN, Cornwall

SW870646, 3½ miles NE of Newquay

St Mawgan's origins can be traced back to the Big Field at Trebelzue on the cliffs above Watergate Bay near Newquay, first used in August 1933 by Sir Alan Cobham's 'Flying Circus'. It was registered as an AA Landing Ground, and in May 1939 Western Airways began using it as a stop on its regular twice-daily services from Swansea to Manchester and Land's End.

However, with the start of the war in September the site was requisitioned by the Air Ministry for development as a satellite of St Eval. Construction started in late 1940 and, despite being bombed in May 1941, it was opened as RAF Trebelzue the following September, consisting of two tarmac runways. It was taken over by Ferry Command at the end of December, and personnel of OADU were detached from Portreath to arrange ferry flights to the Middle East. It was soon apparent that the runways were too short for large aircraft, and after only fourteen despatches it was decided to completely rebuild the station, using land to the east.

Work started in August 1942 to construct three new runways further inland, alongside Trebelzue, which remained operational. The first front-line aircraft to fly from the airfield, a detachment of Mustang Is of 400 (RCAF) Squadron, moved in from Portreath in December 1942. The unit flew escorts to aircraft en route to Gibraltar until rejoining the main squadron at Middle Wallop later in January. A detachment of Mosquito IIs of 264 Squadron, Colerne, also used Trebelzue for a few weeks in January 1943. Other operations included the despatch of twin-engined aircraft such as Beaufighters and Wellingtons to the Middle East, and Henleys of 1 AACU detached from their base at Cleave to tow targets over the ranges at Penhale. On 24 February the station's name was formally changed to St Mawgan.

In June 1943 personnel of the USAAF's 491st Base and Air Base Squadron arrived to prepare St Mawgan for use by the Americans. The opening of the station's main runway on 1 July was marked by the arrival of a USAAF B-24 and a B-17. A period of frenzied activity followed, with the appearance of dozens of aircraft, which were parked on the defunct runways at Trebelzue in preparation for despatch to North Africa. Large numbers of USAAF aircraft followed during August, September and October, making St Mawgan one of the busiest airfields in the country. Two USAAF meteorological B-17s arrived on 5 November 1943, but only stayed for a few weeks as, although OADU deliveries had by then started to slow, arrivals from the USA had steadily increased. With BOAC and KLM also using St Mawgan for some of their Whitchurch services, the airfield became even busier, its dispersals overflowing with aircraft.

Two nasty accidents during December involved Liberators. A USAAF B-24 on its way to Marrakech crashed 2 miles east of St Columb on the 21st, killing four, and on the 28th a fully loaded US Navy PB4Y-1 crashed into the sea shortly after take-off. Thirteen tour-expired crew and passengers who were returning to the USA were killed, and five USAAF men from St Mawgan were cut off by the tide and tragically drowned while attempting to rescue them.

During the spring of 1944 the station's aircraft movements increased as preparations for the invasion built up – on one day in February no fewer than 169 aircraft arrived from the USA. Most were bombers, but the number also included C-47s. In March 1944 St Mawgan began to be used for Transport Command's southbound passenger flights by the Yorks and Dakotas of 24 Squadron, Hendon, and the Warwicks and Dakotas of 525 Squadron, Lyneham. One of the latter's Warwicks, on a service to Algiers, crashed into the sea shortly after take-off in early March, killing all sixteen aboard.

Construction work at the station had carried on throughout this time, and by May the main runway was completed, together with more hardstandings, a new control tower, operations room and Met section. Two T2 hangars were also provided. With routes across France open again, BOAC moved its services to Hurn on 1 November, but total movements for the year still amounted to a staggering 16,110. The first flying unit to be actually based at St Mawgan, 1529 Beam Approach Training Flight, formed at the station on 1 December 1944 with Oxfords to train on the newly installed ILS. The Air Traffic Control School had formed in November 1944 and this became No 1 Air Traffic Control School on 3 January 1945; a ground unit, it used the normal air traffic passing through the airfield for training. It moved to Bramcote in November.

Several large-scale Bomber Command and 8th AF diversions were handled by St Mawgan during early 1945, as it and the other Cornish coastal airfields were often the only ones regularly open during that last winter of the war. With the collapse of Germany, St Mawgan became Transport Command's No 1 Diversion Centre and the UK departure point for heavy aircraft reinforcements to the Far East. USAAF aircraft such as B-17s and B-24s also started to pass through on return to the USA, and another mass movement in June 1945 was that of 165 Lancasters of 6 Group RCAF on their way home to Canada. With the closure of Portreath in September, its traffic transferred to St Mawgan, many of the aircraft supplied to the French to rebuild their air force passing through at this time.

The traffic level reduced during 1946, a highlight being the transit of sixteen Lancasters of 35 Squadron on a goodwill tour of the USA. They departed in July and passed through again on their

Shackleton T4 WB238/N of MOTU, St Mawgan, in 1965.

return to Graveley in late August. Being apparently then no longer required, St Mawgan was closed on 1 July 1947 and put onto C&M. Limited flying then took place by Fingland Aviation, using Ansons, and Plymouth Aero Club, but this was stopped in January 1951 when St Mawgan was reopened as a Coastal Command station.

The Air-Sea Warfare Development Unit moved in from Ballykelly on 4 May with a number of aircraft types including Lancasters, Shackletons, Ansons and Sycamores, engaged on the development of anti-submarine weapons and tactics. On 1 June the School of Maritime Reconnaissance was formed with Ansons and Oxfords as well as Lancasters; working with the ASWDU it became responsible for all air-sea warfare training. No 744 Squadron, FAA, had been formed at Culdrose on 1 March 1954 to act as the Navy's air-sea warfare development unit to work with the RAF's ASWDU, and it moved with its Firefly AS6s and Sea Fury FB11s to St Mawgan on 23 October. Later also equipped with Gannet AS1s and Avenger AS5s, the unit operated until disbanded on 31 October 1956.

No 622 GS had moved in from Harrowbeer in 1955 and flew its winch-launched gliders from the Trebelzue site until moving to St Eval six years later. SAR Whirlwind HAR2s of 22 Squadron arrived from Thorney Island on 4 June 1956. The unit maintained its HQ, engineering base and one operational flight at St Mawgan, its other detached SAR flights being based at seven other airfields across the south. At the end of September 1956 the SofMR was disbanded, its task being taken on by the Maritime Operational Training Unit at Kinloss, but in December two maritime squadrons, 220 and 228, arrived from St Eval with Shackleton MR2s. The former soon re-equipped with MR3s, which required the longer runways at St Mawgan for operations at maximum weight. No 208 Squadron moved in from St Eval in January 1958, exchanging places with 228 Squadron to become the second Shackleton MR3 unit.

Shackleton MR3 XF707 near St Mawgan in about 1970.

X Flight of 22 Squadron was re-designated 1360 Flight on 1 August 1957, and on 1 February 1958 was disbanded to become 217 Squadron. The unit's Whirlwind HAR10s then served in the SAR role during the nuclear tests on Christmas Island before returning to St Mawgan to disband on 13 November 1959. No 220 Squadron was renumbered as 201 Squadron in October 1958 when 42 Squadron arrived from St Eval prior to its closure (still flying Shackleton MR2s, it was not to receive the MR3 until November 1965).

As the premier operational station in 19 Group, St Mawgan then settled down to its surveillance task, covering the South West Approaches and eastern Atlantic. In addition many detachments were made overseas for operational, humanitarian and goodwill reasons. The closure of St Eval confirmed St Mawgan's long-term future, and plans were made for the replacement of its dilapidated wartime buildings. Changing priorities during 1965 resulted in the departure of 201 Squadron to Kinloss in March, followed by 206 in July. However, the MOTU came in the opposite direction to join 42 Squadron, which remained at St Mawgan.

A large hangar was completed in 1969 to house the Nimrod, the first of which arrived in October to enable the newly reformed 236 OCU to start the task of converting Shackleton crews to the new type. On 1 May 1970 No 7 Squadron was reformed at St Mawgan as a target facilities unit. Flying Canberra TT18s, the Squadron worked with various weapons ranges and military units around the country until its disbandment in January 1982. From April 1971 the crews of 42 Squadron began converting to the Nimrod and, once operational, they continued their routine of monitoring Warsaw Pact naval activity, ASW training and SAR, together with Offshore Tapestry fishery protection patrols and oil rig surveillance. Nimrods were shared in a pool between 42 Squadron and 236 OCU, supported by a centralised servicing squadron.

Three Nimrods were kept airborne during the Fastnet Race tragedy of 1979 and saved many lives. To these were added the crew of a Royal Netherlands Navy Atlantique that ditched off the Irish coast in January 1981. In May 1982 two 42 Squadron Nimrods left for Ascension Island to fly SAR and maritime patrols during the Falklands Conflict. St Mawgan was used as a jumping-off point for sixteen Harrier GR3s of 1 Squadron, also bound for Ascension in May.

In 1988 St Mawgan's main runways were resurfaced, and an HAS site was built at the Trebelzue end of the airfield, as the station had been designated as a forward deployment base for Tornado F3 squadrons. However, shortly after these improvements had been completed it was decided to concentrate all maritime squadrons in Scotland, with the result that 236 OCU and 42 Squadron were transferred to Kinloss, the last Nimrod departing from St Mawgan on 9 September 1992. In their place came the SCSR and 3 MHU, their former home at Mount Batten having been closed. The Sea King Training Unit transferred from Culdrose in April 1993, becoming the Sea King OCU on 1 April 1996 and 203 (Reserve) Squadron seven months later. A Helicopter Maintenance Facility (HMF) was also established in the former Nimrod hangar. That St Mawgan still retained importance as a centre for NATO maritime operations was shown when it was selected for the location of an Anglo-American command centre, the Joint Maritime Facility, commissioned in August 1995. This had not been the first post-war US presence at the station, as from the early 1970s the Trebelzue site had been home to a high-security USN facility that stored nuclear weapons for use by the USN and NATO maritime patrol aircraft; this closed in the late 1990s.

Nimrod MR1 XV245 of 42 Squadron on the Trebelzue dispersals in November 1983.

Sea King ZH543 in St Mawgan's Helicopter Maintenance Facility in August 1999.

EC135 G-KRNW, the St Mawgan-based Cornwall Air Ambulance, in 2008.

Late in 1959 Starways of Liverpool had made arrangements to initiate summer tourist flights to St Mawgan, and this was the start of a series of attempts by various companies to run air services to Newquay. By 1962 passenger numbers had outgrown the RAF facilities, but Newquay Council persuaded the Air Ministry to allow construction of a small terminal on the north side of the airfield, near the village of Carloggas. The arrival of British Midland on the scene in 1969 started a decade during which civil operations into St Mawgan finally stabilised, particularly after the take-over of its London-Newquay route by Brymon Airways. By 1977 annual passenger numbers exceeded 25,000 on the Brymon Newquay-London service alone. A new terminal was opened in 1993, and this was extended in 2006. Current operators include Air Southwest, BMI Baby, British Airways, Flybe, Isles of Scilly Skybus, Lufthansa, Ryanair and Swiss International Airlines. Bolkow 105 helicopters (later replaced by Eurocopter EC135s) of Cornwall's Air Ambulance, the first such to be established in the UK, and Trinity House, servicing lighthouses around the South Coast (both operated by Bond Air Services), have operated from a hangar at St Mawgan since 1989.

Although St Mawgan was shortlisted to house the new Joint Combat Aircraft force, in November 2005 it was decided that the JCA would go to Lossiemouth. Plans to close St Mawgan were then announced, with the resident units being disbanded or transferred. The station has been used by various units for training over the years, particularly before deployment to the Gulf or Afghanistan, and this continued, but the draw-down started in late 2006 with the closure of the HMF and culminated in the departure of the Sea Kings of the station's last flying unit, 203 (Reserve) Squadron, for Valley on 12 May 2008. Deployments of other units continued, however, the Harriers of 801 NAS and Tornados of XV Squadron using the airfield later that month. The last flying unit to operate from St Mawgan was 3 AEF/Southampton UAS, which flew its Grob Tutors there during July and August.

Although it closed as an RAF airfield on 30 November, RAF St Mawgan remains as a station, hosting the JMF and the Service Evasion Resistance & Extraction Training Centre, successor to the SCSR. The airfield itself is now under the ownership of Cornwall County Council, and continues in operation as Newquay/Cornwall Airport. The main runway has been reduced in width and resurfaced, a new control tower has been built, and the airfield has been fitted with updated lighting, navaids and new radar. Operators such as Air Southwest have recently increased their routes from Newquay, which is currently one of the UK's fastest-growing regional airports.

Main features:
Runways: 080° 6,000ft x 150ft, 140° 9,000ft x 150ft, 010° 4,200ft x 150ft, concrete. *Hangars:* two T2, two B1. *Hardstandings:* sixty loop. *Accommodation:* RAF Officers 132, SNCOs 98, ORs 1,915; WAAF Officers 12, SNCOs 8, ORs 360.

ST MERRYN, Cornwall

SW889714, 3 miles SW of Padstow

Like many other military airfields, St Merryn originated as a civil one, opening in 1937 under the direction of William Rhodes-Moorehouse, son of the first airman to be awarded the VC, and a pilot with the Auxiliary Air Force. Promoted as Cornwall's first public airfield, the 52-acre field had a large hangar, but was little used before private flying stopped with the declaration of war.

The Admiralty had seen potential in the site and, following a survey in 1939, requisitioned the original airfield together with an additional 550 acres of adjoining fields for the development of an operational flying training station. Four concrete and tarmac runways were laid, a technical site built to the west and a main living site to the north-west. Four large hangars were erected, later supplemented by a number of smaller ones. RNAS St Merryn was opened on 10 August 1940 as HMS *Vulture*, four months after the first aircraft had landed there – a Shark from Roborough, its pilot having mistaken the airfield for St Eval! Land had also been requisitioned early in 1940 at Treligga, a small pre-war airfield to the north-west of Delabole, as a bombing and gunnery range for St Merryn.

The new airfield's first resident was 792 Squadron, formed there on 15 August as a target facilities unit with Rocs, Skuas and Masters. It was joined on 17 September by 774 Squadron from Evanton with Swordfish, Sharks, Rocs and Skuas to provide Telegraphist/Air Gunner training. These two squadrons were to be the main occupants of the airfield until 1943, providing training for the front-line FAA squadrons that would come to St Merryn for short periods of working-up. During their time at the station the two units would go on to fly a variety of types, including Sea Hurricanes, Sea

Swordfish LS373 of 787 Squadron over Beacon Cove near St Merryn in 1943.

Gladiators, Defiants, Martinets, Masters, Proctors, Lysanders, Albacores, Fulmars and Barracudas.

The Luftwaffe soon showed an interest in the new base, a Bf 110 causing some damage on 3 October, two Do 215s bombing on the 9th and two He 111s machine-gunning the camp on the 14th. On 11 November another He 111 made a low-level attack, badly damaging two hangars and injuring two people. Leading Seaman Jack Sleeman was returning from leave just as the last attacker was leaving, and reported to his post at one of the hangars. He found a search party busy at work frantically moving debris looking for a body. When he asked who they were looking for, the surprised searchers replied that it was him!

The first operational squadron to use the airfield, No 829, arrived from Campbeltown on 14 September with Albacores and Swordfish. Operating under Coastal Command Control, it flew mine-laying and bombing operations along the French coast. When the unit moved to St Eval on 7 October it was replaced that day by another Albacore unit, 826 Squadron, also under Coastal Command control, from Bircham Newton. It continued operations from St Merryn, flying at night against coastal targets in Holland, Belgium and France, dropping mines and bombs. No 828 Squadron, also with Albacores, joined it on 25 October, and the following month both units left for Campbeltown to embark aboard HMS *Formidable*.

The first fighter units appeared at St Merryn when the Fulmars of 807 Squadron arrived from Worthy Down for working-up before moving on to Yeovilton on 9 December. More Fulmars were seen when 809 Squadron formed at St Merryn on 15 January 1941, and was joined by 801 Squadron from Hatson four days later. Equipped with Skuas, the latter started dive-bombing training on targets off Trevose Head in preparation for a proposed strike against German battleships in Brest; however, this was called off at the end of March and the Skuas moved to Campbeltown. The Luftwaffe reappeared in April with a low-level attack that caused little damage, but on 5 May six He 111s dropped HE and incendiaries that damaged twenty-two aircraft and injured two ratings. Having satisfactorily worked up to operational standard the Fulmars of 809 Squadron left for Hatson on 10 June prior to embarking aboard HMS *Victorious* for the Russian convoys.

By mid-1941 St Merryn was almost entirely devoted to fighter training, with fleet fighter squadrons flying Fulmars, Martlets and Sea Hurricanes staying for a month or so to work-up for operational deployments. This pattern continued into 1942, and during that year ten squadrons trained at the station before moving onto operations. This included 809 Squadron, which returned to St Merryn on 21 August having been engaged in escorting the Malta convoys aboard HMS *Argus*. At St Merryn it became the first FAA squadron to be trained in army cooperation and on 1 October its B Flight was detached and reformed as 879 Squadron. With six Fulmars it was also intended for army cooperation work, and moved to Charlton Horethorne ten days later.

Another unit formed in October was 748 Squadron, on the 12th, as a Fighter Pool; it operated a variety of aircraft including Spitfires, Fulmars, Hurricanes and Martlets, becoming 10 Naval OTU six months later. Z Flight of 787 Squadron arrived from Lee-on-Solent on 24 February 1943, having been formed a few months earlier to develop the use of rocket projectiles. The flight used the Treligga range for trials with their Swordfish, later also employing Hurricanes and Fulmars.

A major construction programme started at St Merryn in mid-1943 with the decision to base the School of Air Combat there. The main runway was lengthened to 3,810 feet and additional hangars were erected, together with more office and domestic accommodation. The first of the units making up the school, 736 Squadron, arrived from Yeovilton on 2 September 1943 as its Fighter Combat School element; flying Seafires and Masters, it was later to receive Fireflies and Barracudas. Other units formed as the school expanded – 719 Squadron on 15 June 1944 for Air Firing training with Wildcats, Spitfires and Masters, 715 Squadron (from part of 736 Squadron) on 17 August for Air Combat and Fighter Leader training using Corsairs and Seafires, and 709 Squadron on 15 September as the Ground Attack School with Hellcats and Harvards. With all of this activity St Merryn became a very busy station and, with accommodation always at a premium, more building during the year resulted in a new control tower and two T2 hangars. Operations were also mounted during this time, by 816 Squadron flying Swordfish on detachment from Perranporth to patrol the Channel during the Invasion period (from April to August 1944).

By December 1944 the emphasis had changed to training for operations against the Japanese in the Pacific. The School of Air Combat was re-titled the School of Naval Air Warfare, and on 2 January 1945 Nos 719 and 792 Squadrons, together with 780 Squadron at Lee-on-Solent, were disbanded to form 794 Squadron at St Merryn as its School of Air Firing element. In its new guise the school became responsible for strike and torpedo training as well as air combat. Its aircraft types became more varied and the ranges at Treligga were reconfigured to simulate targets that would be encountered in the Far East. The intensity of training increased and was maintained at a high level until the war with Japan came to an end in August.

In the lull after the war St Merryn continued as a training station. No 725 Squadron arrived on 4 August 1945 with Swordfish as an air target training unit and was absorbed by 736 Squadron at the end of December. Also in August, on the 14th, came 748 Squadron from Dale, flying a variety of aircraft including Spitfires, Seafires, Harvards Corsairs and Wildcats to provide a fighter pool. No 741 Squadron formed at the station on 12 August 1946 to fly Seafires in the operational flying training role, and remained until 25 November 1947, when it was disbanded. On 13 August No 796 Squadron formed at St Merryn with Firefly FR1s and Barracuda IIIs to provide flying training facilities for the Telegraphist Air Gunnery School then being formed at the station.

The first control tower at St Merryn, 1943.

St Merryn-based Seafire IBs of 736 Squadron in early 1944; NX890 is nearest the camera.

The Swordfish of 816 Squadron flew operations from St Merryn during the Invasion period.

The station theatre/cinema at St Merryn in August 2005.

The School of Naval Air Warfare continued to operate from St Merryn until March 1948, when it was moved to Culdrose and merged into the Naval Air Fighter School. It was replaced by the Air Armament School, which formed in June to train air and ground armament offices and ratings. In February 1950 No 736 Squadron moved to Culdrose, just as the Sea Fury started to replace the Seafire. Examples of the latter still appeared at St Merryn with RNVR Squadrons, which flew in for their annual weapons training camps during the early 1950s. The Air Armament School closed in early 1952, and in April the last remaining flying squadron, No 796, was split into two, its Barracuda element becoming 759 Squadron. The two units then became the Observers School, and Ansons supplemented the Barracudas until early 1953, when Fireflies and Sea Princes arrived; the school took these to Culdrose when it moved there in November. No 796 Squadron once again became the last remaining flying squadron at St Merryn, but on 9 February 1954 it too moved to Culdrose.

Although the station was paid off as HMS *Vulture* on 14 October 1953 it was immediately renamed as HMS *Curlew*! It then became home to the School of Aircraft Maintenance and the Naval Air Ordnance School, both from Yeovilton, which trained naval artificers, but after a little more than two years they moved out and the station was placed on C&M in June 1955. St Merryn finally closed as a naval air station on 10 January 1956.

Newquay Council expressed an interest in using St Merryn as an airport, but in late 1956 the Air Ministry announced that the site would become an RAF Regiment Depot. However, this and plans for an Army Depot in 1959 never materialised, and on 11 October 1959 63 acres of the airfield were sold, the start of disposal of the whole site. The majority of the airfield returned to agriculture, while some of its buildings were converted into a holiday camp and others were used for farming or light industry. A little flying has continued from the airfield over the years, mainly by homebuilts and microlights. The Cornwall Parachute Centre was established there in May 1979 and flew its Cessna 182 from the airfield for a few years.

St Merryn provided a home for Spitfire Mk IX ML407 for several years. Purchased from the Strathallen Collection by Nick Grace in October 1979, the aircraft was moved into one of its hangars for restoration. This took some six years, and on 16 April 1985 the Spitfire made its first flight from St Merryn's runway, with Nick at the controls. Painted as NU-V of 485 Squadron, the aircraft is now flown from Duxford by Nick's widow, Carolyn.

St Merryn is today remarkably intact. Substantial areas of runway and taxiway are still in place, and several hangars and airfield buildings still stand, together with most of the former admin site.

Main features:

Runways: 014° 3,000ft x 150ft, 056° 3,000ft x 150ft, 105° 3,090ft x 150ft, 147° 3,810ft x 150ft, tarmac. *Hangars:* eighteen 60ft x 70ft, twelve 60ft x 84ft, one 185ft x 105ft. *Hardstandings:* seven. *Accommodation:* RN Officers 181, ORs 1,196; WRNS Officers 13, ORs 502.

A Sandbanks-based Kingfisher of 765 Squadron over Poole in 1942.

SANDBANKS, Dorset

SZ044877, 3 miles SW of Bournemouth

This small seaplane base was commissioned on 15 May 1940 as HMS *Daedalus II*, a satellite of Lee-on-Solent. Situated on the north-west side of Sandbanks, the narrow promontory that forms the eastern side of Poole Harbour, it consisted of a slipway and concrete apron upon which a single hangar was constructed. The hangar could accommodate fourteen Walruses with folded wings, but the only other facilities were a workshop and fuel tanks. On 26 August 1940 No 765 Squadron moved in from Lee-on-Solent to start operations as the Seaplane Training School, to provide Part I of the Seaplane Training Course for Pilots before the students moved on to Part II at Lawrenny Ferry. It flew the Walrus plus a few Swordfish and Seafox floatplanes, which flew from Poole Harbour; the Seafoxes were replaced by Kingfishers in June 1942.

In July 1943 W Flight, 700 Squadron, was formed at Sandbanks with six Walruses and four Swordfish in preparation for an operation in the Azores, but this did not take place and the unit moved to Machrihanish later in the month. The need for seaplane pilots had declined by this time and 765 Squadron started to run down, being disbanded on 25 October 1943. No longer needed, Sandbanks was then paid off.

SHREWTON, Wiltshire

SU076460, 10 miles NW of Salisbury

The airfield at Shrewton was originally intended to house 3 School of Army Cooperation, but, as the unit never actually formed, it was allocated to 1 SFTS, Netheravon, as an SLG. Consisting of a roughly triangular area of land to the north of Shrewton village, it had three good landing runs, but not much in the way of other facilities.

First used by Hinds, Hart Trainers and Audaxes of 1 SFTS in July 1940, it soon became a popular place to practise circuit-planning, approaches, take-offs and forced-landings. Battles also used the airfield, particularly for night-flying with the aid of a goose-neck flare-path. The flares unfortunately attracted attention from the Luftwaffe, a number of attacks being made during August 1940, and again in April and May 1941. Fortunately little damage was caused, with the exception of the night of 12 May, when the main runway was cratered by an He 111, which also hit and destroyed a taxying Battle, injuring its student pilot.

Lysanders from army cooperation squadrons were regular visitors during field exercises, and in June 1941 a detachment of 225 Squadron used Shrewton for night-flying training. When the role of Netheravon changed to that of airborne forces support, the Glider Exercise Unit, later re-titled 296 Squadron, started to use Shrewton for training with its Harts, Hector tugs and Hotspur gliders, and became its major user when 1 SFTS closed on 7 March 1942. The first unit to be actually based at Shrewton was the Heavy Glider Conversion Unit, which formed on 29 June 1942. However, due to the limitations of the airfield the unit moved to Brize Norton a couple of weeks later, before its Whitleys and Horsas were delivered.

The Glider Pilot Exercise Unit was formed at Netheravon from B Flight of 296 Squadron on 20 August 1942 to keep trained glider pilots in current flying practice, and began flying from Shrewton. Much of its flying was at night, and a tragic accident to a Hotspur one October evening, when its tow-rope broke at low level, resulted in the death of Lt Col John Rock, OC 1st Battalion, Glider Pilot Regiment.

No 43 OTU, which had formed at Larkhill on 1 October 1942 for AOP training, briefly used Shrewton during November and December, but it and the GPEU moved out in mid-December to enable the airfield to be upgraded. Three Blister hangars were erected along the north-east boundary of the field and a defensive pillbox, barrack huts and a combined-ranks mess built.

The airfield was reopened in March 1943 and was once again used for glider pilot training. It was upgraded again during the summer to RLG standards and during the autumn was used by the GPEU, then based at Thruxton. The unit's Tiger Moth Flight moved to Shrewton on 15 October. On 1 December the GPEU was disbanded to become the Operational & Refresher Training Unit, continuing to use Shrewton until March 1944 when it moved to Hampstead Norris. Its Tiger Moth Flight remained at Shrewton until 11 November 1944, when it was disbanded.

With the end of the war Shrewton was put on C&M, and retained as an ELG. It was used occasionally by A&AEE aircraft when using Larkhill ranges for weapons trials, but was returned to agriculture in the 1950s. Today the only signs of Shrewton's part in the Second World War are some concrete foundations and its pillbox.

Main features:
Runways: N-S 3,600ft, NE-SW 3,600ft, E-W 3,000ft, NW-SE 3,300ft, grass.
Hangars: three Blister. *Accommodation:* RAF Officers 8, SNCOs 7, ORs 151.

SOUTH CERNEY, Gloucestershire

SP045985, 3 miles SE of Cirencester

Now in the hands of the Army, South Cerney spent more than thirty years as a flying training centre, providing thousands of aircrew for the RAF. Construction of the airfield started in 1936 under the RAF Expansion Scheme, as a flying training station for 3 FTS, a Grantham-based school that was in an area of operational stations and needed to be relocated. When RAF South Cerney was opened on 16 August 1937 construction work was still in progress and only one of its three hangars was ready for use. The school had a variety of biplane types including the Audax, Hart, Hind, Demon, Fury, Wallace, Tutor and Tiger Moth, most of which had to sit around outside until the other hangars were completed. Fortunately the weather was kind at the time.

Audax K7339 is bounced by Demon K5676, both of 3 FTS, near South Cerney in 1938.

Oxfords arrived on 14 June 1938, and the first all-Oxford course, No 24, started on 25 July. From then until the end of the war the type was to be a daily sight at South Cerney, with up to 150 of them being there at any one time. When war was declared on 3 September 1939 No 3 FTS became 3 SFTS, with a strength of forty-four Oxfords and thirty-one Harts. Three Wellingtons of 37 Squadron arrived on 8 September under Operation *Scatter*, but returned to Feltwell on the 20th. The war had also sparked off other events. It was decided to move HQ 23 Group (which controlled advanced pilot training) from Grantham to South Cerney, and it brought with it its newly established Communications Flight, with Proctors and Dominies. By late summer 1940 the Oxfords had increased to more than a hundred in number and, with the Harts gone, the school concentrated on multi-engine training.

A 'vic' of three Oxfords of 3 FTS (L4576, L4574 and L4580) in August 1938.

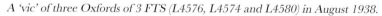

Pupils and staff of 3 FTS with Hart Trainer K5875 at South Cerney in 1938.

Oxfords and Harvards of 15 SFTS arrived in early June 1940, having moved out of Middle Wallop to make room for fighter squadrons covering the South Coast. Its Oxfords were in the circuit with those of 3 SFTS on the evening of 3 June when they were joined by a Heinkel He 111 which dropped six bombs and some incendiaries, fortunately causing no damage. Air raid warnings over the next three nights disrupted the flying programme, and on the night of 29/30 June twenty-two bombs fell to the east of the airfield boundary. More bombs were dropped onto the airfield on the afternoon of 25 July. Fear of invasion resulted in bomb-racks being fitted to the Oxfords, and instructors being on standby to attack enemy troops. At the end of August 15 SFTS moved to Kidlington and shortly afterwards a major change was made to 3 SFTS's training syllabus, from advanced to intermediate training. The Oxfords remained, converting student pilots from single- to twin-engined types, and a new RLG at Bibury eased the pressure on South Cerney. A further role change came in the spring of 1942 when, on 14 March, 3 SFTS was disbanded to become 3 (P)AFU, to give acclimatisation training to pilots trained overseas. Beam-approach training was added later, and to assist with this 1539 (BAT) Flight was formed with Oxfords on 15 April 1943; it moved to Bibury on 13 July and was replaced by 1532 (BAT) Flight, from Hullavington.

The work of 3 (P)AFU and its BAT Flights continued into 1944, satisfying the demand for trained aircrew, and only slowed in the spring of 1945 with the end of the war in sight. In May flying training started to wind down, and in June both BAT flights disbanded, a third flight, 1547 BAT Flight, flying detachments from Watchfield for the AFU until early December. Later that month, on the 17th, 3 (P)AFU was disbanded to become 3 SFTS once again; with Tiger Moths, Magisters and Harvards, it moved to Feltwell in August 1946.

This left South Cerney to 23 Group Communications Flight, joined by the Flying Training Command Instructors School from Wittering on 24 May. HQ 23 Group moved on 1 October to Halton and at the end of, the following February the FTCIS closed. In March 1948 No 2 FTS arrived from Church Lawford with Tiger Moths and Harvards, providing basic flying training courses until May 1952, when it was re-designated the CFS (Basic) Squadron, on Harvards, Prentices and Provosts. On 1 January 1956 the CFS Helicopter Squadron formed at South Cerney with Dragonflies, Skeeters, Sycamores and Whirlwinds, becoming the first RAF unit organised to train helicopter instructors.

CFS (Basic) Squadron moved to Little Rissington in May 1957, and on 22 July the Aircrew Officers Training School arrived from Kirton-in-Lindsey, bringing Chipmunks and Ansons. No 625 GS formed at South Cerney in August 1958 to provide glider training for Air Cadets, using Sedburgh T21 and Cadet T31 gliders. CFS(H) left for Ternhill on 10 August 1961, but the last CFS element resident at South Cerney, the Primary Flying School, formed there on 1 July 1965. Using twenty-one Chipmunks, the school gave initial instruction to newly-commissioned pilots when the all-through jet flying training scheme was abandoned. (Its training was disrupted somewhat during the summer of 1966 when South Cerney provided the venue for the World Gliding Championships.) The PFS left for Church Fenton in January 1967, and with the departure of the

Three Oxfords, L9651, L9703 and L4578, of 3 FTS with Hind K5397 in July 1939.

Aircrew Officers Training School on 21 January 1968 South Cerney was transferred to Air Support Command as a dormitory unit for Brize Norton and Fairford.

No longer needed by the RAF, on 1 July 1971 the station was transferred to the Army, which is still in residence. No 625 GS (which became 625 VGS in 1978) continued to use the airfield until July 1992, when it left for Kemble. Today South Cerney houses the Duke of Gloucester Barracks and is home to 29 Regiment, RLC. It also houses the Joint Service Air Mounting Centre, which coordinates deployments of military units via the nearby RAF stations at Brize Norton and Lyneham. The airfield at South Cerney and most of its buildings remain well-kept, largely unchanged from their Second World War appearance.

Main features:
Runways: 190° 2,925ft, 270° 3,225ft, grass. *Hangars:* three Type C, two Bellman, three 65ft Blister, eight 69ft Double Blister. *Accommodation:* RAF Officers 212, SNCOs 112, ORs 1,640; WAAF Officers 13, SNCOs 8, ORs 382.

STAVERTON, Gloucestershire

SO887218, 3 miles NE of Gloucester

The present Gloucestershire Airport owes its origins to an airstrip opened by the Cotswold Aero Club at Down Hatherley in September 1932. Development options were limited, and in March 1934, when it was proposed to site an airport in the area, 160 acres of land were purchased across the main A40 road by Gloucester and Cheltenham Councils in a joint undertaking. Work started on the airfield towards the end of 1934 and two years later, on 18 November 1936, an operating licence for the airport was issued. Flying had already started, on 25 May, when Railway Air Services' DH84 Dragons started calling in by request on their Birmingham to Bristol route.

The RAF, needing more flying training facilities to support its expansion during the 1930s, wanted to use Staverton. In return for funding improvements, the councils agreed to this, and on 29 September 1936 No 31 E&RFTS was formed; operated by Surrey Flying Services, it flew Tiger Moths, Hart Trainers, Audaxes and Hinds. More military aircraft arrived at the airfield the following year, with the establishment of the Rotol Airscrews Flight Test Department, as an adjunct to the factory built alongside the airfield. The Wellesley that arrived on 17 April was the first of more than ninety aircraft that would be used by the company to develop and test its propellers over the next six years.

The Cotswold Aero Club airfield at Down Hatherley in 1932.

Anson N5331 of 6 AONS in 1941.

A second flying school, the Airwork Civil School of Air Navigation, appeared in May 1939, transferred from Shoreham with its fleet of DH89 Dragon Rapides used to train RAF Observers. Becoming 6 Civil Air Navigation School on 6 August, it was then also flying Ansons. When war came 31 E&RFTS closed to provide more aircraft for other schools and allow more room for the navigation school, which on 1 November was again re-designated, this time as 6 AONS. It then had four remaining Rapides on strength, together with twenty Ansons. The airfield had been officially renamed on 10 September, as RAF Staverton.

On 3 August 1940 No 2 EFTS transferred from Filton to teach novice pilots to fly on Tiger Moths. With the high demand for instructors in 1941 the school became 6 (Supplementary) FIS on 1 November and 6 FIS a couple of months later, then in April 1942 it moved to its RLG at Worcester. Meanwhile in late December 1940 the Folland Aircraft Flight Test Department had arrived at Staverton from Hamble, operating a fleet of the Folland FO108 single-engined flying test beds. These flew from Staverton testing large aero-engines for the manufacturers, and were joined by Glosters, which established a flight test centre in early 1941 to relieve Brockworth for the production-testing of new aircraft.

No 6 AONS was operating at full capacity during the summer of 1941 and had grown to reflect the need for more aircrew, flying sixty-three Ansons and training 240 pupils at any one time. The circuit at Staverton limited its operations, so the school established detached flights at Moreton Valence and Llanbedr to spread the load, all major servicing and support remaining at Staverton. The inevitable title changes resulted in it becoming 6 AOS in 17 January 1942 and 6 (O)AFU eighteen months later, having seventy-two Ansons on its strength by then.

Flight Refuelling Ltd was the next manufacturer to use Staverton; its Flight Test Department, having been destroyed by the Luftwaffe at Ford in August 1940, was reformed there in 1942. Initially sharing a hangar with Folland, it moved into its own Bellman in 1943, where it worked on a number of interesting projects including anti-icing devices, flame-damping equipment, self-sealing tanks and towed-ferrying of fighters by larger aircraft. The company also continued to work on air-to-air refuelling and, after years of disinterest, the Air Ministry suddenly gave it an order in February 1944 to develop equipment for 600 Lancaster tankers and receivers for a projected Far East operation. After much hard work the project was just as suddenly cancelled a year later, as the Allies closed in on Japan.

With losses in bomber crews fortunately not as high an anticipated, and a resulting surfeit of crews, 6 (O)AFU was disbanded on 12 December 1944. This dramatically reduced RAF flying from the airfield, leaving only 44 Group Communications Flight, which had formed on 16 August, to carry on. Most flying was then by Dowty, Glosters and Flight Refuelling, but Staverton's short runways were very tight for four-engine bombers, and there were a number of incidents. On 27 August 1945 a Lancaster of the RAE suffered a hydraulic failure and overran the main runway into Bamfurlong Lane. A similar accident occurred to an FR Lancaster on 11 October after a flight refuelling demonstration for the Ministry of Aviation.

The end of the war saw a general run-down, resulting in the closure of operations by Folland and Glosters, and in early 1946 Flight Refuelling returned to Ford. No 44 Group Communications Flight disbanded on 29 July, leaving the only RAF presence as the RAF Police Dog School, which had opened in the early 1940s, and 7 MU, Quedgeley, which used a number of hangars for storage.

Staverton returned to civilian control on 29 September 1950. Rotol was the sole user of the airfield for several years until March 1953, when Cambrian Airways took over management and Smith Industries Aviation Division moved in. Although Rotol closed its Flight Test Department in 1954, the company merged with Dowty Equipment Ltd in April 1960, and continues to manufacture aviation equipment at Staverton today.

The Skyfame Museum was opened in the former Flight Refuelling hangar by aviation preservation pioneer Peter Thomas in 1963. Its Oxford, Anson and Mosquito were flown regularly together with several other historic types, and became important parts of other collections when the museum had to close due to financial pressure in 1978.

The local councils took over the running of Staverton as an airport in 1962 and various airlines have flown services into it, including Derby Airways, British Midland Airways and Intra, operating mainly to the Isle of Man and Channel Islands. Major improvements to runways and facilities took place in the late 1990s, and today, as Gloucestershire Airport, it is one of the best-equipped General Aviation airfields in the UK. It is also very busy. A number of scheduled services fly from the airport, and it is home to a number of flying schools, helicopter operators such as Bond Air Services, and aircraft engineering companies. The Airport Café, opposite the air terminal, is well worth a visit!

Staverton in mid-2008.

Main features:
Runways: 210° 3,000ft x 150ft, 270° 3,000ft x 150ft, 170° 3,000ft x 150ft, concrete and tarmac. *Hangars:* six Bellman, one MAP Bellman, one EO-Blister. *Hardstandings:* hangar apron 300ft x 80ft. *Accommodation:* RAF Officers 36, SNCOs 122, ORs 421; WAAF Officers 4, SNCOs 4, ORs 315.

EC135 of Bond Helicopters lifting off from Staverton in May 2008.

STOKE ORCHARD, Gloucester

SO925275, 2 miles W of Bishop's Cleeve

The site for a flying training airfield was identified at Stoke Orchard in 1939 and, although it was ready for occupation in early 1941, it was some months before the first RAF unit arrived. In the meantime the Gloster Aircraft Company realised the airfield's potential, and erected two Dispersal Factory Units there during 1940 to support the works at Hucclecote. The final assembly and flight-testing of Hurricanes and later Typhoons took place from the airfield throughout the wartime period.

The first RAF unit to use Stoke Orchard was 10 EFTS, which moved from Weston-super-Mare between 23 and 27 September 1941. Flying fifty-two Tiger Moths, the flying instructors, ground training and support staff got down to work to re-establish courses following the disruption of the move. They had hardly got back to normal when, in the spring of 1942, it was decided that, due to the need for more glider pilots, Stoke Orchard's role would change. Therefore on 21 July No 10 EFTS was disbanded and No 3 GTS formed. Initially equipped with Hotspur two-seat training gliders and Master II tugs to launch them, the school also flew Tiger Moths, Magisters and Oxfords.

The airfield was given an upgrade, and on 4 August 1942 No 1 Course of 3 GTS started. To ease congestion at Stoke Orchard, RLGs were established by the school at Northleach, Aldermaston and Wanborough. Inevitably accidents occurred, mostly to Hotspurs on take-off or landing, but also to powered aircraft hitting obstacles, or developing engine trouble. Although most of the injuries sustained by pupils and instructors were not life-threatening, a number of fatalities did result. The first of these occurred on 17 August, when the pilot of Hotspur HH519 lost control in the tug's slipstream just after take-off, and was killed when the glider crashed into a tree. The tugs also had their share of accidents: Master DL526 crash-landed during a stalled approach on 30 August, injuring its pilot, while three Masters and four Hotspurs were badly damaged in other accidents during the rest of that year. During 1943 there were sixteen serious accidents, mainly to gliders under- or over-shooting. The five accidents during 1944 were mostly during the first half of the year, in the build-up to D-Day.

No 3 GTS made an important contribution to the Normandy and Arnhem airborne operations and continued its work in 1945. However, bad weather had its effects on the well-worn surface of Stoke Orchard and its RLGs during that winter, resulting in a decision to relocate the school. In mid-January 1945 No 3 GTS moved to Exeter. As by then Glosters had also pulled out, flying finished at the airfield. The hangars were used by 7 MU Quedgeley for a few months, but at the end of 1945 Stoke Orchard was closed. It was soon sold off, and quickly returned to agriculture. The outline of the airfield can still be seen today, and a few of the buildings remain in place.

Main features:
Runways: NW-SE 3,600ft, N-S 3,300ft, grass. *Hangars:* four Bellman, seven Double EO-Blister, one Triple EO-Blister. *Accommodation:* RAF Officers 46, SNCOs 116, ORs 483; WAAF Officers 4, SNCOs 8, ORs 189.

STONEHENGE, Wiltshire

SU114421, 3½ miles W of Amesbury alongside A303

Stonehenge looks impressive from any angle, but how many motorists viewing it today from the A303 realise that they are travelling across a former aerodrome built alongside the stones in the dark days of the Great War?

Early in 1917 work started on a new training airfield for the RFC to the north of Salisbury. It was rectangular in shape and covered 360 acres immediately to the west of Stonehenge straddling the main Wyle to Amesbury road. The airfield was situated north of the road and the main technical site, which consisted of six coupled General Service Aeroplane sheds, an Aeroplane Repair Shed, MT sheds, workshops, stores and offices, was built on its southern side. The domestic site of messes and quarters was further south, across the main road. A separate camp for trainee night crews was later set up near Fargo Plantation away from the main airfield.

Although it was built to house two training squadrons, the airfield's first occupant was 107 Squadron, an embryo day-bomber unit formed at Catterick on 8 October 1917 that moved to Stonehenge ten days later to start training. It was joined by two more bomber units, 108 Squadron, formed at the airfield on 11 November, and 109 Squadron, which moved in the next day, having

Stonehenge seen from the north in September 1918.

been formed at South Carlton on 1 November. All three squadrons moved to Lake Down on 2 December to receive their first aircraft, DH9s. They exchanged places that day with No 2 TDS, a day-bomber training unit that flew a variety of types including Shorthorns, BE2s, DH4s, DH6s, RE8s and HP0/100s. It was designated No 1 School of Aerial Navigation & Bomb Dropping on 1 January 1918, although it later dropped the term 'Aerial' from its title. The school was intended as a finishing school for pilots and observers, and comprised two squadrons, one for airmen destined for day-bombers, the other for those going onto night-bombers, principally the twin-engined HP0/400. To fulfil its role the school also later received Avro 504Ks, Pups, DH9s, DH10s, FE2s and Bristol Scouts, as well as HP0/400s. To help provide training on the latter, the RNAS Handley Page Training Flight brought its HP0/400s from Manston in January 1918 and was accommodated on a separate site of four Handley Page and a number of Bessoneau hangars built alongside the A360 in the north-west corner of the airfield. Both the RNAS site and the main technical site were served by branch lines of the Larkhill Military Railway.

No 97 Squadron arrived from Waddington on 21 January 1918, having been formed there as a training unit with various types including the FE2B and DH4, but did not stay long, moving to Netheravon on 31 March. The day-bomber student pilots were given instruction in navigation, cloud flying, formation flying, bombing, gunnery and map-reading, while aspiring night-flyers were also taught night navigation, compass flying and the use of the vertical searchlight. By mid-1918 two Avros and four Shorthorns were being flown for initial checks, forty-eight DH4/DH9s for day-bomber training, and forty FE2Bs and ten HP0/400s for night-bomber training.

The output of the school gradually increased to sixty day and sixty night crews per month, but after the Armistice numbers reduced. Training continued into 1919 but finally came to an end on 23 September when No 1 SofN&BD moved to Andover to be merged with No 2 SofN&BD, becoming the School of Air Pilotage. The school was replaced at Stonehenge by the Artillery Cooperation Squadron, moved in during August 1919 with RE8s, FK8s, F2Bs and Avro 504Ks, although it flew mostly from Worthy Down. On 8 March 1920 the unit was absorbed by the School of Army Cooperation, which reformed that day at Stonehenge. C Flight of 4 Squadron moved in from Farnborough during April 1920, its Brisfits providing artillery spotting, recce and photographic demonstrations for the school as well as bombing and ground-strafing experience for troops training on Salisbury Plain. The SofAC transferred to Old Sarum in January 1921 and RAF Stonehenge was then closed.

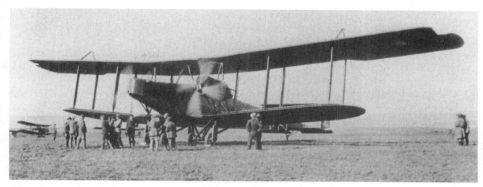

HP 0/400 C9685 of No 1 SofN&BD, Stonehenge, 1918.

A Bristol Monoplane at Stonehenge in 1918.

Aerial view of Stonehenge from the east in 1918, showing its proximity to the stones.

The airfield site was de-requisitioned and auctioned off. Some of its buildings were dismantled but most were sold, the domestic site becoming the Stonehenge Pedigree Stock Farm. The technical site was demolished in 1929, some of the Handley Page hangars being removed for reuse. Parts of one were taken to High Post for the newly established flying club, while other sections went to the Phillips & Powis (Miles Aircraft) factory at Reading and to Old Warden, forming the main hangar that now houses the Shuttleworth Collection. The whole Stonehenge area was eventually cleared of buildings to produce the landscape that we see today – it is hard to believe that a fully equipped military airfield was ever there at all.

Mustangs of 26 Squadron at Stoney Cross in March 1943.

STONEY CROSS, Hampshire

SU246125, 7 miles NE of Ringwood

Built on Ocknell Plain, a plateau to the north of the Cadnam-Ringwood road in the New Forest, Stoney Cross was originally intended as an ALG, devoid of facilities. By mid-1942, however, with construction still in progress, it was decided to develop the airfield as a forward base for fighter and bomber operations, so the contractor, Wimpey, started work on the necessary buildings and installations.

When opened by 38 Wing, Army Cooperation Command, on 9 November 1942, the airfield was still incomplete, and it was 25 January before its first squadron, No 239 with Mustang Mk Is, arrived from Hurn. It was followed, on 1 March, by 26 Squadron, also with Mustangs, from Detling, and by 175 Squadron, bringing Hurricanes from Warmwell. All three then took part in Exercise *Spartan*, a large-scale army cooperation exercise, but operations were difficult because of contractor's activity, three workmen being killed in a collision between a Mustang and their lorry. The Mustangs departed for Gatwick on 7 April, and the Hurricanes for Colerne the following day. Wimpey continued work on the runways, perimeter tracks and dispersals as Stoney Cross was transferred to 10 Group, Fighter Command, with the disbandment of Army Cooperation Command on 1 June 1943.

When the airfield was ready for operations it was not fighters but Albemarles that arrived on 3 June. From 296 Squadron, Thruxton, they spent three weeks crew-training before heading off for North Africa to take part in the invasion of Sicily. They were replaced on 25 August by 297

A B-26 of the 566th BS, 387th BG, in August 1944.

Squadron, also from Thruxton, with a mixed fleet of Whitley Vs and Albemarles. This unit was to stay until 14 March 1944, using Stoney Cross as a forward base for parachute operations; on the first, in September, two Whitleys made a diversionary raid while a third dropped twelve Commandos to attack installations at St Valery in northern France. The troops were later extracted by MTB.

A US Army unit moved into one of the hangars in mid-1943 to assemble Waco CG-4A gliders from their crates for delivery by air to US bases in southern England. On 4 November No 297 Squadron's C Flight was detached to become the nucleus of 299 Squadron, operating Venturas until January 1944 when it received Stirling IVs. The two squadrons then trained with the airborne divisions, and took part in numerous exercises, including *Try Again*. These also involved other airborne forces support squadrons at Hurn and Tarrant Rushton, taking place by day and night, and getting larger and more involved as time went on – on 6 February fourteen Albemarles of 297 Squadron took part in the drop of 1,500 troops of 3rd Para Brigade. Both squadrons also made supply drops to French Resistance units during the spring of 1944 in the build-up to the invasion, and the whole station was working at high intensity when the squadrons were suddenly moved out to make room for units of the USAAF. No 297 Squadron went to Brize Norton on 14 March and 299 to Keevil the following day as the American advance party arrived.

They were from the 367th FG, US 9th AF, which consisted of the 392nd, 393rd and 394th FSs. The main contingent arrived direct from the USA on 1 April to find eighty-five P-38 Lightnings awaiting them on Stoney Cross's dispersals. As only four of the Group's pilots had ever flown P-38s before, an intensive training period followed before the squadrons could be declared operational. This came just over a month later, and on 9 May they flew their first mission, a fighter sweep by forty P-38s drawn from each FS.

Of the twenty missions flown between then and the end of May, a number were spent escorting B-17s on raids into Germany while the remainder were strikes against airfields, gun batteries and other ground targets. For D-Day the P-38s were given the low-level close-support role and flew twenty-seven missions over a four-day period following the invasion. After a week of intensive attacks on the defences of Cherbourg in mid-June, the 393rd and 394th suffered heavy losses on one mission – of the forty-eight aircraft involved, seven were lost and only twelve returned undamaged. However, similar attacks with guns and bombs continued until 6 July when the 367th FG moved to Ibsley to make room for the B-26 Marauders of the 387th BG. The group started to arrive from Chipping Ongar on 21 July, while continuing missions during the transfer. Its four squadrons, the 556th, 557th, 558th and 559th BSs, immediately resumed operations from Stoney Cross, and maintained attacks in support of the Allied beachhead until 1 September, when they moved to Maupertus in France.

Stoney Cross reverted to RAF control on 5 September and was used initially by a detachment of 1 HGSU, Netheravon, to repair glider components retrieved from Normandy and returned by LCT. On 7 October the airfield became a satellite of Ibsley, nine RAF Regiment squadrons moving in to use the accommodation while in transit, and a month later 116 Wing, Transport Command, took over. This heralded a new phase for Stoney Cross, as the Command developed the use of bombers such as the Stirling, Wellington and Liberator as troop transports for long-distance flights overseas. Nos 232 and 242 Squadrons formed on 15 September 1944 to begin training on Wellington XVIs, intended for the shorter routes to Europe and the Middle East. No 232 Squadron was the first to complete the training, then in February 1945 it converted to the Liberator VII and left for Palam in India on the 14th.

On 9 January 1945 No 46 Squadron reformed at Stoney Cross with Stirling CVs and started services on 3 March, flying its first schedule to India on 1 April. No 242 Squadron also received Stirlings in February, adding Yorks in April. The MAP took over No 2 Hangar for the conversion of Stirling IVs to the trooping role, before issuing them to 242 Squadron, supplementing its Yorks; the latter were withdrawn in July. A new passenger and freight building opened in September, in time for the large trooping commitment resulting from the end of the war with Japan.

Aerial view of Stoney Cross in August 2008.

In December No 242 Squadron moved to Merryfield, while 46 Squadron continued services to India, converting to Dakotas from early 1946, and flying its first schedules with the type on 3 March. During 1946 the squadron's routes moved to the Middle East, then predominantly to Europe as it transferred to Manston on 11 October. Following its departure Stoney Cross was transferred to C&M.

No 2 Hangar was used for storage by the Board of Trade for a while and the Home Office retained Nos 1, 3 and 4 for the storage of new Green Goddess auxiliary fire engines. The Forestry Commission took charge of the airfield in 1956 and removed all of the hangars, the control tower and most of the runways and perimeter tracks. The water tower remained in position until 2006 and although two roads crossing the site make use of part of the old runways, much of the remaining runway surfaces and perimeter tracks have since been taken up. A few of the dispersals do remain, however, forming the basis of the Ocknell and Longbeech campsites, open during the summer. An information plaque can be found near the site of the control tower.

Main features:

Runways: 250° 6,000ft x 150ft, 328° 4,560ft x 150ft, 188° 4,200ft x 150ft, concrete and wood chippings. *Hangars:* four T2, six Blister. *Hardstandings:* 21ft x 100ft frying pan, 30ft x 125ft frying pan, eleven loop. *Accommodation:* RAF Officers 164, SNCOs 450, ORs 1,437; WAAF Officers 12, SNCOs 8, ORs 375.

SWAY, Hampshire

SZ287981, 3 miles NE of Lymington

An Emergency Landing Ground was laid out at Sway in the summer of 1940, utilising several fields of Manor Farm and covering about 106 acres. No buildings were erected, accommodation being provided by tents pitched in the north-west corner of the airfield.

The ELG was first used by the Special Duty Flight based at Christchurch, early in August 1940. About ten aircraft, including at least one Battle, were sent to the site for brief radar development trails, tended by a detachment of six groundcrew. The complement was increased to eighteen men in September, with an Anson for communications. The airfield was raided on 23 August 1940 when ten bombs dropped harmlessly into nearby fields, and again on 9 April 1941 when a Hampden was slightly damaged by two bombs.

There were also landings by fighters, usually by pilots dropping in to ask directions, although a damaged Hurricane force-landed in the autumn of 1940 (and was dismantled to be taken out by road). The ELG was abandoned during the late autumn of 1941 after the last aircraft departed.

A Halifax and Horsa take off from Tarrant Rushton for Normandy in June 1944.

TARRANT RUSHTON, Dorset

ST946058, 3 miles E of Blandford Forum

Into the dusk at 2256 hours on 5 June 1944, the first of six Halifax glider-tugs of 298 Squadron left the runway at Tarrant Rushton, each with a Horsa in tow. The gliders carried troops of D Company, 2nd Battalion, Oxfordshire & Buckinghamshire Light Infantry, part of 6th Airborne Division, whose job was to take the important bridges over the Caen Canal and Orne River linking the D-Day invasion beaches of the Normandy coast with the airborne LZs and DZs. Casting off over the objective at 0007 hours, the first Horsa went in, its pilot (Sergeant Jim Wallwork) bringing the glider to a halt 9 minutes later with its nose through the canal bridge's defensive wire. The troops, commanded by Major John Howard, deployed and after a brief fierce battle captured both bridges as planned, holding them against German counterattacks. Meanwhile twenty aircraft of 644 Squadron left Tarrant Rushton on Operation *Tonga*, towing two Hamilcars and fifteen Horsas with a relief force. Three solo Halifaxes dropped bombs on an explosives factory at Caen to create a diversion. More aircraft of 298 Squadron followed up shortly afterwards, towing a further fifteen Horsas and two Hamilcars to the Orne area. Once the Halifaxes had been refuelled they followed up with Operation *Mallard*, each squadron taking fifteen Hamilcars and one Horsa to the LZs occupied earlier in the day. On this eventful day, only two Tarrant Rushton Halifaxes were lost, both by 298 Squadron, one on *Tonga*, the second on *Mallard*.

The airfield at Tarrant Rushton originated in May 1942 when construction started on a plateau to the east of the River Tarrant. Specifically intended for the use of airborne forces, it was handed over by Wimpey to 38 Wing on 17 May 1943. The only Standard Design airfield in Dorset, it had three concrete runways and four T2 hangars, together with a control tower and operational buildings. Although the new airfield was not officially opened until October, the first aircraft actually arrived on 23 September, being Venturas for onward delivery to 299 Squadron, recently formed at Stoney Cross. The first unit to be based at Tarrant Rushton was 298 Squadron, which formed there on 4 November from A Flight of 295 Squadron, detached from Hurn. The unit's initial establishment of seventeen Halifax Vs grew to forty by early February 1944, but on the 23rd it was split to form 644 Squadron. Because of limited accommodation, the latter used Chelveston for much of its training.

The Airborne Forces Tactical Development Unit had formed at Tarrant Rushton on 1 December 1943, with examples of the main types used in the airborne role, but left for Netheravon in mid-January 1944 to make way for more operational units. No 196 Squadron had arrived from Leicester on 7 January for its Stirling IIIs to be replaced by IVs. As well as training exercises it also flew night supply drops of arms and equipment to the SOE, joined by 190 and 620 Squadrons, also flying Stirlings, using Tarrant Rushton as a forward base. During March the airfield became home to 14 and 15 Glider Servicing Echelons of No 1 Heavy Glider Servicing Unit at Netheravon, to support the Hamilcar glider, which was capable of carrying a light tank. Training by the squadrons intensified in the spring of 1944 with a number of large exercises being mounted in the build-up to the invasion of Europe.

On the eve of D-Day the airfield was nose-to-tail with glider/tug combinations ready for action. Its part in Operation *Neptune*, the airborne phase of *Overlord*, is described above, and for three weeks afterwards its squadrons flew re-supply missions to the beachhead. They then reverted to training, punctuated by the occasional bombing mission, SOE supply drop or SAS insertion. Their next major mission came that autumn.

For Operation *Market Garden* on 17 September, Nos 298 and 644 Squadrons flew forty-one tug/glider combinations, fourteen with Hamilcars. They met little opposition, but the re-supply over ensuing days suffered from bad weather and intense flak. The squadrons flew ninety-two sorties over three days, and remarkably did not lose a single Halifax to enemy action. Immediately after the Arnhem operation the Tarrant squadrons re-equipped with Hercules-powered Halifax IIIs and returned to SOE operations, some as far away as Norway. For the last major airborne operation of the war, the Rhine Crossing, they used Woodbridge as a forward airfield from which to fly sixty Halifaxes to the objective.

On return to Tarrant Rushton both squadrons engaged in SOE work over Norway and Denmark, culminating in the landing of the 1st Airborne Division at Copenhagen on 8 May 1945, the day hostilities ceased. This was followed by Operation *Doomsday*, which involved a movement of 7,000 troops and their supplies to occupy Oslo and other major towns in Norway. This was their final operation from Tarrant Rushton, as 298 Squadron left for the Far East during early July, followed as far as Palestine by 644 Squadron in early December.

Halifax III-equipped 190 Squadron was disbanded at Great Dunmow on 21 January 1946 and reformed later that day at Tarrant Rushton as 295 Squadron with Halifax A7s. On 1 April it was disbanded and renumbered as 297 Squadron. Following crew training it flew transport missions before moving to Brize Norton on 5 September when space became available there.

A Lancaster and a Meteor in AAR endurance trials in August 1949.

*An aerial view of Tarrant
Rushton's remains in mid-2008.*

With the departure of the last RAF Halifax, Tarrant Rushton was put on C&M, and declared surplus in December 1947. Six months later it was purchased by Flight Refuelling Ltd., which relocated there from Ford and Staverton, and was to use the airfield as its base for the next thirty years. Shortly after the company's move the Berlin Airlift started, and it was given a contract to carry bulk fuel into the beleaguered city. A Lancaster left for Gatow on 27 July carrying 8,800 gallons of fuel, and more missions to the city followed, which helped to establish the company's post-war reputation.

As a result of the Korean War, 210 AFS was formed at Tarrant Rushton on 5 August 1952, to give refresher training to reserve pilots on Meteor T7s, F3s and Vampire FB5s, which were serviced and maintained by Flight Refuelling. The unit closed again on 29 April 1954, but the RAF's interest in Tarrant Rushton remained and its runways and hardstandings were strengthened as a V-Bomber dispersal airfield. The V-Bombers never arrived, but the airfield remained busy, the company continuing to develop in-flight refuelling systems for a range of aircraft types. It also moved into target systems, developing the Rushton Winch for towing simulated aircraft targets, and a range of aircraft now known as UAVs (including conversion of Meteors and Sea Vixens to unmanned drones, and development of the Australian Jindivik).

As useful as it was, having its own airfield became increasingly expensive, and in the late 1970s Flight Refuelling reluctantly decided to give up Tarrant Rushton and move to Hurn. The airfield was closed for operational flying after the last Sea Vixen flew out on 30 September 1980, but light aircraft and the Dorset Gliding Club continued to use it until the runways were deactivated in January 1981. The site was then rapidly returned to agriculture by its new owners, who demolished more than 300 buildings. The basic structure of the airfield is still evident from the air today, and a T2 hangar still stands. Another survivor is one of the station's Halifaxes, BVII NA337, which was shot down over Norway on 23 April 1945 and crashed into Lake Mjosa. It was brought to the surface some fifty years later and has since been rebuilt for preservation at the RCAF Memorial Museum at Trenton, Ontario.

Main features:
Runways: 010° 6,000ft x 150ft, 080° 4,200ft x 150ft, 130° 4,200ft x 150ft, concrete and wood-chippings. *Hangars:* four T2. *Hardstandings:* fifty spectacle loop. *Accommodation:* RAF Officers 190, SNCOs 530, ORs 1,605; WAAF Officers 10, SNCOs 25, ORs 351.

THRUXTON, Hampshire

SU280455, 5 miles W of Andover

Land was requisitioned from Thruxton Manor estate in 1940 on which to build a satellite airfield for Middle Wallop. There was just enough room for a standard fighter-type three-runway layout, although the main runway had to be restricted to 4,680 feet rather than the usual 6,000 feet. Before construction was complete Thruxton was allocated to Army Cooperation Command as a satellite for Andover. On 22 June 1941 Blenheims of No 2 School of Army Cooperation tested the

Whitleys of 51 Squadron, at Thruxton in February 1942.

runways, but the rough new concrete surface burst three tyres! The opening was delayed until August while tarmac was laid.

The first unit to arrive was 225 Squadron, which moved in on 4 August to fly ASR patrols while specialist rescue units were being established. Detachments from 42 OTU, Andover, then started arriving to use the new airfield for training. The OTU had been formed at Andover on 18 July to train crews for army support duties, with an establishment of eleven Blenheim Is, twenty-two Blenheim IVs, ten Anson/Oxfords and four target tugs. To assist with night-flying training, 26 Blind Approach Training Flight was formed on 3 October within the OTU at Andover with three Ansons and three Blenheims. On 2 November it was re-titled 26 Beam Approach Training Flight and on the 11th moved to Thruxton. By the end of December it had four Oxfords on strength.

At the end of February 1942 Thruxton was selected as the jumping-off point for Operation *Biting*, the first operational paratroop drop mounted from the UK. Fifteen black-painted Whitleys of 51 Squadron were deployed from their base at Lindholme, twelve of which took off from Thruxton on the evening of 27 February, heading for the French coast. The troops of C Company, 2nd Parachute Battalion, were aboard, together with radar expert Flight Sergeant Cox, for their objective was the Wurtzburg radar station at Bruneval near Le Havre. Led by Wg Cdr P. C. Pickard, the Whitley pilots found their objective and successfully dropped ten sticks of parachutists. While the troops secured the area and held off German counterattacks, Flight Sergeant Cox photographed the radar installation, removing some of its components before sappers blew it up. The troops withdrew to the beach and, after an anxious wait, were picked up by the Navy and returned to Portsmouth in triumph with their booty.

Early in 1942 No 225 Squadron had converted to Hurricanes, adding Mustangs to work up in the fighter-recce role. In August it became operational, flying convoy and anti-intruder coastal patrols until the month when it moved to Macmerry in preparation for moving overseas. Meanwhile Thruxton had become one of the forward operating bases for Operation *Jubilee*, the Dieppe raid. To cover the seaborne assault heavy air cover was required, and on 14 August No 226 Squadron flew in its Bostons from Swanton Morley to begin intensive work-up with smoke weapons. Some aircraft had SCIs fitted into their bomb-bays, while others were to carry 100lb phosphorus bombs. They were joined by the Blenheims of 13 and 614 Squadrons, which were also to carry smoke bombs. The force left before dawn on 19 August, heading for the Channel. Locating their targets, the heavy coastal gun batteries overlooking Dieppe, the bombers dropped more than a hundred smoke bombs and sprayed smoke from the SCIs. The German guns were successfully blanketed, although one Blenheim was shot down and several Bostons were damaged. More smoke was laid during the morning to protect the troops fighting ashore, and, with the decision to withdraw later in the day, the bombers returned to lay more smoke. A fourth sortie was made by 226 Squadron to cover the naval forces leaving the beachhead, before the Bostons returned to Thruxton.

The steady expansion of Britain's airborne forces brought more Whitleys to Thruxton when Hurn-based 297 Squadron provided ten aircraft and crews to form 298 Squadron there on 24 August 1942. However, this was a false start, and the unit was disbanded again on 19 October, its aircraft and crews being reabsorbed by 297 Squadron when it moved to Thruxton on the 25th. The unit replaced 42 OTU, which began moving to Ashbourne ten days earlier, leaving behind 1526 BAT Flight. Shortly after arrival 297 Squadron became operational, and flew paratroops on exercises by day, dropping leaflets on *Nickel* raids over northern France by night. Some twenty sorties were flown per month, then in February 1943 the Squadron began tactical bombing by night. In March glider-towing training began, which was put to good use the following month when Whitley/Horsa combinations were used to transport the ground personnel and equipment of bomber squadrons from one station to another on operational transfers. Albemarles joined the unit in July and, with conversion complete, 297 Squadron left for Stoney Cross on 25 August.

Excitement was caused by the sudden arrival of a USAAF B17 on 29 July, which had taken off from Boscombe Down on a chemical bombing trial, but had been diverted because some of the weapons hadn't released over the range. The bomber was quarantined and not allowed to return to Boscombe Down until it had been cleared by RAF officers from Porton Down. In September a detachment of 3209 Servicing Commando moved in to undertake modifications to Typhoons; the fighters were flown in, modified and flown out again, the whole process taking a month. By this time 1526 BAT Flight was using its four Oxfords to train crews on the use of *Gee* radio navigation equipment.

The Glider Pilot Exercise Unit also arrived in September with Master tugs and Hotspur gliders, but after a few weeks returned to Netheravon to make room for 123 Airfield (168, 170 and 268 Squadrons, with Mustang IAs), which arrived in mid-October. No 63 Squadron, from Turnhouse, exchanged places with 268 Squadron in early November, and a week or so later 123 Airfield transferred to Sawbridgeworth. The GPEU then returned, by this time flying Albemarles, Whitleys, Stirlings and Horsas, and on 1 December was re-designated the Operational & Refresher Training Unit. It moved on in late February 1944, with 1526 BAT Flight, to Hampstead Norris, in order to make room for the USAAF, which took over Thruxton as Station 407 on 1 March 1944.

USAAF advance parties had arrived in February to move in stores and equipment ready for the arrival of the P-47s of the 366th FG of the US 9th AF. The Group, which consisted of the 389th, 390th and 391st FSs, transferred from Membury on 29 February. It flew its first mission, a sweep with the Chilbolton-based 368th FG along the French coast, on 14 March, dive-bombed St Valery airfield the following day, and over the following weeks flew sweeps, escorts and ground-attack missions as D-Day approached. On the day itself the Group attacked coastal batteries with 1,000lb bombs, later turning its attention to enemy armour. The 366th FG was one of the first to leave for the continent, moving to Strip A-1/Pierre du Mont, behind Omaha Beach, on 17 June. During its time at Thruxton the Group had shot down twenty-three enemy aircraft, but lost twenty-seven P-47s.

The Group were replaced by 84 Group Support Unit, which arrived from Aston Down on 10 July. This unit maintained a reserve of pilots and aircraft for 84 Group squadrons, and had 110 Mustangs, Typhoons and Spitfires on strength, together with two Austers for communications. It

P-47Ds of the 389th FS taxi into position before take-off from Thruxton on 25 April 1944.

was supported by 1311 Transport Flight, a ferry unit with Ansons, some of which were flown in the ambulance role, and made their first sorties to the beachhead the day after arrival at Thruxton. The Flight was disbanded on 21 July and absorbed by 84 GSU, which left for Lasham four months later

The Austers of 43 OTU, Oatlands Hill, made use of Thruxton for training during this time. I was also used for stockpiling gliders for reuse, and by the autumn more than a hundred Horsas were in open storage on the northern side of the aerodrome. By the end of 1945, however, the glider were being broken up and the airfield itself was declared surplus. The last RAF resident was 9 Mobile Parachute Servicing Unit, which moved in from Ibsley on 29 October 1945, and left for the Middle East on 14 January 1946.

In March 1946 the Wiltshire School of Flying moved in from High Post, and built up a large training fleet, mainly of Tiger Moths, together with a few Proctors. It also undertook conversions of Tigers into four-seat Thruxton Jackaroos, eighteen of which were built by the school's subsidiary Jackaroo Aircraft, between 1957 and 1960. The company also planned to manufacture a new design, the Paragon, but this never passed the mock-up stage. The Wiltshire School of Flying continued to operate from Thruxton until 1967 when Western Air Training took over the airfield.

Motorcycle racing started at Thruxton in 1950, using the airfield's perimeter track, followed by car racing two years later. In 1967 British Racing Circuits took over motor-racing activities at Thruxton, and that winter laid a new 2.4-mile track; this was ready in time for the 1968 Easter Monday International Formula 2 race, which included well-known drivers such as Jackie Stewart and Graham Hill. The circuit has been continually improved over the years and is considered by many to be the fastest track in the UK today; its calendar currently includes the British Touring Car Championships, Formula 3, Superbike and truck racing.

Jackaroo Aircraft had used the old RAF technical site to the south of the airfield, and other light engineering companies have since been based there, including Norton-Villiers Motorcycles and John Edgeley Engineering. Facilities on the airfield itself have been steadily improved, with seven new hangars having been erected for its users since 1976. Activities have included parachuting, from 1973 to 1987, and gliding, from 1977 to 1996.

The airfield became the centre of Operation *Comeback* in 1988. This was a joint HM Customs/Police/RAF surveillance operation to combat a gang planning to smuggle drugs into the UK by helicopter. The gang's Gazelle collected its cargo in Holland and, returning to its base at Thruxton on 4 September, dropped off the drugs in nearby Harewood Forest. Unfortunately for them they were shadowed by two Pumas of 33 Squadron, RAF Odiham, one of which landed Customs officials to arrest the reception party before joining the other to follow the Gazelle. After a high speed cross-country pursuit the Gazelle was forced down at Hurn. Eight gang members were arrested and cannabis worth £800,000 seized.

MBB105 G-NAAB, the Hampshire & Isle of Wight Air Ambulance, at readiness at Thruxton in April 2009.

Western Air Training and British Racing Circuits were merged to form Western Air (Thruxton) Ltd, which took over the operation in 1998 to ensure its continued joint development as race-track and airfield. Thruxton's main E-W runway was partly resurfaced in 1990 to give a usable length of 2,340 feet, and again in 2008, with significant under- and over-runs, together with upgraded lighting. A secondary grass runway of 2,250 feet is also maintained. The main operators from the airfield today are Western Air Flying School (and Flying Club), using four PA23 Warriors, a Firefly, PA28 Archer and Twin Cougar to give flying training up to Flying Instructor and Commercial Pilot level. Other operators include Fast Helicopters, providing flying training and charter, Geminair Services on aerial survey and charter work, and the Hampshire Air Ambulance, flying an MBB105 helicopter, replaced by a Eurocopter EC135 in 2009. Other activities on the airfield include helicopter maintenance, airframe finishing and aircraft restoration.

Many of RAF Thruxton's original buildings remain in use today, including the control tower, T2 hangar, Robin hangar and several Nissen and Maycrete buildings on the old technical site and around the airfield.

Main features:
Runways: 257° 4,680ft x 150ft, 315° 3450ft x 150ft, 020° 3,000ft x 150ft, concrete, tar and wood-chippings. *Hangars:* one T2, nine Blister, one Bessoneau. *Hardstandings:* six Blenheim, twenty-three frying pan. *Accommodation:* RAF Officers 56, SNCOs 122, ORs 946.

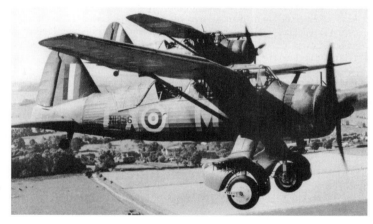

Lysander II N1256 of 225 Squadron, flying from Tilshead in July 1940.

TILSHEAD, Wiltshire

SU021478, 1 mile W of village

Several locations in the Tilshead area of Salisbury Plain have been linked with aviation over the years. The first was an outstation of No 1 Balloon School, RFC Rollestone, set up in 1916. Established on the road between the village and West Down Camp, the two balloons based there were often being taken through the village fully inflated for launch. A field three-quarters of a mile north-west of the village was also used for training during October and November 1918 by RAF artillery observation aircraft.

In 1925 an LG was established on downland half a mile to the west of the village for the use of army cooperation aircraft on exercises. One of the first of these was 13 Squadron, flying the Atlas, and later 16 Squadron (also based at Old Sarum), which flew Bristol Fighters, Atlas, Audax and Lysanders from the field, on short detachments.

The first squadron to be actually based at Tilshead was 225 Squadron, which moved in from Old Sarum with its twelve Lysanders on 1 July 1940. A tented camp was erected for the unit's twenty-eight officers and 355 men, and with two AA gun posts the area became known as Tilshead Lodge Camp.

From here the unit resumed dawn and dusk anti-invasion patrols, looking for signs of enemy activity along the South Coast from St Albans Head to Selsey Bill. Later these patrols were extended westwards and around the Cornish coast, on detachment to Roborough, using St Eval for refuelling.

A Lysander was attacked by an He 111 on 29 July while flying near Weymouth, but escaped in cloud. More serious were the events of 13 August, when another He 111 was spotted near Tilshead. As it ran in over the landing ground, dropping five bombs, it was engaged by AA guns and the rear gunners of two parked Lysanders. A couple of unoccupied tents were destroyed and some huts hit, and although two Lysanders and a Tiger Moth were damaged by shell splinters and machine-gun fire, there were no casualties.

In mid-September 225 Squadron's A Flight was posted to Hatfield to become the nucleus of 239 Squadron, which formed there on the 18th. The aircrew were probably glad to be leaving their tents, which had started leaking due to heavy rain, Tilshead Lodge being commandeered on the 25th to provide dry accommodation. Lysander Mk IIIs started to arrive five days later as the patrol continued. A detachment of 16 Squadron Lysanders arrived from Weston Zoyland for a short detachment in October to carry out army cooperation exercises; these also gradually became the main work for 225 Squadron, and took it as far afield as Okehampton and Staverton. During May 1941 a large exercise simulated an invasion in the Weymouth area, and for three days the Lysanders flew tactical and photo reconnaissance sorties. Eight Lysanders and a Gladiator from 239 Squadron arrived from Gatwick on 24 May to carry out air-firing and bombing on the nearby ranges, and 16 Squadron made another detachment in July for more exercises.

Accommodation at Tilshead was barely improved during 1941. The personnel of 225 Squadron must therefore have been very pleased to receive notice of posting to Thruxton in late July, packing their tents and leaving for their new home in early August. No other units were based at Tilshead, although the LG was used by further exercise detachments until the end of the year when it was handed over to the Army to become part of an enlarged Salisbury Plain range area.

Three SSZ airships at Toller in October 1918.

TOLLER, Dorset

SY540980, 10 miles EWE of Bridport

Part of the network of RNAS airship bases built along the South Coast, Toller sub-station was built during the spring of 1918 and commissioned later in the year by 9 Group, Plymouth. Situated in woodland north-west of Gray's Farm, 1 1/2 miles west of Toller Porcorum, the moorings were well protected from prevailing winds. They were usually occupied by an SS Zero non-rigid airship, on detachment from Mullion on coastal patrols. Toller-based Zero SSZ45 force-landed near Bridport in July 1918, as did SSZ14 in October. SSZ27 was in residence at the end of the war and was deflated at Toller on 3 December 1918. The sub-station was deactivated later in the month, and abandoned in 1919.

Short 184 N9074 of 418 Flight being lifted by the pier crane at RNAS Torquay in 1918.

TORQUAY, Devon

SX919632, near town centre, off A379

When it opened early in 1918, RNAS Torquay completed the chain of flying boat, airship and floatplane bases that stretched out to the Isles of Scilly to cover convoys in the South West Approaches, protecting them mainly from U-boat attacks. Situated in the harbour between South and Haldon Piers, it was one of the most sheltered of the many such bases along the coast of Britain, although entering and leaving the harbour through the narrow gap in the breakwater could be hazardous.

Twelve Short 184 floatplanes were allocated to the base. To house them four small Seaplane Sheds and three Bessoneau hangars were erected, but the site was dominated by a Balloon Shed to house visiting airships, maintained by a detachment from No 16 Balloon Base, Merrifield. Crew rooms, stores and offices were provided on site, but all domestic accommodation was requisitioned in the town, such as the Sea Haven Hotel.

Although a slipway was provided, the floatplanes were usually lowered into the water by crane. Space was at a premium, and only six Short 184s could practicably be based at Torquay, these being taken on charge by 418 (Seaplane) Flight, RAF, when it formed on 15 June 1918. The flight was absorbed by 239 Squadron, which formed at Torquay on 20 August as part of 72 Wing, 4 (Operations) Group. The unit flew largely uneventful patrols for the rest of the war. A second unit, 419 (Seaplane) Flight, was formed on 15 November by 239 Squadron, but by this time hostilities had ended and the unit was transferred to Dundee as part of 249 Squadron.

Eventually flying stopped from RAF Torquay, and on 15 May No 249 Squadron, together with 418 Flight, was disbanded, and the site declared surplus. The slipway was briefly used by Avro 504 floatplane operators to give pleasure flights in the early 1920s. During the Second World War the high-speed ASR launches of 39 Marine Craft Unit were based in Torquay harbour.

Townsend in August 1941 – two Wellingtons can be seen dispersed under the trees.

TOWNSEND, Wiltshire

SU070725, half a mile NE of Yatesbury

A single-runway RLG was established at Townsend in 1938 by 10 E&RFTS, Yatesbury, for forced-landing practice by its Tiger Moths. When the school moved to Weston-super-Mare on 7 September 1940, Townsend was taken over by 10 MU, Hullavington, for aircraft storage; the first arrivals, three Bothas and a Wellington, were received on 29 September. The airfield was titled 45 SLG but, with waterlogging becoming a problem, little use was made of it by 10 MU. In September 1941 aircraft in storage were transferred to other sites and the SLG was closed.

In early April 1942 Townsend was reopened and control transferred to 33 MU, Lyneham, with local defence being provided by troops of the Wiltshire Regiment. Shortly afterwards four Wellingtons arrived, and by the end of the month sixteen aircraft were on site. In July 1942 work on a second runway started and the site was generally improved with the laying of tarmac to improve access to the dispersals. Storage capacity was increased to seventy-six, actual holdings being thirty-three at the end of August, mostly Spitfires and Wellingtons.

Plans were made in the autumn of 1942 to expand usage to take four-engined aircraft, and in September the RLG was transferred to 15 MU, Wroughton. However, shortly afterwards HQ 41 Group, Maintenance Command, ordered that Townsend should be closed. By the end of October all aircraft had been removed and the RLG was never again used for storage.

With the departure of the MU, Townsend was once again used as an RLG, by the pilots of 2 RS Yatesbury for forced-landing practice, as well as by 2 EFTS when it was reformed at Yatesbury in July 1945. When the EFTS departed in 1947, the RLG, no longer needed, was de-requisitioned and soon returned to agriculture. Little sign of it remains today.

The quadrant tower at Treligga in February 1981.

TRELIGGA, Cornwall

SX047848, 1½ miles W of Delabole

First used as a gliding site before the war, Treligga was requisitioned by the Admiralty in March 1940 and laid out as an air-to-surface firing range. Ground targets were placed on the cliffs between Start Point and Tregannick Tail, and inland from the Tail towards Treligga village three rough grass landing strips were marked out to cater for emergency landings by aircraft suffering engine failure or ricochet damage. The only buildings were a tall brick observation tower and quadrant hut in the centre of the range, and living quarters just north of the village.

As a satellite site of RNAS St Merryn the range was named HMS *Vulture II*, and was staffed almost entirely by the WRNS, some twenty girls being accommodated locally in Port Isaac. They operated the quadrant equipment to record the angle of dives and accuracy of aircraft using the range. These included the Fulmars, Hurricanes and Martlets of the Fighter Pool Squadron (No 748) and Seafires and Barracudas of 736 Squadron (the School of Air Combat). Numerous operational units detached to St Merryn also used the facility, and one day in 1944 a B-17 circled the range before putting down on the airstrip; when the Americans stepped out of the aircraft they were no doubt surprised and delighted to find the place staffed by young ladies!

With the increased involvement of the FAA in the Pacific in 1944, Treligga range was reconfigured to simulate Japanese-held territory, modelled on the island of Tarawa, and tanks, bridges and road convoys were provided as targets. After the war the range was in great demand by the School of Naval Air Warfare and by squadrons detached to St Merryn for armament practice. As naval use declined in the early 1950s it was made available to the RAF, and was used mainly by Coastal Command Shackleton squadrons for gunnery practice. With the withdrawal of flying units from St Merryn the range was closed at the end of 1955 and soon reverted to farmland. Today only the quadrant tower remains, standing alone in the middle of a large field.

Main features:
Runways: 045° 2,100ft x 300ft, 105° 2,190ft x 300ft, 165° 2,400ft x 300ft, grass.

Curtiss H12 8662 on its beaching trolley at Tresco in 1917.

TRESCO, Isles of Scilly

SV890149, half a mile S of New Grimsby, Tresco

In an early attempt to provide air cover over the South West Approaches, Short 184 floatplanes were detached to the Isles of Scilly in 1916. They suffered from the weather in their exposed anchorages in St Mary's Roads, and after a brief stay were withdrawn.

Increased shipping losses to U-boats prompted the Admiralty to pursue the idea of an air base in Scilly, and in January 1917 an advance party set up at Porth Mellon (SV908197). By 28 February four Curtiss H12 flyboats were on station, and one of these flew the first operational patrol that day. However, Porth Mellon was found to be too exposed, and when a more suitable location was found on the western side of Tresco, work started on a new base. A rectangular piece of low-lying land covering some 20 acres was requisitioned at New Grimsby, between Hacket Town Lane and the shoreline. A rudimentary flying boat station had been established there by February 1917, consisting of a Bessoneau hangar, slipway, a few wooden buildings and some tents. Personnel were ferried across from St Mary's daily to operate the six H12s on the station's strength.

During the early summer of 1917 No 1 Air Construction Section, RNAS, moved in to build a dispersed hutted camp, together with workshops, flight offices and wooden hangars on the main base. The hangars were used while work continued on two steel-framed seaplane sheds, and an improved slipway was built for the launch and retrieval of flying boats with a track-mounted trolley. A small floating dock was later provided for work on the two Short 184 floatplanes that were added to the station's fleet, and an area to the south-east was laid out to receive visiting airships.

Curtiss H12 8656 sighted a U-boat on 27 May 1917, and attacked it with two 100lb bombs, which hit just forward of the conning tower. The boat sank at a 60-degree angle, its stern coming right out of the water. Two days later the same aircraft attacked another U-boat with four 100-pounders, resulting in a large oil slick appearing on the surface. More action came on 25 June when the crew of 8665 spotted a surfaced U-boat some 10 miles distant. As the flying boat approached, the sub crash-dived, three 100lb bombs dropped on the spot resulting in a huge disturbance on the surface. Further sightings and attacks followed in August and October 1917.

Mishaps were only too common. H12 8652 had to be beached at Newlyn when it started to sink while landing in Mounts Bay on 11 March 1917, and during a gale on 9 May H12 8664

Tresco in 1918, showing workshops in the foreground opposite the main flying boat hangar.

crashed and exploded off Gugh Island, Scilly, its three-man crew being killed. On 5 June H12 8654 landed off Trevose Head near Padstow in the fog; incredibly the aircraft was retrieved by being towed the whole distance back to Tresco, with only minimal damage. The weather was often challenging; gales were a hazard, and on 16 December the wind reached 100mph, lifting three picketed H16s like playthings, smashing them on the beach.

Felixstowe F2A flying boats were received in February 1918, followed by the improved F3. One of the latter, N4341, was patrolling on 10 May when a U-boat crash-dived before the aircraft could reach it, but two 230lb bombs were dropped ahead of its wake, and the area searched. The boat, U-103, escaped, but was later sunk by RMS *Olympic* and its commander captured. During interrogation he produced a fragment of one of N4341's bombs, which had lodged in the submarine casing.

It was intended that twelve F3s be stationed at Tresco, but this was never achieved. Nevertheless a number of units were formed there: first came 250 (Flying Boat) Flight RAF on 31 May 1918, followed by 351 Flight on 30 June, and both were absorbed by 234 Squadron when it formed on 20 August. The Squadron later formed two more flights, Nos 352 and 353, on 15 and 30 September respectively; all came under the command of 71 Wing, Penzance, part of 9 Group, Plymouth.

Searches for missing ships were made and the flying boats sometimes went looking for lost Short 184s, though Atlantic swells gave the latter little chance if they were forced down at sea. Short N2963 was lost in this way on 6 July, and it was September before the body of its W/T Operator was washed ashore near Ushant. Flying boats were not immune to damage either, particularly on take-off, when heavily loaded machines suffered 'bouncing'. A series of bounces resulted in the hull of F3 N4000 caving in on 7 August 1918, and it was beached on Samson; N4001 was not so lucky when it crashed outside the harbour on 22 August.

The last of the thirteen attacks made by Tresco-based aircraft occurred on 11 October 1918, when the crew of H12 N4341 sighted a wake 4 miles ahead of convoy HH71. As usual the submarine dived before the Curtiss could reach the spot, but bombs were dropped anyway. The last wartime patrol from Tresco, a convoy escort, was made on 10 November. Activity then reduced, ceasing on 15 May 1919 when 234 Squadron was disbanded, together with its constituent flights.

The air station was closed, but Scilly remained on the reserve list of flying boat moorings. The Seaplane Development Flight visited the islands in August 1927; this mixed group of flying boats included the new Short Cromarty, which successfully rode out a storm off St Mary's, only to have its bottom torn out when it was taxied onto rocks. Little use was then made of the Scilly moorings until

Felixstowe F3 N4415 outside the hangar in 1918, with the main workshops behind.

the Second World War, when it again became a useful flying boat base. Between 1941 and 1944 detachments of 201, 204, 228 and 10 (RAAF) Squadrons based Sunderlands at St Mary's. Several aircraft were damaged and two were lost in the sudden gales that are a feature of the Isles of Scilly. Sunderland RB-B of 10 (RAAF) Squadron was lucky, however, having force-landed with engine problems on 24 June 1942. It was brought up onto Town Beach and, after being patched up, was towed by Launch RML542 all the way to Mount Batten for repair.

The original RNAS power house still stands on Tresco, together with a number of re-roofed huts. The hangar foundations are in use for farm buildings, but the remains of the slipway have all but gone. Today it is hard to imagine that it was once a busy flying boat base.

UPAVON, Wiltshire

SU152542, 1½ miles SE of village

Upavon, on the edge of Salisbury Plain, is another long-established Wiltshire airfield. In the spring of 1912 it was selected as the site for an airfield on which to base a Central Flying School to train pilots for the Naval and Military Wings of the new Royal Flying Corps.

Formed on 12 May 1912, the CFS opened for flying training on 19 June, with a modest collection of buildings housing seven aeroplanes. The original airfield, built to the south of the main Andover-Upavon road, was provided with eight coupled aircraft sheds, and three larger single sheds were added shortly afterwards. The main camp was to the north of the road and on its eastern edge another landing ground was laid out with six paired aircraft sheds, extending the airfield to a total of 3,324 acres.

No 1 CFS Course started on 17 August 1912, one of its students being Major Hugh Trenchard, later to become 'Father of the Royal Air Force'. Within two years the school had trained ninety-three pilots, but when war was declared on 4 August 1914 almost all of its aircraft and pilots prepared to go to France. The CFS then became a combined advanced flying school and operational conversion unit, with preliminary flying training being provided at Netheravon and Brooklands. Aircraft types flown by the CFS were originally Avro 500s, BE2As, BE4s, Short S27s, Henry Farmans and Maurice Farmans, later supplemented by BE2Bs and BE8s. By early 1916 most of the early types had been replaced by Avro 504Ks, FE8s, Gunbuses and DH2s. An Experimental Flight had been formed in November 1914 to evaluate new aircraft – such as the BE2E and BE12 – but also captured enemy types, together with their weapons. It became the Aeroplane & Armament Experimental Establishment when it moved to Martlesham Heath in January 1917.

Shorthorn No 420 at CFS Upavon on 6 February 1913, with Major Gerrard at the controls.

Several units appeared at Upavon in 1917. On 1 July No 73 Squadron was formed from a nucleus provided by B Flight CFS, moving to Lilbourne eight days later to receive Camels. On 2 July No 72 Squadron formed from A Flight CFS, leaving for Netheravon six days later to receive Pups. It was followed by 85 Squadron, formed from C Flight CFS on 1 August, which went to Norwich on 10 August, then Hounslow, where it got the SE5A. By the spring of 1918 the CFS was producing more than fifty pilots per month for the front-line units. It then had four squadrons – A with SE5s, B with Camels (later supplemented by Dolphins and Snipes), and C and D with Avro 504Ks. Later that year it became responsible for training all flying instructors for RAF flying schools, enabling a standardised training system to be evolved.

BE2As (No 447 nearest) and Shorthorns (including No 431) lined up outside Upavon's hangars in mid-1914, ready for flying.

Bulldogs (J9560 closest to the camera, being refuelled) of 17 Squadron at Upavon in 1932.

Confusion followed the Armistice, with wholesale demobilisation and no clear plan for the future of training. The CFS was disbanded towards the end of 1919 to become the Flying Instructors School, but reformed on 26 April the following year to train instructors on the Avro 504K and Snipe. On 1 April 1924 No 9 Squadron reformed at Upavon for night home defence duties. It received two Vimy bombers before leaving for Manston at the end of the month, exchanging places with 3 Squadron, also formed on 1 April but as a night-fighter squadron with Snipes; it received Woodcocks in May 1925.

A CFS Fury, Tutor, Hart, Oxford and Anson formation near Upavon in 1938.

The CFS transferred to Wittering on 7 October 1926, and its place was taken a week later by another Woodcock unit, 17 Squadron, from Hawkinge. Later receiving the Gamecock, Siskin (17 Squadron only) and Bulldog, Nos 3 and 17 Squadrons operated from Upavon for some time as the only night-fighter units in the RAF. When both moved to Kenley on 10 May 1934 Upavon was allocated to the FAA. The Seals of 821 Squadron arrived on 14 July, and were joined by 801 Squadron with Nimrods in November. Both units (together with 820 Squadron and its Sharks briefly in July/August 1934) used Upavon as a shore base between carrier embarkations until August 1935.

On 1 September Upavon was transferred to 23 (Training) Group, and the CFS returned to its old station. The trusty Avro 504N was replaced by the Tutor, with Hart Trainers and Furies supplemented by a few Ansons for twin-engined training, until Oxfords arrived in November 1937. Handling Flight was formed within the CFS on 8 December 1938 to evaluate new types coming into service, also producing 'Pilots Notes' on each one – which were to become invaluable aircrew aids.

Work started in 1938 on improvements to the station, which still consisted mainly of 1914-18 wooden huts, although the original hangars on the main airfield had been replaced in the 1920s by two A Types. A single C hangar was built alongside them, and another, smaller C Type Aircraft Repair Shed erected on the northern airfield. Workshops, airmen's dining hall, three barrack blocks and married quarters were also constructed during this phase. A Lorenz Blind Approach system was laid out three-quarters of a mile to the east of the main airfield, on Upavon Down, using a separate 3,900-foot grass runway, which, although completed by August 1939, was not brought into use until the following year.

With the declaration of war all aircraft were dispersed and guarded at night by armed RAF personnel. Pillboxes were built, station buildings camouflaged and a Spitfire allocated as Station Defence Flight. Training went on as usual, although some of the courses were cut short due to the demand for new instructors and the appalling weather during that first wartime winter – flying ceased completely for a fortnight early in February 1940 due to heavy frost. The fall of France in May resulted in the arming of training aircraft to repel a possible invasion, with CFS aircraft, including its new Harvards, carrying 20lb bombs on underwing racks. On 14 August 1940 Heinkel He 111s of KG55 raided Upavon, but without damage; one, flown by the Gruppe's Kommodore, was shot down at Dean Hill, to the east of Salisbury, and three aboard were killed, including the pilot.

Magister N3838, Oxford DF233 and Master III W8962 of 7 FIS(A), Upavon, in formation passing over an SLG in 1943.

Both airfields were in constant daytime use by Masters and Oxfords during 1940, although much of the night-flying practice took place at RLGs established at Overton Heath and New Zealand Farm. Handling Flight had left for Boscombe Down in October 1940, which eased congestion. Use of the northern airfield was restricted from 1941, probably for safety reasons, but by the end of that year intensive flying had resulted in heavy rutting of the main airfield. A Sommerfield track runway of 3,000 feet was therefore laid in February 1942, later extended to 3,750 feet, and a tarmac perimeter track added. Ten Blister hangars were erected around the southern margins of the main airfield for additional storage and servicing.

Following a reorganisation and establishment of the Empire Central Flying School at Hullavington, the CFS was disbanded on 1 April 1942 and re-titled as No 7 FIS. It started with OTU instructor courses, using Oxfords and Masters, and when in August the school was re-titled 7 FIS(A) Magisters replaced Masters in its 120-strong fleet. Courses increased to meet the demand for more instructors and beam approach training was stepped up with the formation of 1537 BAT Flight in April 1943, using Oxfords. The FIS and BAT Flight remained in operation at Upavon throughout the rest of the war, finally moving to Little Rissington in May 1946 to become part of the re-established CFS.

Upavon then became the home of 38 Group, Transport Command, which moved from Netheravon, airfield activity then being confined to the Group's Communications Flight and visitors. In October 1948 No 2 Wing RAF Regiment formed at Upavon as HQ for two Light AA Squadrons and a Parachute Squadron. In February 1950 No 38 Group was disbanded and in its place came HQ Transport Command from Bushey Park.

No 38 Group reappeared once again at Upavon when it was reformed in 1960; however, due to a shortage of accommodation it moved shortly afterwards to Odiham. In 1965 a new building was opened alongside the main road (next to the original CFS HQ of 1912) to house HQ Transport Command, re-titled Air Support Command in August 1967. Further changes in August 1972 resulted in Air Support being merged into Strike Command, and 46 Group being formed at Upavon to control the strategic transport force, complementing 38 Group, which controlled tactical airlift.

No 46 Group was merged into 38 Group when it returned to Upavon in November 1975 as the largest Group in the RAF. Flying during this time was by Transport Command Communications Squadron, which formed as a flight in May 1946 with Ansons, later Devons, becoming a squadron in 1960. In April 1964 it was disbanded into the Western Communications Squadron at Andover, but a detachment remained at Upavon. This covered Air Support Command from August 1967, and its successor, 21 Squadron, continued from 1969 until 1976. Gliders took the place of Devons and Pembrokes in Upavon's hangars when 622 GS moved in from Old Sarum in 1978.

Upavon continued as a Group HQ until the early 1990s, when Strike Command at High Wycombe assumed responsibility for all transport aircraft activities. In July 1993, there being no longer a need for Upavon as a Group HQ by the RAF, the station was transferred to the Army. Today, as Trenchard Lines, it is an Army HQ, housing a number of units including the Provost Marshal's

A Viking of 622 VGS taking off at the end of a winch-cable in September 2003, with Upavon's hangars (two Type A and a Type C) in the background.

Department, the Adjutant General's Department, and HQ of the Army Recruiting & Training Division, although there are plans to relocate some of these to another ex-RAF station, Andover.

Many historic buildings remain at Upavon. As well as Trenchard's CFS HQ, the RFC Officers' Mess, several RFC bungalows and the 'mini' Type C Aircraft Repair Shed (in use as a gym) still stand on the north site. On the airfield the 1926 watch office is still in place, although its 1961 successor was removed in 2007. The C Type and two A Type hangars still stand at the time of writing, but, having been inadequately maintained, are due for demolition. Apart from the occasional Hercules dropping in during the week, the airfield is in regular use at the weekends by 622 VGS, which flies Air Cadets in Viking T1 winch-launched gliders, and the Army's Wyvern Gliding Club.

Main features:
Runways: 240° 3,750ft, Sommerfield track, E-W 3390ft, N-S 1,875ft, NE-SW 3,900ft, grass; beam strip adjacent to main airfield 035°, 3,900ft, grass. *Hangars:* two Type A, one Type C1, one GS Aeroplane Shed, one 'mini' Type C, ten Blister. *Accommodation:* RAF Officers 142, SNCOs 216, ORs 529; WAAF Officers 6, SNCOs 8, ORs 344.

Upottery in June 1944, showing C-47s and CG-4As dispersed around its perimeter. The bomb-dump can be seen in the foreground.

UPOTTERY, Devon

ST188101, half a mile SW of Smeathorpe

Also known as Smeathorpe, the airfield of Upottery had a short career, culminating in one momentous event – D-Day. Built in a typical three-runway layout, it was specifically intended for use by the USAAF, originally as a medium bomber base. It was therefore given a large number of loop dispersals and an extensive bomb dump, but only two T2 hangars. The domestic sites of Nissen and Maycrete buildings were dispersed to the north-east. Upottery opened as USAAF Station 462 on 17 February 1944, and it was transports, not bombers, that arrived on 26 April, when the C-47 Skytrains and C-53 Skytroopers of the 439th Troop Carrier Group flew in from Balderton. Consisting of the 91st, 92nd, 93rd and 94th Troop Carrier Squadrons, the group formed part of the 50th Troop Carrier Wing, IXth Troop Carrier Command. Their training continued at Upottery, practising paratroop-dropping and glider-towing with CG-4As and Horsas.

Preserved C-47 43-15211, originally flown from Upottery by Col C. H. Young, OC of the 439th TCG, on D-Day operations, re-visits the airfield in June 2007.

On the night of 5 June the group, led by Colonel C. H. Young, took off for Normandy. The formation of eighty-one Skytrains carried paratroops of the 101st Airborne Division to a DZ near St Mere Eglise, including men of the 506th Parachute Infantry Regiment, whose exploits would be related in Stephen Ambrose's book *Band of Brothers* and the resulting TV series. Heavy ground fire was encountered over Normandy, three Upottery aircraft failing to return. The following day reinforcements were flown in by the group, fifty C-47s towing thirty Horsas and twenty CG-4As. A series of re-supply missions was then flown, beachhead landing strips being used as soon as they became available, and wounded being brought back on return flights. In July the 91st, 92nd and 94th TCSs were sent to Italy to take part in the landings in southern France, leaving the 93rd to maintain the re-supply. The group was reunited in late August, but on 8 September began moving out again, this time to northern France.

The station came under RAF control in October 1944 but was little used until 7 November, when USN PB4Y Liberators from Dunkeswell moved in temporarily while the runways at their base were being resurfaced. Early in January 1945 more USN Liberators arrived, this time from the 107th and 112th Patrol Bomber Squadrons, which took up residence to fly anti-submarine patrols over the eastern Atlantic and Bay of Biscay. U-boat sightings were few and only one attack was made. The units remained until June when they returned to the USA via St Mawgan.

Upottery was taken over by 19 Group at the end of July, but soon transferred to 40 Group, Maintenance Command. Then 265 MU, Collaton Cross, and 225 MU, Warminster, used it for storage, as did 267 MU, Dunkeswell, which took over the site in November 1946. The station was finally closed in November 1948, and soon returned to agriculture.

Upottery airfield is still much in evidence, the control tower and several other buildings still standing. The runways and taxiways survived into the 21st century when work started on breaking them up. Enough of the main runway remained in 2007 to allow Col Young's former C-47, now preserved in the UK, to revisit the airfield.

Main features:
Runways: 270° 6,000ft x 150ft, 210° 4,200ft x 150ft, 330° 4,200ft x 150ft, concrete and tarmac. *Hangars:* two Type T2. *Hardstandings:* fifty spectacle. *Accommodation:* RAF Officers 124, SNCOs 660, ORs 1,396; WAAF Officers 6, SNCOs 18, ORs 300.

UPTON, Dorset

SY990930, 2 miles NW of Poole on minor road off A35

Opened in 1918 just west of Upton House on the Llewellin Estate near Poole, this airship sub-station was built as a mooring-out base for SS Zero non-rigid airships on detachment from Mullion. Although the main site was exposed, some protection was provided by surrounding trees. Had Moreton become operational, Upton would no doubt have been transferred to its control; however, after the Armistice Upton was soon abandoned.

Hurricane IIC of 402 Squadron being bombed up at Warmwell in February 1942.

WARMWELL (WOODSFORD), Dorset

SY760885, 3¹/₂ miles SE of Dorchester

Built for a secondary role, the airfield at Warmwell was later to prove useful as an operational base. It was originally selected as a landing ground for fighter squadrons using the ranges at Chesil Bank, 10 miles to the south off the Dorset coast. The 300-acre airfield was opened with basic facilities on 1 May 1937 as RAF Woodsford, after the nearby village. Its first resident was 6 Armament Training Camp, which flew Tutors and Wallaces to provide target facilities for visiting units. The first of these were the Ansons of 206 and 220 Squadrons, which arrived in July for a coastal defence exercise. They were followed by a stream of other front-line squadrons using the ranges, joined from January 1938 by detachments from various FTSs. On 1 April No 6 ATC was re-titled 6 Armament Training Station, and received more aircraft, including Henleys and Gladiators. To avoid confusion with Woodford, Manchester, the airfield was renamed Warmwell in July 1938, when Auxiliary Air Force Summer Camps were well under way. An admin site was built on the eastern side of the airfield together with two small hangars, and a technical site to the south, based on two Bellman hangars.

During the Munich Crisis of October 1938 Ansons of 217 Squadron were deployed from Tangmere for two weeks to fly coastal patrols. On 25 August 1939 they returned and resumed patrols from Warmwell until moving on to St Eval in early October. On the eve of the declaration of war, 6 ATS was disbanded and merged with 2 AOS Acklington to become 10 AOS at Warmwell, using Harrows Overstrands and Henleys; it was re-designated 10 Bombing & Gunnery School on 1 January 1940.

As training intensified the Central Gunnery School was formed at Warmwell on 6 November to train gunnery instructors; initially flying Battles, Blenheims, Masters and Lysanders, the school started its first course a week later.

The fall of France in June 1940 made the South Coast vulnerable to German attack, but Warmwell was in a good position to provide fighter cover over the Channel and the naval base at Portland. It was therefore transferred to 11 Group Fighter Command as a satellite for Y Sector Airfield Middle Wallop. To make room for the fighters, 10 B&GS was moved to Dumfries on 13 July.

The Spitfire Is of 609 Squadron had transferred to Middle Wallop on 6 July, and immediately began deployments to Warmwell. They flew over in the morning to tented dispersals on the north side of the airfield and remained on 15-minute readiness throughout the day, returning home before dusk. Their first engagement came on 9 July when three Spitfires of B Flight on patrol off Weymouth were vectored onto a formation of Ju 87s. One dive-bomber, flown by the Staffelkapitan of I/StG77, was shot down by Fg Off Crook, but B Flight was jumped by the fighter escort and Fg Off Drummond-Hay was lost over the sea. The intended attack on Portland was, however, broken up and Warmwell had shown its value as a forward base. Unfortunately on the 11th two pilots were lost while protecting a convoy, but on the 13th two Bf 110s fell to the Squadron over Portland Bill.

On 12 July No 152 Squadron, the first full fighter unit to be based at Warmwell, arrived from Acklington with Spitfire Is, and was covered by 609 Squadron while it settled in. Its first operational sorties were flown on 19 July, but the unit suffered its first loss the following day when Plt Off Posener was shot down off the Isle of Wight. Retribution came five days later when a Ju 87 and Do 17 were claimed by Plt Off Wolton, the latter shared with Fg Off Deanesley.

10 Group, newly formed at Rudloe Manor, took over Middle Wallop and its satellite on 4 August. By then eight Blister hangars had been built around Warmwell's perimeter to provide servicing facilities, together with eighteen dispersals. Physical protection was given by six double fighter pens and twelve single pens.

The Luftwaffe kept pressing the British defences, and on 18 August more than a hundred Ju 87s escorted by Bf 109s, attacked Ford, Thorney Island and Gosport. As they withdrew across the Isle of Wight 152 Squadron's Spitfires caught up and claimed eight Ju 87s and a Bf 109. However, on 25 August the Luftwaffe finally managed to penetrate Warmwell. As a large formation of Ju 88s (of II/KG51 and II/KG54) escorted by Bf 110s (of I/ZG2, II/ZG2 and V/LG1) approached Weymouth Bay, it split into three, then made for Portland, Weymouth and Warmwell. Twelve Spitfires of 152 Squadron took off, but it was the Hurricanes of 17 Squadron, Tangmere, that broke up the formation heading for Warmwell. Although only seven Ju 88s got through, they hit the sick quarters and two hangars on the technical site. Nine UXBs caused more problems as they were dropped in the camp area, the last not being detonated until the 27th. Despite this there were no casualties and 152 Squadron claimed three kills and a probable off Portland for the loss of two Spitfires.

The long hot summer of 1940 dragged on with the Warmwell Spitfires in action from Bristol to Bognor Regis, and invasion jitters reaching a peak on 9 September when all defences were manned following a warning from Sector at Middle Wallop. The whole of 609 Squadron moved to Warmwell on 2 October, but had to live under canvas in appalling weather – on more than one occasion the operations marquee and crew tents were blown down. The Squadron made few interceptions during this period and was probably very glad to leave for the comforts of Biggin Hill in February 1941. It was replaced by 234 Squadron with Spitfire Is from St Eval, which flew convoy patrols and bomber escorts.

When the Luftwaffe resumed bombing it was in small numbers, usually at low level. Typical were the single Ju 88 that dropped four bombs on Warmwell on 26 March, and the three He 111s that appeared at low level over the airfield at midday on 1 April. The station workshops received a direct hit in this surprise attack and most of the seven killed and eighteen injured were in this area although a 152 Squadron pilot was killed by a stray bullet while eating lunch in the Sergeants' Mess. Four nights later the Q site at Knighton, $2^1/2$ miles away, was bombed and, with the increase in Luftwaffe activity, it was decided to disperse all non-essential personnel at night. Two attacks on the airfield by single aircraft in May were met with heavy AA fire from the strengthened defences, but the second resulted in a Wellington and Hampden of the CGS being destroyed and the airfield heavily cratered. The heaviest and last raid of all came on 11 May when the alert lasted most of the night; eight aircraft dropped nine bombs, which exploded harmlessly to the north.

No 152 Squadron had left for Portreath on 9 April and the longer-serving resident, the CGS, vacated Warmwell on 23 June for Castle Kennedy. This left the airfield largely free for a new activity, fighter sweeps. The first of these was on 10 July, when twelve bombers escorted by three fighter squadrons left Warmwell to attack radar stations in France. Hurricanes appeared in early September 1941, in the hands of 302 (Poznan) Squadron flying in the fighter-bomber role. The Poles made offensive sweeps over Normandy and Brittany, staying for five weeks. On 5 November the Spitfires of 234 Squadron left for Ibsley, replaced by more Hurricanes – this time flown by Canadians, of 402 (RCAF) Squadron.

During the autumn it had been decided to reopen Chesil Ranges, and 1487 (Target Towing) Flight was formed at Warmwell on 30 October with Lysanders. Units started to arrive for gunnery practice, led by 32 Squadron, which spent five days early in November on this vital practice with its Hurricane IIBs. More Lysanders arrived in January 1942, this time with 276 Squadron, on ASR; based at Harrowbeer, the unit set up several detached flights at other forward airfields. Just as 402 Squadron was leaving for Colerne on 3 March, another Hurricane Squadron, No 175, was forming at Warmwell. After working up for five weeks the unit was declared operational, and flew its first bombing mission, against Maupertas airfield, on 16 April. It was then engaged mainly on shipping strikes, sinking two minesweepers off Cap de la Hague on 15 May. This work continued until the morning of 19 August, when the Squadron took part in Operation *Jubilee*, the Dieppe raid.

Eight Hurricanes of 175 Squadron took off at 0440 led by Sqn Ldr John Pennington-Leigh to attack the Goring heavy gun battery, inland from Dieppe, each aircraft carrying two 500lb bombs. Diving from an altitude of 3,000 feet, the pilots released their bombs at 800 feet right over the target, although smoke obscured the results. All aircraft were recovered safely and a second mission left Warmwell at 1005, its target then being the Rommel Battery to the east of the town. Despite heavy AA fire the aircraft hit the gun position successfully, then took on an He 111 about to attack shipping off the beachhead. The Heinkel and an escorting FW 190 were hit and scored as probables on the Hurricanes' return to base unscathed. The third mission of the day was yet another gun position, this time the Hindenburg Battery to the west of Dieppe. Flying again through heavy defensive fire, the fighter-bombers attacked the guns as Allied ground forces withdrew. One Hurricane was hit and the pilot forced to bail out, but he was rescued unhurt. The other aircraft returned to base at the end of a very successful day for 175 Squadron.

On 1 September another 'Hurribomber' unit, 174 Squadron, arrived to spend three weeks at Warmwell. It had also taken part in the Dieppe operation, but had not been so lucky, losing five pilots, including its OC. Other units appeared at the airfield for APCs, but 263 Squadron brought its Whirlwinds on 13 September for operations. The aircraft had just been converted to carry bombs

Whirlwind I P6979 of 263 Squadron being serviced in its pen at Warmwell in the spring of 1943.

and the unit concentrated on *Roadsteads* before going over to night *Rhubarbs* in February 1943. Apart from short detachments to Harrowbeer, Predannack, Zeals and Manston, the Squadron remained at Warmwell until December 1943 when it converted to Typhoons. The first Typhoons were seen at Warmwell on 21 September 1942 when 266 Squadron arrived from Duxford to fly anti-*Rhubarb* patrols along the South Coast looking for FW 190 'tip and run' raiders. The Squadron sent detachments to Predannack and, though moving to Exeter in January 1943, continued to mount operations from Warmwell until the following September.

During the winter of 1942/43 the Chesil Beach range was used for a series of highly classified *Upkeep* trials to test the initial versions of the bouncing bomb designed by Barnes Wallis, employing Wellington BJ985. After initial drops of wooden mock-ups in December 1942, two further tests were made on 9 and 10 January, the Wellington using Warmwell as its base. Following a further trial on 5 February, which exceeded all expectations, the team moved to Reculver. The test programme was completed in April and the bombs were successfully used on the raid by 617 Squadron's Lancasters in May 1943.

The first American aircraft had appeared at Warmwell in July 1942 when the Spitfires of the 31st FS paid a visit from Westhampnett, but on 22 September 1943 P-47s of the 4th FG arrived on duty, taking off the next morning to escort sixty bombers attacking Vannes airfield in France. They refuelled after the attack before returning to their base.

For much of 1943 the Whirlwinds of 263 Squadron shared the airfield with 257 Squadron, a Typhoon unit that exchanged places with 266 Squadron in January. They also flew *Roadsteads* coastal patrols and offensive sweeps from Warmwell, were also engaged on long-range fighter escorts for B-17 missions, and later in the year started training with bombs. They made their first fighter-bomber attack on V-1 flying bomb sites on 4 January 1944, three weeks before moving to Beaulieu.

In the meantime the Ansons and Walruses of C Flight, 276 Squadron, were kept busy. One mission of note took place on 25 March when a glider on a training exercise was lost over the Channel; a Walrus found it floating 6 miles off Swanage and, alighting, took aboard twelve men. Then too heavy to take off, the Walrus taxied towards the coast until it met a rescue launch, which took off the survivors, enabling the Walrus to return to Warmwell.

The USAAF returned in the spring of 1944 to take over Warmwell as Station 454 of the 9th Air Force. No 263 Squadron had returned on 6 March, this time with Typhoons, when the first P-38s of the 474th FG (428th, 429th and 430th FSs) started to arrive on 12 March. The Typhoons departed a week later as eighty US fighters, their crews and equipment replaced them. No 276 Squadron departed for Portreath on 3 April, but ASR cover from Warmwell was resumed two

Warmwell's old control tower, now a private dwelling, Egdon House, seen in August 2006.

A Belman hangar still in use at Warmwell in August 2006.

weeks later by 275 Squadron, which moved from Valley with Ansons and Walruses, soon adding the Spitfire VC to its fleet. The Lightning pilots resumed training and mounted their first operation, a fighter sweep, from Warmwell on 25 April. They later went over to bombing and strafing ground targets, including a raid on Orly airfield near Paris. Trains and road convoys were also hit. However, the P38s were vulnerable to ground fire and during their fifteen weeks of operations from Warmwell the 474th lost twenty-seven aircraft, all but five to flak. Of the five lost in air combat, three were bounced by FW 190s while escorting B-26s on 7 May. On D-Day the group flew patrols over the invasion fleet, losing two aircraft, believed in a collision. Nonetheless, a 474th formation came across a force of bomb-carrying FW 190s on 18 July, shooting down ten of them for the loss of one Lightning. The Group eventually left Warmwell during the first week of August 1944, the last of the 9th AF's eighteen fighter groups to move to the continent.

RAF units soon began arriving to use the Chesil Beach ranges, and on 27 August No 17 APC moved in from North Weald to provide air-firing practice for 2nd TAF squadrons, with Masters, Spitfires and Martinets. In November No 14 APC also arrived, with Martinets, Hurricanes and Typhoons. The Typhoons of 174 Squadron were the first to complete the fourteen-day course and were followed by a stream of squadrons from the continent, which continued through the winter and spring of 1945 and after VE Day, albeit at a slower rate.

On 7 June thirty-six Spitfires of 310, 312 and 313 Squadrons landed after escorting HM the King and Queen on their visit to the Channel Islands, but the station had already started to run down. No 274 Squadron was reformed at Warmwell with Tempest Vs on 7 September and completed the last air-firing course when it flew out to Germany on the 19th. When 14 and 17 APCs disbanded on 4 October most of their towing aircraft left for Sylt and the station was reduced to C&M. More than sixty squadrons had used Warmwell for armament training on the Chesil Beach ranges during the wartime period.

The last aircraft to land at Warmwell was a Wyvern flown by Westland test pilot Harald Penrose in the late 1940s; he suffered an engine failure and managed to put down between piles of debris on the abandoned airfield. The Ministry of Food took over the Bellman hangars for food storage in 1950 but the station was soon put up for disposal. A housing estate has sprung up on the former domestic site, and the control tower has been converted into a house, but the main airfield has since disappeared as gravel has been extracted from beneath its surface. At the time of writing the Bellman hangars are still in use, for machinery storage.

Main features:
Runways: NE-SW 2,700ft, WNW-ESE 5,040ft, NW-SE 2,700ft, grass. *Hangars:* two Bellman, eight Blister. *Hardstandings:* six double fighter pens, twelve single fighter pens. *Accommodation:* RAF Officers 144, SNCOs 160, ORs 1,934; WAAF Officers 8, SNCOs 10, ORs 284.

A Queen Bee of Z Flight, 1 AACU, on the catapult at Watchet in October 1939.

WATCHET (DONIFORD), Somerset

ST092432, 1 mile E of Watchet off A39

A small grass airstrip was established in 1928 at Doniford, near the town of Watchet on the Somerset coast, this was to provide communications for the Army Camp established alongside the Gunnery Range in Bridgwater Bay, attended by Army units during the summer for anti-aircraft gunnery training. Targets were provided by the RAF from Weston Zoyland, some 19 miles to the east. Hawker Horsley target tugs occasionally put down on the strip, but the more usual users were Avro 504s, Tomtits and DH60 Moths.

Trials with unmanned target aircraft took place at Watchet during the summer of 1937 with the Queen Bee, a pilotless radio-controlled Tiger Moth. The aircraft was fitted with floats, for ease of recovery from the sea, but had to be launched by catapult. The first trials were flown by 1 AACU, based at Biggin Hill, using the catapult of the cruiser HMS *Neptune* anchored in the bay. These were successful, although the aircraft was damaged on landing.

Z Flight of 1 AACU formed at Watchet on 11 April 1938 with eight Queen Bees, plus Tutors and Magisters for communications. A catapult was installed on the gun park at Doniford Camp and the first successful launch of a Queen Bee was made on 3 August. Several aircraft were hit during the summer's firing camp but only one was shot down, another crashing into the sea. The following spring Z Flight returned to Watchet from winter quarters and resumed flying Queen Bees. Drogue targets were also used, towed by the Henleys of A Flight flying from Weston Zoyland. Following the outbreak of war in September 1939 X Flight also moved to Watchet from Henlow as gunnery training increased in tempo. This continued into the winter of 1939/40 without a break as many Army units passed through. The last Queen Bee to be shot down at Watchet was on 22 July 1940, for shortly afterwards X and Z Flights were transferred to ranges in Wales. Targets were then provided by the Henleys of A Flight flying from Weston Zoyland.

The Watchet airstrip remained open for communications and training; the Lysanders of 16 Squadron, also based at Weston Zoyland, used it for short-field landing practice during 1941 and early 1942. It was also a useful emergency strip for tug aircraft if they developed problems over the ranges. Austers became frequent visitors in 1942 and 1943, as did Piper Cubs when US Army units began to use the ranges in 1944.

After the war, closure of the camp and its airstrip seemed imminent, but in July 1947 Watchet became the Light Anti-Aircraft Gunnery School, RAF Regiment. No 15 (LAA) Squadron then moved in from Netheravon, transferring to Upavon in December. It was replaced by 16 (LAA) Squadron, which formed at Watchet on 12 January 1948 and was joined by a number of RAF Regiment Auxiliary LAA Squadrons spending their summer camps there. The defence cuts of 1956 disbanded the RAuxAF and trimmed back RAF Regiment strength, with the result that Watchet was no longer required. The camp was closed in February 1957 and the site is now occupied by a holiday park.

Beaufort II AW304 of the ATDU at Weston-super-Mare in 1940.

WESTON-SUPER-MARE, Somerset

ST344603, 1¹/2 miles SE of Weston-super-Mare alongside A371

Work started on the municipal airport of Weston-super-Mare in February 1936. It was ready for operation by May, when on the 25th scheduled passenger flights were started by Railway Air Services' DH84 Dragons on a Plymouth-Haldon-Cardiff- Weston-Bristol service. A passenger terminal and administrative building was completed in 1938 together with a large side-opening hangar, and in October Western Airways started the first scheduled night services in Britain, flying DH89 Dragon Rapides from Weston. Also in 1938 the RAF opened a School of Technical Training at Locking just a mile to the east, establishing a Station Flight at Weston with Dominies to provide communications.

RAF presence at Weston increased in 1939 when the Air Ministry placed a contract with the Straight Corporation (owners of Western Airways) for the operation of No 39 E&RFTS at the Airport. Flying Magisters, Audaxes and Hart Trainers, it opened on 3 July, but was hardly established when it was disbanded on the eve of the declaration of war and its aircraft transferred to other schools. The company's contract was amended to provide navigation training, 5 Civil Air Navigation School being formed with Ansons that same day. Renamed 5 AONS on 1 November, its aircraft spent much time on navigational exercises over the Bristol Channel and Irish Sea. It absorbed 3 AONS (which had transferred from Kingstown the week before) on 12 June 1940, but with expansion of the Empire Air Training Scheme to include navigator training, 5 AONS was transferred to South Africa. It closed at Weston on 22 August and reopened at Oudtshoorn on 4 November, becoming 45 Air School, SAAF.

Although civil flying had stopped on 3 September 1939, Western Airways was given authority to re-start a Weston-Cardiff service, but this did not last long, the company's facilities then being utilised for the maintenance and overhaul of RAF primary trainers and light aircraft. The airfield was transferred to the RAF on 1 May 1940, and a shadow factory built at Old Mixon, on its western boundary. Production of Beaufighters got under way there in September, though deliveries were slow because of component shortages. A 4,200-foot tarmac runway was laid to aid flight-testing.

Beaufighter production at Old Mixon in 1943.

The place of 5 AONS was taken by 10 EFTS, which arrived on 7 September 1940, having been moved out of Yatesbury to make room for the expanding Radio School. Weston soon became very busy with Tiger Moths, but congestion was eased when Lulsgate Bottom became available for circuit work. Shortage of hangar space remained a problem, with many aircraft having to be stored outside, and a hurricane-force storm on 12 November resulted in eleven picketed Tiger Moths being badly damaged.

To decoy bombing raids away from Weston, a Q site was built at Bleadon, 2 miles to the south. When the first raid on Weston came in January 1941, the Q site was lit before the Luftwaffe could find the airfield, and they immediately homed in on the decoy, heavily cratering it. The site's effectiveness that night was due to the bravery of AC2 Bright, who left the safety of the control bunker when the remote-controlled igniters failed, and lit the decoy fires by hand, a feat for which he was later decorated. The Q site was bombed again in May when more than a dozen incendiaries were dropped on its dummy flare-path; several cows were killed, but there was no damage to the airfield or the town.

Following the closure of Lulsgate for rebuilding in June 1941, Weston became very congested and this forced 10 EFTS to move to Stoke Orchard during September. Weston was then left to Locking Station Flight and the Bristol Aeroplane Company, flight-testing Beaufighters until, on 10 October 1942, No 286 Squadron moved in from Colerne. From its new base at Weston the Squadron flew its Hurricanes, Defiants and Oxfords on detachments throughout the South West to provide target facilities for the training of anti-aircraft units. No 87 GS was opened in the spring of 1943 to teach Air Cadets to fly, under the command of Prince Bira, an exiled member of the Malayan Royal Family. In April 1943 Weston was transferred to Technical Training Command under the control of RAF Locking. The Equipment Training School was established at the airport in August, transferred from Eastbourne. 286 Squadron continued to use Weston as its base throughout the autumn and into the winter of 1943, but on 29 November it moved again, this time to Weston Zoyland, replaced by a detachment of 116 Squadron, Croydon, a radar calibration unit.

In March 1944 a detachment of the Aircraft Torpedo Development Unit transferred to Weston from Weston Zoyland. Using ranges in the Bristol Channel, the ATDU employed a variety of aircraft types, including Swordfish, Beauforts, Beaufighters and later Mosquitoes and Tempests, to drop torpedoes and as chase planes. Meanwhile Beaufighter production had been building up well during 1943, and by early 1944 had reached a peak of eighty-seven per month. A wide range of marks were built at Old Mixon, from the Mark IF fighter through the Mark IV fighter/torpedo bomber to the Marks X and XI anti-shipping and strike aircraft. Production of the Beaufighter finished in September 1945 when Mark X SR919 rolled off the line. Of the 5,564 Beaufighters built in the UK, 3,096 were constructed at Weston, and the type continued in RAF service until May 1960.

Weston-super-Mare in about 1950. The Old Mixon works are at the top (ie western) end of the airfield.

The end of the war meant no major changes for military flying from Weston, as the ATDU ontinued to operate, together with the Locking Station Flight, then flying Proctors. Civil flying vas resumed, initially with scheduled services to Cardiff, as the airfield transferred to the Ministry of Civil Aviation.

With the end of Beaufighter production the Bristol factory built components until, in March 955, it was decided to centralise all Bristol rotary-wing work at Old Mixon. The Helicopter Division moved from Filton, together with production of the Sycamore. This was succeeded by the Belvedere, vhich was still under development when the Bristol Helicopter Division was taken over by Westland Helicopters in February 1960. Production of helicopter spares continued at the factory until 2002.

Three radar-equipped Varsities were stationed at Weston from 1959 for the Radio School at Locking. One was lost in an accident, but the other two were used as flying classrooms for training echnicians until they moved with the school to Cosford in October 1966. Flying continued from Veston-super-Mare airfield until the early 1990s, when it was sold for redevelopment. The Air

Belvedere production at Weston-super-Mare in 1960.

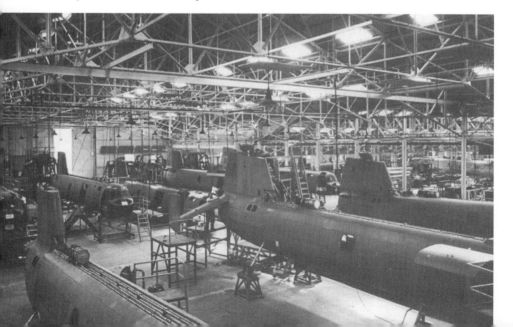

Cadet gliding school, by then entitled 621 VGS, managed to fly on until it was forced to move to Hullavington at the end of June 1993, having spent more than fifty years at Weston.

On the upside, the Helicopter Museum was established at Weston in 1989 with a few helicopters and the support of Westland Helicopters Ltd. It now houses more than eighty on a 4^{1}/$_{2}$-acre site that includes some of the original 1936 airport buildings.

Main features:
Runways: 254° 4,200ft, tarmac. *Hangars:* two O-Blister, four MAP. *Accommodation:* RAF SNCOs 20, ORs 100.

Mustang I of 26 Squadron, one of the first to use Weston Zoyland, in 1942.

WESTON ZOYLAND, Somerset

ST365344, 4 miles SE of Bridgewater

A large field to the east of Weston Zoyland village on the Somerset Levels was selected in the mid 1920s as a convenient landing ground for aircraft towing targets over the Bridgwater Bay gunnery ranges. The Horsleys of 100 Squadron were the first to use the field in 1926, and regular visits followed. In 1929 the Night Flying Flight, based at Biggin Hill with the Anti-Aircraft Defence School, took over target duties with its Horsleys, opening up the LG in May and spending the summer months under canvas. Becoming the Anti-Aircraft Cooperation Flight in October 1931 with Wallaces added to the fleet, it continued to support the range camps, being re-titled the Anti-Aircraft Cooperation Unit in April 1936, and 1 AACU in February 1937.

With the onset of war the seasonal activity at Watchet changed, with training continuing into the winter. A Flight, 1AACU, was permanently based at Weston Zoyland, detached from HQ at Biggin Hill. The Wallaces had been replaced by Henleys, supplemented by Battles, Lysanders and later Defiants.

In November 1939 a detachment of Lysanders from 16 Squadron arrived for army cooperation exercises, returning to base at Old Sarum for deployment to France with the AASF. Following its return to the UK, the whole Squadron moved to Weston Zoyland in August 1940 and started flying dawn and dusk coastal patrols looking for signs of enemy activity. These continued through the winter and covered the whole coastline of the South West, the Lysanders operating from other coastal stations

Warwick CIII HG248 of 525 Squadron at Weston Zoyland in late 1943.

n detachment. No 8 AACU arrived in early August from Filton, flying a varied fleet (including Tiger Moths and Oxfords) on searchlight cooperation training. It left in October, but deployed detachments t Weston Zoyland from November 1940 to March 1942, and again for most of 1943.

On 1 September 1940 Weston Zoyland became self-accounting, but shortage of ccommodation meant the requisitioning of buildings off-camp. In December a detachment of the pecial Duty Flight arrived from Christchurch, to spend almost a year on radar interception trials ith two Lysanders and a Fox Moth. Because of its low altitude, Weston Zoyland was often open hen other airfields were weather-bound, and early in 1941 a number of aircraft landed that were eing ferried to Gibraltar but had to return, often short of fuel. Improvements to the main grass unway and accommodation were therefore speeded up.

No 16 Squadron went through a bad patch in June 1941, when the OC, Wg Cdr Haycock, lost is life in a take-off accident at Roborough on the 9th. Sqn Ldr Walker assumed command and the ery next day his Lysander was attacked by four Bf 109s over Exmouth. Although the Lysander's unner managed to shoot down one of the fighters, it was overwhelmed and destroyed by the emaining Bf 109s, killing both the crew.

When it was decided that Weston Zoyland should become a major practice camp for army ooperation squadrons, 239 Squadron, with Lysanders, arrived from Gatwick on 6 July. As well as ne Watchet range, squadrons were able to use others at Steart Flats for bombing and Lilstock for ir-to-air combat. To add to the target-towing facilities available, P Flight of 1 AACU was formed n 25 August 1941 at Weston Zoyland with Henleys, Lysanders and Defiants, and on 18 October so oo was 1492 (Target Towing) Flight with Lysanders, later supplemented with Masters, Martinets nd Mosquitoes. On 7 February 1942 Mustangs appeared at Weston Zoyland for the first time, with 6 Squadron from Gatwick on an APC; the unit also had Tomahawks, which were being replaced. o 16 Squadron also started to receive Mustangs in April 1942, and began training on their new iounts. Another Mustang unit, 170 Squadron, moved in on 15 June, but within a week had moved n to Hurn. Other Mustang squadrons arrived for APCs during the year, and in October No 16 quadron was cleared for operations and began convoy patrols and coastal sweeps. It hit and estroyed a number of targets, but lost two Mustangs in November and another in December efore moving to Andover on 2 January 1943.

On 1 November A and P Flights of 1 AACU were disbanded and reformed as 1600 and 1601 Anti-Aircraft Cooperation) Flights, remaining at the station to do the same job with Henleys, Iartinets and Defiants. It was joined by No 1 RAF Regiment Anti-Aircraft Practice Camp Target owing Flight, which was formed on 20 January 1943 with Lysanders, but was disbanded on 17 June id re-numbered as 1625 (Anti-Aircraft Cooperation) Flight, with Martinets added to its complement.

Plans for the basing of a Coastal Command reconnaissance squadron at the airfield resulted in general upgrading of the airfield, with work beginning in the spring of 1943. Three concrete unways were laid, together with the construction of hardstandings and dispersals, four main and n smaller hangars, and a two-storey watch office and several operational and technical buildings. he living site to the north-west was enlarged and upgraded.

Weston Zoyland's control tower in July 2005.

With the formation of 2TAF in June 1943, its units used Weston Zoyland for intensive air-firing and ground-attack practice, and as well as Mustangs, Spitfires began to appear. RAF Servicing Commando units also practised working under field conditions at the station. Coastal Command squadrons never appeared, but on 1 September 1943 a new transport unit, 525 Squadron, was formed at Weston Zoyland with Warwicks. By November it was cleared for operations and began scheduled passenger service to Gibraltar. Other changes for the station's squadrons came toward the end of the year. On 18 October No 1492 (TT) Flight was disbanded and reformed as 13 APC with Masters, Martinets and Hurricanes. 286 Squadron, another target facilities unit, arrived on 2 November from Weston-super-Mare with Martinets, Defiants, Oxfords, Masters and Hurricanes. Two days later 587 Squadron, another target facilities unit, was formed following the amalgamation of 1600, 1601 and 1625 (AAC) Flights. Its initial equipment, inherited from the Flights, consisted of Henleys, Martinets, Oxfords and Hurricanes. Both 286 and 587 Squadrons were engaged in a new concept during January 1944 – the towing of target gliders instead of drogues. The trials were successful, but the concept was never taken up.

In February 525 Squadron moved to Lyneham and shortly afterwards 13 APC departed. On 10 April the remaining RAF units, 286 and 587 Squadrons, were transferred to Culmhead to make way for the use of the airfield by the USAAF, and 2,500 beds were set up in the hangars. In the event the Americans were delayed and it was not until after D-Day that the unit allocated to Weston Zoyland, the 442nd Troop Carrying Group, actually arrived. The Group's four squadrons (303rd, 304th, 305th and 306th TCSs) sent forty-five C-47s carrying paratroops of the 82nd Airborne Division from its base at Fulbeck to St Mere Eglise. They then flew re-supply missions into the beachhead until 10 June, then, one by one, moved to Weston Zoyland. Three of the Squadrons deployed to Italy in mid-July to take part in Operation *Dragoon*, while the remaining Squadron, the 306th, flew air freight services to France. The Group rejoined at Weston Zoyland in September ready for Operation *Market Garden*; on the 17th the 442nd TCG flew ninety C-47s taking paratroops of the 101st Airborne Division to take the bridges at Son and Veghel in Holland. They met heavy flak and lost three aircraft, but the following day towed glider-borne reinforcements to the bridgehead. Over the next two days the Group flew more reinforcements and supplies into the area, losing a total of ten aircraft during the operation, then returned to Weston Zoyland to resume re-supply until 4 October, when the C-47s started moving to the continent.

RAF squadrons seemed keen to return, 286 Squadron moving in from Zeals on 28 September as the Americans were packing up. It was followed by 587 Squadron from Culmhead on 1 October. Both units resumed their duties, joined by 1540 BAT Flight in February 1945 flying Oxfords to operate with 6 (P)AFU, Little Rissington, and 3 (P)AFU, Lulsgate Bottom, from July.

Weston Zoyland seen from a microlight in August 2005.

The end of the war in Europe brought changes to Weston Zoyland. A general run-down began, arting with the disbandment of 286 Squadron on 16 May. Its sister squadron, 285, flew in from Jorth Weald on 20 June, only to disband six days later. No 1540 BAT Flight disbanded on 17)ecember. However, the ranges remained open and in April 1946 another target facilities unit, 691 quadron, arrived from Exeter, with Vengeance and Martinet target tugs, Harvards and Spitfire .VIs. It supplemented, then replaced, 587 Squadron, which moved to Tangmere on 1 June, but id not itself stay much longer, transferring to Fairwood Common in July. It was replaced by 151 quadron with Mosquito NF30s, and 222 with Meteor IIIs, but again not for long, 151 disbanding n 9 September, and 222 departing for Tangmere on 2 October.

The airfield was put on a C&M footing for a few years, but reopened for 209 AFS, which formed t Weston Zoyland on 23 June 1952 to train pilots on the Meteor T7 and F4, in case they were needed or the Korean War. Re-titled 12 FTS on 1 June 1954 with Prentices added to its fleet, the unit closed n 24 June 1955. Towards the end of that year Canberras appeared at Weston Zoyland; these were 32s of 76 Squadron from Hemswell, to be prepared for sampling atomic cloud dispersals for the first tomic bomb trials in Australia. Canberra PR3s of 542 Squadron joined them, and together they left or Pearce, Australia, in March 1956. The last units to fly from the airfield were 32 and 73 Squadrons, /hich formed a detachment in January 1957 with 231 OCU to convert pilots to the Canberra B2 om Venoms. At the end of March they departed, flying the Canberras to their new base at Akrotiri.

RAF Weston Zoyland closed in January 1958, but was retained by the Government until 1969 /hen it was sold. A few buildings, including the control tower, remain in place, as well as the unways, which are still in use for microlight flying, providing echoes of the airfield's past.

Main features:
Runways: 285° 5,775ft x 150ft, 048° 3,564ft x 150ft, 343° 4,101ft x 150ft, concrete and wood-chippings. *Hangars:* three T2, one Bellman, one Bessoneau, nine Blister. *Hardstandings:* two 150ft frying pan, thirty-three loop. *Accommodation:* RAF Officers 107, SNCOs 162, ORs 618; WAAF Officers 6, SNCOs 10, ORs 182.

VESTWARD HO!, Devon

S443307, 2¹/₂ miles N of Bideford

Opened in the spring of 1918, Westward Ho! was a landing ground for RNAS DH6s engaged on coastal patrol work. It was situated on a golf course at Northam Burrows, a low-lying romontory at the entrance of the River Taw. Covering some 90 acres, its facilities were basic, with essoneau hangars for the aircraft and a few Armstrong huts for the personnel. A large wooden hed served as guardroom and mess.

A dozen DH6 biplanes were flown from the landing ground by 502 and 503 (Special Duty) lights, formed on 6 June 1918. In early August they were absorbed by 260 Squadron, newly ormed at the station. The DH6s spent their time plodding up and down along the north Devon oast at 20-minute intervals, looking for U-boat activity, but at least keeping them submerged and nable to operate effectively. Westward Ho! was often used by 250 Squadron detachments, who ound it a useful alternative to Padstow.

With the end of the war anti-mine patrols were flown for a while from Westward Ho! to clear the sea-nes of redundant ordnance. After this the station gradually ran down, 260 Squadron disbanding on 22 ebruary 1919 and 502 and 503 Flights on 15 May. The site was soon cleared and returned to the golfers.

A Bulldog display over Whitchurch in 1931.

WHITCHURCH, Somerset

ST595686, 2 miles S of Bristol

The Bristol & Wessex Aeroplane Club was looking for a new home in the late 1920s as its base a Filton was becoming very busy. It found a potential site 2 miles west of the village of Whitchurch which Bristol City Council agreed to purchase as a new base for the club and airport for the city.

The site, which covered 298 acres, was cleared and levelled, and construction began in 1929 Bristol Airport was formally opened by HRH Prince George, Duke of Kent, on 31 May 1930, an scheduled services were initiated by air taxi companies and later by Western Airways, Imperia Airways, Railway Air Services and Crilly Airways with DH84 Dragons and DH89 Dragon Rapides A new terminal building was opened in July 1935 and two years later an additional 104 acres wer purchased to extend the airport to the south and east.

Whitchurch was used as an RLG by 2 E&RFTS, Filton, from 1937, and on 3 December 193 No 33 E&RFTS was formed there. Twelve Tiger Moths were flown by the school, operated unde contract by Charmier Gilbert Lodge and Co Ltd. Audaxes, Hinds and Ansons were later added fo the training of reservists. The airport was requisitioned by the Air Ministry on 30 August 1939 and couple of days later aircraft of British Airways and Imperial Airways began to arrive, evacuate from their bases at Croydon and Heston, which were easy targets for the Luftwaffe. On the day tha war was declared, 3 September 1939, there were sixty large passenger aircraft parked a Whitchurch, including Ensigns, Albatrosses, HP42s, Electras and Ju 52s. No 33 E&RFTS wa disbanded, its aircraft transferred to other FTSs, leaving Whitchurch free for passenger operations.

The Air Transport Auxiliary originated at Whitchurch during this time, when an initial batch c thirty candidate pilots were assembled there for flying tests on Couriers. Many of the male candidate were accepted for ferry duties with the ATA, and they were joined at the end of the year by a numbe of female pilots. Some were then trained to fly military aircraft at CFS Upavon. The ATA wa officially formed on 1 January 1940, its HQ at White Waltham and School at Whitchurch, whic

Whitchurch's hangars, terminal and clubhouse in September 1937, on what later became the south side.

provided training on Tutors, Magisters, Harvards and Blenheims. On 15 February 1940 B Section of No 3 Ferry Pilots Pool (ATA) was set up at Whitchurch to provide a pool of pilots to ferry aircraft from Bristol's works at Filton and Gloster's at Hucclecote, becoming No 2 FPP(ATA) in November.

Following the invasion of the Netherlands, KLM brought its aircraft to Whitchurch, where it resumed services. British Airways and Imperial Airways were merged to form BOAC on 1 April 1940 with Whitchurch as its HQ ('A Base'), and got its schedules together despite a series of setbacks. Two HP42s were blown together and wrecked in a storm on 19 March, while the delivery of DH91 Albatross G-AEVV/AX903 to 217 Squadron was delayed because it was deliberately set on fire; G-AFDI was destroyed in the same attack. The Luftwaffe intervened on 24 November, dropping incendiaries during a heavy raid on Bristol, destroying an Ensign and a DC3.

The scene at Whitchurch in September 1939, following the arrival of aircraft of British Airways and Imperial Airways. An Electra appears in the foreground, then two Lockheed 14s, and behind them a Ju 52, DH91 and two Ensigns, being hastily camouflaged.

Dakota 1 G-AGGB landing at Whitchurch in 1943.

Among the more unusual aircraft to fly from the BOAC base were Curtiss Wright CW-20 G AGDI and FW200 Condor G-AGAY, but most routes were flown by DH91s and DC3s to Foynes the Irish transatlantic seaplane terminal, Lisbon and Gibraltar. The route across the Bay of Biscay was particularly hazardous, although only one aircraft was actually shot down by enemy fighters (on 1 June 1943, with the loss of seventeen passengers and crew).

In the spring of 1941 the Bristol Aeroplane Company started using the south site (or south side for the assembly and storage of Beaufighters, occupying a large factory building, a Bellman and two smaller hangars. The control tower and passenger reception buildings were also on this site, while on the north side a T2 hangar housed BOAC and KLM servicing and another hangar was used by Bristols; a further three hangars were later built alongside them. A new E-W concrete and tarmac runway, of 3,048 feet, was laid during 1941, together with paved taxiways, and the other two grass runways were re-graded. Services to Dublin, the USA and Africa were added, and by 1942 BOAC' fleet operating from Whitchurch included Liberators, Whitleys and Lodestars as well as DC-3s Oxfords and Dakotas also flew from the airport, with BOAC's Central Training School. The airline maintained services from Whitchurch until 1 November 1944, when it moved its main operating base to Hurn, where longer runways were better able to take the York and Lancastrian.

BOAC's Engineering Base remained, however, and continued to use Whitchurch for flying training and Dakota services, while the ATA flew its Anson and Argus taxis to collect aircraft for delivery. In June 1945 the Ministry of Civil Aviation took over Whitchurch, and in September No 3 Ferry Pool closed. BOAC transferred its flying training to Aldermaston in early 1946 and in August its Dakota scheduled services went to other airports. Dakota maintenance operations finally closed in 1948, transferred to Heathrow.

The Bristol & Wessex Aeroplane Club had reopened in 1946, and a number of airlines including Cambrian Airways, started services from Whitchurch. These came and went during the 1950s, but with the expansion of Bristol more houses were built in the Whitchurch area. As this restricted future expansion, it was decided to close Whitchurch and transfer all remaining activity to a new Bristol Airport at Lulsgate Bottom. The last scheduled service left Whitchurch on 13 April 1957.

The site was redeveloped as Hengrove Park, a trading estate whose rents contributed to the costs of the new airport for many years. BAC used the old Bristols north side premises for the maintenance of aero-engines until 1971. The main runway remains in place today, its last use being a Cessna 152 en route to Lulsgate, which put down with a fuel problem in November 1993.

WINKLEIGH, Devon

SS621094, 8 miles N of Okehampton

A stretch of moorland to the north of Winkleigh in beautiful but hilly north Devon was selected in 1940 as a much-needed satellite for Chivenor. Work started on a two-runway airfield that year, but the boggy land surface prevented stabilisation of the runway foundations and it was not until thousands of tons of hardcore had been poured into the sub-soil that it was ready for use.

When RAF Winkleigh was at last ready, Coastal Command had lost interest and it was Fighter Command that opened the station on 1 January 1943 as part of 10 Group. A single T2 and eight Blister hangars provided servicing and maintenance facilities on the north-west side of the field, while the perimeter track gave access to nine dispersals and six fighter pens. A control tower was built to the south-east, near the admin site. Although the opening-up party was in residence, it was not until 24 April that the first aircraft arrived, and that was only visiting. Others passed through, but the airfield had by then no clear use, and on 20 August it was put on C&M.

The first users were the Americans, who arrived in October 1943 for pre-invasion exercises. More than 700 troops moved in, and Winkleigh was designated Station 460 of the USAAF. Landings took place at Braunton Burrows and other beaches along the north Devon coast, and Spitfires of the 12th Reconnaissance Squadron, IXth US Fighter Command, arrived on detachment from their bases at Keevil and Membury, for tactical reconnaissance over the exercise beachheads. They remained until December, replaced by a number of other USAAF units on short-duration detachments until late February 1944.

The first RAF unit arrived shortly after the station was handed back to Fighter Command; this was 406 (RCAF) Squadron, transferred from Exeter on 14 April 1944. The Squadron's Beaufighter VI night-fighters were soon in action, W/O G. F. MacEwan and Flt Sgt C. S. Headley shooting down a Ju 88 off Start Point during a raid on Bristol on the night of 29/30 April. Six nights later, flying one of the unit's new Mosquito XIIs, Sqn Ldr Blackie Williams and Fg Off Kirkpatrick destroyed two Do 217s attacking Devonport with glider bombs. During April a detachment of Defiants and Hurricanes from the peripatetic 286 Squadron arrived at Winkleigh to provide target facilities, and early in May they were joined by an Albacore detachment from 415 (RCAF) Squadron. These eight biplanes flew nightly patrols to prevent E-boats interfering with the invasion fleet then being assembled and exercised off the South Coast, and worked closely with the Wellington XIIIs of 254 Squadron, Davidstow Moor.

On the night of 14/15 May the Luftwaffe returned to bomb Bristol with a mixed force of Ju 88s, Do 217s and He 177s. The crews of 406 Squadron were up in strength to meet them, shooting down four (including a Ju 88 and an He 177), claiming a further three probables and one damaged. By early June the Squadron had six Mosquito XIIs and eighteen Beaufighter VIFs on strength and was flying nightly patrols over the Channel. These were uneventful, as were those on the night of 5/6 June, as the invasion fleet approached the French coast. Night *Rangers* over Luftwaffe airfields resulted in action on 7 June, when a Do 217 went down in flames over Lannion. During July the crews were taken off operations to concentrate on conversion to Mosquitoes, but were also given the task of protecting naval vessels operating off Brest at night. On 21 May they caught seven Do 217s moving in to attack four destroyers off the Breton coast. Williams and Kirkpatrick, flying MM731, closed on one, hitting an engine, which caught fire, the aircraft crashing into the sea. Williams feathered the starboard propeller when he noticed that his engine was streaming coolant, but still managed to catch up with another Dornier and engage it. As the Dornier went down, its port engine on fire, it was hit by another Mosquito and blew up.

By mid-July 415 Squadron had left for Manston, but instead 161 Squadron started to use Winkleigh as a forward base for its black-painted Lysanders to fly clandestine missions into occupied France at night. The last 406 Squadron Beaufighter operations were flown on 9 August, but the unit continued to fly its Mosquito XXXs from Winkleigh until 17 September 1944, when it moved to Colerne. The airfield was then again placed on C&M, but not for long, as in November it was transferred to 23 Group, Flying Training Command. This was in preparation for the establishment of the Norwegian Training Base to train recruits in readiness for the re-birth of the Royal Norwegian Air Force. An initial establishment of Harvards and Oxfords was later joined by a number of Cornells shipped from the Norwegian Flying School at Toronto, Canada. The school operated until 10 November 1945, when it moved to Gardermoen, near Oslo.

Although Winkleigh remained under 23 Group, no further flying took place and it was transferred to the Ministry of Agriculture on 30 June 1948. It was requisitioned again on 15 October 1956, but for whatever reason this came to naught and the airfield was sold off in December 1958. Today its outline remains distinct, and several buildings, including the T2 hangar and the control tower, still stand. On the accommodation sites several buildings have been converted into dwellings.

Main features:
Runways: 270° 4,650ft x 150ft, 003° 4,500ft x 150 deg, concrete and tarmac. *Hangars:* one T2, eight O-Blister. *Hardstandings:* six fighter pens, nine dispersals. *Accommodation:* RAF Officers 82, SNCOs 86, ORs 894; WAAF Officers 10, SNCOs 10, ORs 180.

Winkton; P-47D "Joan the happy hopper" Y8*F of the 404th FG with its ground crew at Winkton in June 1944.

WINKTON, Hampshire

SZ165975, 2¹/₂ miles NW of Christchurch

Having been selected as one of the series of ALGs for use in the build-up and initial phases of the forthcoming invasion, the construction of Winkton airfield was started by an RAF Works Unit in June 1943. Although only 2 miles from Christchurch airfield and 3 miles from both Hurn and Holmsley South, it reflected the urgent need for suitable landing grounds in the area. Hedges were cleared to allow two steel-mesh runways and a perimeter track to be laid across the 300-acre site which took in most of Lower Clockhouse Farm but also extended north of the road between Sopley and Bransgore, which was closed. Facilities were minimal, but by the time of its completion in September 1943 the Luftwaffe already had the airfield marked on its target maps, as Sopley – being not far from the village and GCI station of that name.

The ALG was deliberately left undisturbed in order to allow low-level vegetation to naturally camouflage the steel mesh. Some additional runway reinforcement and dispersals were added by 5005 Airfield Construction Squadron in the spring of 1944, shortly before Winkton was opened by 11 Group. However, its occupants were not to be the RAF but the USAAF, and on 4 April personnel of the 404th Fighter Group, IXth Tactical Air Command, arrived direct from the USA under the command of Colonel W. McColpin, a 29-year-old veteran who had served with one of the RAF Eagle Squadrons. Personnel lived in tents, and when P-47s arrived for the Group's three squadrons (the 506th, 507th and 508th FSs) they were dispersed around the field in the open.

Following intensive training, the Group was ready for operations by the end of the month, and the first of these, a sweep along the French coastline, took place on 1 May. As direct support fighter-bombers, the P-47 pilots gained experience by attacking roads, railways and V-weapons sites. During their first encounter with the Luftwaffe on 8 May an enemy fighter was shot down, and another on the 19th. On D-Day itself the 404th FG flew high-level patrols over the beachheads, a maximum effort resulting in 191 sorties being flown between dawn and dusk. Bad weather then curtailed major operations until the 10th, when forty-eight P-47s left Winkton during the morning to attack artillery positions and bridges. In the evening they turned to the railway system and the 506th hit a road bridge, rail intersection, fifteen trucks and a locomotive, while the 507th cut the tracks either side of two trains then bombed and strafed the stranded locomotives. The 508th cut railway lines near Chartres, set rail tankers on fire, destroyed a locomotive and strafed barracks.

Similar operations continued until early July when the Group started the move to the continent, the main contingent leaving on the 6th. The 404th FG lost eight P-47s in action during its time at Winkton, and another on 9 May, which landed in Eire (in error). Winkton was abandoned following the unit's departure, and once the steel-mesh had been lifted in May 1945 the ALG returned to agriculture. The only sign of its short but active life as an airfield is a memorial on the wall at Clockhouse Farm, used as the Group's HQ.

Main features:
Runways: N-S 4,800ft x 150ft, E-W 4,500ft x 150ft, PSP and Sommerfield track.
Hangars: four Blister. *Hardstandings:* eighty Sommerfield track.

WORTH MATRAVERS, Dorset

SY963770, 4 miles W of Swanage

The Air Ministry Research Establishment moved from Dundee to Worth Matravers early in 1940 and by May was working under the control of the Telecommunications & Research Establishment, whose HQ was at Leeson House, Langton Matravers. The TRE developed such important equipment as IFF (Identification, Friend or Foe) radio installations for aircraft, but during the summer of 1940 one of its priorities was to see whether the British Chain Home radar network could detect gliders, as it was feared that these would spearhead any German invasion.

Trials were started in June using four Scott Viking high-performance sailplanes towed out to sea by three ancient, but adequate, Avro 504Ns using a field near the establishment at Rendscome Farm. The aircraft were flown by the Special Duty Flight based at Christchurch, brought up to the field for each day's flying. Once airborne the glider/tug combinations would ascend to 10,000 feet some 40 miles south of Worth Matravers, where the released gliders, flown by experienced pilots (including world champion Philip Wills), would head back to the English coast. As the trials continued the pilots were tasked with making approaches at progressively lower levels, and on one occasion Wills only managed to clear the cliffs by using upcurrents.

The final trials involved flying the gliders in to approach from the landward side and, once these were completed in August, the aircraft were withdrawn and transferred to the Central Landing Establishment at Ringway. A Magister of 32 MU crashed at Worth Matravers on 14 September 1940, and the airfield continued to be used by communications aircraft for a few months before being abandoned in 1941.

YATE, Gloucestershire

ST706830, 10 miles NE of Bristol

No 3 (Western) Aircraft Repair Depot was established at Yate in 1916 in four large sheds along the southern edge of a large grass airfield. The depot repaired a large number of RFC aircraft during the Great War, ranging from the early BE2 to the Bristol F2B and Sopwith Camel. More than 260 aircraft were also produced at the depot, rebuilt from spares and salvaged components.

Following the Armistice the airfield was abandoned, and the buildings remained empty until 1925 when they were taken over by George Parnall & Co, which built a number of experimental aircraft of its own design. It also licence-built other designs such as the Percival Gull, producing the prototype in 1931, followed by twenty-three more before Percival took over production itself.

Yate in 1941, showing the Fraser-Nash factory.

In 1935 George Parnall sold the airfield to Nash & Thompson Ltd, manufacturers of gun turrets, who with the Hendy Aircraft Co set up a new concern, Parnall Aircraft Ltd, to run the Yate site. Aircraft production continued on a small scale, of designs such as the Heck touring monoplane but the company's main interest became focused on power-operated gun turrets. A large new factory was built in the south-west corner of the airfield in 1938 to produce Fraser-Nash turrets, and this was in full production by the time war was declared. Initially fitted to the Whitley, these turrets were also being fitted to the Wellington, Botha and Sunderland. The airfield remained in use for trials and communications, three Parnall Heck IIc aircraft being used as company hacks.

The Luftwaffe became aware of this activity, and Yate appeared on its target maps. This unwelcome interest resulted in a mission by ten Bf 110 fighter-bombers of Erprobungsgruppe 210 on 27 September 1940. Escorted by forty-two Bf 110 fighters of ZG26, which split to disguise the force's target, they found the factory and began their run-in. However, 10 Group had scrambled the Hurricanes of 504 Squadron from Filton, and they pounced on the Bf 110s as they dived onto their target. The Germans abandoned their attack and jettisoned their bombs to evade the British fighters. During the frantic withdrawal they were attacked by the Spitfires of 152 Squadron from Warmwell and 609 from Middle Wallop, then the Hurricanes of 56 Squadron, Boscombe Down, and of 238 Squadron, also from Middle Wallop. Ten of the Bf 110s were shot down, including the Group's commander, for the loss of one Spitfire.

Part of the original factory seen in July 2008.

However, more attacks were to follow. At lunchtime on 27 February 1941 a lone He 111 followed the railway line at low level and dropped six HE bombs into the factory. The drawing offices and production area were hit, killing fifty-two and injuring many more. This led to dispersal plans, which were accelerated following a further attack by another lone Heinkel on 7 March. This dropped more bombs and machine-gunned the factory, killing three workers and injuring twenty. Within a week the factory was empty, production transferred to a number of sites in the area, including Boulton Mills, Dursley. The main factory was later rebuilt, and used for the manufacture of Lancaster gun turrets as well as airframe assemblies for Lancasters, Spitfires and later Lincolns and Meteors. The company's aircraft continued to use the airfield.

After the war gun turret manufacture continued for a period, until Parnall moved into domestic appliances. The Yate factory is still in existence today, having been extensively enlarged and taking up much of the airfield. The remainder has been sold for housing.

DH1A A1638 of 59 RS at Yatesbury in 1916.

YATESBURY, Wiltshire

SU055710, 4 miles E of Calne

Yatesbury is another Wiltshire airfield dating back to the First World War. The station played an important role during both World Wars, training taking place there on and off between 1916 and 1965.

The site originally consisted of a large field covering more than 500 acres divided roughly in half by a road running from Yatesbury village to the main Calne-Marlborough road. This created two airfields, Camp No 1 at Yatesbury West and Camp No 2 at Yatesbury East. Several hangars were constructed on each, together with technical and admin buildings. RFC Yatesbury was opened in November 1916, its first unit, 55 Reserve Squadron, arriving on the 22nd (a week after its formation at Filton with Avro 504As and Bristol Scouts). It was joined between late April and mid-May 1917 by 59 and 62 Reserve Squadrons from Gosport, and 66 from Wye. These units came under 28 Wing, which formed at Yatesbury on 15 May, being re-titled Training Squadrons on 1 June. They flew a wide variety of aircraft to fulfil their task, including the DH1, DH2, DH6, FE2B, Camel and Pup.

Various reorganisations followed, and squadrons came and went. This culminated in the formation, on 15 July 1918, of 36 TDS, with RE8s and Avro 504Ks taking over No 2 Camp, and 37 TDS taking over No 1 Camp with BE2A, F2B, RE8 and Avro 504K aircraft. Training continued after the Armistice, but by the end of 1919 the airfield had been closed and the land de-requisitioned.

The newly opened Bristol Flying School at Yatesbury in 1936.

In August 1935 the Bristol Aeroplane Company was given the contract for a second RAF Reserve Training School (its first being at Filton), and purchased part of the old western airfield. It refurbished the two 1916 GS hangars and added instructional and accommodation blocks together with ancillary buildings. The new school opened on 6 January 1936 with a fleet of eighteen black-and-silver Tiger Moths, and began training the new generation of RAF pilots. On 1 February 1938 it was re-designated 10 E&RFTS under the control of 26 Group, Training Command, its Tigers supplemented with Audaxes and Hart Trainers for advanced work. The success of the contract led to the award of another to Bristol for a navigation school, which started up as 2 Civil Air Navigation School on 26 September 1938 using Ansons.

Improvement to the buildings on the Western Camp had started in 1937 and a Bellman was later added alongside the 1916 GS sheds. Meanwhile the old Eastern Camp had been re-purchased by the Air Ministry early in 1938 and construction started of a ground training school that eventually covered the old aerodrome. This was opened as No 2 Electrical & Wireless School (E&WS) on 1 December 1938.

Tiger Moth N9181 of 10 EFTS makes a low pass in April 1940 with the student pilot under the hood.

Proctor IV NP184 of 2 Radio School, Yatesbury, in 1943.

The outbreak of war in September 1939 brought major changes to Yatesbury. No 10 E&RFTS became 10 EFTS and its training programme was expanded, as was its fleet, which soon numbered fifty-four Tiger Moths, although its Harts and Audaxes were given up. No 2 CANS became 2 AONS on 11 November 1939, with twelve Ansons on strength. On 14 May 1940 the Bristol Wireless Flight was formed to give flying experience to Wireless Operators under training at No 2 Radio School, which had opened at Yatesbury on 18 January, using Bothas, Dominies and Proctors. No 2 E&WS became No 2 Signals School on 26 August 1940 and its steady expansion, together with that of No 2 Radio School, forced out the other units. 10 EFTS moved to Weston-super-Mare in September 1940 and 2 AONS disbanded on 14 December.

Although RAF personnel had replaced Bristols' instructors by 1942, the company continued to maintain the Proctors and Dominies of the Bristols Wireless Flight, which gradually increased to a peak of 104 aircraft. To rationalise the confusing variety of names being used by wireless-orientated training units, they all became radio schools in December 1942, No 2 Radio School becoming No 9, and No 2 Signals School taking over its title.

Heavy use of the airfield resulted in the need to lay Sommerfield track along the two runways in 1943. A perimeter track was also laid of the same material, linking the dispersals and four Blister hangars to the south-east of the airfield and another two Blisters to the western boundary. The output of trainee W/Ops had outstripped the anticipated losses by the middle of 1943 and a pool was established for trained personnel. Initially 600-strong, this increased to more than 1,600 by October 1944, resulting in additional training to keep them current.

The Bristol Wireless Flight disbanded in July 1945, having trained 18,500 W/Ops during 224,000 hours of flying. It was replaced on the 9th by 2 EFTS, which arrived from Worcester with a fleet of Tiger Moths. The school remained until 30 September 1947 when it too was disbanded. No 2 Radio School continued to train large numbers of radio and radar technicians, and in 1951 was joined by RAF Regiment personnel, the station being used for the formation of 2, 5 and 7 Wings and a number of squadrons. It was also used as a holding area for RAF ground units involved in the Suez operation.

The closure of RAF Yatesbury was announced in 1964 and the air radio element was moved to RAF Cosford. The last course of No 2 Radio School passed out on 21 July 1965, following which the station was put on C&M pending disposal. The station was finally closed in April 1969, the hutted Eastern Camp being demolished by the Air Ministry before it was sold off. Much of the Western Camp remains in place, however, with hangars from 1916 and the buildings of the Bristol School still in place, scheduled for preservation. Aircraft can still be seen over Yatesbury, flying from the thriving Wiltshire Microlight Centre which uses a hangar and airstrip on the southern edge of the former airfield.

Main features:
Runways: 310° 2,916ft, 210° 2,838ft, Sommerfield track. *Hangars:* one Northern Light, three single-span, one Bellman, eleven Blister. *Hardstandings:* three concrete aprons. *Accommodation:* RAF Officers 209, SNCOs 1,479, ORs 5,491; WAAF Officers 16, SNCOs 15, ORs 650.

Yeovil airfield and works in July 1930.

YEOVIL, Somerset

ST540158, 1 mile SW of Yeovil

The longest-serving manufacturer's airfield in Britain, Yeovil has played an important part in the production of aircraft since the First World War. Its origins lie with the decision by Yeovil engineering company Petters Ltd to move into aircraft manufacture in April 1915, to help the war effort. Having been awarded a contract to build Short 184 seaplanes, the company set up a new factory west of Yeovil and named it the Westland Aircraft Works. The first aircraft was finished within eight months and as more were produced (a second contract for Sopwith 1¹/₂ Strutters had followed) the aircraft were crated up and sent off to RNAS Rochester or Hamble for flight-testing and acceptance.

By 1917 it was decided that an airfield should be built alongside the factory and, following the purchase of land, this was ready in April for the first company-built DH4 to be flight-tested. DH9s followed and the company got involved with development work when it was asked to fit a US-built Liberty engine into the aircraft, and this became the DH9A, one of the outstanding aircraft of the Great War. By the time of the Armistice the works had produced 1,100 aircraft for the RNAS, RFC and RAF. The last of these were Vimy bombers, for which the company had built a new erecting shop with an unsupported roof span of 140 feet (then the largest building of its kind in Britain).

The company decided to stay in the aviation business and, with the aid of a contract for more DH9As, managed to do just that. Although there were lean times in the 1920s, Westland managed to produce a number of its own designs, many of which remained only prototypes. Success came in 1927 with the Wapiti, which was ordered by the RAF as a DH9A replacement (it actually incorporated a number of DH9A components) – production was to reach 563. The company's name changed to the Westland Aircraft Company in 1934, and in 1936 it was awarded a contract for its new army cooperation aircraft, the Lysander. It had also received a sub-contract from Hawker to build all 178 examples of its predecessor, the Audax! In 1935 control of the company passed to John Brown Engineering, which immediately invested in new facilities so that when war came – the following year – Westland was in a strong position.

Westland PV6 K3438, the prototype Wallace, at Yeovil in 1933.

After the Lysander came the Whirlwind twin-engine day- and night-fighter, developed and produced in great secrecy – it first flew on 11 October 1938, but it was not until late 1941 that it was officially revealed. Although successful, only 112 were to be produced, due to engine problems. When the Luftwaffe attacked the factory on 15 July 1940 Lysanders and Whirlwinds were in production, and although a number of Ju 88s dropped twelve bombs, they did no real damage. In another raid on 30 September forty He 111s of KG55 escorted by Bf 110s crossed the coast heading for Yeovil. They were intercepted by Hurricanes of 56 Squadron from Boscombe Down and 504 Squadron, Filton, and by the Spitfires of 152 Squadron, Warmwell; the raiders turned away,

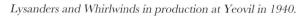

Lysanders and Whirlwinds in production at Yeovil in 1940.

The Merlin HC1 prototype lifts off from Yeovil on flight trials in 1995.

heading for the Channel. A more determined raid on 7 October by twenty-five Ju 88s of II/KG51 escorted by fifty Bf 110s of ZG26 was again intercepted by 10 Group fighters, but forced its way through to drop several bombs on the factory. Although little damage was caused, a direct hit on an air raid shelter resulted in injury some of the workers inside.

As well as manufacturing aircraft of its own design, Westland also sub-contracted for modifications work on Curtiss Mohawks, Tomahawks and Kittyhawks. It produced 700 Spitfires following the bombing of Supermarine's works at Eastleigh, and manufactured eighteen Barracudas before it was switched to Seafire production. It was then made prime contractor for the Seafire and, with Cunliffe-Owen as main sub-contractor, produced more than 2,400 Seafires by the end of the war.

Meanwhile the Welkin high-altitude fighter was put into production, followed by the Wyvern after the war. The company then made the decision to concentrate on helicopters and, after a slow start licence-building Sikorsky designs, produced its own version of the S-55, the Whirlwind. This was followed by the Wessex, then the Sea King. Joint ventures with other manufacturers have resulted in the Sioux, Puma, Gazelle, Lynx, Apache and Merlin. Now teamed with Agusta, Westland is one of British aviation's success stories, still operating from its factory airfield at Yeovil.

YEOVILTON, Somerset

ST550234, 2 miles E of Ilchester

Having been released from the control of the RAF in 1937, the Fleet Air Arm started surveying the West Country for suitable locations on which to build airfields. Yeovilton was decided on as it was not far from the major naval bases on the South Coast. The FAA acquired 417 acres of farmland near Ilchester on 1 July 1939 and work immediately started on what was to become a typical four-runway naval flying training base. However, the land was low-lying and construction was slowed by drainage problems. In May 1940 the airfield was still far from complete when it received its first units, Nos 750, 751 and 752 Squadrons, which made up No 1 Naval Observers School. They had evacuated their base at Ford following raids and brought their Sharks, Ospreys,

Preserved Seafire F17 is seen in July 2007 in the markings of 767 Squadron, based at Yeovilton from 1948 to 1952.

Walruses, Proctors and Albacores to Yeovilton. The station was opened on 18 June 1940 as HMS *Heron* under the Command of Captain H. S. Murray-Smith RN.

One of the first hangars to be erected was for Westland Aircraft, to house the Westland Repair Organisation (known as its Ilchester Factory) for the rebuilding of damaged Spitfires. Yeovilton was intended as the new Naval Air Fighter School, and to this end 794 Squadron formed in August 1940 with Rocs and Swordfish to provide target facilities for the school. This arrived from Eastleigh on 16 September in the form of 759 and 760 Squadrons, which flew a collection of Masters, Rocs, Sea Hurricanes and Sea Gladiators to train fighter pilots.

The Observers School left for Trinidad at the end of September. In the meantime, on 15 September, Yeovilton's first operational squadron, No 827, formed with Albacores, working up until leaving for Crail in early November. It was followed by 807 Squadron, arriving with Fulmars on 9 December for a two-month stay. As well as training, Yeovilton's role expanded to become a shore station for Fleet Fighter Squadrons; the first of these, 804 Squadron, arrived in February 1941, its Martlets and Buffaloes soon replaced by Fulmars and Sea Hurricanes. The unit sent detachments to other air stations and ships as required. No 787 Squadron was formed on 5 March 1941 as the Fleet Fighter Development Unit, and with its three Fulmars and three Sea Gladiators was to develop naval fighter tactics. It also evaluated new types in service, and enemy aircraft as they became available – a Fiat CR42 and Bf 109 were soon seen in Yeovilton's circuit in the hands of the unit's pilots.

In May 1941 No 804 Squadron also took on Hurricanes for CAMship (catapult-launched from merchantmen) deployments to counter FW 200 attacks on convoys. More Sea Hurricanes appeared on 1 August when 801 Squadron formed with twelve aircraft and started working up before deploying on operations, and moving to St Merryn on 6 October. By late 1941 twelve large Bellman hangars and a technical hangar had been constructed, together with many Maycrete and Nissen huts for office and domestic accommodation. Hangars were also erected on new dispersals around the airfield at Manor Farm, Specklington Farm, Bridgehampton and Podimore. Despite this, the saturation of facilities at Yeovilton led to the opening of satellites at Henstridge and Charlton Horethorne.

A Fighter Direction School had been formed in 1941, and a training centre established at Specklington Manor. From a glasshouse built on its roof, embryo controllers learned their trade by directing by radio sailors who were pedalling ice-cream tricycles around Yeovilton's dispersals. With the formation of 790 Squadron at Charlton Horethorne in June 1942, they could progress to the control of real aircraft (Fulmars and Oxfords).

No 807 Squadron became the first to receive Seafires in mid-July 1942, training on Mk IBs while re-equipping with the more advanced Mk IICs. No 759 Squadron steadily expanded, having sixty-six Sea Hurricanes, eight Spitfires, twenty-four Fulmars and fifteen Martlets by April 1943, when it became the advanced flying school component of No 1 Naval Air Fighter School. It was joined that month by 748 Squadron, a fighter pool squadron equipped with Fulmars and Martlets.

On 24 May No 736 Squadron was formed as the School of Air Combat with Seafires. It left for St Merryn in September and was replaced by a new series of squadrons formed to operate the Firefly. The first, 1770 RNVR Squadron, was commissioned on 1 October, followed by 1771 early in 1944. In contrast to most airfields in the South West, Yeovilton had a quiet invasion year with few changes in the training programme. Work on the airfield included camouflaging and the building of more hangars and accommodation.

One of the last wartime arrivals at Yeovilton, on 22 September 1944, was 835 Squadron, which was based aboard HMS *Nairana*, an Atlantic escort carrier with Sea Hurricanes and Swordfish. It had come in to exchange its Sea Hurricanes for Wildcat VIs, but when it rejoined the *Nairana* on 4 October it found that the carrier had been switched to the Russian convoys, and was off to Murmansk. No 748 Squadron moved to Dale in October, leaving the Fighter Direction School and 759 Squadron in residence at Yeovilton. By then the latter had a few Spitfires and Seafires on complement, together with Wildcats. Its Masters were gradually replaced with Harvards, and as Corsairs became available they too were issued to the unit; by early 1945 the Squadron had largely re-equipped with Corsairs, with more than 150 on strength. VE-Day was celebrated in style, but work carried on the following day as the war in the Pacific had yet to be won.

Following VJ Day Yeovilton became a demobilisation centre for the RN and was closed for flying in September 1945, 759 Squadron moving to Zeals. The Squadron returned when Yeovilton reopened in January 1946, only to disband in March. The following month 700 Squadron, the Maintenance Test Pilots School, arrived from Middle Wallop with the Avenger, Hellcat, Wildcat, Barracuda, Firefly, Firebrand and Seafire to teach pupils to test-fly in-service aircraft; the unit disbanded on 30 September 1949. Disembarked Firefly and Sea Fury squadrons were accommodated during 1948-49 and 767 Squadron transferred from Miltown on 8 September 1948 with Seafires and Fireflies to give deck-landing control officer training, staying until 1952. It was then decided that Yeovilton should become the shore base for the fleet's all-weather fighters, and the station was closed for an extensive rebuilding programme, which included the lengthening of the runways, the main one to 7,500 feet.

HMS *Heron* became HQ Flag Officer Flying Training and reopened in November 1953. The first unit to form there was 764 Squadron with Sea Hawks, Seafires and Fireflies, although it disbanded a year later. More important were the series of operational squadrons that formed at or passed through Yeovilton to work up with the new jets, the first being 890 Squadron, the first Sea Venom unit. On 18 October 1956 No 766 Squadron formed as the All Weather Fighter School with Sea Vampires and Sea Venoms. From 1954 to 1956 Sea Furies of various RNVR squadrons were based at Yeovilton, but when the last, 1832, left for Benson in November the station was virtually all-jet. The introduction of the Sea Vixen into service caused the station to close once again for its runways to be strengthened, new hardstandings to be provided and the technical site revamped. The airfield was reopened in January 1958 when 766 Squadron returned, and in November No 700Y Squadron, the Sea Vixen IFTU, was commissioned. Sea Vixen squadrons formed steadily during the following years, and at the beginning of 1961 the Air Direction School arrived, together with the Airwork Services-operated Sea Venoms that it flew. No 766 Squadron, was by then also equipped with Sea Vixens.

In early 1967, with the imminent introduction of the Phantom, Yeovilton was closed once again for runway and hardstanding re-strengthening. It reopened in August 1967 and the following April No 700P Squadron was formed to introduce the Phantom into service. It became 767 Squadron in January 1969 as part of the Naval Fighter School, and on 31 March No 892 Squadron, the operational Phantom unit, was formed – it was soon in the news for making the fastest crossing in the Transatlantic Air Race. No 766 Squadron was disbanded on 10 December 1970 and the run-down of the Sea Vixen squadrons soon followed. By the end of January 1972 only the Airwork Vixens remained in service, and with the Naval Fighter School reduced to 767 Squadron, and 892 often at sea aboard HMS *Ark Royal*, the air station was under-utilised. This was remedied when 707 and 846 Squadrons transferred from Culdrose in May 1971 and Yeovilton became the HQ for the Wessex HU5 Commando Squadrons.

The Naval Fighter School closed in August 1972 as the Phantoms transferred to Leuchars. Airwork Services was joined by the Fleet Requirements Unit from Hurn, the combined unit being renamed the Fleet Requirements & Air Direction Unit on 1 December, with Hunters, Canberra T22s and Sea Vixens. Nos 845 and 848 Commando Squadrons moved to Yeovilton in 1973, 848 disbanding in March 1976. Later that year the Lynx IFTU was formed, becoming 700L Squadron

Yeovilton-based Sea Vixen F(AW)1 XN696 of 899 Squadron in about 1961.

Phantom FG1 XV582 of 892 Squadron, HMS Ark Royal, at its Yeovilton shore base in September 1985.

Sea Harrier FRS1 '122' of 800 Squadron at Yeovilton in July 1987.

on 9 September and the nucleus of 702 Squadron in 1977. The first Sea Harriers arrived for 700 Squadron in June 1979 and further aircraft enabled the formation of 800 Squadron as the first operational unit on 23 April 1980, to be deployed aboard the 'Invincible' Class carriers, while the trials unit became 899 Squadron. Soon afterwards the Sea King HC4, the Commando version of the helicopter, was introduced into 846 Squadron. The FRADU was updated, with Falcon 20 twin jets replacing the Canberras, operated by Flight Refuelling Ltd, which took over the FRADU contract in December 1983. Another change of contractor, to Hunting Aviation, came in 1995 when the unit moved to Culdrose after converting to the Hawk. However, threat simulation and target-towing remained with Flight Refuelling (now FR Aviation), which moved its Falcon 20s to Hurn.

Yeovilton squadrons played a key role in the Falkland Campaign of 1982, with more than 120 of its aircraft involved in assault, communications, transport and logistics, including the sinking of an Argentinian submarine. They also played a vital part in the Gulf War of 1991, providing support to the 1st Armoured Brigade in the desert and to naval forces at sea. From 1992 until 2000 Sea Kings of the Commando Helicopter Force served in Bosnia supporting UN and NATO operations and were also involved in Sierra Leone. Sea Harriers were engaged there too, as well as policing No Fly Zones over Iraq, Bosnia and Kosovo. Helicopters from both the Commando Helicopter and Lynx forces were engaged in operations during the Gulf War of 2003, mounting heli-borne assault by Sea King, and anti-armour missions by Lynx and Gazelle. Aircraft and personnel from Yeovilton continue to provide day-to-day support for operations at sea and on land throughout the world, for example in Iraq, Afghanistan and the anti-drugs effort in the West Indies.

Today the station is one of the busiest military airfields in the UK and one of the largest in Europe, normally housing seven squadrons and around one hundred aircraft. It is also the biggest aviation establishment in the Royal Navy, employing more than 3,000 service and civilian personnel. At the time of writing Yeovilton-based units are the Commando Helicopter Force (845, 846 and 848 Squadrons with the Sea King HC4, 847 Squadron with the Lynx AH7), Heron Flight of 750 Squadron, with Jetstream T.3s, 727 Squadron, with Grob Tutor T.1s, the Naval Standard Flying Wing, with Hawk T.1s, the RN School of Fighter Control, the RN School of Aircraft Control, and the RN Historic Flight, with Swordfish Mk I, II and III, Sea Fury FB11 and Sea Hawk FGA6 aircraft. The station is co-located with the Fleet Air Arm Museum, which houses an incomparable collection of naval aircraft.

A Sea King HC4 of the Commando Helicopter Force flying from Yeovilton in early 1998.

Yeovilton from the east in 2008.

Main features:
Runways: 006° 3,180ft x 100ft, 048° 3,645ft x 150ft, 096° 3,480ft x 100ft, 141° 3,210ft x 100ft, tarmac. *Hangars:* twelve Bellman, one 250ft x 110ft Technical Hangar. *Accommodation:* RN Officers 294, ORs 1,502; WRNS Officers 27, ORs 607.

Defiant TTIII of 286 Squadron, which flew from Zeals between May and August 1942.

ZEALS, Wiltshire

ST780327, 4 miles NE of Wincanton

There were plenty of targets for the Mosquito NFXIIIs of 488 (RNZAF) Squadron on the night of 14/15 May 1944. Patrolling south of Bristol, they found themselves in the path of a German sixty-bomber force heading for the city. Fg Offs Jeffs and Spedding were vectored in to attack a Ju 88; when Spedding picked it up on radar Jeffs moved in the night-fighter until he had visual contact, and a burst from its guns sent the bomber into the sea. The crew hardly had time to recover before they were vectored onto another target, which they claimed as a probable. Flt Lt Hall and Fg Off Cairns similarly dispatched a Ju 188 5 minutes later. This was a good start for the unit, whose score would rise to thirty-four gained between then and 31 August 1944, most of which were made from Zeals during this, the high-point in the station's history.

Whirlwind pilots of 263 Squadron relax at Zeals in June 1943.

Zeals was opened on 21 May 1942 as a fighter station within 10 Group. Its three runways were laid out on a 530-acre grass airfield, an encircling concrete and tarmac perimeter track giving access to a number of dispersals. Most of the buildings were erected on the southern side of the airfield including a control tower, technical site centred on a T1 hangar and eight Blisters on dispersals; the domestic sites were dispersed further south. The first unit to use the newly opened station was 286 Squadron, the main target facilities unit for the South West, which arrived on 26 May; it flew Defiant target-tugs, together with other types such as the Master, Oxford and Hurricane, until returning to Colerne on 21 August. It was replaced on that day by the Ibsley Wing (66 and 118 Squadrons, with Spitfire VBs), which flew in for a few months' detachment. The Wing had taken part in the Dieppe operation a few days before, escorting smoke-laying Bostons, and from Zeals escorted bombers operating over France. Its first operation took them to Cherbourg, covering thirteen Bostons of 2 Group, and fighter sweeps followed. For a brief period in September the Wing went to Predannack for patrol work in the Western Approaches, replaced temporarily at Zeals by 402 and 611 Squadrons, from Kenley and Biggin Hill, both flying the new Spitfire Mk IX. On their return to Zeals the Ibsley Wing resumed bomber escorts with the occasional night patrol, until 23 December 1942, when they returned to Ibsley.

One of the reasons for the Wing's departure was waterlogging of the grass surface due to heavy rain. It left behind 2835 Squadron, RAF Regiment, which provided AA ground defence. Flying resumed again in March 1943 when Spitfire VBs of 132 Squadron and Hurricanes of 174 and 184 Squadrons arrived for Exercise *Spartan*, a close-support exercise with the Army. No 174 Squadron flew Hurricane IIB fighter-bombers, while 184 had Mk IIDs, fitted with 40mm anti-tank cannon. The three Squadrons became 122 Airfield for the duration of the exercise, operating and living in field conditions. When the fifteen-day exercise finished, teams from 14 Works Area moved in to improve drainage on the airfield. This was seen as a convenient time to undertake ground training at Zeals and four newly established RAF Servicing Commandos (Nos 3207, 3208, 3209 and 3210) arrived to set up camp. They undertook military and technical training, using Spitfires, a Kittyhawk and a Typhoon to simulate aircraft servicing in the field.

With the airfield once again ready for use, on 19 June 1943 the Whirlwinds of 263 Squadron moved in to fly *Rhubarbs* along the French coast and over Luftwaffe airfields. On 12 July they abruptly returned to Warmwell and a few days later the Servicing Commandos left for other airfields. This was because Zeals had been allocated to the US 8th AF to receive units arriving from the USA. In October the airfield was transferred to the 9th AF, becoming the 5th Tactical Air Depot for the repair and maintenance of P-47 Thunderbolts. Sommerfield track hardstandings were laid by 500 Airfield Construction Squadron, and the first batch of fifty P-47s arrived just before Christmas 1943. However, with high rainfall and poor drainage it was obvious that the grass surface at Zeals could not endure sustained use by the heavy 'Jugs', and in January they started moving to Chilbolton, which had hard runways. The last USAAF unit to leave was the 21st Weather Squadron, a meteorological unit that had small detachments at most USAAF stations in the UK, with its HQ at Zeals.

The airfield reopened under 10 Group, RAF, on 20 April 1944, this time as a night-fighter base. The Mosquito XIIIs of 488 (RNZAF) Squadron arrived from Colerne on 11 May and made their first successful interceptions a few days later, as described above. Despite Drem and funnel-approach lighting, local topography made Zeals a challenging airfield from which to operate, but the weather remained kind that summer. No 488 operated with 604 Squadron, Colerne, as 147 Wing, and from 6 June flew nightly patrols over the Normandy beachhead. They were joined by 410 (RCAF) Squadron, also with Mosquito XIIIs, from Hunsdon on 18 June and both Zeals's units then flew an average of eight sorties a night, which regularly resulted in successful interceptions. By the end of June the units' Mosquitoes were ranging further afield in defence of Allied forces on the continent, and on 8 July Sqn Ldr March and Flt Lt Eyolfson in MM570 of 410 Squadron shot down one of the new Me 410 twin-engine fighters over the Paris outskirts. They saw Flt Lt Huppert and Fg Off Christie being hit and forced to bail out after shooting down a Ju 88.

Zeals had a good flight safety record, but accidents did occur, and 10 July was an unfortunate day in this respect, when two aircraft crashed. The first was Mosquito HK500 of 410 Squadron, which overshot while trying to land in fog, and came down at Pen Mill, without injury to its crew. The crew of a USAAF Norseman were less fortunate: its pilot requested landing permission at Zeals because of the bad visibility, and while orbiting the airfield hit the very top of King Alfred's Tower, on high ground to the north. All three aboard the Norseman were killed. The Zeals squadrons had come under 149 Wing at the end of June and a few weeks later were joined by the Mosquitoes of A Flight, 604 Squadron, just before the whole Wing was moved to Colerne on 28 July 1944. During its brief stay at Zeals, 604 managed to shoot down a Ju 88 off Granville.

At Colerne, 149 Wing displaced 286 Squadron, which returned to Zeals. By this time the unit was flying Oxfords, Hurricanes, Martinets and a Tiger Moth, supporting AA units across four counties. By September the weather was making ground conditions difficult and, once room became available at Weston Zoyland, the Squadron moved there, departing on 28 September. In October a detachment of 3 GTS moved in from Northleach and soon resumed glider pilot training on Hotspurs, towed by Masters. After a couple of months they too moved on, to be replaced by the Glider Pick-up Training Flight early in January 1945. This unit practised snatch glider recovery techniques with five Dakotas and seven Hadrians, training crews earmarked for Tiger Force, to invade Japan. Five crews were aboard TS435, which took off for Leicester East on 19 February 1945; tragically the Dakota hit a hill shortly after clearing the airfield, resulting in the deaths of twenty airmen, only the pilot surviving. Ibsley became available in the spring, and the GPTF moved there on 21 March.

Dakota CIII TS435 of the Glider Pick-up Training Flight attempting to snatch a wire during training. Tragically, this aircraft flew into a hill after leaving Zeals on 19 February 1945.

Piper Pawnee G-BEHS at Zeals in 1979 while crop-spraying farms in the local area.

Zeals was transferred to the Admiralty in April, and on the 10th the Corsair Familiarisation Flight of 759 Squadron, part of No 1 Naval Air Fighter School, Yeovilton, moved there to be reformed as 760 Squadron. Students were trained at Zeals on the Harvard, Corsair, and later the Hellcat. On 11 April No 704 Squadron was formed at Zeals as the naval OTU for the Mosquito with T Mk IIIs and FB Mk VIs. They were joined by 790 Squadron, which moved in from Charlton Horethorne on 14 April. Part of the Fighter Direction School at Yeovilton, the unit flew Oxfords and Fireflies; shortly after arrival at Zeals, it also received Spitfire VBs and Seafire Is and IIs.

RNAS Zeals became HMS *Humming Bird* on 18 May, and on 25 July a fourth unit arrived in the form of 771 Squadron from Twatt. This was a fleet requirements unit and flew Martinets, Corsairs and Wildcats to simulate targets over the Portland Ranges. However, as autumn set in and the weather worsened, the Navy found conditions at Zeals to be just as unpleasant as their predecessors had. To maintain flying hours, one by one they were found new bases from which to operate. With the war's end the FAA decided to withdraw from Zeals, and on New Year's Day 1946 HMS *Humming Bird* closed. The airfield was reduced to C&M, but not long afterwards was de-requisitioned, and soon returned to agriculture.

Today little remains of the wartime airfield. The western perimeter track is used as a farm road and has seen occasional use as an airstrip for crop-dusters. Some buildings remain on the former domestic site, which is used for farm storage. The control tower still overlooks the former airfield and has been converted into a pleasant dwelling, Tower House.

Main features:
Runways: N-S 4,800ft, E-W 4,250ft, SE-NW 4,250ft, grass. *Hangars:* one T1, eight O-Blister. *Hardstandings:* thirty TE, twelve Sommerfield track. *Accommodation:* RAF Officers 20, SNCOs 180, ORs 1,684; WAAF Officers 6, SNCOs 6, ORs 230.

BIBLIOGRAPHY

Aeroplane magazine (various issues)

Air Britain Aeromilitaria (various issues)

Airfield Review (Journal of the Airfield Research Group – various issues)

Ashworth, Chris, Action Stations Vol 5, Patrick Stephens Ltd, 1982

Ashworth, Chris, Coastal Command 1936 – 1969, Patrick Stephens Ltd, 1992

Ashworth, Chris, Avro's Maritime Heavyweight, The Shackleton, Aston Publications 1990

Barnes, C.H., Bristol Aircraft since 1910, Putnam 1964

Berryman, David, Gloucestershire Airfields in the Second World War, Countryside Books 2005

Berryman, David, Somerset Airfields in the Second World War, Countryside Books 2006

Berryman, David, Wiltshire Airfields in the Second World War, Countryside Books 2002

Brooks, Robin J., Hampshire Airfields in the Second World War, Countryside Books 1996

Bowman, Martin, Mosquito Fighter/Fighter-Bomber Units of World War 2, Osprey, 1998

Bullen, Annie & Rivas, Brian, John Derry, William Kimber, 1982

Channel Islands Occupation Review (various issues)

Cruddas, Colin, In Dorset's Skies, Tempus 2000

Cruddas, Colin, In Hampshire Skies, Tempus 2001

Cruddas, Colin, In Wiltshire Skies, Tempus 2004

Delve, Ken, The Military Airfields of Britain South-Western England, Crowood 2006

Donnelly, Larry, The Other Few, Red Kite 2004

Forty, George, Channel Islands at War, Ian Allen 1999

Franks, Norman, RAF Fighter Command 1935-1968, Patrick Stephens Ltd, 1992

Freeman, Roger A, US Airfields of the Ninth then and now, After the Battle

Hall, Alan W, Boulton Paul Defiant, Warpaint books

Hall, Alan W, Westland Whirlwind, Warpaint books

Hawkins, Mac, Somerset at War 1939-45, Dovecote Press 1988

Howe, Stuart, de Havilland Mosquito An Illustrated History Vol I, Crecy Publishing, 1999

Jarrett, Philip, Airfield of the Second World War, Putnam 1997

Jefford, C.G. RAF Squadrons, Airlife 1988

James, Derek N. Gloster Aircraft since 1917, Putnam 1971

James, N.D.G. Plain Soldiering, Hobnob Press 1987

Johnson, Brian & Heffernan, Terry, A Most Secret Place, Jane's 1982

Kellett, JP & Davies J, A History of the RAF Servicing Commandos, Airlife, 1989

Lake, Alan, Flying Units of the RAF, Airlife 1999

London, Peter, Aviation in Cornwall, Air Britain 1997

London, Peter, In Cornish Skies, Tempus 2000

London, Peter, RNAS Culdrose, Sutton Publishing 1999

London, Peter, U-Boat Hunters: Cornwall's Air War 1916-1919, Dyllansow Truran 1999

Mason, Tim, The Secret Years Flight Testing at Boscombe Down 1939-45, Hikoki 1998

Mason, Tim, The Cold War Years Flight Testing at Boscombe Down 1945 -1975 Hikoki 2001

Mondey, David, Planemakers 2: Westland, Jane's 1982

Morgan, Eric B. & Shacklady Edward, Spitfire The History, Key Publishing 1993

Mowthorpe, Ces, Battlebags – British Airships of the First World War, Wrens Park, 1995

Moyes, Philip, Bomber Squadrons of the RAF and their Aircraft, MacDonald and Jane's 1974

Phipp, Mike, Bournemouth's Airports a History, Tempus 2006

Quarrie, Bruce, Action Stations Vol 10, Patrick Stephens Ltd, 1987

Rawlings, John D. R. Coastal Support and Special Squadrons of the RAF and their Aircraft, Jane's 1982

Rawlings, John D. R. Fighter Squadrons of the RAF and their Aircraft, MacDonald and Jane's 1976

Robertson, Bruce, British Military Aircraft Serials 1911-1979, Patrick Stephens 1979

Saunders, Keith A., RAF St Mawgan, Alan Sutton Publishing 1995

Smith, Graham, Devon and Cornwall Airfields in the Second World War, Countryside Books 2000

Smith, Graham, Dorset Airfields in the Second World War, Countryside Books 1999

Smith, Ron, British Built Aircraft Vol 2 South West and Central Southern England, Tempus Books 2003

Sturtivant, Ray, RAF Flying Training and Support Units since 1912, Air Britain 2007

Sturtivant, Ray, The Squadrons of the Fleet Air Arm, Air Britain 1984

Taylor, John W.R. CFS Birthplace of Air Power, Putnam 1958

Taylor, John W.R. & Moyes P.J.R., Pictorial History of the RAF Vols I – III Ian Allen 1969

Teague, Dennis, Aviation in South West Britain 1909 – 1979, Baron Jay Publishers 1982

Teague, Dennis, & White Peter R, A Guide to the Airfields of South Western England, Baron Jay Publishers

Thetford, Owen, Aircraft of the Royal Air Force since 1918, Putnam 1995

Thetford, Owen, British Naval Aircraft since 1912, Putnam 1977

Thirsk, Ian, de Havilland Mosquito an Illustrated History Vol 2, Crecy Publishing 2007

Thomas, Andrew, Beaufighter Aces of World War 2, Osprey 2005

Thomas, Andrew, Mosquito Aces of World War 2, Osprey 2005

Thomas, Chris, Hawker Typhoon, Warpaint Publishing

Thomas, Chris, Typhoon and Tempest Aces of World War 2, Osprey 1999

Verier, Mike, Yeovilton Defenders of the Fleet, Osprey 1991

Wakefield, Ken, Operation Bolero, Crecy Publishing 1994

Wakefield, Ken, Somewhere in the West Country, Crecy Publishing 1997

Wakeham, Geoff, RNAS Culdrose, 1947-2007, Tempus 2007

Walford, Eddie, War over the West, Amigo Books 1989

Warner, Graham, The Bristol Blenheim a complete history, Crecy Publishing 2005

Watkins, David, RAF Chivenor, Alan Sutton Publishing 1995

Index

RAF Commands

RAF Conversion Units

RAF Operational Training Units

RAF/RFC Squadrons

The Action Stations Revisited Series

Volume 1 Eastern England
9780859791459

Volume 2 Central England and the London Area
9780947554941

Volume 3 South East England
9780859791106

Volume 4 South West England
9780859791212

Volume 5 Wales and the Midlands
9780859791113

Volume 6 Northern England and Yorkshire
9780859791120

Volume 7 North East England, Scotland and
Northern Ireland
9780859791441

Published by Crécy Publishing Ltd
1a Ringway Trading Estate
Shadowmoss Rd
Manchester M22 5LH
www.crecy.co.uk